SIMULATED SELVES

Also available from Bloomsbury

Invention of the Self: Personal Identity in the Age of Art
Andrew Spira

Aesthetics of Ugliness: A Critical Edition
Karl Rosenkranz

Art as Human Practice: An Aesthetics
Georg W. Bertram

SIMULATED SELVES

THE UNDOING OF
PERSONAL IDENTITY IN THE
MODERN WORLD

Andrew Spira

BLOOMSBURY ACADEMIC
LONDON • NEW YORK • OXFORD • NEW DELHI • SYDNEY

BLOOMSBURY ACADEMIC
Bloomsbury Publishing Plc
50 Bedford Square, London, WC1B 3DP, UK
1385 Broadway, New York, NY 10018, USA

BLOOMSBURY, BLOOMSBURY ACADEMIC and the Diana logo are trademarks of
Bloomsbury Publishing Plc

First published in Great Britain 2020

Cover design by Maria Rajka
Cover image © Max Guther

A catalogue record for this book is available from the British Library.

A catalog record for this book is available from the Library of Congress.

ISBN: HB: 978-1-3500-9109-2
ePDF: 978-1-3500-9108-5
eBook: 978-1-3500-9110-8

Typeset by RefineCatch Limited, Bungay, Suffolk
Printed and bound in Great Britain

To find out more about our authors and books visit www.bloomsbury.com
and sign up for our newsletters.

CONTENTS

PREFACE AND ACKNOWLEDGEMENTS

This book forms a companion to *The Invention of the Self: Personal Identity in the Age of Art*. In that book, I explored the notion that personal identity is not a pre-existent truth transcending the circumstances of life, but a psychological and linguistic convention, generated by, and sustained in, a raft of cultural conventions. I argued there that the emergence of the self-sense came to a head in the seventeenth century. Descartes' 'I think, therefore I am' was the perfect expression of the new self-consciousness. At a material level, the most obvious manifestation of the shift was the proliferation of mirrors – a veritable institutionalisation of the experience of self-reference. Although mirrors existed in antiquity and throughout the Middle Ages, they had been elite objects and their reflective power was far from perfect. They only became widespread – granting ordinary people a knowledge of their own faces for the first time – in the seventeenth century. Plenty of other 'instruments of self-reflection', from the reading of intimate letters in private spaces to the notion of 'aesthetic pleasure', were conventionalised at this time.

Western-style democracies are based on the freedoms afforded to individuals by these conventions and they continue to play a key role in the creation of human values; indeed, they are now almost globally accepted as mainstays of our culture. In *The Invention of the Self*, I traced the prehistories of these trends as they evolved to the point at which they began to be taken for granted. In due course, they were identified as natural functions of human culture and were conceptualised as such. However, while their conceptualisation may have confirmed their existence at the level of abstract ideas, it did not guarantee their survival as effective, vital principles in life itself. Indeed, notwithstanding the growing appreciation of their innate value, one of the circumstances that enabled these conventions to be conceptualised was precisely the fact that polarised alternatives to them were also evolving. For instance, the Arts and Crafts revival of ethical craftsmanship was motivated by the perceived *abuses* of human dignity that became part and parcel of the Industrial Revolution; and sharp focus on the psychology of the individual evolved in conjunction with the levelling effect of modern urbanism and the blurred impressionism of statistical analyses in sociology.

These impersonal conditions (industry, urbanism, sociology) co-evolved with the newly conventionalised instruments of personal identity and were therefore in some sense co-dependent with them. But they also had their own histories with their own ideologies that threatened to *undermine* the ground of personal selfhood. That is to say, the self-sense was both perpetuated and eclipsed by them – just as turning on a bright electric light in a candlelit room will, technically, 'add' to the candlelight, but will actually nullify its effect. As a result, as the eighteenth century gathered momentum, the self-sense entered a new phase in its history. This book is about that phase. What happens to the self-sense in a world that generated it, but which no longer revolves around it and depends on it? This is a question that cannot be fully answered because the story it seeks to interpret is still unfolding. The relationship between artificial intelligence and personal identity, for instance, is shifting on an almost daily basis.

As with *The Invention of the Self*, numerous people have helped me bring this project to realisation, and I would like to thank them here. Special thanks are due to Joy Law, Helen Brunner, Malgorzata Sady, Antony Buxton, Carl Gombrich, John Milner, David King, Patrick Bade, Chris McCully, Patrick Walsh and Tim Hyman. Petra Cramsie pored over an early draft of the text and provided much useful feedback – I am extremely grateful to her. Engagement with students over many years has also served as a continually stimulating and illuminating testing ground. The reproduction of images would have been impossible without generous contributions from Jaime and Connie Gonzales, Jeremy Walsh and the Duke of Buccleuch (KT, KBE) – I am most grateful to them. Thanks are also due to picture librarians and image holders from all over the world for their patience and efficiency; to Max Guther for the marvellous image that appears on the cover (capturing the typical and predictable aspect of modern 'freedoms' so well); and to Liza Thompson, Frankie Mace, Lucy Russell and others at Bloomsbury for seeing the book through production. Finally, I am hugely grateful to my friends and family, for their support and belief in the project over many years.

CHAPTER ONE

Introduction

The notion that human beings have personal 'selves' is so ingrained in us – in the 'West', at least – that we rarely question it. At the most basic level, we think we know who we are. Even if we subscribe, at a theoretical level, to the notion that, after fifty years of post-structuralist and postmodernist philosophy, the self has been 'deconstructed' and rendered conditional or provisional, the discourse of personal identity retains its position at the heart of western culture.[1] Generally speaking, we consider ourselves to be the consistent 'subject' of our thoughts, feelings and beliefs, even if our thoughts, feelings and beliefs may constantly change (as in 'I can't make up my mind'); and, from a purely practical point of view, we know what our name is, who our family and friends are, where we live, what we own, where we like going, what we like doing, reading and eating. Although there are, of course, innumerable exceptions to these basic buildings blocks of self-awareness, and although they are perpetually shifting, each of them contributes in the long term to a relatively continuous sense of self. The theory of deconstructed selfhood is not, therefore, always underpinned by practice. Indeed, because the western world is pervaded by conventions – practical, institutional, social, linguistic, psychological – that are based on the presumption of coherent and enduring selfhood, it would be difficult to live without the 'mask' of a self, even if one wanted to; even to *think* beyond it is difficult because by activating the thinking mind, and operating as rational subjects, we affirm its existence and automatically slide into the 'grooves of convention' that have developed around it. Thus, even though it is frequently upheld that the sense of a 'personal self' – the sense of a 'me' or 'I' – is 'merely' a social and psychological construct – that is to say, a kind of *illusion* – the implications of that intuition could be realised more deeply. To do this, it is necessary to consider, firstly, how, when and why the self-sense was constructed in the first place, and secondly, how, when and why the self-sense began to *lose* its coherence and integrity, whereupon it could be *seen* to be constructed. These questions have frequently been discussed *abstractly* – from psychological and philosophical perspectives – and they have been raised by anthropologists in relation to non-European cultures. But they have rarely been addressed in relation to the material culture of Europe and the European tradition in which they germinated, constituting a kind of 'anthropology of selfhood in the West'. This is what the present project sets out to do. The first question – how, when and why was the self-sense constructed? – was addressed in a companion volume, *The Invention of the Self: Personal Identity in the Age of Art*; the second question – how, when and why did the self-sense begin to lose its coherence and integrity, whereupon it could be seen to be constructed? – is addressed in the present one.

The origin of the self has been variously traced back to antiquity on the one hand and to the emergence of empirical philosophy in the seventeenth century on the other.[2] It has also been associated with the 'discovery' of the individual, both in the twelfth century and the fifteenth.[3] While classical notions of the self can in many ways be said to provide a 'prehistory' of the modern self, these later periods can be said to cover 'early', 'middle' and 'late' aspects of the same phenomenon. Indeed, it is arguable that the sense of a personal 'self' evolved in conjunction with a swathe of cultural conventions that co-evolved with it over several centuries. These conventions both accommodated the burgeoning self-sense and precipitated it in subsequent generations.

Despite ancient precedents, a continuous notion of selfhood, leading directly to the *modern* self-sense, can be said to have first acquired form in the twelfth and thirteenth centuries. Originally manifest in initiatives that turned against the collectivised interests of the Church and were therefore considered – by the Church – to be 'heresies', the impulse to incarnate a self-sense was subsequently manifest in numerous different ways. In the late Middle Ages, increased engagement in personal devotion began to complement collective participation in ecclesiastical ritual. A discourse of personal conscience, eased by confession but sometimes at odds with the doctrines of Church, also began to emerge. Changes to the domestic environment reflect a new appetite for private spaces among the laity, and for the solitary and self-reflective activities to which private spaces were conducive, such as silent reading and study. In the fifteenth and sixteenth centuries, the formation of the self was accompanied by the development of the 'artist' as an archetype of selfhood, and of the notion of 'art' as a medium of self-expression. Painters, traditionally afforded the lowly status of craftsmen, were reconfigured as 'artists', a new role invested with the elevated status of the liberal arts. Whereas a 'craftsman' was a mere technician, an 'artist' was a more creative and imaginative individual, akin to an ancient poet. Moreover while artists were directly involved in developing artistic conventions in which the experience of individual selfhood was implicit and legitimised – for instance, through the use of optical verisimilitude in representation (in contrast to medieval stylisation) and the development of portraiture – they also put these conventions at the disposal of their viewers, thereby extending the possibility of a highly personalised mode of experience to that constituency too.

Although traces of the self-sense became more common at this time, it was not, arguably, until the seventeenth century that the self's awareness of itself became explicit and self-authenticating. Manifest signs of self-reflexivity (for instance, self-portraits and autobiographies) were generated from the fifteenth century onwards, but it was only at this later date that self-awareness became circular, authorising itself from within its own experience – as consummated in Descartes' epoch-making observation in 1637 that 'I think, therefore I am'. Besides becoming independent, the self-sense also became *widespread* at this time. Institutionalised in the new word 'self-consciousness' (in Britain), its dissemination was epitomised by the proliferation of mirrors, which had hitherto been expensive luxuries, available only to the elite. New forms of behaviour and expression – reflecting the legitimisation of personal emotion and private pleasure on their own terms, without regard for 'higher' sources of valorisation – also became current. In the late seventeenth and eighteenth centuries, the self-sense became so habitual in culturally progressive circles that it became the fundamental ground of experience; that is to say, in normal circumstances, all experiences seemed to be naturally rooted in a sense of 'I' as their subject. This privilege was extended throughout western society in the nineteenth century, when primary education became universally available and the mechanical production of an abundance of cheap commodities enabled people from all walks of life to participate consciously in the process of identity formation. Indeed, it did so to the point at which the presumed existence of personal identity became coterminous with mental and cultural conventions at every level. On the one hand, *new* cultural forms were continuously generated to accommodate and propagate new aspects of personal selfhood (most recently, personal blogs and selfie sticks); on the other hand, it was perpetuated by *historic* conventions (traditions, institutions, buildings, language, modes of communications, etc.) and the sheer momentum of the cultural habits that these conventions supported. In so far as it was sustained by conventions in this way, the experience of a self-sense itself became a kind of convention.

Despite the fact that the notion of personal selfhood has become engrained in western culture to the point at which it is unnoticeable, it is nevertheless arguable that in many significant ways it has run its course. While it continues to function as an official component in human societies – for instance, as the subject of human rights and/or as a responsible legal entity – the objectivity of its existence is ever more open to debate. Why does this matter? In some ways, it doesn't – it is expedient to accept it. Just as we allow ourselves to identify, and use, certain objects as 'functional items' despite knowing that they are merely conglomerations of atoms, or to be moved by a film despite knowing that it is no more than light flickering on a screen, so we are perfectly happy to function as 'selves' despite accepting that the self is ultimately a construction. Having said that, although the self may be an 'effective myth' – an 'illusion, or fantasy, that works' – it does not always work *well* and there is therefore plenty of reason to scrutinise it. While it may serve as the apparent subject of personal dignity, responsibility, creativity, etc., it is also a source of political, social and psychological anxiety – from ideological and religious conflict on the world stage, to personal fear of identity theft, death and non-existence. It is the purpose of this book to explore the extent to which shifting historical circumstances have relativised the value the self-sense, amounting in some formulations to its disintegration, but also to consider why, despite exposing it as a conditional convention of mind and culture, we continue to cleave to it as if it was an absolute truth.

While the concept of the self lends itself amply to philosophical and psychological *analysis*, through logic and introspection, this is not the approach taken here. Indeed, *Simulated Selves* makes little reference to theoretical discourse. This is partly because an abundance of theoretical perspectives on personal identity have been published in recent years. But, more significantly, it is also because the argument of the book is rooted in the perception that the self-sense is generated by cultural processes rather than existing in itself as an object of contemplation, and that it waxes and wanes as they do. For this reason, the book attempts to present its subject in such a light that the material reveals the structures it conceals according to its *own* logic – as it acquired them in the course of its history – without having to conceptualise them as philosophical abstractions; for it is arguable, paradoxically, that a theoretical analysis of the self presupposes the kind of rational coherence in the self-sense of the analyst which the analyst is, at the same time, employed to question; and even if a man looking at himself in a fragmented mirror will see his face fragmented, his eye will only ever see itself clearly. In order, therefore, to avoid the circularity of direct self-analysis, *Simulated Selves* attempts to identify the self-sense and its demise from the *traces* it has left in the historical environment. That is to say, it does not focus on what the self consciously sees in itself, or says of itself; for whatever it sees is subject to its capacity to see, and is therefore solipsistic. On the contrary, it looks, more obliquely, for accidental evidence of selfhood – and, above all, of its suggested disintegration, dispersal or 'undoing' – in the body of conventions that have grown up around it and in conjunction with it; such conventions act like a slowly evolving mould, carrying the self-sense as a *range of possibilities*, over and above the comings and goings of individuals, into the future. 'Undoing' here has a double meaning, suggesting both enervation and incapacitation. On the one hand, the word refers to the deposition of the self-sense from its seat of absolute power or freedom in the life of the individual, leading to anxiety; on the other hand, it refers to the increasing inability of the self to determine its own future, or do what it wants, with regard to certain key areas of its life – such as controlling personal data that is accrued about it online, or making an impact on political situations. Nor is it as instrumental in the process of personal decision-making as it has habitually been thought to be. Disempowered, therefore, in real terms, it has become something of an *expedient*; it is useful to imagine it – so useful, in fact, that we overlook the fact that this is what we are doing. But, given that its power and freedom may not be what they seem to be, it is highly constructive to interrupt ourselves – to reflect on the fact that we imagine our selves, and to explore, and hopefully understand, why we do so.

Various challenges present themselves. Firstly, the subject involves both positive and negative evidence. While it may be possible to identify the *presence* of selfhood, because the self seems to be reflected in its objects, it is difficult to identify its *absence*, for the simple reason that the absence of a phenomenon can only be surmised in relation to an expectation (based on knowledge), past experience or imagination. Two solutions have been taken to this problem. One is to examine the disintegration of the objects in which the self has arguably invested itself and with which it disintegrates symbiotically; this is the subject of the fourth chapter on the changing status of 'art' over the last two centuries. The other is to observe the emergence of other, larger-scale conditions of identity formation – communal, institutional, national and social – that have arguably overshadowed the notion of personal identity by usurping the power of the individual to control his or her life and experience. The first of these emerging conditions is changing attitudes towards the forces of history and evolution. An opening chapter on the 'narrated self' charts how historiographical conventions developed to reflect the emergence and existence of the self by increasingly crediting it as a source of agency in historical processes. Reaching its apogee in the seventeenth and eighteenth centuries, the dominant agency of the self was subsequently eclipsed by the vision of 'objective' forces in history that overruled it, signalling its relegation to a peripheral role, or, in extreme cases, to no role at all. Other conditions that consign a diminished role to the self in the life of the individual, and which are addressed in their own chapters, are the institutionalisation of art appreciation (chapter 3); the development of utilitarianism in design and the mechanisation of the processes of object production (chapter 5); the depersonalisation of the media of communication (chapter 6); and the fragmentation of the self by psychoanalysis (chapter 7). The final chapter addresses the extent to which the self-sense is sustained as a mental construct in linguistic conventions.

Given the scope of the project – more 'continental drift' than 'microbiology' – there is the obvious danger of generalisation. A study that chooses to cover such an enormous amount and variety of material is inevitably going to find itself voicing opinions that can easily be challenged by exceptions and variations. Standing on the edge of the Grand Canyon, it may be difficult to imagine that the earth is round. Conversely, it is perfectly legitimate to argue, from that perspective, that the earth is not absolutely round. This problem only increases as one approaches the twenty-first century when the evidence becomes infinitely vast and various. Moreover, we only need to compare our own *experience* of a given moment to our retrospective *descriptions* and *analyses* of it, as it slips from 'memory' into 'history', to realise how profoundly artificial and stylised our representations of the past are. Generalisation, therefore, is an occupational hazard in all histories, but it is to be hoped that the pros (the usefulness of generalisation as an instrument of reflection) outweigh the cons (the undue protection it offers to preconceived ideas). The book also makes choices about which cultural trends to focus on, and in which regions. Allowing for a certain amount of osmosis, the guiding principle here has usually been to go where the 'pulse' of any given development has been especially strong, in the knowledge that many of its effects would in due course spread and become representative of wider trends. That the classical style in architecture only became fashionable in England one hundred years after it was revived in Renaissance Italy, or that psychoanalysis took root in Spain long after it was developed in Vienna, or that there was no branch of Starbucks in Italy until 2018, reflect the uniqueness and idiosyncrasy of all historical occurrences, but they do not invalidate the albeit easily overgeneralised observation that architectural classicism, the practice of psychoanalysis and American consumerism have all become ubiquitous in Europe and the West. And so it is, arguably, with the self-sense and its 'undoing'. Although there is an infinite number of potential reflectors of personal identity in the world, which we, as self-conscious individuals, are profoundly conditioned to recognise and use, the infrastructures of other 'scales' or 'denominations' of identity are also growing in their influence, but we are less inclined to see them because we do not see ourselves reflected in them.

CHAPTER TWO

The Narrated Self: Time and the Dramatisation of Historical Agency

Surely one of the frames of reference that accommodates the self-sense most securely is the concept of time. On the one hand, it is from the notion of a 'future' that the self derives its sense of its *possibilities*, which are only realisable in the future: it is from its possibilities that it derives its sense of *freedom* and *potency*, in which its identity as a conscious, causal subject resides. On the other hand, it is from the 'past' that it derives its sense of its character, via memory and reflection. It is arguable that the notion of time as a *personal experience* – in the present moment and in the course of everyday life – was only fully abstracted, becoming an independent function of the self-sense, between the thirteenth and seventeenth centuries. During the course of this period, natural and religious markers of time (from changing light at dawn and dusk, to the ringing of church bells) were superseded by automatic timekeeping devices – mechanical clocks and watches. While mechanical clocks and watches were developed for the sake of their accuracy and autonomy, so – conversely – their accuracy and autonomy facilitated the creation of a mental environment in which the possibility of personal freedom and potency, in which the self-sense inheres, was abstracted and rendered perfectly independent of circumstances.[1]

So much for the personal experience of time. Similar changes took place with regard to the perception of the overall temporality of the world, via the construction of *historical time*. In today's world, the discourse of history embraces a broad range of cultural conventions through which it is possible to articulate and reflect upon the ambitions, desires, dreams, accomplishments, failures and capacities of human beings. Whether conceived as a straight line, modelled on the course of a life from infancy and youth to maturity and old age, or as a spiral, modelled on the recurrence of days, months and years, history is a primary medium through which the human sense of self identifies and expresses itself, both in its individual and collective manifestations. However, while the practice of researching and exposing history may seem – to us – to concern 'what happened in the past', as if the past was a homogenous pre-existent space, furnished with occurrences that recede into the distance and are available to be discovered and interpreted (Fig. 2.1), it is equally possible to argue, conversely, that the organisation of events within a 'temporal' structure involves the *creation* of the notion of the past, thereby constituting the creation of a mental environment in which the identity of society, as defined and legitimised by its 'history', can seem to cohere. It is arguable that we are so profoundly habituated to, and invested in, this conception of historical time that we completely overlook the extent to which it is a mental construction. While this proposition may seem impossible to sustain in a world in which historical phenomena are seen to be 'objectively real' (independent of the mind that apprehends them), it becomes more plausible when seen in relation to the foothills of modern European historiography, at a time when objective conventions for recording and recalling the past were only just coming into existence. At this early period, it can be seen that not only do historical records provide us with information about the past (information that is consciously selected for recording), but the *changing ways in which the past is recorded* reflect fundamental attitudes – which are *not* always conscious – towards the nature of historical agency. Regardless of the contents of historical writing, the *models of historical time* that are used at any given period reflect, firstly, the laws that are believed to govern history (discernible from the patterns that are identified in it) and, secondly, the forces that are believed to drive it forward. The purpose of the present chapter is explore not so much the changing *content* of historical narratives but the changing *models of historical time* in which such content is framed, for it is in these that the underlying attitudes of individuals towards their own role in history are most clearly revealed. And it is in the strength, or weakness, of this self-reflective impulse that their appetite for a sense of personal identity is most clearly reflected.

FIGURE 2.1: Emma Willard, *The Temple of Time*, 1846, print, A. S. Barnes & Co., 51 John Street, New York.

Of course, the earliest records of the past were perpetuated orally. Indeed, until the thirteenth century, oral eyewitness accounts were often considered to be more authoritative and trustworthy than 'incidental evidence' (which required interpretation and was therefore subject to error). Both in the transmission of the past and in courts of law, they were preferred because they were grounded in first-hand experience. Moreover when passed down through the ages, such accounts created an oral tradition which was given precedence because, despite their ever-growing distance in time from the events they related, they were nevertheless rooted in present testimony ('How do you know?' 'Because someone *told* me!' 'And how did *they* know?' 'Because somebody told them!'). Such oral records survived to the extent that they were presently remembered and recited; indeed, they *only* survived to the extent that they were presently remembered and recited. Although they served their purpose, they existed in no other form and were therefore unable in themselves to furnish an abstract historical framework that existed independently of them. Although it is of course only possible to speculate, it is arguable that corresponding conditions applied to the sense of a personal self in individuals. In the absence of an enduring framework – networks of co-ordinates in the environment that seemed to reflect the self to itself, enabling it to acquire the sense of historical continuity that is integral to its nature – the ability of a self-sense to realise and articulate itself remained minimal.

It was through the relationships between inscriptions, monuments, images and documents that an *enduring* framework of historical time was first imagined; and it was arguably through this material infrastructure that the possibility of personal identity was initially institutionalised, albeit in embryonic form and only for the elite: individuals became able to define themselves by placing themselves in a historical context. Among the earliest surviving 'objective' records are those of ancient Sumer and Egypt – carved into stone or written on papyrus in the third and second millennia BCE. In this milieu, historical time was measured locally – mainly in relation to lists of kings, whose reigns were of variable length. To the extent that events were dated at all, they were placed against this background: 'such-and-such a ruler reigned for thirty-four years; in the tenth year of his reign such-and-such event happened'. But because descriptions of dates recommenced with each new reign, it was impossible to articulate a homogenous overarching sense of ancient time; it remained partial and fragmented. In the ancient Greek and Roman republics that followed, the *fixed* annual tenures of leaders ('archons' and 'consuls') ensured that the periods named after them were at least of regular length. In the third century BCE, some Greek writers established a larger scale of reckoning time by supplementing dates associated with leaders with dates since the first Olympic Games, which, they agreed, began in 766 BCE; the winners of races were sometimes named, as points of reference.[2] Similarly, from the third century BCE, some Romans dated events from the foundation of Rome (753 BCE). Despite transcending the limitations of systems based on the circumstances of living individuals, the highly localised nature of each of these systems continued to preclude the possibility of a unified vision of historical time. In the fourth century after Christ, the Christian theologian Eusebius of Caesarea attempted to surmount this problem. In his *Chronicon* of around 325 CE, he juxtaposed lists of rulers and events from different kingdoms (Assyrian, Greek,

Roman, Hebrew) in tabular form, in order to calculate the synchronicities between them. Aided by the newly accessible format of the codex (which, in itself, precipitated a more structured way of thinking than the roll it replaced), Eusebius created an abstract framework in which to conceptualise a unified notion of historical time; the earliest surviving copy of the text dates to the fifth century (Fig. 2.2).[3]

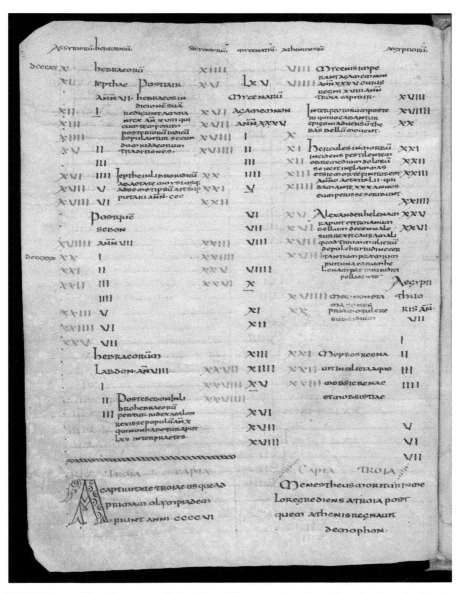

FIGURE 2.2: The *Chronicon* of Eusebius of Caesarea (translated into Latin and edited by St. Jerome in the fifth century), around 699, Fleury (France), Burgerbibliothek Bern, Cod. 219, f. 26v. Photograph: Codices Electronici AG, www.e-codices.ch.

A similar development towards an abstract notion of historical time is reflected, at around the same period, in the computational tables that were originally devised to help calculate the date of the movable feast of Easter. Determined by the movements of the sun and moon – like the dating of the Jewish feast of Passover on which they were based – these tables consisted of lists of dates, unfolding from the time of writing *into the future*. This system, promulgated by the English monk Bede in the eighth century, prevailed for centuries. For instance, a calendrical manuscript that was produced in Durham in around 1120 gives the dates of Easter at least as far ahead as 1253; for years in the future, the right-hand column of the table, which notes the state of the moon on Easter Sunday, is left blank (Fig. 2.3).[4] Because these dates were as yet unclothed by narrative, they merely 'marked time', subjecting what would otherwise have been thoroughly indeterminate and impossible to apprehend to regular measurement and extension. When written on a page as a list, such tables acquired a spatial dimension, facilitating and even encouraging conceptualisation.

Similar constructions of temporal sequences can be found in early collections of annals in which historical events are listed by year. Although these lists originated in antiquity, they did not gain a permanent foothold in Europe until the seventh century, when records of events began to appear in the margins of computational tables, as afterthoughts. In the early twelfth-century calendrical manuscript mentioned above, records of events were added until 1199 (Fig. 2.3).[5] The feature that renders these records most clearly as markings of time rather than meaningful narratives with a sense of agency is the fact that, in many cases, no connection whatsoever is made between the listed events, which can easily pass from a battle, to the death of a king, to a miracle, to a good harvest, to the sighting of a comet or eclipse, without comment. Such events were originally added to calendars relatively soon after they happened, without necessarily presupposing a sense of historic time extending abstractly into the past. They were therefore records of the *present*, for the sake of posterity, rather than reflections on the *past*. It was only subsequently, when they were copied as groups of dates (sometimes edited with the benefit of hindsight) that they seemed to reflect and create a sense of extended time. This effect was reinforced by the fact that in some collations of annals, years are listed even if no event is recorded for them, thereby establishing nothing more than the passing of time itself. Nor did these sequences of events have an ending; they were to be copied and continued indefinitely, by anonymous writers with no particular agenda of their own.[6] Indeed, the role of many annalists was simply to *update* the records of their predecessors.

As the Roman Empire slid into decline, the parameters within which its sense of historical time was constructed became increasingly Christian. Thus, while unifying the chronologies of disparate kingdoms, Eusebius's vision of history also traced the demise of world views that competed with the Christian one. Indeed, his *Chronicon* prepared the way for his *Ecclesiastical History*, which was explicitly conceived to promote Christianity. Significantly, although the *Chronicon* begins with Abraham (the earliest event for which Eusebius could find synchronicities in other traditions), subsequent versions of Jerome's much-copied translation, modification and continuation of the text include an '*exordium*' or false beginning (adapted from the Old Testament) that takes its starting point back to the creation of the world, or the birth of Adam, therefore placing all of history firmly within the context of sacred,

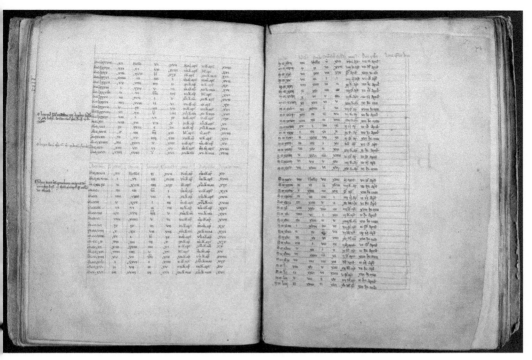

FIGURE 2.3: Bede, 'Writings on the calendar, and other astrological texts', 1125–50, Durham. University of Glasgow, Special Collections, MS Hunter 85 (T.4.2), ff. 26v and 27r.

biblical time and indeed within the context of the whole of time; consistent with the scope of this vision, the future was calculated up to the Last Judgement and the end of the world.[7] Reflecting this ideological shift, Paulus Orosius – theologian and friend of St. Augustine – used the construction of history as an instrument of Christian propaganda, as specifically reflected in the title of his most celebrated work, *Seven Books of History Against the Pagans* (416–17). The Christianisation of chronology was further advanced in 532 when, following the initiative of the Scythian monk Dionysius Exiguus, the calculation of the dates of Easter first came to be made in relation to the incarnation of Christ rather than the accession of Emperor Diocletian (or any other secular dating system). This measuring of dates from the time of Christ was applied to all historical events by Bede in the eighth century (though the practice did not become standard in Europe until the fifteenth).

The sanctity of historical time was further underpinned by the notion of 'sacred history'. This notion, which – like the method of dating Easter – was inherited from Judaism, enshrined the view that the future was predetermined, as prescribed in the scriptures (especially the Book of Revelation), and that it would unfold in keeping with, and as a manifestation of, God's will. Indeed because Christian belief was *rooted* in historical phenomena – the sin of Adam and Eve, and the death and resurrection of Christ – and because Christians considered their religion to be a living sign of the maturation of a historical process that had begun in the time of the Old Testament (implicit in the name of the 'new' one that superseded it), there is a case for saying that Christianity, and the cultural milieu that it spawned, was (and is) fundamentally *historiated*. Historical consciousness was essential to its vision of itself, and a sense of historical time was therefore sewn into the fabric of the European sense of identity that developed from it. With regard to the past, many Christian commentators believed that past events were not only manifestations of God's will in themselves; they were also prophetic codifications of future events, such that the historical process constituted a progressive revelation of God in the world, unfolding according to pre-existent patterns. The Calabrian monk and mystic Joachim of Fiore (c. 1135–1202) identified a Trinitarian structure in history comprising three overlapping eras: an age of the Father, which unfolded – subject to numerological patterns concealed in the Bible – as the Old Testament; an age of the Son, the New Testament, which corresponded in its structure to the Old Testament; and an age of the Holy Spirit, which Joachim believed was soon to commence. The theory of sacred history represented a vision of the future in which the individual self had no significant personal part to play. In his *History of the English People* (written in 1135), the chronicler Henry of Huntingdon used the convention of historical thinking as a template with which to project his sense of time a thousand years back into the past, to the year 135, and a thousand years forwards into the future, to 2135, and even into the fourth and fifth millennia after Christ. One of his reasons for imagining the expanded space of historical time in this way was to highlight the insignificance of man in the unfolding of history and the futility of worldly striving.[8] Man had no power over his destiny, and his perception of historical time made no provision for the discourse of personal identity.

The same implication of 'selflessness' is present in the tradition of 'martyrologies': compilations of the names and stories of early Christian martyrs, listed chronologically by the dates of their deaths and ritually recited during services from the fourth century. Although the early martyrs (first venerated as such in the second century) were individuals, they were also 'selfless'. On the one hand, they were guided by visions or were the instruments of God's miracles; and on the other hand, they died for Christ. The tradition of martyrology developed into a broader tradition of hagiography, which added the life stories of saints who did not die for their faith to those of the martyrs. It reached its apogee in Jacobus de Voraigne's *Golden Legend*, a comprehensive anthology of saints' lives assembled in 1260. Significantly, Jacobus also organised the lives of the saints chronologically – in keeping with the so-called 'epochs' of world history, and the liturgical calendar – such that, besides telling copious stories about the saints (a primary source for image-makers for the next three centuries), his text also reflected his belief in the sacred logic at work in the unfolding of history. Most of Jacobus's narratives were miraculous. Thus, although the cult of saints revolved around individuals, it did not focus on their *personal* independence or identities; on the contrary, it focused on the ways in which Christian values or the will of God operated in them.

The pious selflessness that constitutes the content of hagiographies, and which was intended to inspire their readers by example, was also implicit in the manner in which they were expected to be received. The fact that saints were the instruments or beneficiaries of miracles – one of the proofs of their sanctity – indicates that readers were expected to *believe* their stories and respond to them with selfless piety and devotion to God, rather than to *analyse* or *study* them rationally as examples of human conduct. That the 'lives' of the saints were intended to mediate a preconceived truth about the role of Christian faith in the world, at the expense of facts if necessary, rather than record a sequence of events in an apparently objective, documentary way, is corroborated by the fact that, as with annals and chronicles, writers were accustomed to simply *copying* their narratives from earlier texts, hallowed by the status of tradition, rather than reviewing them in the light of new evidence (though fanciful 'improvements' were sometimes introduced, out of piety). For the coverage of more recent events, eyewitness accounts were considered to have the advantage of direct experience. As we have seen, an eyewitness made a story more *believable*; it was as if an event that was actually observed, without having to rely on secondary evidence, was speaking for itself. Thus, because they were primarily expected to *believe*, readers as well as writers were subject to a frame of reference in which the sense of a personal self, realised through the exercising of its critical faculties, was only minimally, if at all, active.

The universally held belief that the course of an individual's life was dependent on the will of God – rather than on personal volition or control – was paralleled by the belief that his salvation was irrevocably subject to God's grace; he played no role in his own history. In the fifth century, St. Augustine had definitively argued that it was *impossible* to be saved without grace. He articulated this notion in response to the contemporary moralist Pelagius, who maintained that, in order to accrue the merit that legitimises salvation, individuals must exercise free will – a view that came to be seen as a heresy on account of its apparent presumptuousness and arrogance. In the middle of the eighth century, the Augustinian view was put forward in an extreme form by a Saxon monk, Gottschalk of Orbais, who maintained that the fates of both the blessed and the damned were predestined, to the point at which individuals had no freedom whatsoever to influence their salvation.[9] To all intents and purposes, therefore, they had no functional self-sense. From this perspective, there was no point in following the dictates of the Church or practising a virtuous life, for what difference would it make? In 748 and 749, Gottschalk's views were refuted and condemned at councils by the most senior clerics in the kingdom, including Rhabanus Maurus, the archbishop of Mainz. Following the personal interest of Emperor Charles the Bald in the controversy, efforts were made to define the paradoxical relationship between the necessary grace of God and the responsibility of the individual. Arriving at an unstable compromise (subject to infinite modifications and qualifications over several years), it was held by many that though there is nothing an individual can do to assure his own salvation, the impulse to sin (or to not respond to God's grace) is nevertheless not created by God. There had to be, or seem to be, some function or capacity in man that was responsible for it.

The identification of the circumstances in which such a condition might exist proved to be highly problematic. On the one hand, it *had* to exist, in order for man to be responsible for his actions; but on the other hand, it *could not* exist without implying that God, who created everything, had created man's capacity for evil and was therefore in some sense responsible for that evil. The latter implication was unacceptable; to suggest that evil was somehow created by God was to fall into the dualistic Manichean heresy. While it was understood that the ability to do good was an extension of God's grace in man, there must somehow be a psychosocial state in which it is possible for that which is 'not good' to be effected, without being caused by God. It took several centuries for that state to evolve; it is arguable that it constitutes the sense of a personal self, and that the discourse of personal identity evolved, or was generated, to accommodate the conceptualisation and exercise of humanity's freedom in the world.

Having accepted, despite its worrying implications, that man was responsible for his actions and therefore must be free to make choices, the debate revolved around the precise location of that freedom in the soul: did freedom lie in the intellect, which was therefore free to direct or misdirect the God-given appetites of the will? Or did it lie in the will, which was therefore free to follow, or neglect, the God-given wisdom of the intellect? Or did it lie in the 'rational appetite', a combination of the two? Equally debatable was the moral status of man's freedom. Was man naturally sinful but 'free' to do good, or naturally good and 'free' to sin? The doctrine of original sin suggested that he is naturally sinful (on account of the Fall) and that his freedom is therefore constituted by his ability to seek salvation. But it had already been established that all good actions were a manifestation of God's grace rather than human freedom; and besides, to suggest that man is free to effect his own salvation smacked of Pelagian wilfulness. If, conversely, man is naturally good (contradicting the doctrine of original sin), then his freedom – the freedom to err from the true path, as illuminated by the Church – is a dangerous and potentially sinful condition.

Significantly, it was exactly when arguments against the heresy of Gottschalk were being articulated – outlining the scope of the individual to take responsibility for his own actions – that the earliest efforts to legitimise the independent behaviour of lay individuals were made in European culture. While annals and hagiographical texts overlooked the individual will, tacitly identifying the forces that drive the historical process as being both impersonal and sacred, there is a case for finding early manifestations of the self-sense, as an independent agent, in the first 'biographies' of laypeople, which were also written at this time. While secular biographies had been written in antiquity – most famously Suetonius's *Lives of the Caesars* (121 CE) – the genre subsequently fell into abeyance, until the ninth century when the *Lives* of the Carolingian emperors Charlemagne (c. 742–814) and his son Louis the Pious (778–840) revived the genre. The *Life* of Charlemagne, written by Einhard (one of Charlemagne's courtiers) in around 817–30 – shortly after Charlemagne's death in 814 – gives a detailed account of the emperor's life, from his military and political successes to aspects of his personal appearance, habits and demeanour. As such, as a secular history book, it is precocious. Having said that, although Einhard justifies his work on the grounds that he knew Charlemagne well and was therefore uniquely placed, and even obliged, to record his life for posterity, many of the details of the work – for instance, the emperor's eating and drinking habits, his attitude towards his daughters' education and even his appearance – were based on Suetonius's *Caesars* (especially the life of Augustus), which Einhard was emulating on account of its noble antiquity.[10] Thus, although the work has pretensions to 'portraying' Charlemagne and ascribing independent agency to him, it is not, in any developed sense, personal. On the contrary, it was part of the apparatus of leadership, serving a political purpose rather than portraying an individual personality; it was above all required to associate Charlemagne with the emperors of classical Rome and to make a case for the legitimate succession of his son Louis the Pious, for whom two contemporary *Lives* also survive.

These written histories of the Carolingian kings represent some of the earliest efforts to find value in the actions of lay individuals, albeit subsumed in the conventions of statecraft and religious orthodoxy. That this was a key part of their aim is reinforced by the evolution of a second, equally distinctive genre of writing, the 'mirror of princes', that advised Christian kings and princes of the fundamental association of virtue with good deeds; examples of the genre, which clearly reflected the view that individuals *could* make an impact on the unfolding of events, were often directed at specific people (including Louis the Pious and his immediate descendants) at the beginning of their reign.

Some ancient *Lives* – for instance, Thegan's *Life of Louis the Pious* (837) and Asser's *Life of King Alfred* (893) – commence with a roll call of ancestors and then follow the format of annals, listing events year by year. By being listed in this way, the identities of their subjects are constructed according to the conventions of history-making. Indeed, it is arguable that one of the key ways in which the burgeoning sense of self was justified at this very early stage was through 'historicisation' – by being grafted on to the stock of the past and, above all, by manifesting that connection and making it *visible*. The most immediate sign of this trend was the tabulation of genealogies: diagrammatic visualisations of family lineages. In some cases, this meant documenting knowledge that had been remembered and recited orally for generations; according to the twelfth-century *Passio Sancti Aetheberhti*, two minstrels sang songs to King Aethelberht of East Anglia (d. 792 or 794) about his royal lineage as he made his way to Hereford.[11] In other cases, it meant constructing knowledge (deleting unhelpful details as required, according to Bede).[12] Usually it meant mixing the two.

The purpose of genealogical tables was not only to identify an individual's ancestors; it was also to articulate the antiquity of his or her lineage and attach it to a noble source. The earliest surviving example, demonstrating that the Holy Roman Empress Cunigonde of Luxembourg (c. 975–1040) was a descendant of Charlemagne, dates to soon after 1014 (Fig. 2.4). In creating such a structure, the subject of the lineage projected a source of nobility into the remote reaches of historical time in order to subsequently appropriate it, as if it was *inherited* and therefore – crucially – inalienable. As early as 1096, Fulk IV le Rechin, Count of Anjou, wrote a history of Anjou in which he said of his own inheritance: 'I, Fulk . . . have desired to write down how my ancestors came by their honour and held it until my own time, and how I myself have held it, by God's grace.'[13] Fulk's identity and, above all, his nobility were reinforced by his ability to historicise himself. But the practice of genealogy was also underpinned by its association with sanctity. Not only was genealogy used in the Bible to trace the lineage of Christ (back to Adam and Abraham, by the evangelists Luke and Matthew respectively), but from the ninth century, the lineages of noble kings, including King Alfred, were traced back to the very first man, thereby perfecting their claims to the throne by linking them visibly to biblical sources.[14] In the eleventh century, the genealogy of Christ was represented in visual form for the first time.[15] The image was based on an Old Testament passage in which the Prophet Isaiah declared: 'And there shall come forth a rod out of Jesse [the father of King David], and a branch shall grow out of his roots.'[16] Because the Latin word for 'rod' – *virga* – resembles the word *virgo*, meaning 'virgin', the births of David and Christ were mapped on to each other, in a typically medieval fashion, to the

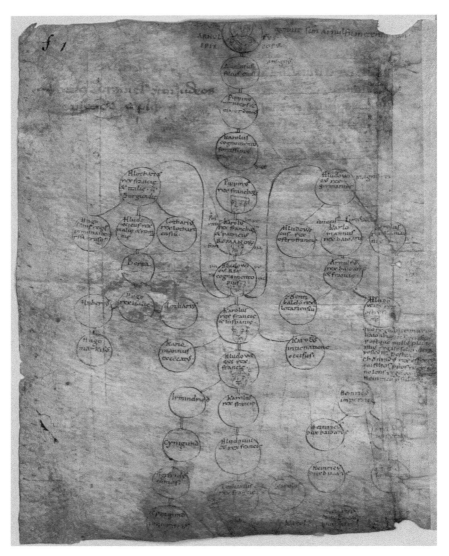

FIGURE 2.4: The 'Bamberg table' or 'Tabula genealogica Carolingorum', after 1014, Regensburg (?), 19 × 14 cm. Bayerischen Staatsbibliothek, Munich. BSB Clm 29880(6. This the earliest known diagram of a genealogical sequence. Cunigond (Cynigund imperatrix) is shown in the bottom left roundel; Charlemagne (Carolus Rex) is shown in the central column, sixth roundel down from the top.

extent that Christ was seen to have been born from the rod of Jesse, by equivalence as well as by descent; his advent was therefore seen to be implicit in, and predetermined by, the Old Testament. In the twelfth century, this rod blossomed into the 'Tree of Jesse', a fully peopled family tree that illustrated Christ's long descent from Jesse through David, Solomon and the Virgin Mary (Fig. 2.5). The 'tree'

FIGURE 2.5: The 'Tree of Jesse', from The Lambeth Bible, around 1140, South of England. Lambeth Palace Library, MS3, f. 198r.

concept, requiring successors to ascend from their ancestors rather than descend from them, was widely depicted throughout the Middle Ages; it mostly appeared in illuminated manuscripts and stained-glass windows (notably in Chartres and Canterbury cathedrals). At the end of the century, Peter of Poitiers' *Compendium historiae in genealogia Christi* (*The Compendium of History in the Genealogy of Christ*) elaborated on the genealogy of Christ by enhancing it with a historical commentary, derived from the Bible. Because the unbroken continuity of Christ's lineage was integral to the concept of Peter's work, and because diagrams 'commend themselves to the memory by habit', Christ's genealogy was sometimes presented visually as a unified structure on a long parchment roll (Fig. 2.6), setting a precedent for the genealogical rolls of English kings that were produced from around 1260.[17] In one example of the latter from around 1461, Edward IV is represented at the top of a tree that is clearly based on a 'Tree of Jesse' (though, in this case, the tree is rooted in Henry III, the foundation of Plantagenet rule in England). Nearby, scenes from the king's life are juxtaposed with scenes from the Old Testament that are thereby made to anticipate them typologically. In both cases, methods of Christian exegesis are used to demonstrate that Edward's identity as ruler is based on the apparent necessity of *historical* logic (Fig. 2.7).[18]

Some of the earliest efforts to articulate a sense of personal identity in terms of family relations were practical. While genealogies were intended to display the lineage of a family, linked by marriage, to legitimise its claims to status, power and landownership, 'ancestor lists', linked by blood, were also produced to ensure that people did not marry individuals that were too closely related to them. These lists, which identified the degrees of separation between relatives (siblings, cousins, in-laws, step-relations, etc.), were based on a generic structure of kinship relations, salvaged from classical sources by Isidore of Seville in the seventh century, and disseminated throughout the Middle Ages in elaborate 'consanguinity tables' (Fig. 2.8). In 948, the Synod of Ingelheim recommended that all Christians produce lists of their own ancestors in order to check the degree of kinship between them and their prospective spouses. In the early twelfth century, Bishop Ivo of Chartres pronounced a marriage 'consanguineous' (having too much shared blood) after consulting an ancestor list provided by the family.[19] While such lists were recommended by the Church to avoid incest, they could also be used to help identify lines of inheritance (though the required distance of kinship between spouses was sometimes ignored by nobles that were keen to keep property within the family). In this respect – and because of their diagrammatic structure – 'ancestor lists' resembled family trees, implicitly articulating the extensive *historicity* of a family's identity, as well as its bloodlines.

From the beginning of the thirteenth century, the use of genealogical tables as instruments of identity formation was supplemented by the use of coats of arms. Coats of arms had developed in the previous century as a language of visual insignia with which to identify knights who were completely concealed by their armour during battles and tournaments. As a result, they were associated with military prowess and valour. In due course, they came to be conferred on courageous individuals by their lords, as signs of loyalty, privilege and chivalry. Indeed they eventually became so associated with noble and heroic behaviour that, from the fourteenth century, Christ himself was seen to have had one, composed of the *Arma Christi*, or instruments of

FIGURE 2.6: Peter of Poitiers, *Compendium historiae in genealogia Christi* (*The Compendium of History in the Genealogy of Christ*), 1275–99, parchment, 72.2 × 26.0 cm. Free Library of Philadelphia, Lewis E 249A-B. Free Library of Philadelphia, Rare Book Department.

FIGURE 2.7: Genealogy of Edward IV, 1460–70, England, parchment roll, 175.0 ×
53.5 cm. British Library, London, Harley MS 7353, f. 011. © The British Library Board.
Based on the 'Tree of Jesse', the tree shows Henry III reclining at the bottom (centre) and
the opponents Edward IV and Henry VI at the top (top right and left respectively).

the Passion (Fig. 2.9). Some writers even interpreted the Crucifixion as a kind of battle
or joust in which a chivalrous Christ, with a shield emblazoned with his coat of arms,
fought to win the heart of his lady, the pious Christian's soul.[20]

Although coats of arms were awarded to individuals, the process of 'knighting'
was originally a practical transaction, without much ostentation – somewhat like the
giving of modern-day 'bonuses' – and it was therefore little cultivated as a means of
identity formation. However, as it developed throughout the twelfth century, it

FIGURE 2.8: Table of consanguinity from Gratian's *Decretum*, around 1270–1300, Italy, probably Naples, thirteenth century, ink, tempera and gold on parchment, 28.9 × 21.2 cm. The Cleveland Museum of Art, purchase from the J. H. Wade Fund, 1929.435.2.

became increasingly honorific and elaborate. Although the details could vary enormously, beneficiaries were typically invested with helmet, shield, lance and horse by their lord as a reward for heroic services, sometimes on the battlefield, but sometimes at court ceremonies. As coats of arms were passed on from one generation to the next, they became formally heritable; as a result, and especially when the use of gunpowder finally put an end to man-to-man combat, rendering total body cover

FIGURE 2.9: The arms of Christ, from the Hyghalmen Roll, around 1447–55, Cologne, Germany, College of Arms, London MS M. 5b, ff. 1v–2r. Reproduced by permission of the Kings, Heralds and Pursuivants of Arms.

unnecessary, they came to be seen as badges of honour per se, associated more with lineage than with military achievement. Moreover, they were associated with *families* rather than individuals, to the extent that the honour or shame earned by an individual was frequently ascribed to his kin. Having said this, because only one person was permitted to bear a given coat of arms at a time, variations on the fundamental design were introduced to identify the roles of individuals within the family structure, especially the eldest son who was heir to the title of lord. First appearing in the thirteenth century, these variations (called 'differences' or 'marks of cadence') consisted of the addition of small details, such as a label, crescent, star or cross, to the 'undifferenced' design.[21] On a microscopic scale, they constituted embryonic signs of abstracted individuality – though, as they were attached to the individual *role* rather than the individual *person*, they remained impersonal, accommodating the *idea* of personal identity rather the *experience* of it.

As coats of arms came to be associated with family honour rather than military exploits, they began to be used in other contexts, enhancing buildings, chattels and – most significantly in the present context – chronicles and genealogical rolls, where, by virtue of being inserted into a representation of historical time, they functioned as badges of a specifically *historiated* sense of identity. Accordingly, the text of chronicler-monk Matthew Paris's *History of the English*, written in 1250–5, is punctuated with coats of arms, which are placed in the margins at the points at which their bearers appear in the narrative (Fig. 2.10). In this particular instance, the shields do not simply *represent* their bearers, marking time; they are also made to *tell their stories*: they are given crowns at coronations and mitres at elections, and are turned upside down at deaths, accompanied by the instrument of death if there was one (e.g. a crossbow or broken lance). A genealogical roll of the kings of England and France, produced in France in 1467–8, explicates the historicist implications of coats of arms

FIGURE 2.10: The death of Richard I and coronation of King John, in *Historia Anglorum, Chronica Majora, Part III*, by Matthew Paris, 1250–5, Royal MS 14 C VII, f. 85v. British Library, London. © The British Library Board.

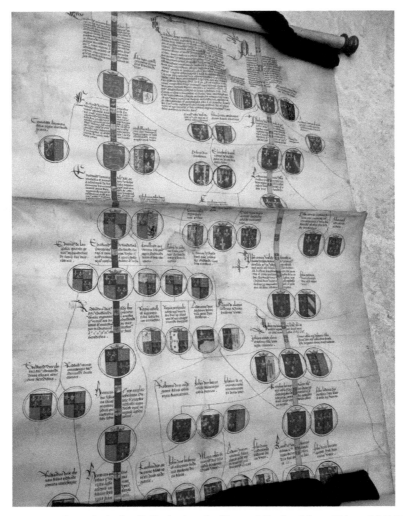

FIGURE 2.11: Genealogical roll displaying the kings of England from Edward I (1272–1307) to Edward IV (1461–83), and the kings of France from Philip IV (1285–1314) to Louis XI (1461–83). About 1465, France, vellum, 125 × 63 cm. The Newberry Library, Chicago, Case MS 166. The lines of succession of England and France are arranged in vertical columns, with intermarriages and other connections criss-crossing in the centre.

by assembling them into a family tree, thereby highlighting the legitimising continuity of a family's honour in the clearest possible way (Fig. 2.11). The potential of coats of arms to legitimise identity by historicising it is even more explicit when they were attributed retrospectively to individuals who lived before the existence of heraldry – for instance, King Arthur or Brutus of Troy (the legendary founder of Britain) – from whom honour and legitimacy could then be seen to be inherited. An ingeniously designed genealogical roll dating to around 1465 traces the lineage of the

FIGURE 2.12: Chronicle of the History of the World from Creation to Woden, with a Genealogy of Edward IV', 1461–4, England, vellum, 477.8 × 46.0 cm. Free Library of Philadelphia, MS Lewis E201. Edward IV (mounted on horseback) is shown above God and the Temptation of Adam and Eve. Free Library of Philadelphia, Rare Book Department.

recently crowned King Edward IV back to Adam and Eve, carefully documenting its passage through the Old Testament and a number of British, French and Saxon kings, many of whom have had coats of arms attributed to them posthumously (Fig. 2.12). The roll was clearly intended to prove that the king's right to the throne was predetermined by scripture, history and the logic of symmetry, for – as an inscription at the top of the roll professes – while Edward was intent on consolidating his identity as the king, he was also keen to highlight that 'this is the Lord's doing'.

The reality of the past was thrown into sharp perspective when the possibility of pictorial representation came into view. It was one thing to *mention* one's ancestors, but quite another to *depict* them, given that it was not known what they looked like. This issue came to a head in the fifteenth century when naturalistic styles of representation became common, whereupon the ordinary objects of optical experience had to be taken into consideration, alongside sacred subjects that were perpetuated by tradition. The new genre of portraying living people – itself a powerful sign of the developing self-sense – was, of course, fed by the artist's actual viewing of the sitter. However, with regard to historical people who pre-dated the age of naturalism, leaving no accurate visual record of their appearance, what should an artist do? What face and body type should he choose? This was a problem that had never arisen before because, for most of the Middle Ages, image-makers used generic facial types for all people, whether dead or alive. Moreover, the surviving descriptions of the appearances of early medieval individuals (mostly rulers) were of little use, as they were invariably generalised. Charlemagne, for instance, was described by his biographer Einhard (who knew him intimately) as being:

> large and strong; his stature tall but not ungainly, for the measure of his height was seven times the length of his own feet. The top of his head was round; his eyes were very large and piercing. His nose was rather larger than is usual; he had beautiful white hair; and his expression was brisk and cheerful; so that, whether sitting or standing, his appearance was dignified and impressive. Although his neck was rather thick and short and he was somewhat corpulent this was not noticed owing to the good proportions of the rest of his body.[22]

As we have seen, the purpose of this description was as much to associate Charlemagne with Emperor Augustus, as described by Suetonius in *Lives of the Caesars,* as to evoke a realistic impression of him. William of Malmesbury's description of William II was even more laconic. According to his *Chronicle of the Kings of England* (c. 1125), William was: 'well built; his complexion florid, his hair yellow; of open countenance; different-coloured eyes, varying with certain glittering specks; of astonishing strength, though not very tall, and his belly rather projecting'.[23]

Early depictions of individuals are no more informative than verbal descriptions. Moreover, because the visual representation of individuals had not yet been raised to a level of significance, examples of the genre are scarce. With the exception of coins, which bear highly simplified, stylised profiles of the presiding ruler, no contemporary representations of Charlemagne survive. A rare thirteenth-century tapestry of him still shows him as generic type (Fig. 2.13). His descendants, especially his grandson Charles the Bald, realised the political potential of having themselves depicted, but the images they patronised are also rare (seen only by the elite) and too

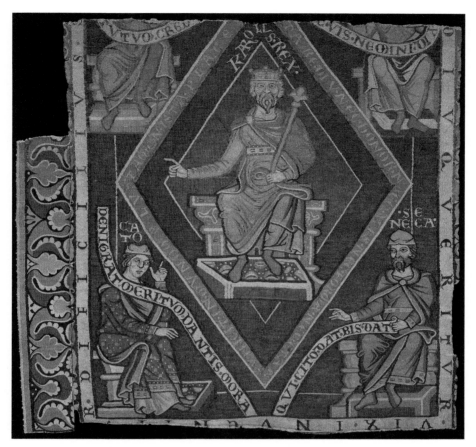

FIGURE 2.13: Charlemagne enthroned. The Karlsteppich tapestry, second half of the thirteenth century, linen and wool, 158 × 163 cm. Lower Saxony Domschatz Halberstadt, Inv. Nr. 520. Landesamt für Denkmalpflege und Archäologie (State Office for Historic Monuments and Archaeology), Sachsen-Anhalt. Photo Juraj Lipták.

generalised to give a personal likeness; indeed, despite his ancient nickname, it is not even known whether Charles the Bald was bald or not. In the ensuing centuries, images of kings became increasingly common. But although they signified that the monarch was *worthy of representation*, they did not aim to resemble him.

When the need for realism in portraits did eventually evolve, there were various options. In some cases – involving classical heroes or patron saints – the problem was solved by using the faces of patrons, flattering them by association in the process. In others, artists used their own faces or those of their friends and fellow artists. A third alternative was simply to make the image up, adapting ideas from one or more anonymous models, or from the example of other prestigious portraits, or from what little documentary evidence survived. The latter was the fate of many of the early kings of England, who were represented in a realistic style for the first time in the sixteenth century – for instance, in Thomas Talbot's *Booke Containing the True Portraiture of the Kings of England*, published in 1597, or Renold Elstrack's *Baziliologia* of 1618 (Fig. 2.14). These publications were key sources for the series of royal portraits that lined the 'long galleries' in great houses of the period, institutionalising historical thinking among the ruling class while also enabling them to demonstrate their allegiance to the monarchy (Fig. 2.15). In such cases, the use of a plausible and

FIGURE 2.14: Renold or Reginold Elstrack (Elstracke), King William I, from *Baziliologia, A Booke of Kings, being the true and lively effigies of all our English kings from the Conquest untill this present*, 1618, engraving, 17.7 × 11.2 cm. National Portrait Gallery, London.

FIGURE 2.15: The Brown Gallery with rows of sixteenth- and seventeenth-century portraits at Knole, Sevenoaks, Kent. © National Trust Images/Andreas von Einsiedel.

even convincing image – represented *as if* it was based on observation – was more important than actual verisimilitude; besides, their inaccuracy could not be proven. Some people, however, used representations that were *known* to be wrong. Soon after 1520, the owner of a fifteenth-century manuscript of the *Chronicle* of John Harding (d. 1465) added an author portrait to the book, but, because he did not know what John Harding looked like, he reused a woodcut print of George III, prince of Anhalt-Dessau, by Lucas Cranach the Younger, in its place. He even added an invented coat of arms and inscription to the image: 'The portrature [sic] of John Harding: maker of these chronicles.'[24] In this somewhat formulaic expression of identity, it appears that the mere registration of Harding as a visible individual was sufficient, over and above his actual appearance and personality.

While such images gave the *impression* of 'truthfulness', projecting the capacity for 'naturalistic experience' into the past, they were not what they seemed to be. Despite pretending to be based on observation – inviting viewers to engage with the characters they portrayed in a realistic way by depicting them as real individuals with personal narratives, rather than as stock types – they were in fact presupposing, and exploiting, the credulity of the viewer in a purely 'medieval' way. This uncritical stance was challenged in the fifteenth and sixteenth centuries. Just as the new valorisation of human rationality and experience resulted in the birth of naturalism in painting – representing the world as it appeared to optical vision, rather than as perpetuated by tradition – so it led to the development of new historiographical conventions that were increasingly conceived around the validity of *objective evidence*. Conversely – and more significantly in the present context – just as naturalistic painting addressed and evoked an empirical function in the individual viewer, rather than a conformist, credulous one, so the new ways of thinking about history and historical time presupposed, and accommodated, a mindset that implicitly ascribed a degree of personal freedom and protagonism to the individual, and therefore to itself. The possibility of self-reference and personal identity was implicit in these new ways of thinking.

Throughout the Middle Ages, perceptions of truth were seen through a lens of Christian belief. Phenomena were not evaluated on their own terms and they were not therefore rated per se as evidence. On the contrary, their truth value was evaluated in terms of their compliance with Christian doctrine. Moreover, as we have seen, until the thirteenth century, narratives were often perpetuated orally because, no matter how far back the oral tradition went, it was rooted in first-hand experience and therefore 'must be true'. The possibility of distorting the facts, let alone challenging them, was not highlighted by such a mode of transmission; if it had been, the pervasive belief in miracles and veneration of relics would have been impossible. How could it have been otherwise, in a world in which the theft of a relic was considered legitimate because it could not have happened if the saint in question had not blessed it? Moreover, in courts of law a person's innocence was not necessarily tested by assessing the evidence; it was often tested by forcing a miracle – that is, by subjecting the accused to an ordeal, by water, fire or scorching hot iron, and judging them on the auspicious signs of the outcome (for instance, whether their skin was marked or not). In the fifteenth century, however, questions were increasingly asked about the evidence that supported a wide range of traditional claims; and, in due course, individuals began to look for independent signs in the world that would enable them to build an impression of the past that was based on observation, interpretation and understanding, rather than ritual repetition and belief. When commissioned to paint a commemorative picture of Charlemagne in 1510, for instance, the Nuremberg artist Albrecht Dürer did not simply follow precedents in the traditional manner; he also looked for *evidence* of the emperor's appearance (Fig. 2.16). Because there was no surviving record of the emperor's face (apart from the rather generalised descriptions of his biographers), Dürer's rendering of the face could never make claims to historical 'accuracy', though it is realistic. It simply presents a traditional facial type, prevalent since the twelfth century, in a modern way. However, the costume he used for the emperor was based on survivals that were thought to be the actual garments and regalia of Charlemagne.[25] By using them as models, therefore, Dürer was clearly attempting to bring an unprecedented degree of historical realism to the work; more broadly, he was subscribing to a mode of history-making in which statements or suggestions of fact were subject to empirical verification, addressing and evoking the powers of rational discrimination in the subjects that engaged with them. That the imperial costumes were subsequently discovered *not* to be associated with Charlemagne does not spoil his intention. The concept of evidence was acquiring value even if the wherewithal to prove its soundness was still emerging.

The new need to support apparent statements of historical fact with evidence was most urgently felt in relation to Christ himself, for Christ was as much a historical

FIGURE 2.16: Albrecht Dürer, *Charlemagne*, 1511–13, paint on lime wood, 215 × 115 cm. Germanisches Nationalmuseum, Nuremberg.

figure as he was the son of God. Now that naturalism in painting had become standard, it was necessary to ask – and answer – the question: what did Christ actually look like? Christ's appearance had hitherto been provided by tradition: the familiar long-haired, bearded figure. Although this image had only originated in the fifth century (superseding a short-haired, beardless figure), it had satisfied the faithful for a millennium. Now, however, *to satisfy the rational mind*, it was necessary to have proof. There was already *some* evidence (or assumptions that were taken as evidence): for instance, St. Luke was believed to have painted Christ and the Virgin from life, producing an image that became the first in a chain of replicas that amounted to an eyewitness tradition, although Christ was an infant at the time. Another source was the Veil of Veronica, a towel on which Christ was believed to have wiped his face on the way to Golgotha, leaving a magical impression on it; but the image was miraculous (surviving as a relic) and therefore impossible to verify rationally. Moreover, neither tradition could be traced back further than the sixth century. It was extremely timely, therefore, that in the thirteenth century a historical document that described Christ's appearance in detail was 'discovered'. What is significant about this much-copied and sometimes illustrated document – the 'Letter of Lentulus' sent by Publius Lentulus, Governor of Judaea at the time of Christ, to the Roman Senate – is not the information it conveys; this conforms to the image perpetuated by tradition, while going into enough detail to suggest first-hand experience. It is more the fact that it was conceived to address an individual for whom truths could no longer be accepted on trust; they need to be backed up with evidence. In order to do this, the Letter of Lentulus created a circumstance in which the very real humanity of Christ was no longer at odds with a secular, rational understanding of historical time, and therefore implicitly exclusive of the 'experiential self'; on the contrary, it was now revealed to be consistent with such an understanding. And that being so, it implicitly accommodated a model of subjectivity, or *self-sense*, which – still within the overall context of Christian belief – was thereby expected, and empowered, to exercise its rational faculties freely. The fact that the document was a forgery is, again, ironic, but it does not undermine its significance. More to the point is the fact that it was fake *evidence* rather than a fake *miracle*.

The significance of the increased dependence on objective evidence was not only that it reflected the use of observation and rationality on the part of pioneering scholars, but also that it awakened these critical faculties in the minds of their readers. Indeed, by presupposing the use of rational discrimination, it provided a mental environment in which the mind of the subject was implicitly active and inclined to cohere into a sense of self. What passed for evidence in the Middle Ages was anything that confirmed the preconceived doctrines of the Church, or served its purposes, because the 'truth' of the Church was invested in those doctrines and purposes. A sense of historical context, and the ways in which context may have contributed towards the significance of historical phenomena, was not yet important. Moreover, contradictions were not necessarily analysed to the point at which they were resolved; they could equally well be further complicated by the 'discovery' of new qualifying circumstances, or by reference to other doctrines of equivalent status, or by miraculous intervention, thereby postponing the problem indefinitely. Indeed, the logic of miracles, omens and visions was an *alternative* to evidence; it could solve *any* problem; and, at its most extreme, it rendered the whole realm of worldly phenomena irrelevant. The outcome of this approach was that each observation existed in its own private context or 'space' in which it seemed to make sense. But when those 'spaces' were placed together, they did not blend into each other, creating the expanded impression of a singular conceptual space; the logic of one contradicted the logic of the other, giving rise to a sense of space that was fragmented and incomplete: although one can *stand on* a chair and one can *lift* a chair, one *cannot lift a chair while standing on it.* But this did not matter, precisely because the sense of a homogenous overall 'conceptual space', against which one might notice the inconsistency of individual observations, did not exist; nor did the coherent 'noticer' of such inconsistencies. The individual relationship of any given observation to the Christian truth that it was required to manifest was sufficient to justify it.

What we see happening from the fifteenth century onwards, however, is a desire to evaluate observations not simply in relation to the truth they are believed to manifest, but in relation to each other; that is to say, to ensure that the overall space in which they are made is consistent and homogenous, as judged, not on principle, but by newly critical faculties of observation and analysis in the minds of the individuals that apprehend it. So, for instance, while texts *were* written in the fourth century, and medieval grammar *was* used in the eighth century, eighth-century grammar was *not* used in the fourth century. Therefore, a new explanation had to be developed to account for the *Donation of Constantine*, a document which purported to have been written in the fourth century despite using eighth-century grammar and vocabulary. In 1440, it was discovered by the humanist scholar Lorenzo Valla, using a rational assessment of historical evidence, that this document, in which Emperor Constantine was said to have surrendered political power to the papacy, was a fake, whereupon a new 'space' or frame of reference in which the discrepancy could be resolved (without damaging the papacy's pretensions to truthfulness too much) had to develop; namely, an understanding that what had once seemed to be 'proof' (because unquestioned) might now turn out to be 'fake', and that other arguments for papal supremacy would therefore have to be found. Historical context *was* important in this instance and it presupposed a degree of historical consciousness in individuals; this historical consciousness in turn presupposed a historiated sense of self that was located in, and looked back in time from, the present time.

The appetite for a consistent and comprehensive sense of historical or temporal space was paralleled by an equivalent appetite for a unified sense of *pictorial* space in the visual arts. Until the fifteenth century, pictorial space was either non-existent or highly inconsistent. The conventions used in the representation of forms were maintained by tradition (by copying precedents, as with texts), and required no analysis of optical experience. In the fifteenth century, however, pictorial space became increasingly consistent and homogenous, owing to the use of linear perspective (a coherent system of parallel lines, or 'orthogonals', receding towards a distant vanishing point) and descriptive modelling (the realistic lighting and shading of forms). While the development of these conventions gave rise to a completely new type of art, their more hidden significance was the provision of conditions under which reason and observation, and *the self-sense that was implicitly active in them*, became a current and legitimate means of assessing the world – at the expense of unquestioning belief in the authority of the Church. The conventions of historiography unfolded, from a position that presupposed belief to one that presupposed reason, in exactly the same way. While they can on the one hand be seen to have developed in order to facilitate a more objective perception and evaluation of historical evidence, they can equally well be seen to have developed as a function of the burgeoning self-sense, which generated conventions through which to see itself extending coherently into the world, and thereby to realise itself as a coherent entity.

Throughout the Middle Ages, chronologies, annals, sacred histories, genealogies and heraldry were created as intellectual media through which to conceptualise the notion of the past, and to find – and place – meaning in that notion. They constituted models of historical time in which the passage of the years was organised into a series of regular relationships that seemed to reflect or embody a meaningful principle. Above all, they were constrained to demonstrate the influence of God's will or providence in the destiny of the world, either as revealed in the intelligence of numerical patterns that appeared in the fabric of historical time, or by direct miraculous intervention. From the eleventh century, chronology was also visualised in elaborate genealogical tables. The purpose of these tables, which could be apprehended in a single glance, was to promote the unity of a family, extended over time and sealed by blood and marriage, and to secure the rights of its heirs to inherit property and power. While some of these tables claimed to manifest the will of God in keeping with traditional values by tracing their subjects back to biblical ancestors, not all of them did. They also begin to reflect a shift of interest towards the role of the individual in the unfolding of history. Indeed, in 1580, the historian Reiner Reineck promoted the use of genealogies as an instrument of historical research precisely because they structured historical time, not in terms of God's will, but in terms of human action: 'anyone can see that histories chiefly deal with the persons who did things, and that they must be separated out into families'.[26] Increasingly, educated people were beginning to assess their fortunes from a secular perspective, ascribing agency to independent human individuals for the first time.

As a result of this shift towards human agency, the annalistic form of chronicle, structured by year, began to decline, in favour of narratives that were conceived more flexibly around the causes and consequences of historical events. The oral transmission of truths was increasingly supplanted by a critical evaluation of material evidence, mostly in the form of documents but also through historic inscriptions, coins and artefacts.[27] Offering a direct parallel to the visual arts, the key developments originated in Florence. Thus, although the humanist historian Leonardo Bruni adhered to a year-by-year structure for his pioneering *History of the Florentine People* (1442), following the annalistic form of the Florentine *Chronicle* by Giovanni Villani (1300–1348), he dispensed with the providential view of the latter in favour of a secular view of historical change, inspired by Cicero and Livy, that revolved around human action; the human drama was played out not so much against the will of God (though of course, God's will was always found, if sought) but against the random and erratic vagaries of fate and fortune, sometimes personified as a blind woman to suggest the lack of an 'agenda'. Moreover, well into the sixteenth century and beyond, it was believed that not only personal destinies but history itself – from revolts and plagues to the historical evolution of different religions – were subject to the regular but ever-changing relationships between the planets, and to the anomalous appearance of comets (and could therefore be predicted by experts in the art of astrology). In 1554, Girolamo Cardano controversially ascribed control over the characteristics of Christianity to the nature and behaviour of Jupiter and Mercury.[28] But many people also rejected astrology. The Dominican preacher Savonarola (1452–98) and the humanist philosopher Pico della Mirandola (1463–94) railed against it on the grounds that it eclipsed the free will of both God and man.[29]

The alternatives to divine providence, planetary influence and blind fate were, at first, limited. One option was developed by Bruni, whose revival of the classical convention of putting fictive speeches into the mouths of historical protagonists highlighted their personal involvement in events, while also giving readers the impression that they were experiencing the action as it was happening. The use of direct speech (which could be seen as a reimagining of the oral tradition without the intermediate voices) added a rhetorical flourish not only to the imagined thoughts of historical characters but also to the *re*presentation of their speeches by the writer. Indeed, the historian's task increasingly depended on his mastery of rhetoric. The role of this ancient art was not just to make his texts more elegant and literary, as speeches; it was also to make them more affecting and effective, as historical narrative. For the purpose of history-making was itself changing, away from the mystical presentation of history as an exposition of the will of God in an extended temporal form, towards the presentation of it as a body of examples of social, political or personal action to be used by its consumers in a practical way – as models (positive or negative) in the process of self-fashioning. It had, therefore, to be inspirational.

The classical art of biography, revived as an elite form of accolade by the Carolingians, was also reinvigorated at this time, and largely for the same reasons. *Collections* of biographies were especially telling as they highlighted the *genre* of biography as much as the individual characters under consideration. Inspired by Plutarch's *Lives* and Suetonius's *Lives of the Caesars*, the genre institutionalised the reality of the self-sense by reconfiguring history around the morality and temperament of individual people. In the mid-fourteenth century, Petrarch and Boccaccio both wrote collections of biographies, mostly of illustrious or ill-fated characters from antiquity. Petrarch stressed the effects of personal virtue, as opposed to fate or fortune, on the unfolding of events; his *On Famous Men* (*De viris illustribus*), begun in 1338, was partly intended to accompany a gallery of thirty-six painted portraits of Roman heroes belonging to his patron.[30] Boccaccio's *Fates of Illustrious Men* (*De casibus virorum illustrium*) also highlighted the individuality of famous people, but it underlined how even the fortunate can fall. In around 1360, Boccaccio also wrote a pioneering text, *On Famous Women*. In around 1395, Filippo Villani (nephew of the Florentine chronicler) modernised the genre of collective biography by including a series of brief biographies of *contemporary* celebrities (including painters, but not sculptors) in his patriotic history of Florence. In his *Lives of Three Illustrious Florentine Poets* of 1440, Gianozzi Manetti turned the genre on itself by writing the biographies of biographers (Petrarch, Boccaccio and Dante). In 1512, the historian Paolo Giovio began collecting painted portraits of eminent individuals, both living and dead. Subscribing to the Roman belief, quoted by the humanist Poggio Bracciolini, 'that the images of men who had excelled in the pursuit of glory and wisdom, if placed before the eyes, would help ennoble and stir up the soul', he put them on public display in a private museum, built especially for the purpose.[31] By the time of his death in 1552, his 'temple of virtue' numbered 484 portraits, each accompanied by a brief biography. It was subsequently dispersed, but not before copies of many works were made by Cristofano dell'Altissimo for Cosimo I de Medici; these have been on display in the Uffizi Gallery, as a single sequence running the length of the First Corridor at architrave level (interspersed with larger portraits of Medici family members), since 1587 (Fig. 2.17). Thirty years later, Paul Ardier, a counsellor at the court of the French king Louis XIII, was inspired by this precedent to commission a series of 327 paintings of illustrious individuals whom he perceived to have influenced the history of France since 1328 for a gallery at the Chateau de Beauregard, where they have been on display ever since. Other ways of cataloguing individuality also developed. Archduke Ferdinand II of Austria (1529–95) showed his esteem for the individuals he admired by collecting the armour they wore on significant occasions and displaying them, alongside his own, in his *kunstkammer* at Schloss Ambras, both as relics of historical events and as portraits of their protagonists. Paradoxically, the collection of horoscope readings that the astrologer Girolamo Cardano produced from the 1530s – the lives of prominent individuals (including Savonarola, Pico della Mirandola and himself), as determined by the astrological conditions that prevailed at the times of their births – also amounts to a set of biographies. Clearly by the time Vasari wrote his *Lives of the Most Excellent Painters, Sculptors and Architects* in 1550, celebrating the elevated status of artists, the tradition of collective biography was well established.

The transition to a paradigm in which personal virtue was recognised as being instrumental in the unfolding of an individual's life – thereby presupposing the existence of a self-sense endowed with the freedom and responsibility to make

FIGURE 2.17: Benedetto Vincenzo de Greyss, *Galleria Imperiale de Firenze* (showing copies of the Giovio portraits installed in the Uffizi Gallery, above the windows), 1748, drawing on paper, 37 × 52.5 cm. Osterreichische Nationalbibliothek, Vienna.

choices – was by no means straightforward. Despite continued assurances that free will was compatible with the foreknowledge of God, the shift put pressure on the Church. For instance, discussions about the relative values of the 'active' and 'contemplative' lives increasingly concluded in favour of the active life, in service to one's family and society, at the expense of monastic seclusion; contemplative laymen, such as Petrarch, were accommodated in the newly evolving role of the 'secular scholar'. In his *De Professione Reliogosorum* (1442), Lorenzo Valla regarded a virtuous life in the world as superior to the monastic life under vows because it tested free will, rather than childishly abdicating responsibility for it.[32] Significantly, Erasmus's humanist recommendation that individuals take responsibility for their actions led to charges of Pelagianism. To conservative theologians, his initiative seemed not to be based on the example of the saints, who surrendered their wills unreservedly to God, but on arrogant wilfulness. Such forthright individuality could, however, be seen from another perspective. Successful mercenaries, employed by the Italian city states due to their lack of standing armies, were honoured with grand equestrian monuments, despite the fact that they put money and status before morality; some such monuments – for instance, Paolo Uccello's painted monument to the English mercenary Sir John Hawkwood – were even placed in churches (in Florence Cathedral in 1436, in this instance).[33] Niccolò Machiavelli (1469–1527), who disapproved of mercenaries (but only for strategic reasons), positively encouraged leaders to impose their wills on history. His notorious *The Prince*, in which he advocated an unflinching pragmatism, even if the process involved the transgression of social and moral ideals, was written in 1513. One way around this moral problem was to enlarge the pool of acceptable behavioural models. The revival of interest in classical precedents was partly fuelled by this need. Where the saints had been self-deprecating, many figures from ancient history could be seen to set a precedent of courageous, responsible and heroic thought and behaviour. Such associations presented a respectable case for the discourse of personal freedom and selfhood – even for Christians, if interpreted 'correctly'. Some pagan gods and goddesses could also be used as positive role models.

Alexander the Great, for instance, was revered both for his military prowess and his magnanimity. In the early Middle Ages, the legendary king was usually invested with negative associations of ambition and pride, largely on account of the legend that he flew towards heaven in a chariot drawn by griffins that were motivated by lumps of meat that he dangled in front of them (Fig. 2.18). In the thirteenth century, however, his significance began to change. Initially, he was included among the 'Nine Worthies', a group of stock characters from the past – three Christian, three Jewish and three pagan – selected to epitomise the universal virtues of chivalry; Alexander was part of the pagan contingent, alongside Hector and Julius Caesar (Fig. 2.19). This convention thrived throughout the Renaissance. By the fifteenth century, the potential for using the writing – and especially the *studying* – of historical narratives as an instrument of self-fashioning had been developed to such a level that privileged individuals could articulate their own identities by identifying with historical heroes and appropriating their qualities *allegorically*. In a pair of tapestries depicting the military exploits and heroic deeds of Alexander – commissioned by Philip the Good, Duke of Burgundy, in Tournai in around 1459 (and now in the Galleria Doria

FIGURE 2.18: The celestial journey of Alexander the Great, pulled by gryphons, one of
the Rolls Plaques, about 1160, the Meuse Region, champlevé enamel, 10.2 × 10.2 cm.
Victoria and Albert Museum, London.

Pamphilij in Rome) – the faces of Alexander and his father, Philip of Macedonia, are
based on the faces of Philip the Good and his son Charles the Bold, who Philip
considered to be a 'new Alexander'. For the same reason (using the past to *construct*
the present), the costumes of all the figures in the tapestry are contemporary.
Machiavelli also considered Alexander to be a model conqueror. Not only was he
worthy of emulation on account of his own achievements, but he also wisely learned
from his predecessors:

> But to exercise the intellect the prince should read histories, and study there the
> actions of illustrious men, to see how they have borne themselves in war, to
> examine the causes of their victories and defeat, so as to avoid the latter and
> imitate the former; and above all do as an illustrious man did, who took as an
> exemplar one who had been praised and famous before him, and whose
> achievements and deeds he always kept in his mind, as it is said Alexander the
> Great imitated Achilles, Caesar Alexander, Scipio Cyrus.[34]

FIGURE 2.19: Daniel Hopfer, *The Three Worthy Pagans (Hector, Alexander the Great and Julius Caesar)*, after Hans Burgkmair, about 1516, etching, 15.2 × 22.1 cm. Metropolitan Museum of Art, New York, The Elisha Whittelsey Collection, The Elisha Whittelsey Fund.

To render him more apt and useful as a role model, Alexander's prowess was complemented by associations of magnanimity. His 'celestial journey' was no longer a sign of his pride; it was reinterpreted (in conjunction with his legendary exploration of the ocean depths in a glass, submarine-like vessel) as a sign of his intellectual aspiration and curiosity. In the sixteenth century, the exemplarity of Alexander's character was further enhanced by signs of generosity and restraint, as conveyed by Paolo Veronese's painting *The Family of Darius before Alexander*, painted in 1565–70 (Fig. 2.20). In this work, Alexander is shown forgiving the wife of his defeated adversary Darius for mistaking his counsellor and friend Hephaestion for himself; as a sign both of his gentility towards Darius's wife, and of his respect for his friend, Alexander says: 'He is also an Alexander', implying – not only within the story, but also for the viewer and patron of the painting (whose features may well have been used in it) – that he too can 'become an Alexander' by virtue of a courageous and magnanimous life. As in the Alexander tapestries, the participants wear modern costume (with the exception of Alexander, who wears armour based on classical precedents).

Such a *gracious* way of exercising free will was typical of Alexander. On another occasion, he is represented – with the same calm magnanimity that he showed Darius's wife – giving his lover Campaspe to the painter Apelles, who fell in love

FIGURE 2.20: Paolo Veronese, *The Family of Darius before Alexander*, 1565–7, oil on canvas, 236.2 × 474.9 cm. National Gallery, London.

with her when painting her. This subject (the new popularity of which also reflects the increased status of painters in this period) was depicted by Francesco Morandini for the *studiolo* of Francesco I de Medici in the Palazzo Vecchio in Florence in 1571, reflecting the Grand Duke's own munificent patronage. However, not all heroes were able to realise and express their freedom with the same equanimity as Alexander; some of them had to strive for it, and the patrons that emulated such dynamic heroes were seen, accordingly, to have achieved their honour by making the same heroic effort as their models. The man-god Hercules was a case in point. His numerous labours offered patrons a wealth of opportunities to associate with immense strength, for while it was flattering that virtue should seem to come to them naturally, as if bestowed upon them by grace, it was also becoming to seem to have achieved it through manly struggle – of which only elite patrons were, by implication, capable (indeed, the word 'virtue' was derived from the Latin word for manly strength or 'virility'). Images of the labours of Hercules, therefore – sometimes adorning extensive cycles of tapestries – were widely commissioned. The inscription on a portrait of Erasmus, painted by Holbein in 1523, indicates that the scholar considered the challenge of translating the scriptures from Greek into Latin to be 'Herculean'.[35] Moreover, the he-man was also renowned for choosing virtue over pleasure – often manifest, according to ancient sources, as two alluring women (for instance, as depicted by Annibale Carracci for the Farnese *camerino* in Rome in 1596, Fig. 2.21). Not only did he project an image of strength in the service of virtue, but he enabled Herculean patrons to harvest maximum credit from their strength by being seen to use it freely, as the fruit of personal choice. Even when such pride was seen as arrogant, it could still be heroic and courageous. Such was the fate of the revived archetypes of Sisyphus and Prometheus, both of whom used their cunning and ingenuity to trick the gods and secure their independence. Sisyphus

FIGURE 2.21: Annibale Carracci, *The Choice of Hercules*, 1596, oil on canvas, 166 × 237 cm. Capodimonte Gallery, Naples

cheated death twice and was condemned to engage in the hopeful but eternally fruitless task of pushing a rock up a hill; nearing the top, he always lost his grip and the rock rolled back down to the bottom again. Prometheus stole fire from the gods and gave it to mankind. Fire was subsequently interpreted as an independent source of imaginative fury or genius in man; nevertheless, Prometheus was punished for his hubris by being chained to a rock and having his liver pecked at by an eagle. Despite their humanoid folly, in both cases these strongmen's independent and determined striving for perfection could be seen as praiseworthy, as an allegory of indomitable spirit despite the fatality of the human condition.[36] In the *studiolo* of Francesco I de Medici in the Palazzo Vecchio in Florence (1570–2), Prometheus is depicted at the very centre of the iconographic programme, in the middle of the vaulted ceiling, where he reflects the anxiety and aspirations of his patron. Although he is shown chained to a rock, he also holds a flare and is being given a large mineral orb by the goddess Nature, symbolic of her transformative and alchemical intelligence.

The heroes, and occasionally heroines, of antiquity served as the perfect precipitate for the development of a personal sense of self, increasingly inspiring the privileged individual to make his or her own rational choices, free of traditional authority. But while they represented alternatives to, or modifications of, Christian ideals, they also constituted ancient authorities of a kind and, as such, they were frequently credited as much for their antiquity as for the actual quality of their example. Indeed, the quality of their example occasionally came under scrutiny. Ironically, it was precisely by virtue of the personal freedom that classical precedents had bequeathed to their emulators that the latter became *able* and *inclined* to reflect on, and question, their models' reputations. So while histories continued to be written as examples of political and moral practice – using the full range of rhetorical devices to make them persuasive – historians also began to analyse the evidence on its own account, regardless of its potential contemporary application, and jettisoning the rhetoric where necessary. Intensive research slowly revealed the foibles of heroes that were once unimpeachable. In his epic poem *Orlando Furioso* (1516), Ludovico Ariosto claimed that 'Aeneas was not as pious, nor Achilles as strong, nor Hector as valiant as their fame suggests . . . nor was Augustus as holy or benign as the trumpet of Virgil proclaims.'[37] The behaviour of the gods and goddesses, who were often lustful, jealous, violent and vengeful, also left much to be desired. Even ancient historians, once thought to be the epitome of style and grace, were found to be unreliable. For instance, the convention of putting speeches into the mouths of historical characters in order to convey their significance more effectively – a classical practice that was revived in the early Renaissance to differentiate humanist historiography from the medieval chronicle tradition – eventually came to be seen as inappropriately imaginative and was challenged. Some moderate writers conceded that such speeches were legitimate if the 'decorum' of the person making them was respected (i.e. if they were 'appropriate' to the circumstance), but others insisted that they were downright false. The Roman historian, Quintus Curtius Rufus, was widely criticised for giving the same kind of speech, all written with the same declamatory flourish, to a variety of character types in his *Story of Alexander the Great*, one of the key sources for knowledge of Alexander in the Middle Ages and Renaissance. As early as the 1440s, Leonello d'Este had empathised with Alexander – identifying with his sickness when he was himself ill – but he was also disillusioned by the many contradictions in Curtius's story.[38]

The tradition of inventing speeches for historical figures had been revived because it 'humanised' history. It continued to operate within a broadly moralising framework, like medieval historiography (albeit subject to a less distinctly Christian end), but it also conceived history around the role of the individual in the unfolding of events. Significantly, as 'invented speeches' became controversial, the one area in which they came into their own was on the stage: in 'chronicle dramas' or history plays which constructed and delivered the narratives of history, both literally and metaphorically, in terms of the individual protagonist. The most significant examples of this genre, which originated in the historical 'mystery plays' of the Middle Ages and came to a head between the 1580s and 1620s, were the history plays of Christopher Marlowe and Shakespeare. While such dramas drew their narrative material from chronicles, they focused on the outcomes of the positive and negative thoughts and actions of individuals, and their relationship to fate and fortune. Although they continued to serve a moral purpose, they also constituted a powerful new medium for the conceptualisation, expression and *enjoyment* of personal identity.

While the imagination was given free rein in new genres of literature – secular plays and eventually novels – it was increasingly driven out of historical writing, which gravitated towards the other end of the 'factuality' spectrum. Concrete evidence became increasingly important as the foundation of history's value as an instrument of instruction – even among Christian hagiographers, some of whom (for instance, the Bollandists and Maurists in the 1620s) were pioneering in the rigour of their research methods. It is ironic, therefore, that exactly when great efforts were being made by historians to ensure that their narratives were based on exhaustive, reliable evidence, drawn from a wide variety of primary sources that were thoroughly tested against each other and newly cited in footnotes and references, a radical new question arose: why do we need to measure ourselves against the past *at all*? Not only were the heroes of the past increasingly found, by studying the evidence, to fall short of the ideals projected on to them, but the whole idea of valuing the present in relation to a historic precedent, rather than on the basis of its own innate value, began to seem arbitrary. Could a situation not simply be judged on its own merits? Could self-evident and therefore infallible truths not also be found? Questions of this kind were originally asked by philosophers in relation to the natural world – for instance, medicine or botany (to what extent were the ancient authorities Galen and Pliny still valid?). For while moral and aesthetic issues might not lend themselves to ultimate verification, as the criteria were impossible to pin down definitively, physical issues *did*: they could be assessed according to their material construction and current functionality. Moreover, precisely because physical phenomena were judged on their functionality, there were plenty of examples of practices in which the 'moderns' were seen to have advanced on the 'ancients'; indeed there were many examples of revolutionising inventions (printing, gunpowder, telescopes, etc.) that did not even exist in antiquity. Thus, where religious superstitions had been supplanted by the methodical rationality of classical antiquity – exemplified by Aristotle, Galen and Ptolemy, who were invoked to help liberate the medieval mind from credulity – it was now the turn of present-time empiricism to supplant the nostalgic idealism of the antiquarians in favour of a realism based on experiment and experience. This line of thought came to a head with Descartes, for whom truth consisted of only that which was *presently known* to be true – that is to say, his own existence: *I think, therefore I am*. Nothing but his self-evident existence was absolutely certain, and therefore nothing else could be rated as an absolutely reliable source of knowledge. This judgement included historical evidence. Descartes maintained that, no matter how much evidence there may be, the past can never be known accurately and certainly as a truth; and no amount of respectable authority can remedy this. From his perspective, historical knowledge, therefore, was a purely practical, comparative resource, with no fundamental epistemological value.

While this sequence of attitudes towards the past – progressing from 1) dogmatic and sacred, to 2) exemplary and moralising, to 3) evidence based and objective, to 4) superfluous – may seem to challenge and contradict each other, each of them constitutes a conventional frame of reference in which a new model of identity could be accommodated, and, as such, they belong to the same extended narrative: the evolution of a sense of personal self, and its development towards an ever-greater degree of self-reference and autonomy. For in each of these historiographical modes, a new capacity for self-awareness is active and, therefore, a new sense of self is arguably implicit. To recap: the development of secular historiography in the fifteenth century marked a departure from Christian histories that presupposed the impersonal mentality of religious belief. However, the writing of history continued to serve a moral purpose, providing examples of positive and negative behaviour that offered scope for personal self-fashioning. To the extent that moralising histories presupposed the existence of an elevated ideal, they also subjected the sense of self to an external source of determination that – despite being rational – was not entirely personal; it was expected to conform to a preconceived exemplar. The growing insistence, from the mid-sixteenth century, that historical narratives be consistent with ever-greater quantities of objective evidence, even at the expense of its moral implications, accommodated and exercised a model of selfhood that was more rooted in personal experience of objective evidence than common idealism. The concept of chronological time that this model of selfhood presupposed was systematically objectified and homogenised, to accommodate the ever more complex relationships that it established between the various fragments of evidence that it discovered; it dispensed with theories of cyclical history and numerological correspondence within the timeline of history, because neither theory is supported by concrete evidence. To the extent that it was aspiring to be evidence based, it was in line with Descartes' analytical 'scientific' method.

But despite being empirical with regard to evidence, and thereby finding its own capacity for objectivity reflected in its historiography, the self-sense was still reliant on *external* resources – the imagined and incomplete vision of times other than the present one (the only time that is actually experienced) – as a medium of identity formation. And no matter how concrete the evidence consulted was, the picture of historical time that it was used to construct was still imaginary, and the sense of identity that was implicitly active in it, and identified by it, was also, to that extent, imaginary. It was for this reason that Descartes rejected history as a source of knowledge: the evidence on which it was based was provisional, and the fact that it might be a complete phantasm, as in a realistic dream, was not even taken into consideration. His own enquiry, on the other hand, required that the evidence be absolute and incontrovertible; his truths had to be *self*-evident. As a result, what he considered to be evidence was uniquely found within consciousness itself, rather than in the outside world of time and space, and the self-evident truth that it proved was *only* his own existence. *He had proven (to himself) that his self existed.* The implication that the 'quest for historical truth' was, beneath the surface, an artificial act of self-fashioning and identity formation, rose to the surface and became explicit, whereupon the self-sense sloughed off the mythical skin of historicity (the felt need to historicise itself in order to ennoble itself) to which it had been attached for so many centuries.

The obverse of Descartes' pioneering realisation of self-consciousness was the implication that everything of which he was conscious *but not 'as himself'* must be unconscious, and therefore mechanical, and therefore subject to physical laws. These laws were clearly objective, because they fell outside the sphere of his subjectivity, and were therefore consistent and immutable, in which case they must be intelligible and explicable – whereupon a new era in the history of science began. However, not everyone agreed with Descartes, not least because the implications of his realisation were unfavourable with regard to religion; while he himself attempted to maintain a belief in God, partly out of expediency, his theories paved the way for atheism. Moreover, although he succeeded in discrediting all claims to knowledge that were not consciously apprehended as self-evident (i.e. all knowledge other than the certain knowledge that the knowing 'I' currently has of its existence), he could not, and did not, account for the impact that consciousness may have on other beings which, he had concluded, were subject to objective laws. Indeed, his presupposition was precisely that the outside world was *only* subject to objective laws, regardless of the possibility that there may exist subjects of consciousness other than himself that he could not therefore experience. Moreover, although he appreciated that subjective feelings or 'passions' formed a natural part of human beings and could have a significant impact on their thought and behaviour, he considered them, broadly speaking, to be mechanical, playing no part in the perception of objective truth.

One of the most outspoken critics of Descartes was the Neapolitan jurist and professor of rhetoric Giambattista Vico (1668–1744). While both philosophers identified the same categories of knowledge – subjective knowledge of mental activity and objective knowledge of nature – they ascribed very different values to them. Descartes considered knowledge of nature to be true because natural phenomena were subject to objective, immutable laws and could be apprehended as such; the mind, on the other hand, was subject to all kinds of whimsical inconsistencies and none of its ideas (beyond its knowledge of itself) could be proven. Vico, by contrast, took a more practical approach and insisted that natural phenomena could *not* be understood by man because they were fundamentally unintelligible – not because they were too 'difficult' or 'obscure' to be understood, but because intelligibility (to man) was not one of their attributes; they were only intelligible to their maker. The products of the mind, by contrast, were intelligible to man precisely because they were constructed *by* the mind and were therefore directly and innately aligned to the mind's capacity to understand them. The truths they contained were valued on the basis of their knowability rather than their supposed objectivity. The stuff of human history, therefore, was not, for Vico, an erratic and incomplete fantasy, unable to yield objective truths; on the contrary, it was an immense resource, providing both an infinite amount of information about the past and an infinite number of clues that reflected the changing capacities and inclinations of the human mind over many centuries. The key question was how to interpret these clues. Because mentalities changed over time, as they do in individual human beings during the course of their lives from infancy to old age, Vico deemed it inappropriate to judge their fruits by the standards of his own day; they had to be evaluated in relation to the capacity and inclinations of the minds that generated them. But given that the minds of those times no longer existed, how could their capacities and inclinations be known? It was one of the tasks of his *New Science* (published in 1725 and in several revisions) to answer this question. In this pioneering work, Vico provided a hermeneutical tool that would enable historians to interpret the past in newly relevant and revealing ways – in keeping with the conditions that prevailed in the past, rather than solipsistically in relation to the present. Thus it was anachronistic to regard an ancient phenomenon like Homer as a uniquely inspired proto-modern seer to be emulated by aspiring philosophers, when in all likelihood 'he' was the personification of numerous rough-and-ready bards who, over many centuries, sang songs that were eventually brought together and written down under the name of a single man.[39] Conversely, it was misguided to criticise the cultures of ancient civilisations for lacking rational clarity when the mindsets that prevailed in their times had not yet developed the linguistic and institutional infrastructure with which to accommodate the degrees of mental abstraction necessary for such clarity; on the contrary, such cultures thought *mythically*, expanding their capacity for understanding and expression by using language poetically and metaphorically, rather than analytically. Indeed, it was the fabric of language itself – not just the narratives it told, but also the very webs of words from which it was made – that embodied the mindsets that used it; etymology was especially illuminating in this context. Thus, while the mind could only understand phenomena that it generated (what Vico called the 'civil world', as opposed to the illegible 'natural world'), so the phenomena that it generated reflected the mind that created them, retroactively (or, as Ralph Waldo Emerson pithily said, albeit in a very different time and place, 'all facts of history pre-exist in the mind as laws').[40] The two phenomena – the mindset and its culture – evolved together.

Vico's 'science' proposed that, to the extent that sequences of ancient customs and institutions could be pieced together and interpreted correctly by historians, they constituted a history of the human mind: for 'the principles of the civil world [all cultural phenomena] can and must be discovered within the modifications of the human mind'.[41] When applied *to his own time*, his theory suggested that the perceptive apprehension of cultural conventions would constitute a *current vision* of the human mind; for, despite being current, contemporary conventions were also generated historically and were therefore subject to the same possibilities of interpretation as ancient ones. It is not surprising then that, in his autobiography, Vico wrote about himself in the third person, as 'he', reflecting on himself not as a subjective self but as a specimen of society (albeit an unusual one), subject to historical conditioning. Even his own ability to reflect on the past, in the characteristic way that he did, amounted to a kind of mental convention that had emerged historically (for instance, in reaction to Descartes' dismissal of history) and was therefore worthy of a historian's attention.[42]

Vico's philosophy is significant in the present context because it highlights the changing role of historiography in the process of identity formation. Vico had criticised historians, past and present, for using history as a reflective instrument with which to define *themselves* as much as the past. What he called the 'conceit of scholars' was the illusion among scholars (ignorant of the evolution of mentalities) that the aspects of the past that they valued had *always* been valued; this oversight enabled them to think that they understood the past (because they understood their own values), when in fact the opposite was true: they were using an *association* with the past, about which they were actually quite deluded, to confer dignity on their values. Vico also claimed that Descartes had taken a position on history that was as much about himself as about 'truth', for by denying the contribution of past philosophers to the development of his own knowledge of certainty, he was taking all the credit for it. Like the 'historians' that used the past to find precedents for their own prejudices, he was, in his own way, using history (by denying its value) to reflect a highly personal sense of self.

Vico's philosophy of history, by contrast, did not revolve around the *personal* sense of self; indeed, it is one of many signs that the currency of personal identity was beginning to be eclipsed at this time – on the one hand, by *communal* denominations of identity, and on the other hand, by *impersonal* agency in history.[43] Vico perceived the narratives of history to reflect not the will of God, the effect of fate, fortune or chance, or the efforts and ingenuity of individuals, but the *general mentalities of human societies*. Although individuals could control their immediate actions, they had no direct control over their overall mindset; nor could they control the customs and conventions to which their actions were subject. On the contrary, these customs arose from the common ground that universally underpins the diversity of human actions (both positive and negative): out of the lust of individuals developed the common institution of marriage; out of family relationships developed the practices of civil law; out of fear of natural phenomena, such as thunder and lightning, arose the notion of 'the gods' and religious belief in them. What Vico was sensing, without articulating it explicitly, and what his own work was reflecting, was the emergence of the disciplines of *psychology* and *sociology*. Firstly, he was acknowledging the impact of mental activity on all human behaviour; it is no accident that the discipline of psychology was indeed being articulated at this very time (albeit in Germany, beyond the sphere of Vico's influence). And secondly, he was observing the instrumental power of societies at the expense of the individuals of which they were composed.

Vico's influence was limited in his own time, partly due to his unfashionable response to Descartes, but he was not alone. The French jurist and political philosopher Charles-Louis de Secondat, Baron de Montesquieu (1689–1755), also upheld that human culture and history were subject to impersonal conditions, or laws, emerging from tradition and customs, rather than political ideals, which emerged from the imaginations of individuals (including God, the archetypal individual). Like Vico's *New Science*, which may have influenced it, Montesquieu's *Spirit of the Laws*, published in 1748, identified the determinative impact of social laws on human activity; by generating and submitting to these laws, individuals surrendered their freedom to the collective 'identity of society'. But it also acknowledged the effect of climate, soil and food resources, thereby ascribing agency to *nature*. Because each society experiences different geographical conditions, this observation laid the ground for the articulation of national and ethnic identities in a way that abstract moral ideals – which could be applied to people regardless of local conditions (as, for instance, attempted by Kant) – did not.[44] Unlike Vico's work, *The Spirit of the Laws* was widely printed and hugely influential.

Both Vico and Montesquieu made occasional references to 'providence' as the guiding principle of history, though there is little to suggest that this word had religious connotations for either of them, as it had for their predecessors. Nor did they acknowledge the ability of God to intervene in the course of events 'miraculously' or in response to petitionary prayer. Indeed, although they were both faithful Catholics, they generally believed religions to have originated as cultural conventions. Given that the Inquisition was still active in eighteenth-century Naples, it may have been prudence that prevented Vico from suggesting that Christianity was also a cultural convention. In 1751, *The Spirit of the Laws* was added to the list of books forbidden by the papacy for suggesting that the chief virtue of Christianity was as a source of social cohesion, moral integrity and benevolence, rather than for any privileged access to a higher truth that it might offer.

The French economist Anne-Robert-Jacques Turgot (1727–81) was equally ambivalent about the use of the notion of providence. In 1750, when he was a student of theology at the Sorbonne in Paris, he wrote a discourse on the positive contributions that Christianity had made towards the human race, but later that year he abandoned his career in the Church. His *Philosophical Review of the Successive Advances of the Human Mind* and *On Universal History*, written a few months later, were clearly based on the Christian concept of providence, in that they both describe a historical trajectory that is universally and inevitably directed towards a positive end. But what makes them significant in the present context is that they newly orientate the logic of history around the secular idea of *progress*. Like Vico, Turgot maintained that the unifying agent in history was not so much the actions of human beings, which on the whole were self-centred and irrational, but the *capacity* for rationality that co-evolved with them and informed the institutions they generated: laws, forms of government and conventions of language.[45] It was therefore the rational identity of *society* as a whole – rather than that of individuals – that such historical conventions were seen to reflect and promote. The development of language, for instance, was determined collectively. Evolving from sounds, through words, fables and concepts, to mathematical theorems, it facilitated the expression and realisation of ever-greater degrees of rational clarity among individuals; but it did not impose it on them.[46] Individuals, therefore, were *free* to be rational, albeit within social constraints that they were not free to alter. Unfortunately they were not always able or inclined to take advantage of that freedom. Even in the rare cases of geniuses who *did* make use of their freedom, the emergence and fruition of rational clarity was subject to conducive social conditions.

Turgot's view of the actual nature of the agency in history was somewhat generalised and vague. The course of history was not dictated from without by providence (though he does occasionally refer to it), nor was it determined from within by an internal human drive; moreover, the 'perfection' towards which it was 'inevitably' directed was never clearly defined. Accordingly, the model of personal identity that his vision of history accommodated was indeterminate – neither passive to the will of God, nor the master of its own destiny. But the individual *was* at least free. Indeed, it was precisely because Turgot displaced the capacity to change history from the individual will to the overall mentality of society, subsuming the possibility of human selfishness and folly within the whole, that he was able to reconcile the notion of an inevitable trajectory in history with the individual's moral freedom to act rationally and virtuously, or not. In this respect, his position was characteristic of his time, occupying the space between the final dismantling of extraneous structures of authority (expressed in its most essential form by Descartes, but not widely realised until the middle of the eighteenth century) and the clear formulation of an independent alternative.[47]

That alternative, eager to surface, was *reason*. While acknowledgement of the fundamental value of reason was latent throughout Turgot's writing, it was not prioritised. Turgot seemed more concerned to communicate *that* there is a unifying rationale in history besides providence and human volition, than to say *what* it is. This was not the case with his follower, friend and biographer Nicolas de Condorcet, who stressed in his *Outlines of an Historical View of the Progress of the Human Mind* (written almost fifty years later than Turgot's works on progress) that *reason* is the guiding principle of history. This shift was important for several reasons. Firstly, the mechanisms of historical development became *intelligible* by virtue of the fact that they were fully rational, and could therefore be analysed scientifically, like the physical world. Indeed, if the tools of arithmetic and probability theory were applied to them, they could be understood precisely; Condorcet attempted to demonstrate this point in relation to the probable lengths of the reigns of the seven ancient kings of Rome and the probable accuracy of the historians who recorded them.[48] It would then be possible to implement rational policies that would steer mankind with some degree of certainty towards a state of perfect happiness. Secondly, the shift meant that all traces of external agency in the historical process could finally be erased. For the more the determinants of history were invested *in the historical process itself*, the less scope or need there was for external influence. On this account, Condorcet was, unlike Turgot, highly critical of the Church and of all religions, presenting them as the enemy of reason and freedom.[49]

Paradoxically, one outcome of Condorcet's appeal to reason as the immanent principle of progress was that the freedom of the individual to influence his or her own destiny was subtly qualified. Although Condorcet passionately defended the freedom and rights of man, he also upheld the ideal of their fusion with the interests of society as a whole. Reflecting on the potential of 'the moral and political sciences' to rationalise the 'motives that direct our sentiments and our actions', he asked: 'what is the object of the improvement of laws and public institutions, consequent upon the progress of these sciences but to reconcile, to approximate, to blend and unite into one mass the common interest of each individual with the common interest of all?'[50] The obverse of Condorcet's view of the natural rationality of progress was that there was little for the individual mind to do other than embrace it or submit to it, albeit freely. Because its benefits were obvious to the rational man – having been revealed to him by statistical analysis – the pursuit of them was less likely to involve a moral dilemma, requiring the torturous exercise of free will. Indeed, Condorcet speculated that, by applying probability theory, or calculus, to ordinary, everyday decision-making, it would become possible to predict events, suggesting that free will is not quite what it seems to be. Given that decision-making already naturally involved a sequence of evaluations and judgements, based on the frequency of past occurrences and the probability and expectation of their recurrence, there was a case for saying that it was itself a kind of calculation process that – ideally – enabled reason to 'speak for itself' automatically. Despite appearances then, the arena in which the individual was truly free *as an independent agent* was limited.

The growing use of statistical analysis to identify patterns in cultural conventions, and of probability theory to predict outcomes, reflected a further shift of focus away from the individual towards the tendencies of society as a whole. For those philosophers that found evidence of the rational progress of humanity in gradual changes to the overall character of society, rather than in the accomplishments of individuals (which could vary significantly without impacting the whole), the agency in history increasingly seemed to be operating at a collective level. The sense of selfhood implicit in this understanding was that of a 'passenger' whose freedom consisted in his rational assent to the inevitable operations of reason in the world. These inclinations were established on a more formal footing following the French Revolution in 1789. In 1793, the date from which historical chronology was measured – the date of Christ's birth, which implicitly Christianised the whole of history – was changed to 1792, the year in which the French Republic was founded. Inaugurating the 'era of liberty', historiographical conventions were reconfigured to reflect the impact of reason on world history; the system survived until Year XIV in the Republican calendar, 1806.

During the most heated years of the French Revolution (1793–4), in which antagonism against irrational and autocratic structures of power came to a head, extremists elevated the benefits of reason to such a level of 'absolute truth' that they ceased to be seen as an opportunity to exercise free will, but became the object of a cult, in relation to which the self-sense was implicitly invited, and tacitly required, to sublimate itself. Ironically, despite rejecting the credulous and irrational trappings of religion – above all, the belief in a deity – the Cult of Reason gave rise to a number of 'expressions' that were manifestly religious in their origin. Despite assurances that reason and its concomitant virtues were abstractions and 'parts of ourselves', the authorities organised festivals in which 'goddesses of liberty' (represented by actual members of the community, to avoid confusion with Catholic idols) were revered in churches that had been converted into 'temples to reason' (Fig. 2.22); approximately

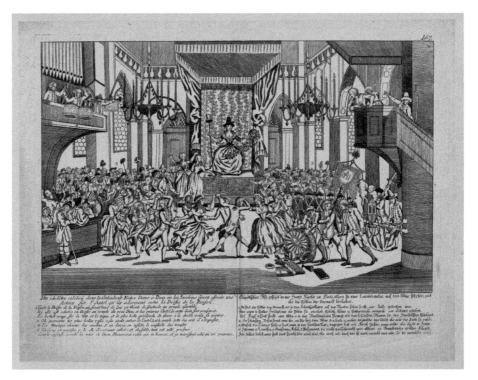

FIGURE 2.22: 'Idolatrous . . . festival celebrated in the Cathedral of Notre Dame in Paris, where the Jacobins put an actress on the altar and worshipped her as the Goddess of . . . Reason', engraving, 1793. Bibliothèque Nationale de France, Paris.

one thousand such conversions were registered with the authorities.[51] In some cases, sculptures of Christian subjects were reworked into representations of revolutionary ideas. At St. Sulpice in Paris, for instance, stone crosses and papal keys were turned into Republican swords and bundles of fasces.[52]

While appearing to dissociate from religion in their outward significations, such conventions left room for traditional patterns of thought and behaviour that were religious in their psychology. Indeed, despite aspiring to transcend the pitfalls of arbitrary personality, the very fact that 'reason' was conventionally regarded as the function of a *mind*, and eventually of a 'supreme being', encouraged people to identify it with a centred principle or being of some kind, from which a transformative influence seemed to emanate into the world like light, informing the course of history.[53] The implication that the effects of the 'principle of reason' were transformative subtly suggested a kind of volition, which in turn reflected a tacit belief in its anthropomorphic character. This belief rendered it easy to personify the principle (for instance, in its manifestation as 'liberty'), subtly inducing people to continue functioning in relationship to it as personal selves. However, given that the 'deification of reason' was ultimately founded on imagination and belief, it too was irrational. Some rational philosophers therefore continued to seek a condition of life and history that they considered to be truly independent of the mindset that had hitherto shaped it into a discrete object (however minimally and abstractly) in order to find itself (as a discreet and subtle subject) reflected in it.

The refusal to imagine a discrete 'principle' of life and nature – detached *from* life and nature, and raised above them in the form of God or spirit – resulted in a theory according to which 1) the only extant entity in the universe is matter and 2) the behaviour of matter is subject to natural laws that manifest in different ways in different phenomena – in keeping not with a transcendental principle, but with the particular, characteristic structures of those phenomena. Human beings were no exception. According to this atheistic view, promoted most persistently and openly by Paul-Henri Thiry, Baron d'Holbach, from the 1750s onwards and published anonymously in his *System of Nature* of 1770, natural laws pervade the material realm indiscriminately, determining the motions of human bodies and minds as much as those of stones and plants. On the one hand, such laws presuppose no individual source of motion from outside themselves; on the other, they leave no space for individual configurations of matter (including individual human beings) to act independently of those laws, i.e. 'freely'. In antiquity, according to Holbach, human beings had fallen under the shadow of ignorance, gullibility and fear, and had begun to create abstracted deities to account for the phenomena they did not understand. Firstly, they personified the forces of nature to such a degree of independence that they became disconnected from their source; and secondly, they projected human motives on to these personifications such that they seemed to behave like human beings, expressing the entire range of human passions, usually in their most exaggerated and idealised form. By abstracting the timelessness and diversity of nature in this way, eventually personifying it as a single overriding God, human beings created a blueprint for the immaterial and immortal soul, with which – given the irrational fear of death that evolved with it – they were only too keen to identify. They also began to see their world in corresponding terms of narratives that were more susceptible to free interference from gods and men than they were to the influence of natural laws. For Holbach, by contrast, the material realm was evenly pervaded by the forces of nature, leaving no room for autonomous action. The soul was not an independent agent with free will, but a collection of effects necessarily caused by the particular configuration of material circumstances that constituted the human structure. It was merely a function of the body, which was in turn a transient constellation of atoms within the ever-changing fabric of matter as a whole. In fact, although Holbach used the word 'soul' occasionally, it scarcely existed for him. There was no need to interpret the world in such a way that it suggested or evoked an independent sense of self in individuals, each with its own destiny. On the contrary, if reason was allowed to function naturally – based on experience and rooted in sensation, rather than focusing on impossible fantasies or being cultified like a religious object – a harmonious and healthy course of events would inevitably unfold.

Given that the history and volition of human beings was being sublimated in the processes of matter (by some precocious writers, at least), it is no accident that the mechanisms and processes of natural history should have also come under scrutiny at this time – not least because humanity increasingly seemed to be subject to them. Significantly, at a moment when secular history was, for the first time, being developed into an independent university discipline, inaugurating a century of intense 'historicism', the expansion of historical thinking to include the creation of the earth and the evolution of life forms placed the individual in a context that looked far beyond his social and cultural, let alone personal, identity.[54] For centuries it had been widely believed that the natural world was created by God as a graded hierarchy of distinct creatures, ranging upwards from inanimate stones, plants and fishes to animals, human beings and angels; this fundamental structure, created approximately five thousand years ago (according to calculations based on the Bible), was complete and had not changed. But as individuals became interested in phenomena for their own sake – as *evidence* of their causes rather than as general signs of the ingenuity of God – alternative theories about their nature and origin became necessary. Naturalists became inclined and able to interpret fossils, which had hitherto been kept as incomprehensible objects of wonder in cabinets of curiosity. For instance, because the fossilised skeleton of the American mastodon did not resemble the skeleton of any living creature, the French naturalist Comte de Buffon (1707–88) concluded, in his *Des Epoques de la Nature* (*The Epoch of Nature*) published in 1778, that it must have become extinct, probably due to climate change. By the end of the century, the pioneering palaeontologist Georges Cuvier (1769–1832), a successor to Buffon at the Jardin des Plantes in Paris, had discovered enough fossils of creatures that were not to be seen in the world to conclude that *many* species of animal must have become extinct, despite the fact that such a termination was not mentioned in the scriptures and did not seem to tally with God's originally complete plan for creation. Because of the perfect functionality of the skeletons that Cuvier studied, and the lack of seemingly transitional examples, he rejected the view then gaining ground in Paris that, by adapting to changing circumstances over vast periods of time, some species might have gradually changed their structures. Instead he ascribed the extinction of creatures to exceptional catastrophic changes to the circumstances of the earth, of which the biblical Deluge was merely the most recent. The role of God as creator and controller of the universe remained intact according to this view, even if it was more complex than it had been thought to be.

Other naturalists interpreted the evidence in a completely different way. In his *Animals Without Backbones* (1801), Jean-Baptiste Lamarck (1744–1829) rejected the notion of extinction. He ascribed the differences between fossils and living creatures to the fact that ancient creatures had mutated into contemporary ones and, conversely, that contemporary creatures had evolved from ancient ones, which had themselves evolved from primitive organisms. Although Lamarck was not an atheist, the role of God as creator was clearly in jeopardy here. In explaining his theory, Lamarck maintained, firstly, that natural forms were innately programmed to develop from simplicity to complexity, and secondly, that the manner of their development was determined by their environments. Changing environments (climate, predators, food sources, etc.) required creatures to adapt their behaviour. If such adaptations were repeated for long enough over many generations, they would lead to modifications in the fundamental structure of creatures that would be inherited by their offspring, and would therefore become instinctive.[55] Functions and features appeared and disappeared depending on how much and how effectively they were used. Thus the necks of giraffes grew longer, over many millennia, as they reached for higher and higher leaves, to the point at which the inner configuration that was spontaneously created in them by their altered behaviour became constitutional.

Lamarck's theory met with various challenges. Some critics, including Cuvier, ridiculed it on the grounds that it seemed to suggest that creatures could manipulate the bodies and instincts of their descendants by wilfully altering their own circumstances;[56] on this basis, generations of blacksmiths should be able, eventually, to give rise to offspring with strong arms. This view, however, was a caricature of Lamarck's theory, which never proposed that the transmission of habitual characteristics could be voluntary. His position was clear from his statement that the environmental process also occurs among microscopic life forms that have no nervous system or brain and, therefore, no capacity to will outcomes.[57] Others maintained that the very principle of tracing a species' instincts to the ancient encounters that its progenitors had with new environments was flawed. In 1839, the British politician Henry Lord Brougham (1778–1868) argued that the progenitors of a wasp that provided grubs for its offspring and then died before they hatched could never have learned the behaviour from experience as they can never have experienced its outcome and purpose. He ascribed the behaviour to the direct guidance of God. Charles Darwin, on the other hand, used the same data as evidence in support of his theory of natural selection.[58] Qualifying his subscription to Lamarck's view of changing environments as a stimulus to mutation, Darwin proposed that mutations were spontaneous and random and that only the strongest and best-adapted members of a group would survive the challenges of the environment to pass on their characteristics to their offspring. According to this model, the environment was more influential on the *survival* of a creature than on its *formation*.

The significance of both of these views was that they ascribed a kind of intelligence to nature itself. Earlier views had tended to see all action as an outcome of the intelligent will of God – albeit subject, to a greater or lesser degree, to natural laws. The notion of the 'will of God' was a seminal one because although – to the extent that it was all powerful – it withheld the possibility of free will and personal identity from man, it did nevertheless generate an overall discourse of personal identity (by ascribing the chief attribute of personal identity – free will – to God). The views of Lamarck and Darwin, on the other hand, suggested that the processes of nature were *themselves* intelligent; although both writers were reluctant to address the religious implications of their theories head on, they implicitly left no space for an external agent: the role of God was at best honorary; it was certainly non-executive. The challenge for them, therefore, was to account for the automatic presence of intelligence in nature without implying or requiring the existence of a miraculous or transcendental source of any kind.

The theory of evolution achieved this (albeit without explaining creation). According to conventional models of history, events (mainly human narratives) were seen as discrete phenomena that unfolded against the background of their environment; but according to the theory of evolution, it was the *environment* that was unfolding. Human history no longer formed an independent narrative with its own dramatic centres. It formed *part* of a greater whole; it was symbiotically involved in the dynamics of the environment – throughout which intelligence was diffused, without centre or source – and it co-evolved with it as one of its functions. Nor could historical phenomena be seen against the abstracted backdrop of a regular timeline; on the contrary, the evidence of geology burst the banks of the timelines that had been created for humanity and stretched them beyond the limits of the imagination. In the same way, the notion of *instinct* came in for renewed scrutiny and refinement. It was by virtue of this notion that natural intelligence was able to manifest in specific creatures without recourse to the will of God or indeed to any subjective mind or self-sense.

The phenomenon of inborn knowledge in animals had been observed in antiquity and was, by general consent, ascribed to the Creator; but for many years the difference between an inborn inclination to behave in a certain way (especially evident among the newly born) and an inborn knowledge of ideas (for instance, of what is 'good') was unclear. The confusion came to a head in the seventeenth century. While Descartes could not bring himself to dispel the notion of innate ideas, such as that of 'God', despite pressure from within his own philosophy to do so, John Locke championed the idea that each human being was born as a *tabula rasa* and subsequently acquired all knowledge from experience rooted in sensation. Locke's 'sensationalist' followers were relieved to realise that people are merely conditioned by their environments, rather than predestined to pay for the transgressions of their ancestors (and that they could therefore be *positively* conditioned by positive environments and education, resulting in certain 'progress'). But they also had ulterior motives for ascribing all knowledge to sensation – to prove the redundancy of all other sources of knowledge, especially as manipulated by the Church. For this reason, they denied the possibility of instinctive knowledge and, fearing its apparent similarity to innate ideas, looked for ways to avoid it. Erasmus

Darwin, for instance – grandfather of Charles – ascribed the otherwise incomprehensible ability of newborn creatures to feed, stand, clean themselves, etc. to vaguely equivalent experiences that they must have had, or witnessed, during gestation.

It soon became apparent, however, that the evidence against this view was overwhelming and, as mistaken associations of instinct with innate ideas of a religious kind were dropped, the notion that some practical knowledge was inborn and automatically transmitted from parent to offspring was increasingly accepted. Following Darwin's publication of *On the Origin of Species* in 1859, the notion that species *evolved* also became widely accepted. However, the questions of inheritance and adaptation were by no means straightforward, especially in the case of man, which Darwin had tactfully avoided mentioning in *The Origin* until the last page. The notion that man might have evolved from a more primitive ape-like species – not addressed directly by Darwin until he published his *Descent of Man* in 1871 – was taken as an insult by many people who considered the possibility that they *personally* may have descended from an ape to be a slur on their dignity. But it also intensified doubts about the role of God in creation and the foundations of Christianity. Indeed, from an existential perspective, it raised questions about the identity of man altogether. If individuals did hot have their own purpose-made personal selves, on what ground did their morality stand?

In order to deal with this problem, new compromises were advanced. While it was increasingly accepted that the physical anatomy of man had evolved, it was upheld by many that his *mental* abilities (his intelligence and capacity for emotion and morality) had not – at least not in the same way. Traditionally associated with the soul, these faculties developed independently. In his essay *On the Origin of Human Races* (1864), the naturalist Alfred Wallace (who developed a theory of natural selection at the same time as Darwin) maintained that, when man's mental faculties had evolved to the point at which people became concerned to protect the weak and unfit on moral grounds, the survival-of-the-fittest mechanism was overridden and the law of natural selection therefore ceased to apply to the human body. Subsequently, the mind, which continued to evolve independently of the body, became the chief instrument of survival, existing on a different plane:

> From the time when the social and sympathetic feelings came into active operation, and the intellectual and moral faculties became fairly developed, man would cease to be influenced by 'natural selection' in his physical form and structure . . . From the moment that the form of his body became stationary, his mind would become subject to those very influences from which his body had escaped.[59]

Following his commitment to spiritualism in 1865, Wallace took a more conservative view, maintaining that, even before human civilisation had become complex, early man's brain was so developed that it must have been intended for purposes beyond the merely practical, and must therefore have been designed by a higher will.[60] While this view appeased some Christian critics of evolution, it was rejected by one of Darwin's most stalwart supporters, the biologist Thomas Huxley, on the grounds that the practicalities of mere survival under primitive conditions must have required as much, or more, brain power as the demands of modern life did for most 'ordinary Englishmen'.[61]

Darwin, who was also horrified by Wallace's capitulation, refuted the notion of man's independent mentality by finding copious examples of rational, emotional and moral behaviour in animals that resembled that of human beings, and of instinctive behaviour in human beings that resembled that of animals. Rejecting Sir Charles Bell's theory that, alone among creatures, human beings were endowed with facial muscles specifically designed for the expression of emotion,[62] Darwin documented expressions of emotion that were common to man and animals – for instance, smiling, laughing and crying among dogs and apes – placing the species at different points on the same scale.[63] He also traced the origins of religion beyond the earliest human animism to the animal kingdom. Ever sensitive to evidence from the most diverse sources, he regarded his own dog's initial anxiety that a parasol lying on the lawn flapping in the wind might be a threat, as a sign of its capacity to assign spiritual agency to inanimate objects and therefore as a sign of embryonic religiosity in animals.[64] The devotion of dogs to their masters, often reflected in dependence, submission and propitiatory offerings, lent itself to the same interpretation (Fig. 2.23).[65] Religious sentiment need not therefore have been *planted* in man by God; it may have developed organically as a form of cultural adaptation.

With regard to morality, Darwin proposed that conscience was rooted in the primal conflict between individual and social instincts that was spontaneously experienced by animals – for instance, when under threat while defending their young. Prior to a certain developmental stage, the experience of conflict, and therefore of choice, did not occur. At the other end of the scale, the institutionalisation

Fig. 6. The same in a humble and affectionate frame of mind. By Mr. Riviere.

CHAP. II.   THE PRINCIPLE OF ANTITHESIS.   53

FIGURE 2.23: Charles Darwin, *The Expression of Emotion in Animals*, engraving by J. A. Riviere, J. Murray, 1872. Wellcome Images.

of thought and communication in enduring signs – also rooted in animal behaviour – enabled conflicting motives to be objectified, rationalised, modified and resolved, with reference to the concept of 'conscience'. As the possibility of choice evolved and became *conscious*, so the possibility of morality came into existence. Moreover, by manifesting a difference between individual and social interests, moral conflict was an innate reflection of a *self-sense* because it implicitly pitted a personal sense of self against a communal one; indeed, it was arguably the capacity for moral action that *constituted* the sense of personal self. For some commentators, 'goodness' was an objective truth created by God, who also created the moral sense in individual men and women, exercised in the context of religious belief; these phenomena transcended the vicissitudes of evolution. For Darwin, however, morality was a *collective* and *evolved* instinct, inherently related to an individual's curbing of his or her own drives for the sake of the community as a whole, even to the extent of putting the individual's own survival at risk. To demonstrate the *natural* source of this apparently altruistic tendency, Darwin made reference to sterile worker bees, which cannot pass their characteristic traits on to their offspring because they do not have offspring. This theory seemed to challenge the fundamental notion that species' traits are passed on by descent through natural selection. He resolved this problem by proposing that the worker bees' survival instinct is realised through the survival of the *community*, rather than themselves, and that their traits remain heritable in the community through their parent queens and drones. Indeed, it is always the communities (the species) and never the individuals – even the fittest ones – that survive.

Because Darwin's view of the moral impulse was *evolved*, *instinctive* and *rooted in the interests of the community*, it was impersonal. It was not rooted in a self-sense, and did not necessitate or presuppose the existence of a self-sense. Indeed, it presented a model of the world to which a sense of personal self was peripheral. Some of Darwin's followers went so far as to suggest that self-consciousness was simply a product of evolution: consciousness began to reflect on itself, as a natural reflex, when the mental apparatus of human beings was sufficiently evolved to do so. In his *Mental Evolution in Man* of 1893, George Romanes, Darwin's last research assistant, used the evolution of species (from protoplasmic organisms to anthropoid apes) and the development of individual human beings (from ovum to child) as prototypes for the evolution of the human mind (from primal reflex to self-consciousness), drawing direct parallels between the various stages of their growth (Fig. 2.24). The development of the theory of evolution into a universal law was undertaken by the philosopher Herbert Spencer, who extended it beyond natural history and psychology to sociology. Indeed, Spencer maintained that, like – or *as* – natural organisms, *all* the products of human culture *evolved* from a state of simple homogeneity to one of complex heterogeneity. In his essay 'Progress: Its Law and Cause', published in 1861, he proposed to show that 'this law of organic progress is the law of all progress. Whether it be in the development of the Earth, in the development of Life upon its surface, in the development of Society, of Government, of Manufactures, of Commerce, of Language, Literature, Science, Art, this same evolution of the simple into the complex, through successive differentiations, holds throughout.'[66]

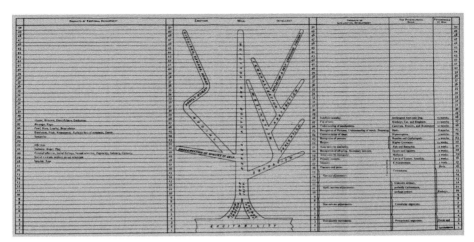

FIGURE 2.24: George J. Romanes, *Mental Evolution in Animals: With a Posthumous Essay on Instinct by Charles Darwin*, London, 1883. Wellcome Collection.

Although, in a political context, Spencer attempted to safeguard the rights of the individual, his theory of universal evolution marginalised the role of free will. Accordingly, it radically altered the potential significance of history. Spencer observed with dismay that this shift was not reflected in changes to the teaching of history in schools, which stuck to a biographical model. In his essay 'What Knowledge is of Most Worth?' (1861), he commented: 'The biographies of monarchs (and our children learn little else) throw scarcely any light upon the science of society. Familiarity with court intrigues, plots, usurpations, or the like, and with all the personalities accompanying them, aids very little in elucidating the causes of national progress.'[67] For some progressive thinkers, the subject of history did cease to revolve around individual protagonism, looking instead towards the development of government policies, class systems, social customs, institutions, etc.. In France, for instance, the French Revolution had given a new practical urgency to the study of history that lasted throughout the nineteenth century. Efforts were made to identify and understand the forces that shaped the past, with a view to managing them more effectively in the present. In the early 1820s, the prolific historian and politician François Guizot (1787–1874) gave lectures at the Sorbonne on the *History of the Origins of Representative Government in Europe*, in order to give historical objectivity and legitimacy to the liberal, socially orientated values that he would later attempt to introduce to French government policy. Aiming to avoid both the exclusive individualism of the elite and the mindless wilfulness of the masses, his histories focused on what he considered to be the 'civilised' precedents in which human rights, duties and responsibilities played a leading role.[68] Likewise Jules Michelet (1798–1874) was driven, partly due to his rediscovery of the works of Giambattista Vico in 1824, to place the French nation, culture and people as a whole – rather than the prominent individuals – at the centre of his seventeen-volume *History of France* (1833–67). The writing of history was of more than purely political significance for him. He believed the development of historical self-consciousness (which he embraced as a personal mission) to be the medium through which humanity identified itself, thereby separating itself from the indeterminate chaos of nature and enabling it to evolve towards higher levels of unity. However, following the 1848 revolution, which revealed the depths of class inequality that still existed in France, he became disillusioned by the ability of humanity to realise its potential for unity and turned his attention towards subjects of natural history. Originally perceiving nature to be a threat to the purposeful progress of human civilisation (as he conceived it), he eventually accepted the intelligence of its purposelessness – of which human history was but a part – and its value as a condition of perpetual change.[69]

Michelet put an emotive, almost visionary spin on the momentous logic of the historical process. His exact contemporary, the philosopher Auguste Comte (1798–1857), took a more rigorous approach to the subject, insisting that his conclusions were systematically rooted in material evidence, unencumbered by romantic speculation. Not only did his new science of society – called 'sociology' from 1839 – project agency into society at the expense of the individual, but its development as a discipline was, Comte argued, the result of an evolutionary process. This process saw man advance, in keeping with his rational capacity, from the study of inorganic material (astronomy, physics, chemistry) to organic material (biology), to the study of societal material (sociology).[70] Man's understanding of the forces at work in any given science was also seen to have evolved beyond a personal, anthropomorphic frame of reference: 'causes' that were originally personified as gods, operating from above, and later conceptualised as abstractions, could now be recognised to be impersonal 'laws' innate in phenomena; and they were to be studied as such, i.e., scientifically. With regard to the emotional, intellectual and moral condition of mankind, the practice of phrenology was embraced by this 'positivist' philosophy because it regarded these phenomena as physiological and, apparently, measurable (Fig. 2.25). By associating them with the physical proportions of the skull – and, by implication, of the brain – phrenology rendered the differences between individual personalities and intelligence numerically commensurate with each other, thereby attempting to reveal a unified principle of character formation that transcended personal inclination (Fig. 2.26). But the discipline of psychology was not acknowledged in this way; nor was it necessary. As a measure of the extent to which human behaviour could be read as the manifestation of social trends, rather than personal initiatives, the sociologist Emile Durkheim (1858–1917) attempted to understand the high incidence of suicide by analysing the rate, location and circumstances of its occurrence, rather than the inaccessible states of subjective psychology that seemed to underpin it.[71]

The historian and literary critic Hippolyte Taine (1828–93) adapted Comte's impersonal positivism to the arts. While Taine maintained that every work of art or literature can be seen to reveal something of the 'inner man', 'soul' or 'psychology' of its individual maker, such work is not an *expression* of the individual maker and, therefore, a sign of his selfhood. Rather it is an expression of the conditions under which he was working and which caused him to be the way he is – just as natural phenomena such as crystals are subject to the conditions that form them. As Taine set forth in the introduction to his *History of English Literature* (1864–9), these conditions prevail at three key levels: *race*, *milieu* and *moment*.[72] 'Race' refers to the 'innate and

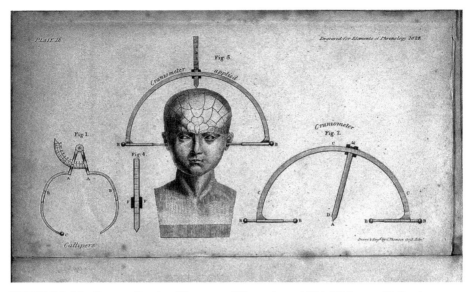

FIGURE 2.25: George Combe, *Elements of Phrenology*, 1824. Wellcome Collection.

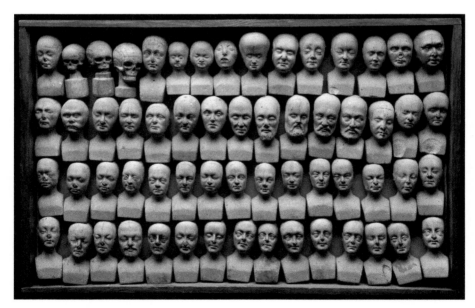

FIGURE 2.26: Wooden case containing sixty small phrenological heads, William Bally, Manchester or Dublin, 1831. Wellcome Collection.

hereditary dispositions' with which man is born. These structural characteristics, accumulated by communities of people over many centuries, are transmitted internally and are only very slowly altered by circumstances in the world. 'Milieu' refers to these 'circumstances in the world', ranging from geographical and climatic conditions to social and political ones. Finally, 'moment' refers to the legacy from the past that has accumulated in the present moment, differentiating it from all other moments and investing it with unique potential, or 'momentum'. It was these conditions, rather than any self-expressive agenda on the part of the artist, that determined the work of art. In a lecture that he gave in 1864 at the École de Beaux-Arts, where he was professor of art history, Taine described how even the artist's own disposition was prescribed by his cultural circumstances; this situation would be reflected in the artist's work, thereby giving socially minded art historians grounds for analysing it scientifically:

> Just as there is a physical temperature which, by its variations, determines the appearance of this or that species of plant, so there is a moral temperature which, by its variations, determines the appearance of this or that species of art. And as we study the physical temperature in order to comprehend the advent of this or that species of plant . . . so it is necessary to study the moral temperature in order to comprehend the advent of various phases of art.[73]

In another lecture of the same year, Taine described the impact of melancholy or cheerful environments on artists, clearly associating their prescriptive effects with natural selection: 'In every simple or complex state, the social medium, that is to say, the general state of mind and manners, determines the species of works of art, in suffering only those which are in harmony with it, and in suppressing other species through a series of obstacles interposed and a series of attacks renewed at every step of their development.'[74]

Each of these historians deflected the 'instrument of historical change' away from the individual, towards social and cultural circumstances. Although personal identity was disempowered, it was typically superseded by national identity and, in the case of Comte, by an identity of mankind; both of these types of community were invested with a 'truth value' in which the disempowered individual could vicariously participate. Such impersonal models of history continued to reflect an anthropocentric agenda, albeit at higher levels of denomination, and, although they reduced the immediate value of the personal self-sense, they were nevertheless able to accommodate an inverted perception of it. The theory of evolution, on the other hand, extended no privilege to humanity; even the 'identity of mankind' – and its steady progress towards social or political stability (let alone salvation) – was unprotected by it. On the contrary, subject to the evolutionary model of narrative, historical events were no longer 'discrete forms' that unfolded *in time*, as if time was a vacuous, pre-existent space to be 'filled'. On the contrary, time unfolded *in forms*, existing, not abstractly, but only to the extent that it manifested as change in matter, or, more broadly, in the total material of life. Conversely, matter ceased to be inert and subject to distinctive stages of progression; it was inherently dynamic and in a state of flux, informed by the momentum of history (the inwardly accumulated force of its movement) such that it manifested states of 'becoming' rather than states of 'being'. There was nothing external to itself, or objective, against which it could be measured, and it did not revolve around a subject or principle; nor could it be observed by a dispassionate onlooker. Herbert Spencer's philosophy had pointed in this direction, without perhaps meaning to; for by maintaining that all historical developments are subject to the law of evolution, Spencer implicitly contextualised his own capacity to realise the evolutionary nature of history as a cultural product that evolved, rather than as the ultimate key to a new science. He further intimated this by claiming that, despite having now become an innate characteristic, the unique ability of man to apprehend space and time had originally evolved. Writing of the evolution and heritability of man's psychological capacities, as early as 1855, he said:

> The simple universal law that the cohesion of psychical states is proportionate to the frequency with which they have followed one another in experience, requires but to be supplemented by the law that habitual psychical successions entail some hereditary tendency to such successions, which, under persistent conditions, will become cumulative in generation after generation, [sufficient] to supply an explanation of all psychological phenomena; and, among others, of the so-called 'forms of thought.' Just as ... the establishment of those compound reflex actions which we call instincts, is comprehensible on the principle that inner relations are, by perpetual repetition, organized into correspondence with outer relations; so, the establishment of those consolidated, those indissoluble, those instinctive mental relations constituting our ideas of Space and Time, is comprehensible on the same principle.[75]

When Spencer suggested that the capacity of the human brain to apprehend space and time had evolved, he was probably refuting a belief that he (wrongly) attributed to Kant, that they were created by a supernatural agent and somehow installed in man. Nevertheless, his suggestion did sow a seed for the notion that the coherence of time and space – the very skeleton of his own philosophy – may be conditional, co-evolving with the mind or self-sense that generated them. Not only did his theory of evolution enable history to unfold without recourse to the human will, but it also raised the possibility that the entire narrative structure of history may be mythical, for it brought the notion of time itself into question. This was not a possibility that Spencer addressed himself. But it *was* addressed by one of his one-time admirers, the French philosopher Henri Bergson (1859–1941).[76] Bergson immersed himself in Spencer's mechanistic philosophy until around 1883, when he noticed how profoundly conceptualised and artificial the model of time that was used in the conventional exposition of history and evolution had become, at the expense of experience. He illustrated the absurdity of reducing time to a sequence of units, like a strip of film, by reference to the paradoxes of the ancient Greek philosopher Zeno. In one of his paradoxes, Zeno observed that for an arrow to travel from point A to point B, it must travel through the midpoint C, between A and B; but to travel to the midpoint C, it must travel through the midpoint between A and C, and so on *ad infinitum*. The arrow cannot therefore arrive; it cannot even move; in fact, all movement is impossible. Bergson raised this point in order to show how logic is flatly contradicted by experience, and is therefore fundamentally flawed as a method of enquiry. In its place, he foregrounded the value of experience and intuition, even if it inevitably involved a sacrifice of theoretical clarity and consistency. On the grounds that Zeno's arrow does in fact arrive at its destination, Bergson proposed that the essence of an action lies in its wholeness rather than the fragments to which thinking reduces it. Just as the present 'moment' – *as experienced* – cannot be measured as a 'second' or other finite unit of time (though it may seem to be measurable *to the intellect*, as it appears on the regulated line of time 'between' the past and the future, having been placed there *by the intellect*), so the 'duration' of an action cannot be reduced to the sum of its parts.[77] Bergson inverted the current understanding of time. Conventional evolutionary thinking saw time as a pre-existent line which, by analogy with space, extends into a distance (Fig. 2.1). Numbers could be used to measure it, structuring it in such a way that it could acquire intellectual (historical) meaning. Bergson proposed, by contrast, that numbering was the means by which the indeterminate body of duration was fragmented and robbed of experiential value; it was the intellect's application of numbers to experience that turned it into a tunnel of time.

More significant than Bergson's theory of duration is the methodological shift in the mode of enquiry that it presupposes. The theory implies that the essence of a complete action cannot be apprehended by the thinking intellect, because it is not reduced to intelligible fragments. On the contrary, it presupposes a different mode of apprehension – namely, intuition – which accordingly presupposes a different kind of subject, a subject that cannot be apprehended by intellectual reflection, without being transformed thereby into a finite fragmentary object. Indeed, although Bergson referred to a 'deep' inner self (complementing a 'surface' self that was shaped by its interactions with the outside world), he was chronically unable to describe it without either turning it into a conditionally generated convention (like the surface self) or arbitrarily attaching imagined attributes, such as 'openness' or 'creativity', to it (like an object of religious belief). Given that it lay beyond the limits of self-consciousness (within which the subject objectifies itself), there were in fact no grounds for identifying it as a 'self' at all.

It was in order to reflect a self-sense that experience was conventionally required to be measurable and subject to historicisation – the notion of time gave it *existence*; the notion of history gave it *meaning*. But this requirement was rarely pushed to its logical conclusion. If time was a line, it *must* have a beginning; it could not exist as a coherent object without one, for if it had no beginning, what exactly was it and from where would it extend? But if it had a beginning, how did that beginning originate, and what preceded it? To suppose a source would require 'religious' belief. Time, therefore, can be neither finite nor infinite. This conundrum is unsolvable. But the impasse may not lie in the *object* of enquiry; it may lie in the *subject*, or mode, of enquiry. Indeed, Bergson turned the problem around and wondered if it may not be the apparatus used to undertake the enquiry (namely the rational mind) that was confusing, rather than the issue under consideration – not from pretensions to piety or humility, but because the rational mind was innately limited by its capacities and, therefore, inevitably inclined to project the characteristics of its capacities on to its experience. The most significant of its 'capacitating' characteristics, in the present context, was its compulsive inclination to reduce experience to linear, binary differences – nominally, to 'evaluate' and 'know' its experience functionally, in terms of discrete objects and their spatial and temporal relationships to each other, but, more fundamentally, *to find itself reflected in it*.

Bergson pushed the discourse of time to the point at which it undermined itself. Although rationality could make some provisional sense of temporal phenomena within the limited discourse of analytical thinking, it could not account for the fundamental fact of the creation of the universe – not least because it was itself a product of creation. In his best-known work, *Creative Evolution,* published in 1907, Bergson wrote: 'Deposited by the evolutionary movement in the course of its way, how can it [our thought] be applied to the evolutionary movement itself?' The fact of creation could, at best, be intuited *in experience*, though the subject of that intuition – the sense of self that experience implied – remained ever elusive and indeterminate to the point at which its existence became questionable.[78]

It has been the purpose of this chapter to show how the changing conventions used over the last two thousand years to create and organise a sense of the past have implicitly accommodated shifting models of identity. The first significant step in this process was the institutionalisation of knowledge of the past in enduring forms (clay tablets, coins, inscriptions, etc.). This is not to say that knowledge of the past did not exist prior to its institutionalisation; just that that knowledge died with the people who held it, unless it was institutionalised outside of them, or passed on orally. Obviously, we will never know what 'facts' (in the broadest possible sense of this word) we have, for this reason, missed. Over and above the information that they preserve and canonise, these institutions of knowledge gradually accumulated to such an extent that overriding systems and principles of knowledge preservation could be developed, eventually becoming consolidated into conventions of thought and memory. One of the most crucial of these conventions was the establishment of chronology: how do we measure time? While chronology may seem to manifest or express the hidden linear structure of pre-existent time, it may also be seen to *impose* a linear structure on an otherwise indeterminate phenomenon, transforming it *into* time. Either way, what does the 'structuring of time' say about the people who engage in it? So endemic has the inclination to temporalise experience become that we cannot *not* engage in it.

The inclination to see the world in terms of an unfolding human narrative – in terms of 'history' – emerged in antiquity and laid the foundations for a model of identity in which the self-sense was seen to be extended in time. As Christianity became the state religion both in and after the Roman Empire, this inclination was subjected to belief in the providential role of a Christian God in the world, to the extent that any scope for the self-sense to conceptualise itself by reference to its independent 'freedom to operate in time' or its 'freedom to influence its future' was lost. St. Augustine's *City of God*, written in the early fifth century, rendered the city of Rome, and the pagan values it stood for, redundant. However, during the course of the next fifteen hundred years, there developed conventions that accommodated a notion of human identity that accorded value to the agency of individuals in the historical process. These conventions first appeared in relation to families, as reflected in the development of genealogies and coats of arms in the twelfth century; but from the fifteenth century they began to appear in more personal contexts – by association with antique precedents, by promoting dramatic narratives (including personal biographies) instead of annalistic chronicles, and by exercising the faculty of reason, instead of belief, in relation to historic evidence. Such practices precipitated and sustained a sense of personal self; indeed, it is arguable that they were generated, albeit subconsciously, for this very reason. In due course, that self-sense became sufficiently established in the culture to seem natural and automatic. Indeed, Descartes' rejection of history as a source of valuable knowledge is a testimony to his conviction that the self-sense was self-authenticating, needing no external source to support it. In a certain sense, then, the self had finally been formed – in that it knew itself to be real – whereupon it became a profound and abiding figment of the imagination. What Descartes failed to account for was *everything else* – namely everything that was *not* known, by the self, to be itself – which he consigned to the realm of mechanical nature. To subsequent writers, this solution seemed unacceptable or at least incomplete. It raised, but did not answer, the question 'who created the machine?', and if the answer was 'God', it merely returned to the irrational medieval position of belief. In due course, the intelligence and agency that were conferred on the personal self were extended, by virtue of 'impersonal reason', to society, culture, nature and, in some cases, all of matter, to the point at which the identity of the individual was absorbed into the identity of a greater whole. Especially when applied to social history, the theory of evolution made allowance for the view that, although individuals were not significantly in control of their destinies, nor was the world directed from without by a guiding hand; on the contrary, it evolved in keeping with the impersonal characteristics of its own substance and structure. Indeed, especially when taken to its logical conclusion, the theory of evolutionary history no longer supported a sense of self, let alone God; it provided no scope for a self-sense to assume responsibility for itself and affect its future. Bergson reinforced this position with reference to the psychology of perception, according to which the perception of time as a projected frame of reference, in which the self might at least see itself reflected as a temporal or historiated phenomenon, was discredited. Under such circumstances, the self/time equation no longer made sense.

This is not to say that the notion of self-sense ceased to arise at this time. Of course it arose, and in numerous forms. Only, it was supported by very different contexts with very different agendas, including historiographical ones; for although materialist, monist and evolutionary theories were widely read and discussed throughout the nineteenth century, they remained controversial until the twentieth, and their deepest implications (regarding the transpersonality of historical agency) were rarely allowed to penetrate the core values of the culture. By contrast, novels, which certainly stimulated personal passion and fantasy, flourished; and the *historic* novel emerged as a new genre. Spearheaded by Sir Walter Scott's Waverley novels from 1814, authors working in this new genre clearly historicised the narratives of the personal self, deliberately subscribing to conventions associated with factuality, but they did so in a self-consciously *fictional* manner. The liberties that they sometimes took with the facts for the sake of 'dramatic truth' (rather like the inventors of historical speeches in the fifteenth century) attracted criticism from professional historians; so did the historicist paintings of the period, which often included objects from later periods among their accoutrements, as if it was the concept or impression of historicity, rather than historical truth itself, that mattered.[79] Professional historians, by contrast, were becoming increasingly academic and rigorous – though it is arguable that, for many of them too, the encounter with historical phenomena remained a profoundly *imaginative* process. For instance, while Thomas Carlyle popularised the notion that history was shaped by exceptional individuals with his *On Heroes, Hero-Worship and History* of 1840, he did so in a style that was highly literary and rhetorical, as if he were writing drama. Self-expression also thrived in the visual arts, albeit subject to momentous and significant changes (as discussed in chapter 4). At one end of the creative process, cultural space was given to individual creative artists more wholeheartedly and expectantly than ever before, and at the other end, monuments to national heroes (inspired by Carlyle's 'great man theory') were erected in every proud town.

A powerful sense of self was also perpetuated by the sheer momentum of tradition, language, habit and belief. However, given the tumultuous state of Europe at the time, there is a case for saying that the renewed adherence to a philosophy of the personal self that unfolded in France at the beginning of the nineteenth century was a thoroughly expedient development; not unlike a character from a novel, the self had a role to play. For instance, many conservative individualists reacted *against* the rationalist atheism of the sensationalists and materialists, who ascribed all causality not to the free will of a self, or providence, but to the laws of nature or physics. These conservatives explained the violence of the French Revolution by reference to the absence of a moral principle in such views. Therefore, a sense of subjectivity that could be held responsible for its actions – or even a 'soul', long since superseded by the rational 'mind' – needed to be reinstated as a matter of principle. As a result, Christianity underwent a revival – in its institutions, its culture, its psychology and its role models. The aristocratic concept of monarchy, as a secure source of political stability, was also gradually restored – firstly when the republican Napoleon became first consul and then emperor (in 1799 and 1804 respectively), and then when the royal line of Louis XVI was re-established (in the person of his brother Louis XVIII in 1814). For the philosopher Maine de Biran (1766–1824), both of these institutions (God and monarchy) were consonant with the idea of a self – indeed, they were arguably projections of the self concept – and he promoted them in relation to each other accordingly.

Although Maine de Biran claimed to derive his notion of the self – the *moi* (me, in French) – from pure introspection, it is arguable that he also took other circumstances into consideration when developing it. Besides resonating with his reactionary political and religious views, he regarded the existence of the self as a *logical* necessity: it was impossible, he claimed, for knowledge to be generated passively from sensations (as the sensationalists had maintained); some innate inclination towards such a process *must* pre-exist them. Although, in pursuing this line of thought, Maine de Biran was overlooking the sensationalists' observation that the very language used to articulate a sense of self was itself conventional and therefore subject to cultural development, he nevertheless upheld that the latent element of will in man's capacity for knowledge constituted the self. His notion that the self-sense was an expedient that was formed under pressure from society also seems to render it conditional. It is therefore arguable that, despite his evident commitment to the *idea* of the self, Maine de Biran's actual self-sense was a convention of mind that was somewhat *at odds* with the cultural environment in which he hoped, but failed, to find it reflected. Despite his confessions of selfhood, the theoretical status of his self-notion is suggested by both his thought and experience. On the one hand, he accepted that any moral component in the self could only be developed in relation to society (and was not, therefore, innate), for it was only for the sake of others that the self would be motivated to curb its spontaneous inclinations. On the other hand, his private journals clearly reflect his own personal struggle to incarnate a solid self in himself, in the face of incursions from the outside world, as well as his own uncontrollable thoughts, which he sometimes found unbearable. Indeed, it was his failure to realise a sense of self – evidently a desirable ideal, rather than a known truth – that turned him back towards religious belief (which *presupposes* a sense of self and therefore facilitates its performance).

Maine de Biran was a deeply introspective character and few of his writings were published during his lifetime. He did, however, host a philosophical society through which his ideas were disseminated. One of his keenest followers was the philosopher Victor Cousin (1792–1867), who, like him, used a method of introspective observation to identify and magnify the *moi* that both men believed to exist *a priori* in all individuals. Also like Maine de Biran, Cousin had various external agendas that supported his position. These included his attitude towards private property. He maintained that the volitional core of the *moi* was realised both in its possession of itself and in its appropriation of objects; exploiting the double meaning of the word, the impulse to own *property* was one of the *moi*'s natural *properties*.[80] A key area in which Cousin differed from Maine de Biran was in his insistence on the social impact of the *moi*. Although, like his former mentor, Cousin maintained that the self-sense was polarised against the sense of community, defining itself by difference, he also argued, unlike de Biran, that it was an integral part of the community, defining itself by participation in that community. Cousin initially spread his ideas by teaching: he began lecturing at the Sorbonne in 1815, often to packed houses, and many of his lecture notes and his students' notes were published.[81] But his influence in France only became pervasive when, in 1832, as a member of the Royal Council of Public Instruction, he was charged to reform the teaching of philosophy at *lycées* across the country. He did this by introducing a module on psychology into the curriculum (a change that remained in place until 1874).[82] This new subject was to address such issues as 'consciousness and the certitude appropriate to it', 'voluntary and free activity', 'the phenomenon of the will and all the circumstances surrounding it' and the '*moi*, its identity and unity'. One of the key methods to be used was introspection. Experiential knowledge of the self was to be taught in schools.

Given Cousin's 'doctrinaire' approach to the project, however, there is a case for saying that his *moi*, like that of Maine de Biran, was as much a convention of mind, reacting against the anarchy of revolutionary impersonality and 'selflessness', as a deeply experienced reality. While some impression of how students responded to his programme can be gleaned from the few exam papers that survive, the evidence of the policy's immediate impact is slim.[83] Moreover, despite his repeated references to introspection, Cousin left no substantial evidence that he had thoroughly engaged in the practice himself (unlike Maine de Biran), and many of the textbooks produced to teach the practice spend more time describing what students should see than how they should look. Therefore, it is also arguable that, while clearly believing in the existence of the *moi* (and indeed extending a quasi-religious aura to it), he was using the idea of the self as an instrument with which to define, but also control, a certain tranche of the community – principally the growing bourgeoisie (especially the propertied, male bourgeoisie). For the more he propagated his idea of the *moi*, substantiating a self-conscious collective, the more institutionalised and subject to the impersonal forces of collectivisation it became. This was Cousin's 'innovation'. His *idea* of the self was not new; in its presumed objectivity, it was a revival of the Cartesian *ego*. Nor was his contemplative method new; a form of introspective contemplation had clearly been used not only by Maine de Biran but also by the sensationalists – for instance, Condillac – when analysing the nature of sensation. But whereas Condillac had attempted to reveal the content of consciousness in *itself* (concluding that it was all derived from sensation – though consciousness itself, and its subject, remained indeterminate), Cousin placed his *moi* in a *relational* context where it served a social, political and moral purpose. On the one hand, it stood against the atheism and anarchy of materialism; on the other, it legitimised centralised control of social processes. Indeed, by identifying consciousness not with the primitive level of 'spontaneity' that he associated with members of the working class and peasantry, but with educated 'reflexivity', Cousin's notion of the self became the mental mechanism that generated, and came to epitomise, the bourgeoisie; it was as if, like a computer program, it could be downloaded into the mind.[84]

During the course of the nineteenth century, the locus of historical agency shifted from the vision and will of exceptional individuals towards social and evolutionary forces. Just as the burgeoning concept of society depersonalised the notion of identity, so the theory of evolution depersonalised, and even dehumanised, the process of history. The reality of the personal self, as reflected in its efficacy, was therefore diminished and, according to extremists, annihilated. The *moi* of Maine de Biran and Cousin constituted a vigorous attempt to refute this conclusion, but, in so far as its existence was defended as a theoretical necessity and in relation to its external, societal contexts rather than 'in itself', it did not entirely succeed, for it was presented as a conditional truth, rather than an absolute, self-authenticating one. As a result, it does not contradict the 'undoing' of the self being described here; on the contrary, it corroborates it, albeit in a complicated and paradoxical way, by acknowledging the instrumentality of society in the economy of the self-sense at this period. In fact, the significance of the *moi* lies elsewhere – in its anticipation of psychoanalysis. While the attempt to establish the personal self as an objective truth did not bear fruit, the method of introspection used to identify it certainly did. When the discipline of psychoanalysis eventually emerged, it found a highly *subjective* impression of selfhood, though not necessarily a very coherent or continuous one.

The investment of agency into the notion of society, both at the expense of individuals and in relationship to them, gave rise to numerous cultural manifestations. On the one hand, it led to the identification of the 'public' and the formation of institutions that embodied it; in this context, the role of ordinary individuals was of secondary concern and, with the exception of artists who represented them on the public stage, their idiosyncrasies were insignificant. On the other hand, the personal self-sense, now left to its own devices – as society and its institutions evolved independently of it – began to disintegrate. Psychoanalysis evolved to meet this challenge. The emergence of infrastructures that reflect and accommodate these shifts will be the subject of the ensuing chapters.

CHAPTER THREE

The Publication of the Self: the Sublimation of Personal Identity in Publicity and Art Appreciation

When we conceptualise the Renaissance, we tend to think of Raphael, Leonardo da Vinci, Michelangelo, Titian, Holbein and the individuals they portrayed: popes, doges, kings and queens, Erasmus, Machiavelli, Luther. It was they who contemporary and subsequent historians have monumentalised as instruments of historical change, because it was they, among many others, who seemed to give form to their sense of themselves as individuals by expressing their ideas, effecting political change and making, commissioning and appreciating works of art. But we forget that this opportunity to exercise a sense of personal identity was limited to an extremely small circle of privileged, high-profile individuals. The works of art that epitomise the Renaissance for us – the Sistine Chapel ceiling, the *Mona Lisa*, Titian's mythological paintings – were seen by very few people other than their patrons, and it is highly likely that over ninety-nine per cent of the population would never have heard of the artists who produced them. The reality was that, unless an individual was privileged enough to engage with the elite new media of self-definition and self-reference, he or she remained subject to the principles of identity formation that had prevailed in the Middle Ages. For a majority of people, the parameters of their identities were controlled by the aristocracy, who owned the land they lived and worked on, and the Church, who controlled their spiritual destinies. From their point of view, therefore, there was no such thing as a 'Renaissance'. Both in the community and at home, there was very little scope for the propagation of a sense of selfhood. At one end of the spectrum, there were few public amenities such as schools, hospitals, shops and factories. At the other end, most individuals were illiterate, with little private access to knowledge, and they shared rooms, and often beds, for sleeping in. In the eighteenth century, this situation began to change. The possibility of articulating a sense of personal identity became increasingly vested in conventions that revolved around a less privileged class of people, thereby undermining the elite status of personal identity and making it more accessible to a far wider range of individuals.

One of the most significant signs of this shift was the evolution of the notion of the 'public'. Whereas the majority of the population had hitherto formed part of an indeterminate mass of anonymous peasants living in the countryside, the 'public' consisted of a community of self-conscious and aspirational individuals, increasingly living in towns, whose personal interests and potential were newly reflected in a wide range of cultural institutions; indeed, the public acquired its identity from the cultural institutions that served its interests. For the most part, these institutions arose in the cultural sphere long before they were represented in a political one. Environments that facilitated a new kind of sociability were the first to emerge. Coffee houses, for instance, began to appear in the 1640s – in Venice in 1645, London in 1652 and Paris in 1672. Their potential for the expression, dissemination and creation of popular, anti-monarchical sentiment is reflected in the number of initiatives taken to close them down.[1] Exhibition spaces also emerged, providing what would become 'middle-class' people with an opportunity to have 'aesthetic' experiences and to make 'aesthetic' judgements – and thereby to activate their sense of themselves as 'aesthetic subjects' – for the first time.

One of the earliest occasions on which the notion of the public was explicitly accommodated as an entity in its own right occurred in Paris in 1678, when Jean Donneau de Visé, editor of the journal Le Mercure Galant, gave his readers a voice for the first time. Le Mercure Galant was founded by Donneau de Visé in 1672 and, as a literary periodical offering commentaries on life at court and critiques of contemporary literary culture, it can lay claim to being the first newspaper in France.[2] What made it unique and highly controversial was that, besides providing information about contemporary literary events, especially novels, it also encouraged its readers to respond to what they read, sending the editor their thoughts about the issues it raised. Many of their views were then published in the journal, thereby promoting an ongoing debate in which readers were actively and explicitly involved. In taking this initiative, Donneau de Visé created a cultural convention through which amateur readers, hitherto expected to remain respectfully and silently compliant, were empowered to pass judgement on works of literature. This privilege had traditionally been reserved for formally acknowledged academics, who, predictably, met the initiative with considerable resistance. Indeed, the right to judge was so invested with elite status that many writers of noble stock considered it demeaning to publish their works at all in case they should be inappropriately exposed to the scrutiny of anonymous amateurs; they preferred to circulate them privately, often in salons.

One book that particularly stimulated the public imagination was Madame de la Fayette's Princesse de Cleves, often considered to be the first novel to explore the emotional and psychological content of a romantic narrative. When this work was published in 1678, Donneau de Visé asked his readers to consider the wisdom of the princess's fatal confession of her love for another man to her husband, and to write to him sharing their views about the various issues it raised, both in relation to the novel and in relation to their own lives. In this way, Donneau de Visé was not only encouraging them to develop their own positions vis-à-vis a range of emotional situations, but was positively enshrining the possibility of public opinion in a cultural form (the periodical) that existed independently of his readers' individual responses. Reflecting the great appetite for such an opportunity, Donneau de Visé received between five and six hundred letters, selections of which he published in every edition of the periodical for a year.

With regard to visual art, a parallel shift towards involvement of the public was reflected in the concern for public access that became an integral feature of the Academy of Fine Arts in Paris. This institution had been founded in 1648 in imitation of Italian art academies, at the expense of the traditional guilds of painting. Its concern for the public took two principal forms. The first was a series of monthly lectures (*conférences*) given by senior academicians on various aspects of the theory of painting; significantly, these lectures, which were intended to substantiate the intellectual dimension of painting over and above its traditional status as a mere craft, were open not only to academicians and artists, but also to any interested member of society.[3] The second was the regular display of work by academicians (inaugurated in 1663 and reduced from running every year to every two years in 1665) in their meeting rooms in the Louvre, on view to all comers.[4] While these occasions were originally extremely popular, attracting unexpected numbers of visitors, they were discontinued from 1673 partly due to lack of enthusiasm on the part of the academicians, many of whom, like elite writers, objected to having their work judged by amateurs. With a few minor exceptions, they were not reinstated until 1737, when a new programme of 'Salon' exhibitions was organised (named after the rooms in the Louvre in which they took place), in which artists from a variety of backgrounds were able to submit their work to a panel of judges for display in public exhibitions for the first time.[5] In the present context, the importance of this development lies in the way in which the identity of the public, previously excluded from cultural life, became formally instituted in a prestigious convention. The role of the public was not merely passive to the works of art on display, as it was, to all intents and purposes, in relation to religious art on display in churches; on the contrary, in this instance, they were required to validate the exhibits they saw with their approval, and thereby to authorise them as legitimate works of art. The public's role as agents in the 'completion' of a work of art was stated in the official booklet published to accompany the Salon of 1741: 'As the votes of the enlightened public bestow on each kind of work its true value, it is out of these assembled opinions that reputations are made. What more equitable means could one find to place the public in a position to decide with justice than the exhibition of various objects which are the outcome of the Academy's work?'[6]

While these developments appeared to invest the notion of the public with cultural value and identity, they were, in fact, based more on idealism than on real conviction. Although the public's judgement was certainly being invoked, adding an ethical and socially legitimising dimension to the activities of the Academy, its existence was nominal. In reality, the Academy's attitude towards the public was often condescending, regarding it as both pretentious (attending the Salons in order to be seen there, rather than to engage knowledgeably with the art) and uncultured (seeking scandal above all). Partly because the Academy and the public did not always see 'eye to eye' about artistic matters, several visitors to the Salons took it upon themselves to critique the exhibitions on behalf of the public and, on many occasions, to publish their views, often anonymously, in public journals. As a result, the Salons were the events that gave rise to the first professional art criticism. Not only were these writers writing for the public (explaining the significance of the works on display to them) and on behalf of the public (expressing to the artists what the public required from painting), but they were themselves members of the public, rather than academicians – a fact that, needless to say, attracted much dismissive comment from the Academy. While the best-known critic of the Salons was Diderot, who critiqued eight Salons between 1759 and 1771, the writer credited with initiating the tradition of popular art criticism was Étienne La Font Saint-Yenne, a member of the court at Versailles, whose *Reflections on some Causes of the Present State of Painting in France* was written in response to the Salon of 1746 and was published as an anonymous pamphlet in 1747. At the beginning of his review, La Font comments not only that the public have a right to judge works of art, but that it is in their collective identity as a public, rather than as individuals, that the perspicacity and accuracy of their judgements is most manifest:

> An exhibited picture is the same as a book on the day of publication, and as a play performed in the theatre: everyone has the right to make his own judgement. We have gathered together the judgements of the public which showed the greatest amount of agreement and fairness, and we now present *them*, and not at all our own judgement, to the artists, in the belief that this same public, whose judgements are often so bizarre and unjustly damning or hasty, rarely errs when all its voices unite on the merit or weakness of any particular work.[7]

While the ascription of cultural value to the identities of 'middle-class' individuals was reflected in the institution of public exhibitions and the (nominal) legitimisation of public critiques, it was also reflected in changing attitudes towards the subject matter of art. In the second half of the eighteenth century, there was a reaction against the mid-century predilection for the 'rococo' style that mediated pleasurable sensations, devoid of preconceived intellectual programming, on the grounds that it was irresponsible and self-indulgent. In place of these insubstantial works, critics advocated a return to subjects that were morally principled and orientated towards the well-being of society as a whole, inaugurating the 'neoclassical' style. La Font was such a critic.

While La Font's substantiation of the public as an agent of cultural value in Paris constituted a challenge to the Academy's monopoly on cultural authority, so his comments on the 'current state of painting in France' also took issue with the frivolity of rococo art. Writing when the style was at the peak of its fashionability, he took particular exception to what he regarded as its excessive appetite for novelty and ornamentation, at the expense of the meaningful historicity and classical *gravitas* that was characteristic of the preceding baroque age. Significantly, he identified one of the key causes of the decline in French painting as the proliferation of mirrors, 'which were comparatively rare in the last century and are extremely abundant in this [one]' and which epitomised and facilitated the realisation of a sense of personal identity in the late seventeenth century. While La Font was sensitive to the marvels of mirrors, he rued the fact that they now 'monopolised the decorations of salons and galleries' and had 'banished the finest of the arts from our apartments; the only refuge left to it being to fill in a few miserable gaps, overdoors, overmantels and the tops of a few pier-glasses, reduced in height for the sake of economy'.[8] The relegation of painting to these secondary areas had also led to a banalisation of its subject matter, which now favoured trite decorative groups of the elements, seasons, senses, arts or muses that required 'neither genius nor imagination'. Even for ceilings, which were once glorious arenas of allegorical painting, the 'material whiteness of plaster carved into filigree work . . . often gilded' was now being preferred to 'embellishments of an intellectual character, requiring some consideration and knowledge'. In the light of this development, painters who could have been working on ennobling subjects in the grand classical manner were often limited to painting portraits that merely flattered the eye without addressing the soul and that – like mirrors, but even more beguiling because they do not tell the truth – were largely motivated by self-love.

Although La Font was happy to challenge the Academy, he highlighted what he perceived to be the self-indulgent and degenerate hedonism of the modern (rococo) style by offsetting it against the classical grandeur and principled restraint of the academic Louis XIV style that preceded it. Indeed, all criticism of the rococo style, which was vociferous from the 1740s onwards, recommended solving the problem by reviving the classical style in one way or another. With regard to subject matter, for instance, the traditional academic hierarchy of genres, which had been neglected in recent years by painters of *fêtes galantes* (such as Watteau), was revived. The supremacy of classical history painting was restored at the expense of portraiture, paintings of everyday scenes, landscapes and still lifes. But, while the reaction against rococo laxity was entirely compatible with nostalgia for the order and nobility of baroque classicism, and could to some extent be articulated as a revival of that ideal, the internal dynamics of the new classicism were in fact very different from the internal dynamics of the old. Seventeenth-century history paintings had been largely allegorical, resonating with the self-aggrandising agendas of the elite and using exaggerated rhetoric to impress a sense of the status and power of their patrons (usually monarchs or political leaders) upon their viewers. The history painting of the 1760s and 1770s, by contrast, did not revolve around private patrons. On the contrary, while it was still required to reclaim the dignified associations of classical antiquity, it was motivated by a desire to produce art that engaged with, and responded to, the values of the public – and when public interest began to manifest in consumption, so the productivity of artists ceased to be subject to the patronage of privileged individuals for economic reasons too.

Just as the privileged individual had been accommodated by the sensuous and decorative imagery of the rococo style, so the emerging public also sought forms of art that reflected a coherent sense of its identity. Whereas the individual self was reflected to itself by its personal sensations and pleasures, the cultural forms that accommodated the identity of the public submitted the appetites of individuals to its own collective interests and socialised them; it turned individuals into 'citizens'. These new cultural forms embodied, and revolved around, a cohesive principle that maintained a relationship between individual members of the public and the public as a whole. As the idea of the public was increasingly realised, this principle – infused with a feeling of moral responsibility – was nurtured in its individual members as a sense of a commitment to a communal, rather than a personal, ideal.

The painter whose work first reflected this moralising trend was Jean-Baptiste Greuze (1725–1805). Greuze perpetuated certain key aspects of rococo art – its air of familiarity, attentiveness to personal sensibility and absence of grandiosity – but he rejected its elitism, triviality and self-indulgence. Soon after his appearance in Paris in around 1755, he was acclaimed for restoring an element of dignity, self-respect and pathos to painting without allowing high-minded iconography or rhetoric to alienate the public. His most successful works, which dominated the Paris Salons for the next ten years, represented scenes from everyday life, especially family life, often placing emphasis on the relationship between fathers and children. In this respect they show the influence of Chardin and other genre painters of the period who meditated on the quasi-existential simplicity of ordinariness. However, in Greuze's genre works, the participants – each of whom manifests a distinctive psychological state – are usually configured in such a way that their gestures and expressions of feeling can also be read as a dramatic narrative. In each case, there is at least some degree of psychological transaction or conflict, requiring resolution. Indeed, each work, staged as a tableau, was clearly designed to engage with the personal experience of its viewers, encouraging them to decipher and evaluate its psychological, social and moral implications. As such, the paintings identified their viewers as being worthy and capable of moral judgement – indeed, it institutionalised this capacity – implicitly inviting them to participate actively in the cultural process.

The Village Bride is a case in point. According to Diderot, who wrote about the painting extensively in his critique of the 1761 Salon where it was first exhibited, The Village Bride attracted such large crowds that it was almost impossible to view it.[9] The extent to which it resonated with the public is further suggested by the fact that it was very quickly engraved and disseminated in the popular affordable form of print (Fig. 3.1). The work depicts the moment at which a father hands over one of his daughters, and her dowry, to her new husband. The occasion, which is being recorded by a notary, is witnessed by the whole family, each member of which expresses a different emotional response: the bride is torn between her old and new roles; her mother weeps helplessly; her sisters are more pragmatic, looking on with detachment. Above all, the father, suffering the 'loss' of his daughter with dignity, urges his son-in-law to take responsibility for her, and the young man listens attentively and respectfully, suggesting his earnest promise of commitment and care. The emotional core of the image resides in the fact that both of these male figures are required to act with a degree of self-restraint in relation to each other's sacrifice – the former by relinquishing his daughter, the latter by relinquishing his freedom to live as a single man. Indeed, it was precisely through this appeal to act with altruism in favour of a greater good that Greuze captivated his public, for, by highlighting the possibility of moral improvement in a given situation, he was putting the transpersonal interests of the collective before the personal interests of its individual members. And by giving form and precedence to the interests of the collective in this way, he reflected the power and authority of the public to itself, and thereby became instrumental in its realisation and expression of its own identity and status.

Despite the fact that critics praised Greuze for his ability to capture the dramatic core of what was otherwise a familiar occasion, this form of 'dramatic realism' was relatively short-lived. What it initially gained in pathos, through its perceived ability

FIGURE 3.1: Jean-Jacques Flipart after Jean-Bapiste Greuze, *L'Accordée de Village (The Village Bride)*, 1770, engraving, Tournus, Hôtel-Dieu, Musée Greuze. Photo: © RMN-Grand Palais/Thierry Ollivier.

to express earnest and sincere emotion, it lost in dignity, through its bourgeois sentimentality and trite moralising. Greuze himself sensed this and tried to rectify the situation by altering both his subject matter and his style. His effort was largely concentrated in a single work – *The Emperor Septimius Severus rebuking his son Caracalla for attempting to assassinate him* – which he submitted to the Academy in 1769 (Fig. 3.2). In this work, he replaced his typically contemporary subject matter, now perceived to be overfamiliar and banal, with a historical episode from classical antiquity, thereby immediately reclaiming a degree of austerity and dignity by association. This device had been deliberately abandoned by rococo painters in favour of the immediacy and spontaneity of meaningless sensory pleasure. Its revival in the second half of the eighteenth century reflected a growing interest in, and appreciation of, history as an independent progressive force, over and above the will of God and the whims of individuals, as outlined in the previous chapter. Greuze also replaced his characteristically lively and sensuous manner of painting, partly inherited from his capricious rococo predecessors, with a more restrained and structured classical style that was clearly derived from that of the supreme idol of the Academy, Nicolas Poussin. Thus, the composition is sparse and rectilinear, simplifying

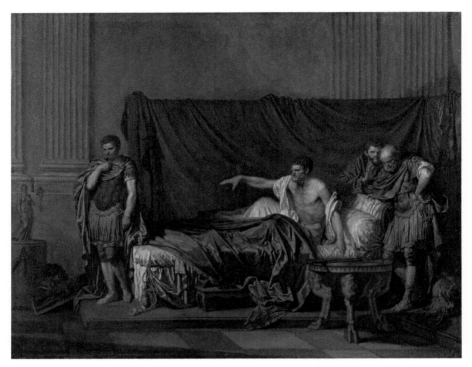

FIGURE 3.2: Jean-Baptiste Greuze, *Septimius Severus reproaching his son Caracalla for trying to assassinate him*, 1769, oil on canvas, 124 × 160 cm. Musée du Louvre, Paris. Photo: © RMN-Grand Palais (Musée du Louvre)/Michel Urtado.

the sinuous interweaving of lines and feelings in *The Village Bride* to brutal, intractable extremes, and the subject matter is bleak. The classical columns in particular serve both to set the scene in a grand Roman setting and to add rigour to the composition.

Although the subject matter and composition of the work are sufficiently austere to restore the prerequisite degree of nobility to the art of narrative painting, the work continues to revolve around a simple moment of confrontation between two family members (substantiated, for the sake of narrative realism and depth, by a secondary level of reaction from witnesses), exactly as in *The Village Bride*. However, where *The Village Bride* depicted a delicate moment of diplomacy, couched in a world of personal sensitivities, *The Emperor Septimius Severus* elevates the exercise of self-restraint to a heroic level of self-transcendence. Septimius's son Caracalla has attempted to kill him, for which the emperor only *rebukes* him, when he could quite legitimately have had him executed for attempted regicide. Instead, at some risk to his own life (knowing that Caracalla or his followers could repeat their crime), he manifests the heroic virtues of tolerance, forgiveness and trust. He surrenders the impulse to act on his personal anger, which is amply conveyed by his expression and gesture, for the sake of social stability and family loyalty.

FIGURE 3.3: Jacques-Louis David, *Combat of Mars and Minerva*, 1771, oil on canvas, 146 × 181 cm. Musée du Louvre, Paris. Photo: © RMN-Grand Palais (Musée du Louvre)/Philippe Fuzeau.

The painting was, in fact, a dismal failure for Greuze, partly because it was strategically contrived to ensure his acceptance into the Academy at the most elevated level of 'history painter', for which his simple genre paintings had not qualified him. Because his presumptuousness, based on ten years of huge popular acclaim, was offensive to the Academy, he was only accepted at the lower level of 'genre painter', which amounted to a rejection. As a result of this snub, Greuze withdrew from exhibiting at the Salon altogether and returned to his previous style, never again attempting to paint in the grand manner. Ironically, however, although *The Emperor Septimius Severus* was ridiculed by critics at the Salon, it did set a precedent for a type of painting that was eventually to succeed in treating moral subjects in a powerful and dignified manner. The champion of this genre was Jacques-Louis David (1748–1825), who was praised by his followers for raising history painting to such a level of purity and perfection that it embodied timeless ideals. Significantly, the earliest works that David submitted to the Salon were painted in a sensuous and softly glowing style that is closer in sensibility to the works of Greuze than to his own later neoclassical works. For instance, his *Combat of Mars and Minerva*, exhibited in 1771, was clearly influenced by the light-hearted style of Boucher (who briefly taught him) and, besides showing a similar taste for voluptuousness, also shares Boucher's convivial, trivialising approach to mythological subject matter (Fig. 3.3). The dramatically outstretched hand and limp wrist of Minerva, pronouncing defeat over Mars, is remarkably similar, both in rhetorical intent and in feebleness, to the hand of Septimius Severus in Greuze's flawed epic.

It was not until the 1780s, after five years of exposure to neoclassicism in Rome, that David developed a mature and convincing neoclassical style. Inspired by the pioneering art historian Johann Joachim Winckelmann's celebration of Greek and Roman sculpture as representations of ideals that transcend the imperfections of the manifest realm, he began to eliminate all traces of contingent sensuality and sentimentality from his work. Most significantly, his subject matter began to focus on ancient acts of heroism in which individuals sacrificed themselves or their interests (sometimes in the form of their family members) for the sake of the greater good. Where baroque artists such as Charles Le Brun had used noble classical precedents to help them inflate the personal status and grandeur of their patrons, often explicitly casting them as the individual conquerors of their enemies or the elevated rulers of their subjects, David revived the same range of ennobling sources (neglected by rococo painters in the meantime) to sacrifice the personal identities of his protagonists in favour of their identities as members of a public. The most acclaimed of David's classical history paintings was *Oath of the Horatii* (1784), in which three brothers swear selfless allegiance to Rome before engaging in battle with the Curatius family, despite the fact that one of their wives is a member of the Curatii and one of their sisters is engaged to one of them. Although the Horatii won the battle, only one of the three brothers survived. On his return, he found his sister weeping over the death of her Curatius fiancé and killed her for her lack of selfless patriotism; he was condemned to death for the crime, but was spared following an appeal from the Roman people. Three years later, David painted *The Death of Socrates* in which the ancient philosopher is shown committing suicide (Fig. 3.4). Having been condemned for his unorthodox ideas and for supposedly corrupting the youth of Athens, Socrates was required either to renounce his philosophy and go into exile or to poison himself. Rather than renounce the truth of his teaching, he chose the latter option, sacrificing himself for the sake of an objective good. In the same spirit, *The Lictors Bring to Brutus the Bodies of his Sons* (1789), painted on the eve of the French Revolution, depicts a scene following the command of the Roman leader Brutus that his own sons should be executed for attempting to overthrow the Roman Republic. While Greuze's Septimius Severus had shown a degree of selfless tolerance towards his son in similar circumstances, Brutus was utterly – and, in his own way, selflessly – unrelenting in his attitude towards his own sons. Where Greuze had tried and failed to develop a discourse in which personal subjectivity or selfhood was powerfully and convincingly sublimated in the interests of the public, David succeeded. It is no surprise, then, that when, in 1793–4, the revolutionary government contemplated introducing a national civic costume to be worn by all men – as an expression of each man's function as a member of society, rather than his personal preferences – they commissioned David to design it (Fig. 3.5).

The intense, almost aggressive impersonality of David's iconography in his epic historical works (which make a pointed exception, typical of the time, of the women depicted) was also reflected in their style, which eliminates all scope for subjective engagement. In each case, the scene is set in a rigorous rectilinear space, defined by rigid architectural lines; even the people and objects in the space are ranged along planes that are parallel to the picture surface, as on a classical relief. They are static and

FIGURE 3.4: Jacques-Louis David, *The Death of Socrates*, 1787, oil on canvas, 129.5 × 196.2 cm. Metropolitan Museum of Art, New York, Catharine Lorillard Wolfe Collection, Wolfe Fund.

distinct, subjected to the overall schema of the work. Nothing is random, wayward or occasional; nothing invites or even permits the viewer to melt into a pleasurable reverie. Even the brushstrokes, which are restrained and smooth like enamel, deny the viewer any opportunity to indulge his or her personal inclination towards sensual or self-expressive experience. Indeed, although some of the pictorial conventions of personal experience are firmly in place (the human narrative, the sense of naturalistic space, etc.), the psychological principle of personal experience – that is to say, the *sense* of personal self – is sublimated within them. It no longer exists as an independent entity of value; it is only acceptable to the extent that it is subject to the whole.

While the association of self-sacrifice with classical discipline was explicitly forged in the narratives of neoclassical history painting, it was also implicitly present in the decorative and utilitarian arts of the period, invisibly pervading the environment, as it does in David's painted interiors (for which the artist had 'antique' chairs specially made). The rococo style had replaced the ostentatious grandeur and formality of the baroque style with whimsical spontaneity, subjectivity and sensuality. Reacting against the perceived triviality and self-indulgence of this style, neoclassical designers restored the dignity of baroque classicism, but, filtering it through the experience of rococo elegance, dispensed with its sumptuousness and pomposity (Fig. 3.6). Where baroque forms had been conceived around a rhetoric of *gravitas* and status, neoclassical ones tended to revolve around a rhetoric of levity and sensibility, refinement and restraint. On pieces of furniture, for instance, fine, tapering legs were intended to suggest that the function of *support* was effortlessly

FIGURE 3.5: Dominique Vivant Denon, after Jacques-Louis David, *Civic Attire of a French Citizen*, 1794, etching, 30.1 × 17.5 cm. Metropolitan Museum of Art, New York, The Elisha Whittelsey Collection, The Elisha Whittelsey Fund.

FIGURE 3.6: Armchair, Georges Jacob, around 1780–5, carved and gilded walnut, embroidered silk satin, 102.2 × 74.9 × 77.8 cm. Metropolitan Museum of Art, New York, Gift of Samuel H. Kress Foundation.

accomplished with grace and ease, as if the pieces were standing on tiptoes; this impression of lightness stands in stark contrast to the theatrically 'burdened' supports of their monumental predecessors, in which swelling forms are frequently made to bulge under the apparent weight of their loads. The ethos of classical discipline and self-sacrifice was distilled to an essence and concentrated in a vocabulary of rigorously restrained but highly evocative antique motifs. Austere architectural features, such as fluted columns, bases, capitals, etc., which are suggestive of built institutions and therefore of civic order, were common, as were ancient weapons – arrows, spears, shields and *fasces* – which were frequently used, without a narrative context, to symbolise courage and commitment to public welfare. In post-revolutionary France, where ostentatious signs of affluence became dangerously unfashionable, the neoclassical style was pared back even further, giving rise to the severe and rigorous Empire style (evident, for instance, in the chair in Fig. 3.5). But a bold austerity, suggestive of military discipline on the one hand and domestic virtue on the other, also spread across Europe, informing the Central European Biedermeier and British Regency styles, among others. In many cases, the telltale signs of the classical style – fluted columns with capitals and bases – were so stripped of superfluity, and so reduced to their geometrical essences, that they became entirely 'abstract', leaving nothing but fluting (Fig. 3.7). Indeed, unless one was already familiar with the genesis of such designs, it would be impossible to tell from their appearance alone that they were classical; in such cases, the classical call to self-sacrifice was only implicitly present. Just as the sense of individual self was sublimated in a collective

FIGURE 3.7: Regency hall bench or window seat in the manner of Charles Heathcote Tatham, around 1815, British, Cuban mahogany, 43 × 106 cm. Michael Lipitch Antiques.

sense of the public, so the self-sacrificial implications of classical restraint were absorbed into the metabolism of the environment, leaving little trace on the surface.

David's works are typical examples of the kind of 'cultural form' that evolved in the second half of the eighteenth century, in France and throughout Europe, to accommodate a sense of public identity. Not only does their iconography specifically promote the priority of public welfare over personal preference, but, more subtly (and like all the most culturally validated paintings of the time), they were first exhibited in a context – the public Salon – that was specifically intended to acknowledge and activate the public by inviting them to respond, and thereby engage in the cultural process (Fig. 3.8). Indeed, several of them were commissioned to hang permanently in the Louvre, which was being adapted at the time to serve as a public museum of art, and they were immediately transferred there when the Salon closed at the end of the season. Their role in the Louvre was to graft contemporary art on to the stock of historical art (mainly from Italy) and thereby to make the cultural primacy of contemporary France seem historically inevitable.

This institutionalisation of the history of art in public museums was of great significance. While the Salon had created *occasions* in which the cultural identity of the public was implicit, but which generated no dedicated architecture and left no permanent trace, public museums institutionalised the cultural identity of the public at the highest possible level, whether adapted from a royal collection (as in the Louvre) or newly founded (as in the National Gallery in London). Moreover, at the Louvre, the new art historical self-awareness of the displays reflected and precipitated a historical self-awareness in its public, linking the notion of public identity to the impersonal 'logic' of the historical process (as we saw in chapter 2); by virtue of this act, the identity of the public acquired a dignifying history and context. Although the Louvre was not the very first public museum to structure itself according to an

FIGURE 3.8: Pietro Antonio Martini, *The Salon of 1785*, 1785, etching, 27.6 × 48.6 cm. Metropolitan Museum of Art, New York, A. Hyatt Mayor Purchase Fund, Marjorie Phelps Starr Bequest.

'objective' art historical principle, it was to become the grandest and the most politically charged, and it set a standard for public museums all over Europe.

Until the eighteenth century, collections of cultural treasures had mostly been privately owned and many of them were encyclopaedic, including natural and artificial treasures as part of a single synthetic vision of the universe – that of their owner. For instance, in a sixteenth-century *kunstkammer* (cabinet of curiosities), it would not have been unusual to find a conch shell juxtaposed with a bronze sculpture of a sea god, on account of their shared marine connections and prophylactic properties. Indeed, many collectable objects, such as mounted nautilus cups, were decorated with subject matter that explicitly expressed the connection between natural materials and classical mythology; it was these links that gave them meaning. In such a context, luxury objects were often valued for their exoticism (their technical and poetic ingenuity, and the precious materials from which they were made), rather than as works of 'art' per se. Even small pictures were collected as curiosities and kept in cabinets; they were not necessarily displayed in dedicated gallery spaces. Indeed, in some cases, pictures of objects were used as substitutes for the objects themselves, when originals could not be found. Accordingly, with a few rare exceptions, the status of painters remained relatively low at this time. Works of art were only collected as independent commodities at the most elevated level.

Such courtly collections enabled their owners to articulate their understanding of the world by creating their own unified, rationalised microcosm of it, thereby substantiating their sense of a personal self in which that understanding seemed to inhere. But they were also contrived as demonstrations of education, wealth and power – mostly to other educated, wealthy and powerful people – and were presented accordingly, in displays that highlighted their exclusive rarity and decorative splendour. In the seventeenth century, when the first substantial collections of paintings began to be assembled, it was the overall impact and status of the collection that determined the principles of classification and display, thereby subtly propagating the identity of the collector before that of the artists exhibited. The juxtaposition, in such a context, of a sixteenth-century religious painting originally created for an altarpiece in a church and a seventeenth-century still life, was an indication of the extent to which the identity of a painting as a luxury object, rather than as a primary means of communicating religious or moral ideas, had begun to prevail. Similarly, the symmetry of the hang of a collection of paintings, densely packed together and mounted in lavish carved and gilded frames, often took precedence over any historical links that might exist between individual works. This convention persisted until the end of the eighteenth century. At Corsham Court in Wiltshire, much of the collection of old master paintings is still displayed as it was when it was first hung in around 1770. Bearing in mind that the Methuens who conceived the picture gallery were Protestant, the abundance of Catholic and even papal subjects in the collection demonstrates the extent to which the originally religious status of the pictures had been superseded – and even annihilated – by their status as 'works of art'. Having said that, the fact that they were displayed in a strictly symmetrical manner, with little regard for their subject matter, date or style, and that some of them were even extended or cropped in order to conform to the overall effect of symmetry, indicates that they were primarily required to contribute towards the impression of a prestigious gallery. Ultimately, they constituted a manifestation of the owner's identity – as an appreciator and owner of art – as much as an attempt to understand the gallery's content on its own terms.

Towards the end of the eighteenth century, as the effects of the enlightened 'objectification of knowledge' began to take root, efforts were made to classify works of art according to more consistent and measurable principles of relationship and difference: date, place of origin, style, artist, etc.. Such principles were intended to rise above the merely decorative and status-related potential of elite objects, and the inconsistent subjectivities of their owners, and to reveal a coherent and objective development in the history of art itself. Encapsulating this shift, in 1787 Catherine the Great of Russia demanded that a silver 'cameo cup' that had been given to Peter the Great by King Frederick IV of Denmark in 1716 be dismantled so that its eclectic mix of two hundred cameos, which dated from antiquity to the Renaissance and were mounted on the cup randomly, could be classified and stored according to rational historical principles. Peter had kept his eccentric cup (known from a watercolour produced before its dismantling) in his *kunstkammer*. Catherine laid out her greatly enlarged collection (which, at almost fifty thousand objects by the time of her death, amounted to a miniature museum) in serried ranks in five cabinets – made in the grand but restrained neoclassical style – that she had commissioned especially for them.[10]

One of the first large-scale collections to be reconceived along these lines was that of the Hapsburgs in Vienna.[11] This imperial collection had been built up around the encyclopaedic *kunstkammer* of the reclusive Rudolph II (1552–1612), whose extraordinarily diverse collection of natural and artificial wonders epitomised the Renaissance notion of '*kunstkammer* as microcosm'. Indeed, Rudolph's attitude towards collecting appears to epitomise the notion of collecting as a pathological act of identity formation. It was as if he was attempting to recreate the universe, in microcosmic form, as an object of his own understanding, in order to perfect and immortalise his sense of himself in relation to it. In subsequent years, as the status of painting increased, Rudolph's successors supplemented his *kunstkammer* with a large, if somewhat inconsistent collection of pictures. By the end of the eighteenth century, their rather haphazard approach to collecting and displaying works of art had become anachronistic and, in 1778, Emperor Joseph II commissioned a Swiss art dealer and printmaker, Christian von Mechel, to reorganise the imperial collection of paintings according to artist and school, in such a way that they should not only be impressive but above all instructive to the public, constituting a 'visible history of art'.[12] A catalogue of the collection, including an informative ground plan of the new galleries, was also published at this time, in 1784 (Fig. 3.9).

In Paris, similar changes were also planned for the Louvre, which, prior to the French Revolution, was both a royal palace and home to the Royal Academy of

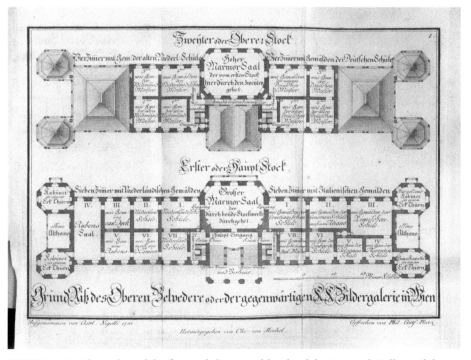

FIGURE 3.9: *Floor plan of the first and the second levels of the Imperial Gallery of the Belvedere Palace in 1778*, published in Christian Mechel's catalogue of the collection, Vienna, 1783. Photo: Alice Hoppe-Harnoncourt.

Painting and Sculpture, where the regular Salons were held. Parts of the French royal collection of historic paintings had already been put on public view in the Palais de Luxembourg in 1750, but the hybrid arrangement of the works there still suggested an audience of privileged initiates, including some artists, rather than the general public.[13] It was not until after the French Revolution, when the royal collections became the property of France and the Louvre was opened as a national museum, that a fully art historical display was first attempted. Significantly, although initiatives to open the Louvre as a public museum had been taken as early as the 1770s, its actual opening on 10 August 1793 – exactly one year after the fall of the French monarchy – was celebrated as a republican festival: it was immediately made to embody a sense of French national identity, rather than the identity of the monarchy, and to effect a regeneration of the people by initiating them into a new state of historical self-awareness (Fig. 3.10).

The introduction of a new system of art historical classification in public museums was significant because it reflected the realisation of a new principle around which such collections were believed to acquire cultural meaning and value. On the one hand, it instituted a belief in the linearity and coherence of history; on the other, it

FIGURE 3.10: Hubert Robert, *Project for the Transformation of the Grande Galerie of the Louvre*, 1796, oil on canvas, 112 × 143 cm. Musée du Louvre, Paris. Photo: © RMN-Grand Palais (Musée du Louvre)/Jean-Gilles Berizzi.

placed unprecedented importance on individual artists and their schools, rather than on the preciousness, status or subject matter of works of art. The institutionalisation of the concept of the artist at this level of social prominence was especially significant in the present context because it reflected the crystallisation of a new archetype in the imagination of the public – that of the unique, creative and even prophetic individual. It is arguable that this archetype evolved as a complement to the chronically homogenised and deindividualised identities of members of the public; it served as a compensatory projection of the ideal of personal identity – otherwise sublimated in the identity of a public – on to an object that was generated specifically to carry and process that projection. As such, the elevation of the 'artist' to the level of a heroic individual, working and suffering for the benefit of the people (in keeping with the neoclassical ideal of self-sacrifice), constituted a further subtle institutionalisation of the personal self – not just for the self-selecting elite this time, but at the level of the people as a whole – although in this instance, the sense of self that it reflected was largely inverted and projected, and, therefore, for the most part subconscious. It was only through the appreciation of art and culture – newly made available in public places – that the self-sense of the burgeoning majority could rise to the surface and become manifest. By the beginning of the twentieth century, this mediation of cultural value via the public experience of visiting museums and galleries had become so complete that it trumped the private experience of art; thus, when the *Mona Lisa* was stolen from the Louvre in 1911, people came flocking to see the space it had vacated. The self-sense had come to feed on the *concept* of art, reinforced in the minds of individuals by subscribing to it in public, as much as the *experience* of it. The development of the concept of art, and of the archetype of the artist, will be explored in the next chapter.

CHAPTER FOUR

The Disintegration of the Self: the Origins of Abstraction and the Deobjectification of the World

Although the status of painting had been raised to that of a liberal art during the sixteenth century, it was not until the early nineteenth century that artists fully ceased to depend on commissions and, therefore, on the agendas of patrons. Artists became ever freer to express the content of their own minds, however removed from 'objective' principles of taste that content may have been. As a result, their work came to embody a Romantic ideal of self-sufficient subjectivity, whose sources of creativity lay within itself. At the same time, the notion of the 'artist' crystallised into an archetype that functioned as a surrogate form of self for those innumerable consumers of art who were otherwise removed from the elusive objects of artistic contemplation and who increasingly constituted their 'public'.

While the sheer number of people included in the 'public' enabled unprecedented numbers of individuals to participate in the 'cultural process' and to identify themselves accordingly, it was of course impossible for each one of them to sustain a sense of personal *distinctiveness* within the group as a whole, for the emerging signs of distinctiveness were constantly being devalued or neutralised by the fact that they were shared by others; the experience of an intensely felt sense of personal selfhood therefore remained virtual for them. To compensate for this fact, individuals felt constrained to project their sense of themselves outside of themselves, on to some form of external agency. It was for this reason that the role of the artist was raised to the level of an archetype at this time – to embody the possibility of personal creativity that was implicitly being denied to the undifferentiated society of ordinary individuals in their own lives. While the notion of the public enabled individuals to participate in the cultural process, albeit anonymously, the romanticised archetype of the artist – and indeed the notion of art as a whole – enabled members of the public to realise a sense of their personal identity, albeit vicariously, as a fantasy, or in the realm of the imagination.

The archetype of the artist continues to be effective today, stretching the possibilities of 'individual freedom' beyond conventional levels of social acceptability and consummating it in works of art. Art became the zone in which the sense of self was most perfectly accommodated; indeed, because the notion of art emanated directly from the self as a unique medium of self-realisation and self-communication, it was perfectly and innately structured to reflect the self to itself. Moreover, because it seemed to necessitate the self in this way, it was invested with a quasi-sacred power, adopting the functions of religion that Enlightenment rationalists had attempted to wrest from Christianity. However, as soon as the archetype of the artist was in place, and the temple to art as a 'repository of truth' was built – both metaphorically and architecturally (for instance, in national museums) – its coherence came into question and it slowly began to unravel; and as it unravelled, so the coherence of the subjective self that seemed to find itself reflected in it (albeit vicariously on the part of the art-viewing public) began to unravel too.

The shift in the role and function of art is first reflected in the changing relationship between its subject matter and its style. From the sixteenth to the nineteenth century, the arts of painting and sculpture had largely revolved around the visible representation of discrete objects (including imaginary phenomena, such as mythical figures or angels) in a coherent sense of pictorial space. The style of a work was primarily used to enhance its iconography, in which the primary significance of the work was invested, although it did of course modify the significance of iconography by contextualising it in a particular manner; it was the role of the artist to convey this significance with insight and feeling. In the nineteenth century, this began to change. Towards the end of the neoclassical period, a budding appreciation of subjective experience gave rise to a sensitivity to the evocative mood of artworks at the expense of their high-minded references to objective ideals. In subsequent years, this trend towards the autonomy of artistic experience would continue, manifesting as a growing interest in the expressive potential of the language of art per se, at the expense of its content. The process culminated at the beginning of the twentieth century with the realisation of an art that was 'non-objective' in the sense that it had no 'objective' content (or subject matter) and was, therefore, independent of all external sources of meaning. Most important in the present context is the fact that, by ceasing to define itself in relation to an objective frame of reference, non-objective art undermined the principal co-ordinates of subjectivity, or the sense of a personal self, thereby putting fatal pressure on a cultural convention that had served as the keystone of European culture for over five centuries.

While the devolution of the notion of 'art' seemed revolutionary in its day, coming to a head at the time of the First World War, it was not as unprecedented and reactionary as it first appeared to be. On the contrary, its constituent parts had already existed for many years, lying dormant and dispersed as seeds of possible meaning in the disciplines of an earlier age. An iconic moment in the prehistory of abstract art was reached in 1839 when the discovery of the principles of photography led some commentators to suggest that the role of painting as a means of representing the objective material world had come to an end. On first seeing a daguerreotype, the painter Paul Delaroche is said to have exclaimed: 'From today, painting is dead!'. Although the academic painting tradition continued to thrive throughout the nineteenth century, the advent of photography did indeed present it with a significant challenge – putting many painters of miniature portraits out of business, for instance – and styles of painting that departed from optical realism developed accordingly. Indeed, some commentators maintained that painting could now focus on its 'proper' function, which was to explore the 'higher regions of the mind',[1] to represent the invisible world of feelings and ideas that cameras could not capture, and thereby to create cultural forms for hitherto unrecognised dimensions of human experience. In due course, the insistence on creating a convincing illusion of pictorial space was indeed relaxed; objects that inhabited that space, and had done so for over three centuries, were no longer required to look perfectly coherent and discrete – and, more significantly, the subjective self-sense no longer sought to find itself so coherently reflected in them.

In the twenty years that followed the invention of photography, the pros and cons of the medium were hotly debated. Because photography provided viewers with an opportunity to experience sights that they could not have otherwise witnessed, with a degree of verisimilitude that no painter could have ever dreamed of achieving – for instance, in distant lands or from hot-air balloons – it broadened the parameters of human experience beyond the scope of painting and was, therefore, ascribed a certain primary value. Indeed, although photography was originally seen to be too realistic, in a purely technical way, to be expressive, familiarity did eventually acclimatise viewers to the artistic potential of the medium and, in 1863, it was legally acknowledged to be an 'art form' that deserved to be exhibited at the annual Salons alongside the traditional media of painting and sculpture.[2] But because it involved highly specialised technical processes, it was initially regarded as a scientific method for recording data, rather than as a medium of artistic expression. From the point of view of many artists, photography was generally considered to be an aid to painting, at best. Indeed, the earliest photographic processes were invented by painters – Daguerre, a virtuoso in France, and Fox Talbot, an amateur in England – who had used the traditional camera obscura as an aid to tracing images. Because photographs were able to capture the visual 'truth' of an object 'with unbelievable exactitude and finesse . . . with almost mathematical precision',[3] it was suggested that they could be used in place of preparatory sketches and engravings as sources of visual information for painters. Even Ingres, the portrait painter par excellence, is known to have used daguerreotype photographs of his sitters, especially commissioned from Nadar, to speed up and simplify the process of painting. Moreover, because much of the detail recorded in photographs was not even noticed by the photographers that took them, many people, requiring art to show signs of personal genius and inspiration, denied them the status of art. The fact that photographs seemed to provide unquestionable factual information about the visual world and could be predictably reproduced in significant numbers gave them a further air of impersonal objectivity. Such observations lent weight to the claim that they were, ideologically speaking, products of the Industrial Revolution, perfectly suited to commercial consumption by an anonymous public, rather than as catalysts of refined aesthetic experience for the discriminating and self-conscious art lover. This association is understandable if one considers how the tendency of silver nitrate to darken in response to light was first used to record images by one of the sons of Josiah Wedgwood, whose ceramics factory, Etruria, in Staffordshire, was one of the definitive institutions of the Industrial Revolution. Having been brought up among the leading scientists of the time, Thomas Wedgwood's unsuccessful efforts to fix projected images on 'white paper, or white leather, moistened with a solution of nitrate of silver' were first described by Humphrey Davy in 1802. Moreover, he was said to have experimented with quicksilver and silver nitrate in the preparation of glazes for his father's lustrous 'silvered wares' as early as 1790.[4] These apparent pretensions to scientific status eased the pressure on painting to make the same claim, freeing it up to take a looser, more experimental approach to its subjects.

While the development of stylised modes of representation coincided with the evolution of photography, it also derived legitimacy from its association with medieval and early Renaissance painting. The revival of interest in medieval culture had originally occurred, in the mid-eighteenth century, as a result of its ability to reflect proto-Romantic, anti-classical dimensions of experience that were not entirely measurable and explicable, albeit in a rather superficial and naive way. This shift of priorities had also led to a revived interest in Christianity, partly as an expression of dissociation from the rationalism of Enlightenment philosophy. Having originally functioned as a whimsical alternative to the classical style, the revived medieval style now acquired religious, moralising associations. The legitimacy of interest in Christianity was further corroborated by an appreciation of the quality of its art and it was, therefore, just a question of time before the mysterious allure of the Middle Ages and the excellence of Christian art combined their forces to stimulate a taste for medieval art as a new epitome of 'spiritual culture'. It was in this context that, despite its unclassical pictorial conventions, medieval painting came to be respected as a model for contemporary artists. The fact that painters were content to mix elements of early Christian, Byzantine, Romanesque and Gothic art with aspects of Italian painting from the fourteenth and fifteenth centuries (from Giotto to Fra Angelico to early Raphael) is of secondary significance. More important is the fact that Christian precedents were now being used to legitimise and even sacralise the employment of highly abstracted styles of painting in commissions of 'high' art, thereby introducing those styles into the currency of contemporary culture at a respectable level. The fact that many such commissions were for murals in churches, to be seen from a considerable distance by many people simultaneously, provided an additional functional rationale for simplifying their style and highlighting their graphic impact.

One artist who dedicated his career to the revitalisation of Christian painting was Hippolyte Flandrin (1809–64) – once his father had been persuaded by a phrenologist to allow his thirteen-year-old son to 'realise his true nature', as revealed by the shape of his skull, by becoming an artist. Jean-Auguste-Dominique Ingres, Flandrin's teacher, had taken some steps towards the pious sensitivity of the Middle Ages by eschewing classical subject matter in favour of Christian themes from the works of medieval authors such as Dante, but his style remained resolutely classical. Flandrin went a step further. Having been awarded the Grand Prix de Rome in 1832, he spent several years in Italy, where he immersed himself in early Christian, medieval and Renaissance art. On his return to France in 1838, he devoted himself to the decoration of churches with monumental murals, using an eclectic range of medieval and Renaissance 'Christian' styles. For instance, in the basilical church of St. Vincent de Paul (from 1848) in Paris, he painted a long, unbroken frieze of statuesque saints and martyrs proceeding solemnly towards the altar (Fig. 4.1). Although the frieze itself is conceived in an austere but rich neo-early Christian/Byzantine manner, after models in Rome and Ravenna, the static classicising style of the figures is reminiscent of the work of fifteenth-century Italian artists such as Masaccio and Mantegna. While the gilded background is iconographically appropriate in that it symbolises

FIGURE 4.1: Interior of the church of St. Vincent de Paul, Paris, showing the frieze by Hippolyte Flandrin, 1848–53.

the otherworldly sanctity of the blessed (as in Byzantine mosaics), it also serves the more significant purpose, in the present context, of limiting the illusion of the pictorial space. This is also true of the backgrounds in Flandrin's extensive cycle of paintings in the church of Saint-Germain-des-Prés (1855–63), where gold grounds are complemented by backgrounds of deep azure blue, derived from the fresco cycles of Giotto in Assisi and Padua painted in around 1300 (Fig. 4.2). Significantly, where Giotto's uniformly blue grounds represented a transitional stage between the symbolic abstraction of early medieval painting and – to the extent that they represent skies – the naturalistic representation of three-dimensional space that was characteristic of early Renaissance painting, Flandrin's blue grounds represent a step in the opposite direction: away from literal worldly naturalism, towards abstraction. Moreover, the revival of interest in the stylised conventions of late medieval and early Renaissance art also reflects a shift away from the implicit attempt of fully naturalistic painting to pose as an extension of the viewer's present experience – by virtue of its verisimilitude and dramatic rhetoric – towards a more symbolic and ritualistic mode of experience in which meaning is increasingly created, not in response to a series of convincing optical illusions, but in keeping with an interiorised code of otherworldly symbols and associations.[5]

While the revitalised church espoused medieval and early Renaissance stylisation for religious reasons, and artists tended to espouse it for its expressive potential, dealers, collectors and museum authorities valued it for its romantic associations and historical significance. The connoisseurs responsible for the new national picture galleries (for instance, in Paris, London and Munich) had hitherto found the edifying values they were looking for exclusively in the naturalism of High Renaissance and baroque art. However, the growing inclination to give a complete picture of the history of art, rather than focus on 'grand masterpieces', led to acquisitions of paintings that were chosen specifically to illustrate the unsophisticated conditions of art from which the Renaissance emerged, thereby throwing its heroic achievement into clear perspective. In 1857, for instance, Sir Charles Eastlake, the first director of the National Gallery in London, bought two 'primitive' works – by Margarito of Arezzo (c. 1263–4) and Duccio (c. 1315) – solely for their historical importance (Fig. 4.3). By the standards of the time, works of this kind were simply too stylised and abstracted to have any artistic value of their own. The work of Piero della Francesca (c. 1415–92), by contrast, was slightly more accessible because, although it was static, hieratic and calculated to the point of being artificial, it provided its viewers with the basic familiar reference points of three-dimensional objects placed in a unified naturalistic space (Fig. 4.4). Towards the end of the 1850s, therefore, Piero's reputation began to change; where he had previously been neglected as a rather second-rate artist (despite Vasari's praise of him) because of the apparent stiffness of his drawing and the naive absence of rhetorical devices in his paintings, efforts were now made to track down examples of his work, and between 1861 and 1874 his *Baptism*, *St. Michael* and *Nativity* entered the National Gallery collection. By slow degrees, the stylised language of early Renaissance art was translated into contemporary currency. Despite its lack of naturalistic, dramatic expressivity – in fact, *because* of that lack – it developed into a medium for the expression of contemporary values.

FIGURE 4.2: Interior of the abbey church of Saint-Germain-des-Prés, Paris, showing murals by Hippolyte Flandrin, 1855–63. Photo by David Iliff.

FIGURE 4.3: Margarito d'Arezzo, *The Virgin and Child Enthroned with Narrative Scenes*, 1263–4, egg tempera on wood, 92.1 × 183.1 cm. National Gallery, London.

FIGURE 4.4: Piero della Francesca, *The Nativity*, 1470–5, oil on poplar, 124.4 × 122.6 cm. National Gallery, London.

The appreciation of early Renaissance painting was originally justified on the grounds of its religious innocence, solemnity and directness. By around 1860, the archaic painterly conventions used to capture these virtues were becoming sufficiently familiar to accrue their own expressive power and to become part of the stylistic vocabulary of contemporary artists, regardless of their religious background. The early work of Edgar Degas (1834–1917), for instance, clearly reflects the influence of the fifteenth-century paintings that he had copied as a student in Paris in the early 1850s, and which he encountered again between 1856 and 1859 when he lived in Italy. He was particularly precocious in his appreciation of Piero della Francesca, and his *Semiramis Building Babylon* of 1861 is clearly indebted to Piero's frescos of the Legend of the True Cross, which he saw at the church of San Francesco in Arezzo in 1858 (Fig. 4.5). Several aspects of this painting recall Piero's precedent, which legitimised Degas' formal innovations by investing them with historical dignity: the earthy but muted palette, the structured clustering of the figure group, the airy levity of the figures, the delicate hesitancy of the gestures, the graphic effect of the flattened profiles, the frozen, expressionless quality of the faces, the heavy eyelids, half closed as if caught unawares or lost in contemplation. Although Degas originally set out to be a history painter (aiming to revitalise the tradition with works such as *Semiramis*), in around 1865 he decided to become a painter of contemporary life. As a result, he became one of the first artists to apply an abstracted style of painting, hitherto associated with the symbolic function of religious art, to scenes that had no significant symbolic content. For this reason he is considered to be one of the first 'modern' artists, in conjunction with Edouard Manet, whom he met in around 1864, and the Impressionists (Monet, Pissarro, Renoir). Despite exhibiting with the Impressionists

FIGURE 4.5: Edgar Degas, *Semiramis Building Babylon*, 1861, oil on canvas, 151 × 258 cm. Musée d'Orsay, Paris. Photo: © RMN-Grand Palais (Musée d'Orsay)/Hervé Lewandowski.

in all but one of their celebrated exhibitions between 1874 and 1886, on account of their shared experimental approach to the purely painterly or 'formal' properties of painting, Degas rejected the term 'Impressionism' and its associations. He was more rooted in the academic tradition than Monet and Pissarro and was not interested in working spontaneously *en plein air*, as they were. On the contrary, where the Impressionists were primarily concerned with capturing the effects of light, he was preoccupied by the relationships between forms and shapes, and by their role in the compositional dynamics of a painting. Moreover, he was also more interested in the psychological potential of iconography (focusing on anonymous people, especially women), although he never returned to narrative painting as such.

Apart from Renaissance (and other old master) painting, two other sources encouraged Degas to abstract his style: Japanese *ukiyo-e* prints and photography. Japanese prints had been flooding Europe, sometimes incidentally – as wrapping paper for porcelain – since the opening up of Japan to European trade in 1854. Such exposure to oriental art was not unprecedented in Europe. Above all, in the eighteenth century the use of asymmetry in Chinese imagery and the inclination of such imagery to include the human figure as a mere *part* of nature – rather than as a dominating controller of nature (as reflected in the taste for formal parterre gardens in the French style) – had been instrumental in the development of the rococo style and of picturesque gardens. The same unclassical features were characteristic of Japanese prints and they were hugely influential on artists, especially the French Impressionists, in the 1860s and 70s. Although artists had been painting exotic oriental subjects for many years, their works had been largely executed in a conventionally academic style; it was only towards the middle of the century, as the stronghold of classical naturalism began to weaken, that artists also became interested in the artistic devices used in Japanese prints, and began to integrate them into their own work on their own account, without making explicit reference to their exotic source. Indeed, it was acknowledged by several writers that Japanese prints were not merely 'influential'; they positively precipitated the drive towards abstraction in European art.

Degas, who collected Japanese prints, was a case in point. While he was highly sympathetic to the understated charm of the transient, semi-neglected 'floating world' (*ukiyo-e*) of everyday life depicted in these works – for instance, scenes from the theatre and of women in their private spaces (Fig. 4.6) – he did not exoticise his own images of these subjects by associating them with Japan. On the contrary, he indigenised them – again, in parallel with the Japanese precedent – by locating them in the most ordinary and even banal contexts: those of his own unremarkable urban environment (Fig. 4.7). Indeed, in contrast to academic history painting, which revolved around the meaning of dramatically staged narratives, their iconography seemed to be meaning*less*, signifying nothing of value. Moreover, Degas' casual approach to subject matter was complemented by the apparently arbitrary, indifferent way in which he presented it. Rather than focusing on his subject matter as if he had specifically chosen to study it on account of its significance, and placing it in the centre of the image where the viewer could see it and engage with it clearly, as in classical painting, he frequently presented oblique views of his subjects in which his figures are no more demanding of the viewers' attention than the walls or floors against which they are placed. In direct proportion to the diminished 'iconicity' of

FIGURE 4.6: Kitagawa Utamaro, *A
Woman with a Cat*, around 1793–4,
Japan, polychrome woodblock print on
paper, 38.4 × 25.9 cm. Metropolitan
Museum of Art, New York, H. O.
Havemeyer Collection, bequest of
Mrs. H. O. Havemeyer.

FIGURE 4.7: Edgar Degas, *Woman Bathing
in a Shallow Tub*, 1885, charcoal and pastel
on light green woven paper, 81.3 × 56.2
cm. Metropolitan Museum of Art, New
York, H. O. Havemeyer Collection, bequest
of Mrs. H. O. Havemeyer.

his subject matter is the increased importance that the artist ascribed to design and
composition. Moreover, just as the understated nature of his subject matter was
consonant with the subject matter of 'floating world' prints, so his feeling for purely
compositional considerations was indebted to their aesthetic principles. For instance,
his experimentation with asymmetrical, even lopsided designs, which seem to be
randomly cropped regardless of their subject matter, clearly reflects his admiration
for the compositional strategies of Japanese printmakers (Fig. 4.8). Likewise, his
treatment of three-dimensional objects (including human forms) as coloured shapes
without shadows, sometimes circumscribed and flattened by black outlines and
placed against a grid of rectilinear elements (architecture, furniture, picture frames,
etc.), was partly due to this source. This relationship became all the more clear in
around 1865, when Degas began to place his figures against off-centred views of the
corners of rooms because of the abundance of diagonal lines – also much loved by
the Japanese – that they offered.

    Another source that was integral to the development of Degas' stylisation was
photography. According to Paul Valery, who knew the artist at the end of his life,
Degas 'loved and appreciated photography at a time when artists despised it or did

FIGURE 4.8: Edgar Degas, *Mary Cassatt in the Louvre*, 1879–80, etching and drypoint on paper, 30.4 × 12.6 cm. Rijksmuseum, Amsterdam.

not dare admit that they made use of it'; he was one of the first artists to 'see what photography could teach the painter'.[6] The medium was of interest to him partly because a key element of it was, or seemed to be, absolutely or objectively realistic in the sense that it involved a process in which objects were reproduced, by virtue of the direct effect of light on a surface of silver nitrate, without being manipulated – in the moment of exposure – by the personalising agenda of an artist. In that moment, reality seemed to reproduce itself, and consequently the personal role of the maker in the production of the image was momentarily qualified. At the same time, because some photographs inevitably included elements of arbitrariness and accidental subject matter – for instance, the series of *Vues instantanées de Paris* produced by Hippolyte Jouvin from 1861–5 (Fig. 4.9) – they could also be seen to represent a mode of seeing that was radically different from that of the highly controlled pose-orientated compositions of academic painting. By accommodating aspects of experience that are involuntary and impersonal in this way, such images implicitly ignored, and even excluded, the deliberate and self-conscious viewer, clearly neglecting to reflect him to himself. The discourse of the self-sense was suspended in them.

The impression of a decentralised self-sense, both on the part of the maker and the viewer, is especially clear in photographs in which figures were unintentionally cropped at the edges – a feature which, as in Japanese prints, had the effect of downplaying the importance of human narrative in the overall economy of the image. A similar effect was created by photographs of moving figures which, because of the relatively lengthy exposures being used in the 1850s (several seconds), could appear blurred and suggestively dematerialised. Having said this, as it became possible to work with exposures of a fraction of a second, from around 1860, so it also became possible to take instantaneous 'snapshots' that could abstract fleeting moments from sequences of actions that the human eye could not see on its own. In producing such

FIGURE 4.9: Hippolyte Jouvin, Stereographic image of 'Le Pont-Neuf, seen from the quai des Grands Augustins', 1860–70, 8.6 × 17.2 cm. Library of Congress, Washington.

unpredictable images, the camera defied the natural tendency of the mind to synthesise its myriad, fragmentary impressions into a sustained vision of an object as a coherent and legible continuum, and provided insight into the imperfect interstitial spaces that exist in between identifiable moments of self-awareness. Most photographers *tolerated* these side effects rather than actually *sought* them out, as they still aimed to control as much of their images as possible. It was, nevertheless, through these imperfect works that images of unselfconscious people, oblivious of the viewer and forgetful of themselves, and sometimes caught in awkward and ungainly postures, became part of the visual currency of the time. In 1863, the American writer Oliver Wendell Holmes observed this effect while looking at 'a number of stereoscopic views of the streets of Paris and New York, each of them showing numerous walking figures, among which some may be found in every stage of [this] complex act'. He commented that 'no artist would have dared to draw a walking figure in attitudes like some of these', had they not already been identified and therefore, to some degree, normalised in photographs.[7] In the same year, Ingres and Flandrin interpreted the evidence in the opposite direction, blaming photography for what they perceived to be the 'decline' in the quality of academic drawing at the Salon.[8]

Although neither Degas' banal subject matter, nor his 'uncomposed' compositions, nor his apparently casual and 'blurred' brushwork were at all random, he used the *look* of randomness, made familiar by the unintentional elements in photography, for poetic reasons. On the one hand, this look deepened the feeling of uncontrived naturalness in his work; on the other hand, it weakened the impression of deliberate and meaningful coherence in the objects of his attention. This combination of effects is reflected in numerous works – for instance, *La Coiffure*, painted in 1896, by which time Degas had himself experimented with photography (Fig. 4.10). Firstly, the subject matter – a woman combing another woman's hair epitomises the profound ordinariness of everyday life. The insignificance of this subject matter is enhanced by the women's total lack of self-consciousness in relation to what they are doing – an indifference that is powerfully transmitted to the viewer of the painting, not least by the closed eyes of the seated woman, her head tilted back in a deeply absent-minded, quasi-ecstatic state, and the delicate and vulnerable position of her raised arms. The impression that her attention – and indeed her sense of self – are dispersed beyond the confines of her body and mind, is passionately evoked by the way that the fiery colour of both her hair and her clothing spills beyond her form, on to the curtains and walls of the room, and indeed into the very air and atmosphere around her, allowing the suggestion of physical dissolution and formlessness to signify a state of psychological indetermination; it is as if she is disintegrating physically and psychologically into the environment that contains her. By understating the value and coherence of his subject matter in this way, Degas undermined its inclination to reflect meaningful coherence in the personal identities of the viewers that engaged with it, while also revealing the uncontrived naturalness of the formless state of consciousness that pre-existed (and pre-exists) those identities.

Because many of Degas' subjects are sensuous, naked women who are evidently unaware of the viewer's presence and therefore vulnerable, his works have often been construed as voyeuristic, as if the artist and therefore the viewer are hidden from the subject, spying on them, secretly gratifying a private fantasy, as in so many

FIGURE 4.10: Edgar Degas, *Combing the Hair (La Coiffure)*, 1896, oil on canvas,
114.3 × 146.7 cm. National Gallery, London.

sixteenth- and seventeenth-century paintings of nudes. He has also been accused of
misogyny on the grounds that his work attempts to control the sexual availability of
women. But this interpretation is not supported by the visual evidence; it projects a
partial narrative on to the subjects, presuming that they seem unaware of the viewer
because they have not noticed him, without completing it by considering where that
voyeuristic viewer might actually be located. The fact is that in most examples of
Degas' work in which the subjects seem to be unaware of the viewer – for instance,
his paintings of women ironing, washing, combing their hair or rehearsing ballet
positions – the point of view from which the scene is implicitly observed is so close
to the subjects (sometimes scarcely more than a few feet away) that, if the internal
logic of the paintings is correctly followed, it would be impossible for them not to
notice him. Moreover, it is often so high above them that he would also have to be
floating in the air to see them. It is arguable, therefore, that, although the women are
obviously shown as being visible, they are also shown as *not being seen* and they
cannot, therefore, be objects of voyeurism. On the contrary, they are as truly alone
in their private spaces as they seem to be, occupying an imaginative space that is
explicitly inaccessible to the physical eye, and in which disembodied vision functions
not as voyeurism but as a poetic metaphor for a mode of insight into the invisible
nature of the interstitial world. In the same way, because the viewpoint presupposed
by the pictures cannot represent the natural human eye, nor therefore does it

implicitly locate the viewer in front of the painting. Although the viewer's space is implicitly acknowledged by the illusion of pictorial space, the possibility of a viewer's actual presence there is positively resisted. Indeed, paradoxical though it may seem, the implication of the paintings is that there is *no* viewer. That is to say, the personal identity of the viewer is not registered in them – in stark contrast to sixteenth- and seventeenth-century images of nudes in which voyeurism is built into the pictures' narratives, and especially to any picture in which eye contact is made with the viewer. On the contrary, according to the internal logic of the paintings, personal identity is necessarily and innately non-existent in them; it is only as a non-viewer, as a non-self, that their presence is possible. This feeling for the non-existence of the self is perfectly reflected in, and induced by, the virtual non-existence and non-recognition of the personal identities of the women depicted – and in the apparently random way in which they are observed. At most, the women are characterised by their disinclination to be identified as discrete objects and thereby to accommodate and reflect coherent significance. While in most naturalistic painting the personal identity of the viewer is presupposed and supported by the coherent objectivity of the painting's subject matter (which functions as one of many co-ordinates that locate him, allowing him to say: 'the object that I see exists as a coherent object, therefore I must exist, as a coherent subject, to perceive it'), in this instance, the existence of the viewing self is undermined by the fact that the subject matter of the paintings is in a perpetual state of designification and disintegration.

The apparent dissolution of subject matter – most significantly, of people – into their environment became one of the most characteristic conventions of avant-garde painting in France in the late nineteenth century. Both iconographically and stylistically, it signified the incipient disintegration of personal identity. This trend was clearly reflected in the work of the Nabis, a 'brotherhood' of mostly French artists (including Maurice Denis, Paul Sérusier, Pierre Bonnard and Edouard Vuillard) that came together in the 1890s to restore a decorative and aesthetic dimension to the arts, which they believed had been sidelined by the excessively literalist approach of academic illusionism; the name of the group, derived from the Hebrew word for a prophet, reflects their sense of mission. Firstly, as in Degas' work, many of the figures in the Nabis' works are depicted in insignificant genre situations (reading, sewing, bathing, having breakfast, etc.). The apparently casual and even careless ways in which they were arranged on the picture surface – i.e. often blurred or 'crudely' cropped – reinforces the initial impression that they scarcely attracted the painter's attention and that they are scarcely worthy of the viewer's. These features – partly inspired, as with Degas, by Japanese prints and photographs – artfully contribute towards the sense of negligible selflessness that such figures convey. Moreover, the way in which the forms of the figures are made to dissolve optically into the environments that contain them further underlines their lack of independent value. In Vuillard's case, this lack of distinctiveness was achieved in two key ways. On the one hand, he reduced people and objects to shaped fields of evenly spread decorative patterning (inspired by Japanese prints); his favourite motifs – women wearing patterned dresses, decoratively upholstered furniture, bouquets of flowers, elaborate wallpapers, etc. – lent themselves particularly well to this kind of treatment (Fig. 4.11). On the other hand, he limited his use of colours to a narrow band of tonalities, allowing for only minimal contrast

FIGURE 4.11: Edouard Vuillard, *Music*, 1896, oil on canvas, 212.5 × 154 cm. Petit Palais,
Musée des Beaux-Arts de la Ville de Paris. Photo: © RMN-Grand Palais/Agence Bulloz.

between them. In conjunction with the quasi-random cropping of his work, this combination of effects was designed to understate the subject matter, which in extreme cases can scarcely be distinguished, in favour of the evenly decorated surface of the image as a whole. As with much of Degas' work, Vuillard's paintings revolve around a paradoxical state of impersonal or selfless presence. Not only did he depict individuals in indeterminate states of being, but he did so in an apparently casual way. Moreover, he also promoted a quasi-existential frame of mind in his viewers by offering them an artistic experience in which the intellectual or narrative appeal of subject matter was completely eclipsed by the aesthetic effect of decorative appearance. In this way, his work induced its viewers *by aesthetic means* to empathise with the indeterminate state of being realised in the figures in it, rather than to relate to them as robust 'individuals with personal identities'.

The inclination of the Nabis to distance themselves from the overpolarised and dramatised encounter between the subjective viewer and the objective work of art – an encounter in which the 'theatre of the self' was performed – was reflected in the fact that many of their members also made designs for the more ephemeral media of decorative murals, books, prints, programmes and posters, as well as the 'minor' arts of textiles and furniture (including folding screens, again based on Japanese precedents). Because these media were not isolated by the iconic status cultivated through the concept of 'fine art', they were able to act as media through which the regenerative principle of creative work could be integrated into the practices of everyday life. In its own discreet way, this shift set a precedent for the dismantling of the iconic monument of 'art' and the structures of personal identity invested in it. The medium of colour lithography, used principally for public advertisements, was particularly well suited to the Nabis' interest in the decorative and graphic potential of the picture surface as it relied on a limited number of flat, unmodulated colours for its effects. Because of this characteristic, lithography was inherently ill suited to the detailed representation of naturalistic space, which it tended to flatten, and, therefore, it was also instrumental in the development of the visual language of abstraction. Moreover, because lithographic posters were both public (displayed on hoardings all over major cities) and ephemeral (often advertising theatrical occasions and, therefore, lacking the iconic aura of 'art'), they were particularly well placed to disseminate their innovative effects throughout the cultural environment, establishing new possibilities, expectations and norms of experience among the public, without controversy or resistance. Their potential as secret agents of change was reflected in a contemporary description of the 'task' of Jules Chéret, who pioneered colour lithography in France in the 1860s and reached his peak as a poster designer in the 1890s, as the 'subconscious education of public taste'.[9] Chéret's posters certainly popularised the effects achieved by contemporary painters. But some of the subjects that they covered – which the designer clearly integrated into his work – also underline how the formal innovations occasioned by lithographic posters could be associated with a subtle dismantling of the mind, with regard to both perception and understanding. Loie Fuller's 'serpentine dances', performed in voluminous swirling dresses with ever-changing polychromatic light effects, seemed to dematerialise and abstract the form of the human body (Figs 4.12, 4.13); Chéret clearly relished the breakdown of clarity that her amorphous performance offered him.

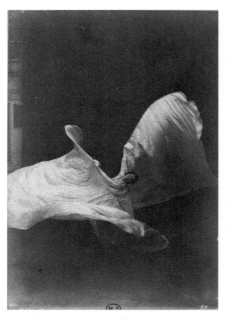

FIGURE 4.12: Loie Fuller, 'Serpentine
Dance', photograph, 1896.

FIGURE 4.13: Jules Chéret, *Loie Fuller at
the Folies Bergère*, colour lithograph, 1893.
Victoria and Albert Museum, London.

    The Nabis implicitly challenged the notion of high art on three accounts. Firstly, by channelling their creative energy into design and decoration, they challenged the attitude that had dissociated poetic imagination from the 'banal functionality' of the applied arts since the Renaissance. Secondly, they undermined the primacy of iconography in their work, allowing both its objects and the pictorial space that its objects seemed to occupy to decompose and become diffused to the point of becoming unrecognisable. In this way, they reduced the significance of human narrative and the fantasy of personal identity that such narratives animated; both literally and figuratively, they 'defaced' the individual. And thirdly, they abstracted the visual language of their work to the point at which it became autonomous and independent of the subject matter that it seemed to depict. As Maurice Denis prophetically proclaimed, in 1890: 'Remember that a picture, before being a battle horse, a nude woman, or any interpretation you want, is essentially a flat surface covered in colour assembled in a certain order.'[10] Although they never formulated the concept of abstraction as such, the Nabis' work certainly constituted a 'subconscious education of public taste', preparing the public for the convention of 'abstract art'.

    Degas and the Nabis anticipated abstraction by seeming to neglect their subject matter to the point at which it became both poetically and optically indeterminate, often leaving little more than a 'flat surface covered in colour assembled in a certain order'. The key Impressionists, by contrast, anticipated it in a completely different way. While the work of Degas and the Nabis addressed apparently insignificant subjects in such an apparently casual manner that they seemed to slip into a quasi-existential state of negligible insignificance, the Impressionists – especially Claude Monet, Camille Pissarro and Alfred Sisley – attempted to isolate the experience of seeing, regardless of its subject matter. For them, the optical effects of light were more interesting than the poetry of faded meanings, to the extent that, eventually, subject matter ceased to constitute the primary content of art.

Because the Impressionists favoured subjects that were saturated in natural light, they focused on outdoor subjects, especially landscapes; and because they were primarily interested in capturing the actual effects of light, rather than in composing conventional paintings in a studio according to established formulae, they painted *while* outdoors, *en plein air*. They were not, however, the first painters to take this immediate, technical approach to the experience of seeing. In the late eighteenth century, William Gilpin, who conceived the notion of the 'picturesque', encouraged amateurs to make on-site sketches of picturesque scenes in order to 'fix their impressions' in their mind. By 1802, John Constable was also producing outdoor sketches of landscapes – in his case, to work up into finished paintings in the studio. Moreover, in 1814 he resolved for the first time to produce finished works in the open air. In that year, he wrote to a friend: 'I am determined to finish a small picture on the spot for every one I intend to make in future . . . this I have always talked about but never yet done . . . my mind is more settled and determined than ever on this point.'[11] He made this move partly to free himself from the overwhelming influence of his predecessors (especially Claude Lorraine and Gainsborough) and partly because of his growing belief that painting was a science as much as an art, and that it was as reliant on objective observation as on poetic sensibility. As he asserted in a lecture that he gave at the Royal Institution in London in 1836: 'Painting is a science and should be pursued as an inquiry into the laws of nature . . . Why may not landscape painting be considered a branch of natural philosophy, of which pictures are but the experiments?'[12] This orientation is reflected in the fact that his celebrated paintings of clouds (Fig. 4.14) are as much studies of meteorological phenomena, often with date, time and weather conditions annotated on the back, as they are evocations of poetic associations (as they would have been for painters of the picturesque). In this respect, he represents a distinct departure from the characteristically romantic mode of the German painter Caspar David Friedrich. When Goethe asked Friedrich and a number of other German artists for images of different cloud formations – which had been recently classified according to their technical properties by the amateur meteorologist Luke Howard – Friedrich indignantly refused on the grounds that clouds are inherently formless and free, and that to attempt to subject them to types would be to 'undermine the whole foundation of landscape painting'.[13]

Constable's innovations were better received in France than in England, and it was there, after the successful display of several of his paintings, including *The Haywain*, at the Paris Salon of 1824, that his example was first followed. For instance, when Delacroix first saw his work shortly before the opening of the Salon that year, he made last-minute alterations to his monumental *Massacre at Chios* (also exhibited at the Salon), adding lively touches of freshness and luminosity to its

FIGURE 4.14: John Constable, *Study of Cirrus Clouds*, around 1822, oil on paper, 11.4 × 17.8 cm. Victoria and Albert Museum, London.

smooth glazed surface. Although Delacroix also made sketches in the open air, he tended to apply his new insights to imaginative works executed in the studio, subjecting them to the demands of a dramatic narrative. It was not until the subject matter of a painting ceased to take precedence over its style that the experience of 'pure seeing' could become an end in itself. Proponents of the theory of the picturesque had begun to make a claim for the independent expressive potential of the 'mode of representation', as distinct from its content, at the end of the eighteenth century.[14] But the shift only became established in the 1830s when a new generation of landscape painters, partly inspired by the free handling of paint that they witnessed in the works of Constable and Delacroix, started to work systematically from nature – a process that was greatly facilitated by the sale of paint in small, portable metal tubes patented by an American painter, John G. Rand, in 1841, in place of unreliable pigs' bladders.

In contrast to the classical landscapes of Claude and the picturesque views of British landscape painters, these artists – called the Barbizon school after the village outside Paris where they used to work – abandoned the Romantic interest in the poetic associations of landscape in favour of direct communion with nature as immediately experienced. Their works revolved around the resources of the local countryside. Unlike their predecessors, they did not feel the need to travel to evocative locations, such as Italy or Scotland, which carried iconographic associations with classical or picturesque ideals. Nor did they make use of rhetorical compositions (for instance, dramatic asymmetry, leading the eye artfully into the background) which, because of their predictable emotional associations, could amount to a kind

FIGURE 4.15: Charles-François Daubigny, *A River Landscape with Storks*, 1864, oil on wood, 24.1 × 44.8 cm. Metropolitan Museum of Art, New York, bequest of Benjamin Altman.

of iconography. On the contrary, their works were thoroughly undramatic and unsensational, both in their subject matter (fields, trees, forests) and in their compositions; these often focused on a centrally placed feature set against a strictly flat horizon that provided no scope for imaginary meandering. In place of these distractions, they offered intimate perceptions of nature itself, captured in lively, textured brushstrokes that embodied the spontaneity and sensitivity of the artist. Charles-François Daubigny – who converted a ferryboat, *Le Botin*, into a floating studio in 1857 to establish himself at the heart of nature – was a leading proponent of this approach. In the 1860s, his work became increasingly loose, rendering an even and overall 'impression' of a scene (according to contemporary critics), rather than treating it with precision (Fig. 4.15). The more he attempted to imitate, rather than define, the fleeting changes of light that he observed, the more rapidly he applied his brushstrokes, which, as a result, became more and more broken, discontinuous and summary, and less and less descriptive of detail. It was this aspect of the Barbizon school – the way it began to allow the medium of painting to become independent of its subjection to subject matter – that inspired the Impressionists. The picture surface was no longer a translucent screen through which to see the subject matter of the painting; in some sense it *became* the subject matter of the painting, the very site on which the artistic content of the image was negotiated.

An important difference between the Barbizon painters and the Impressionists was the fact that, whereas for the former the lively texture of the surface evolved as a side effect of their desire to experience nature freshly and immediately, for the latter – especially Monet and Pissarro – it became the deliberate *rationale* of their art. Although Monet and Pissarro applied individual brushstrokes as gestural registrations of individual optical perceptions, as had the Barbizon painters, they also began to place coloured brushstrokes strategically in relation to each other on account of the autonomous effects of the optical relationships between them. Rather than blend neighbouring brushstrokes, using glazes and halftones to create an illusion of perfectly graded shading on objects, in order to give a convincing impression of their solidity, they reduced their objects to a series of fragmented perceptions. Indeed, Monet was so much more interested in the experience of perception and the effects of light than in objects per se that he could be said, to all intents and purposes, to have abandoned subject matter. On one occasion, he advised:

> When you go out to paint, try to forget what objects you have before you, a tree, a house, a field, or whatever. Merely think, here is a little square of blue, here an oblong of pink, here a streak of yellow, and paint it just as it looks to you, the exact colour and shape until it gives your own naive impression of the scene before you.[15]

Reminiscent of the speculations of eighteenth-century *philosophes* who sought to understand what it was possible know on the basis of optical experience alone, without the help of remembered knowledge, Monet even said on one occasion that 'he wished he had been born blind and then had suddenly gained his sight so that he could have begun to paint in this way without knowing what the objects were that he saw before him'.[16] His lack of interest in subject matter is clear from the paintings themselves. In an overwhelming majority of cases, the key characteristic of his subjects is not their recognisability and associations, but their capacity to be pervaded by atmospheric light and to register changes of light in the minutest detail. Not surprisingly, therefore, his favourite subjects were the formless luminosity of water, the sky, clouds, mist and steam; as far as natural forms were concerned, he constantly returned to the filigree and airy structures of leafy treetops, flower beds and meadows deep with wild flowers and long grasses. To the extent that he painted solid objects at all, he favoured those with intricately fragmented surfaces in which changes of light could be observed from moment to moment. To suggest that his paintings of haystacks have a social implication, as they would have done for the realist painter Jean-François Millet, or that his paintings of Rouen Cathedral are related to the Gothic revival would be to misread them (Fig. 4.16).

One of the key ways in which Monet attempted to magnify the impression of light in his work was through the use of complementary colours – that is to say, through combinations of the simplest and most immediate colours into which pure light can be divided (as in a rainbow). The principal pairs of complementary colours include one of the so-called 'primary' colours (red, yellow or blue) and one of the 'secondary' colours (green, violet or orange), which themselves consist of a combination of the other two primary colours. Thus, the complementary colour of red is green, which is composed of blue and yellow. When these basic colours (the three primary colours, or a primary colour and its secondary) are combined as coloured light (for instance, from spotlights), they produce white light; when they are combined as coloured substances (such as paint), they move in the opposite direction along a scale of greys towards blackness. Thus, when red and green paints are mixed, they produce a colour darker than themselves – brown – but when they

FIGURE 4.16: Claude Monet, *Haystack (Effects of snow and sun)*, 1891, oil on canvas, 65.4 × 92.1 cm. Metropolitan Museum of Art, New York, H. O. Havemeyer Collection, bequest of Mrs. H. O. Havemeyer.

are *juxtaposed* rather than mixed, the coloured rays that each of them emits is synthesised in the eye as *light*, creating an impression of brightness. It was largely for this reason that Monet became interested in the expressive potential of the picture surface at the expense of its subject matter. Although he was originally inspired by the spontaneity and expressive freedom of gestural painting, as explored by the Barbizon painters, it was ultimately the effects of juxtaposing loose, independent brushstrokes in complementary colours, in response to momentary experiences of light in nature, that pushed him to the brink of abstraction.

The fact that colour was not simply a property of objects to be observed and reproduced, but that its effect was also subject to the mechanisms of perception, had been appreciated throughout the nineteenth century. Newton's theory of colours, which had wrested the rainbow from the realm of medieval wonder and superstition two hundred years earlier and elevated the study of colour to the level of an objective science for the first time, had maintained that colour was a physical function of light. In so doing, he was contributing towards the construction of the dualistic paradigm according to which objects are discrete entities with measurable qualities, distinct from, and perceivable by, corresponding subjects or 'selves', which are themselves objectively extant entities. By virtue of their interdependence, such objects and subjects polarised and reinforced each other; according to Kant, they could even be seen to necessitate each other. Goethe, on the other hand, noticed that certain aspects of the human experience of colour occur independently of the objects being seen and are, therefore, subjective – for instance, the 'after-images' that arise when one closes one's eyes having looked intensely at an object for a prolonged period of time. Thus, if one gazes at a red object for, say, a minute, one's eyes will become acclimatised to seeing red, and will adjust themselves accordingly, to the extent that if one then looks at a bright white surface, they will be more sensitive to the components of its light to which they have not yet adapted – i.e. all the colours other than red, especially its 'complementary' colour, green; the white surface will, therefore, seem to be green until the eye rebalances itself. Goethe used this observation to undermine the theory that objects (and, therefore, subjects) have absolute distinctive properties, on the basis of which they are typically differentiated from one another; for just as the mechanisms of the eye contribute towards one's optical experience of objects, potentially rendering them as 'functions of the eye', might not the mechanisms of the mind contribute towards one's apparent knowledge of objects, rendering them as 'functions of the mind'?

The theory of complementary colours was first systematically published by the French chemist Michel-Eugene Chevreul, who, as director of the dye works at the Gobelins tapestry factory from 1824, discovered that certain undesirable effects in the factory's products were not due to the discolouration of the dyes themselves, as first thought, but to the way that the eye reacted to colour relationships. Having realised that the eye brings its own unforeseen after-images to the perception of colours, he was able to identify which colour relationships had undesirable secondary effects, with a view to avoiding them. He published his conclusions in 1839 in his work *De la loi du contraste simultane des couleurs*. With regard to painting, one of the first artists to integrate knowledge of the 'non-objectivity' of colour perception into his work was Eugene Delacroix, who described his interest in the fact that shadows tend to *look* purple by virtue of their contrast to the yellow of sunshine, despite the fact that when closely examined, out of view of the sun itself, they are not purple. The influential art critic Charles Blanc claimed that Delacroix had deliberately juxtaposed complementary colours in his works, in knowing anticipation of their luminous after-effects. In his influential *Grammaire des arts du dessin*, first published in 1867, Blanc outlined Chevreul's theories and applied them to Delacroix's *Women of Algiers* of 1834 (Fig. 4.17), though Delacroix had in fact acquired his knowledge of the science of colour perception from his painter friend J. F. L. Mérimée in the early 1830s, before the publication of Chevreul's ideas:[17]

> Delacroix did not prepare his most exquisite, refined, rare tones on his palette before placing them on the wall; he spontaneously calculated the future effect of the composition; he made them *result* from his combinations. In the painting of the *Women of Algiers*, a rosy chemise sown with little green flowers gives rise to a third indefinable tone which cannot be named with precision and which a copyist would never be able to capture if he tried to compose it in advance and to raise it on to the canvas at the end of the brush.[18]

Delacroix's use of complementary colours was especially well suited to the commissions for murals that preoccupied him from the mid-1830s onwards. Indeed, it is arguable that part of his interest in the technique lay in its ability to sustain an

FIGURE 4.17: Eugene Delacroix, *Women of Algiers*,1834, oil on canvas, 180 × 229 cm. Musée du Louvre, Paris. Photo: © RMN-Grand Palais (Musée du Louvre)/Thierry Le Mage.

impression of brightness and clarity over a considerable distance, at the expense of detail if necessary. Blanc commented on the 'marvellously rich effects' that Delacroix was able to achieve in the vast cupola of the library in the Senate in the Palais du Luxembourg (1840), compensating for the lack of natural light by using the 'play of colours to create artificial light'. While admiring the freshness of the rosy tones that Delacroix had used to depict the skin of one of the nudes in the cupola, he was informed by one of the artist's friends who had seen him working on the painting: 'you would be surprised if you knew which colours produced the rosy flesh tones that ravish you. They are tones which, seen separately, would have appeared, as dull, if you'll excuse me, as the mud in the streets.'[19]

While Delacroix used complementary colours as a means to an end – in order to make his narratives more visible and dramatic – the Impressionists used them as an end in themselves – to create light for its own sake. Although Delacroix was instrumental in detaching colour from objects – in recognising its independent expressive power – he continued to subject it to the exigencies of iconography. As such, he contributed towards the creation of the *vocabulary* of abstraction before it cohered as a *language* – and, consequently, he was hugely influential on the next generation of painters. However, just as the anti-classical asymmetry and apparently arbitrary cropping of so much modern painting had been encouraged by Japanese prints, so it was again in response to Japanese prints – a catalyst that was entirely free of the associations and momentum of the western European tradition – that colour was finally liberated from its secondary role as descriptive of objects, and that its independent expressive potential was realised as artistic currency. The fact that contemporary artists had no understanding of the original cultural context and significance of such images enabled them to respond to their juxtaposition of unmodulated fields of bright, flat colour from a purely aesthetic point of view. Indeed, some critics claimed that it was the example of Japanese prints that enabled Impressionism to happen at all. For instance, Theodore Duret, who was a friend of several Impressionist artists, commented in 1886: 'well, it may seem strange to say it but it is nonetheless true that before the arrival among us of Japanese picture books, there was no-one in France who dared to seat himself on the banks of a river and to put side-by-side on his canvas, a roof frankly red, a white-washed wall, a green poplar, a yellow road, and blue water'.[20] Moreover, besides their extraordinary and unprecedented visual impact, the fact that Japanese prints were non-European added to their appeal as a source of influence, as it helped the Impressionists to detach themselves from the rigorous demands of their own tradition and thereby emphasise the freshness, originality and modernity of their work. Edmond de Goncourt (one of the Goncourt brothers whose joint writings helped popularise the taste for Japanese art) explained in 1884: 'When I said that *Japonisme* was in the process of revolutionising the vision of the European peoples, I meant that *Japonisme* brought to Europe a new sense of colour, a new decorative system, and, if you like, a poetic imagination in the invention of the *objet d'art*, which never existed even in the most perfect medieval or Renaissance pieces.'[21]

In the second half of the nineteenth century, there was scarcely a progressive artist in France who was not influenced by Japanese art in one capacity or another. Whether it was the audacious juxtaposition of bright zones of colour, the decorative patterning and flattening of surfaces, the abrupt cropping of forms or the oblique and evocative treatment of unremarkable iconography (or a combination of these), Japanese prints served as an inspiring and legitimising precedent for departing from the classical tradition of reproducing the optical appearance of visual objects in a 'meaningful' way. Indeed, the Impressionist painters were frequently referred to as *japonistes* during this period. In some cases, artists introduced Japanese devices into their works by incorporating Japanese objects or prints into them – for instance, Manet's *Portrait of Emile Zola* (1868) or Van Gogh's *Portrait of Père Tanguy* (1887, Fig. 4.18). But in most cases these devices were fully integrated into the artists' work to the extent that there is nothing manifestly exotic about them. Indeed, an excess of *japonisme* was seen by some commentators to undermine the realism that otherwise made the new techniques so contemporary and affecting.[22]

Despite their common responsiveness to Japanese prints – as well as to Delacroix, the Barbizon school and photography – it is misleading to think of Impressionism as a unified whole. The series of eight exhibitions of 'Impressionist' paintings that were held between 1874 and 1886 appears to suggest an intentional unity between the exhibitors, and the label 'Impressionist' (coined as a negative term by a journalist after the first exhibition, and adopted as a title for the shows at the third) appears to

FIGURE 4.18: Vincent Van Gogh, *Portrait of Père Tanguy*, 1887, Musée Rodin, Paris.
Photo: © RMN-Grand Palais (MNAAG, Paris)/Thierry Ollivier.

identify them as a club; but they were, in fact, a very disparate group of artists (with different exhibitors in each exhibition) and they responded to the opportunity for change in very different ways. This situation became especially clear when the Impressionist exhibitions came to an end, and even the illusion of unity ceased to be projected into the public domain. For instance, Paul Cézanne, who had worked in a light and airy Impressionistic manner in the 1870s and who exhibited in two of the early exhibitions, began to transform his brushstrokes from spontaneous textured gestures into more calculated building blocks, in order to introduce a more coherent and comprehensive sense of structure to his work (Fig. 4.19). Having begun his career as a profoundly Romantic painter, treating dramatic imaginary subjects in a passionate and brooding manner (after Delacroix), he eventually came to focus on the experience of optical perception and, therefore, on the natural world around him. But unlike Monet, who he criticised for being an undiscriminating 'seeing machine' ('just an eye, but what an eye!'), he was intent on developing the art of painting into an independent expressive system. Left to its own devices, the view of nature was random, as if seen through the viewfinder of a camera. To become art, it also had to be subjected to higher laws of perception, which were able to reveal the unifying principle or inner structure of a view.

At the other end of the spectrum, Paul Gauguin, who exhibited at the last five Impressionist exhibitions, became less and less interested in the optical experience of nature and more and more interested in the decorative effects of the picture surface. Not surprisingly, he was influenced by the indigenous tradition of mural painting, promoted by Hippolyte Flandrin. Moreover, Gauguin's interest in decorative painting extended beyond the impressive flatness of its forms to the naive mystique of the medieval art that influenced it. Indeed, following his abandonment

FIGURE 4.19: Paul Cézanne, *Still Life with Apples and Pears*, c. 1891–2, oil on canvas, 44.8 × 58.7 cm. Metropolitan Museum of Art, New York, bequest of Stephen C. Clark.

of any pretensions to Impressionism, Gauguin became interested in what he perceived to be the raw and unsophisticated culture of so-called 'primitive' societies, using their example as a precedent on the basis of which to create his own intensely direct, natural and pure art. It was these qualities that attracted him first to Pont-Aven in Brittany, where he savoured the ancient simplicity of Breton life and culture, and eventually to self-imposed exile in Tahiti, where he hoped to experience a primordial paradise, unspoiled by the deceptive and decadent veneers of European 'civilisation'. As a result of these adventures, he became associated with the symbolist movement, which reacted against the 'materialist banality' of mere realism, in favour of an evocative associationist genre that transformed the world into a veiled representation of an immaterial truth. It was also against this background (and with the help of Japanese prints) that he was inspired to liberate the artistic elements of colour and shape from their traditional obligation to describe objects, and to restore to them their ancient ability to function in a more directly expressive 'primitive' capacity (Fig. 4.20).

FIGURE 4.20: Paul Gauguin, *Ia Orana Maria (Hail Mary)*, 1891, oil on canvas, 113.7 × 87.6 cm. Metropolitan Museum of Art, New York, bequest of Sam A. Lewisohn.

Cézanne and Gauguin were instrumental in transforming painting from a descriptive tool into an independent medium of communication with its own expressive potential and, as a result, they were phenomenally influential on the subsequent history of art. The only other painter to have had a comparable impact on the development of art into an independent language (but who did not exhibit in any of the Impressionist exhibitions) was Vincent Van Gogh, whose exuberant and passionate brushwork can be said to have achieved for the surface texture of paintings what the work of Cézanne and Gauguin achieved for their structure and colour (Fig. 4.18). While these Post-Impressionist artists were highly divergent and idiosyncratic individuals, what they had in common was, firstly, their fundamental dissociation from academic insistence on reproducing the appearance of objects in an 'accurately' illusionistic manner (despite their profound knowledge of, and respect for, artistic tradition) and, secondly, their elevation of the technical means of art beyond a purely descriptive role, to the level of an independent language. Gauguin and Cézanne were especially influential, partly due to the large posthumous exhibitions of their work that were held in Paris in 1903 and 1906 (Gauguin) and in 1907 (Cézanne), and two major trends developed in their wake: Fauvism and Cubism.

The first of these trends, Fauvism, was largely inspired by Van Gogh and Gauguin and it revolved around the application of bright, flat colours in textured, painterly brushstrokes. Having first experimented with the disciplined pointillist style of Georges Seurat, several artists working in this manner (led by Henri Matisse and André Derain) eventually allowed their instincts to take precedence over colour theory and, as a result, when they exhibited their highly impulsive and exuberant works together for the first time in 1905, they were dubbed *fauves* (wild beasts, Fig. 4.21). The Fauves were more concerned with the expressive effect of bold, sensuous shapes in bright, unblended colours than with the associations of the scenes and objects that their colours were nominally required to represent. Consequently, the impression that their work gives of 'coherent objects' in 'naturalistic space' is often highly abstracted and, indeed, in many paintings, it is unrecognisable. Instead of offering coherent objectivity, the amorphous shapes and sinuous lines that they used ensured that the eye travelled over the surface of the paintings in a fluid and sensuous manner, stimulating a unified but ever-changing and uncircumscribable continuum of feeling. While Gauguin's use of colour was clearly a liberating precedent for these artists, so was his interest in 'primitive' cultures. Indeed, it was surely as a result of his example that they became able to find expressive power in the tribal arts of Africa and Oceania (Fig. 4.22). Under his influence, they also became the first artists to collect tribal art, using it to inspire and legitimise their own explorations – both of shape and colour on the one hand, and of the irrational forms of experience that they accommodated and precipitated on the other. Not only did tribal art provide the Fauves with visual precedents for the uninhibited use of colour, form and pattern, but they also invested these features with profound spiritual significance and potency, thereby raising their work beyond the level of mere decoration to the level of ritual, where they provided access to otherwise unknown realms of sacred and psychological space.

In contrast to the seamless sensuality of Fauvism, Cubism involved the representation of visual objects as highly calculated and articulated structures,

FIGURE 4.21: Henri Matisse, *Still Life with Vegetables*, around 1905, oil on canvas, 38.4 × 46 cm. Metropolitan Museum of Art, New York, Jacques and Natasha Gelman Collection. Photo: © SCALA, Florence. © Succession H. Matisse/DACS 2018.

FIGURE 4.22: Anonymous, 'Fang Mask (Gabon)', early twentieth century, wood, 42 × 28.5 cm. Musée National d'Art Moderne, Centre Pompidou, Paris. Photo: © Centre Pompidou, MNAM-CCI, Dist. RMN-Grand Palais/Image Centre Pompidou, MNAM-CCI.

assembled not as indeterminate realms of feeling, but as aggregates of fragmented perceptions, sometimes experienced from a range of different viewpoints, that rigorously punctuated the movement of the eye as it passed over the picture surface. Taking its lead from both the disjointed, faceted forms of 'primitive' art (especially African tribal masks) and the highly disciplined constructions of Cézanne, it made a radical contribution to the deconstruction of the traditional presumption that objects of perception are coherent and discrete, and thereby challenged the notion of the subjective self that seeks to find itself coherently reflected in those objects. The first signs of Cubism appeared in the work of Pablo Picasso in 1906–7; the style was then developed by Picasso and Georges Braque, who had been a Fauve until he met Picasso in 1907. As with the Fauves, albeit in a very different way, tribal art provided Picasso with a precedent for using a radically new and anti-classical visual language to embody new forms of intelligence and experience (Fig. 4.23). It is significant, however, that although he was fascinated by the primal and supernatural associations of tribal art, he was not particularly interested in the specific roles that tribal artefacts played in their original contexts (as ritual objects at initiations, funerals, etc.).

FIGURE 4.23: Pablo Picasso, *Portrait of Ambroise Vollard*, 1910–11, oil on canvas, 92 × 65 cm. Pushkin Museum, Moscow. © Photo SCALA, Florence. © Succession Picasso/ DACS, London 2018.

Indeed, it is ironic that Picasso derived so much of the visual language of Cubism – a thoroughly avant-garde style that challenged the conventions of classical naturalism – from objects that were originally made to honour and appease spirits and thereby to function as stable protectors of orthodox hierarchies of power. Moreover, although Picasso was also inspired by the formal properties of tribal masks, he was not, by his own account, particularly appreciative of the aesthetic subtleties of individual examples; once he had integrated the principle that tribal masks revealed to him, he was glad to be inspired as much by artefacts made for tourists as by ancient and revered treasures. It is also significant that by finding inspiration in tribal art – and thereby ascribing cultural value to it – Picasso was not only finding a precedent for his own developments; he was also educating the public into an appreciation of the aesthetic and cultural value of these objects. If artists had not demonstrated in this way how radically stylised images, from tribal artefacts to medieval imagery, could be seen to be consistent with modern European experience and feeling, it would have been entirely natural and conventional for people to continue to find them 'primitive', 'ugly' or 'badly made', as many conservatives, conditioned to think of the ideal beauty in terms of classical naturalism, did throughout the nineteenth century.

While their association with tribal art enhanced the Cubists' aspirations to tap 'pure', 'untouched' sources of creativity within themselves, and enabled them to dissociate from the academic tradition by seeming to destroy the classical ideal of coherent objectivity in a 'barbaric' manner, their receptivity to the work of Cézanne underlined the way that they also continued to work within the western European tradition. Indeed, while tribal art may have inspired them to abandon any inclination to conform to *external* conventions, the inheritance from Cézanne taught them to ensure that their compositions retained *internal* coherence. When Picasso and Braque first began experimenting with Cubism, they adopted Cézanne's earthy palette of greens and ochres, and painted coherently structured objects in space as he had done. However, at the height of the first key phase of the style between 1908 and 1912, they reduced their palette to a narrow band of browns and greys to isolate the purely structural dimension of their compositions. Indeed, given the extent to which they distanced themselves from the more sensuous and colourful Fauves, there is a case for seeing their development as a continuation of the line-versus-colour debates that flared up in the sixteenth century (between the Florentines and the Venetians) and in the seventeenth century (between the Poussinists and the Rubenists).[23] One of the effects of the reduction in the Cubists' palette was to minimise the range of contrasts between colours and tones, and thereby to reduce the impression of difference that existed between objects and their backgrounds. The impression of 'object distinctiveness' was also weakened by the fact that the fragmentation of objects enabled them to dissolve into, and be penetrated by, the space that contained and surrounded them. It was further undermined when areas of space itself – and not just the objects in that space – were subjected to the same process of fragmentation, reflecting the transitory, flitting way in which the eye perceives them, while also introducing a greater degree of evenness to the overall picture surface. Thus, the abiding effect of the Cubists' attempt to represent the world as it is actually perceived – i.e. as a dynamic sequence of fragments, and not merely as a static abstraction – was that objects and the objective space they occupied were deconstructed into 'moments of perception' to the point at which they were scarcely identifiable as distinct objects. Although Cubism aimed to synthesise these dispersed sequences of perceptions into an artificial whole, its fundamental and primary communication was that the coherence of objects – and, therefore, the coherence of the subjects that seek to find themselves reflected in them – is provisional. Neither object nor subject are static entities that exist in themselves. On the contrary, they exist (or seem to exist) in states – or rather, as *processes* – of perpetual construction and deconstruction that are only held together as unities in memory, or in the artificial synthesis of mental abstraction.

It is significant that neither Matisse nor Picasso nor Braque ever actually ventured beyond the realm of abstraction – the representation of objects in an abstracted manner – into non-objectivity. That is to say, no matter how extremely stylised their work became, it was always representational; it always had subject matter. Moreover, despite the fact that all three artists developed pictorial languages that were truly avant-garde in their time, their subject matter remained highly traditional throughout their lives. Considering the amount of controversy they caused at this early stage in their careers (enough for some to suggest suspicious parallels between Picasso's 'iconoclastic' work and the contemporary theft of the *Mona Lisa*), it is ironic – and perhaps suggestive of a fundamental conservatism at the heart of their work – that they largely restricted themselves to subjects which had been mainstream for artists since the seventeenth century: portraits, nudes, still lifes and landscapes. Indeed, a part of their reputation as leaders of the avant-garde is due to the immensity of the influence that they had on their contemporaries, who in many cases took their experiments far further than they did themselves.

A case in point was Robert Delaunay (1885–1941), a largely self-taught painter mostly living and working in Paris, who was initiated into the language of modern art by way of pointillism and Fauvism. In his mature style, from around 1909, Delaunay transformed his textured and painterly patches of opaque colour, derived from the Fauves, into crisper, translucent facets, derived from the Cubists, fusing the two styles and taking them to a different level. Like the Cubists, he considered himself to be developing a new way of seeing and perceiving; however, unlike the Cubists, who he regarded as excessively preoccupied with physical objects and their structures, he focused on light and the relationships between colours, partly as a result of the influence of Chevreul's theory of complementary colours, which he had studied intensively. Accordingly, he ceased to build his compositions around the perception of structure in objects, but built them around colour relationships – to the extent, in fact, that colour relationships eventually became the very content of his work. This shift away from the representation of physical objects was presaged by the fact that his early subject matter differed radically from that of the Cubists. On the one hand, it revolved around the defiance of gravity, and on the other hand, it was often specifically modern – the soaring vaults of medieval churches and church towers, but also leaping rugby players, Ferris wheels, aeroplanes and the Eiffel Tower, the last two of which were icons of progressive technology and modernity (Fig. 4.24). Moreover, much of Delaunay's subject matter consisted of objects in which the sense of 'constructedness', and therefore the scope for deconstruction,

FIGURE 4.24: Robert Delaunay, *L'Equipe de Cardiff*, 1913, oil on canvas, 326 × 208 cm. Paris, Musée d'Art Moderne de la Ville de Paris. © 2018. Photo: Josse/Scala, Florence.

was explicit; unlike the opaque and uniform objects used by the Cubists, such structures were typically seen against the sky and were, therefore, inherently penetrated by light and air. In his series of paintings of *fenêtres* (windows, 1912), the form of the Eiffel Tower can usually be picked out in the distance, though in some cases it is indistinguishable. As in the pictures of Ferris wheels and aeroplanes, his subjects eventually became little more than an excuse for painting the sky and bright sunlight. Indeed, in 1913, the insubstantial circular forms that were at first provided by Ferris wheels and the spinning propellers of aeroplanes (which Delaunay used to watch taking off and landing at the aerodrome at Buc near Versailles) became detached from their sources and began to multiply like independent ripples of light emanating from the sun. This shift gave rise to a series of 'pure' paintings of overlapping concentric circles of light and colour called *Discs* (1913); some of these paintings are themselves round (Fig. 4.25). The fact that they continue to be structured but do not actually represent objects (rather like actual colour wheels) reflects the extent to which Delaunay's work became 'fully abstract' at this time. However, although the artist accepted that his work was not figurative, he denied that it had no subject matter, for although it was organised according to internal principles (the laws of colour relationships, rather than the perceived structures of objects), it was still based on the experience of looking.

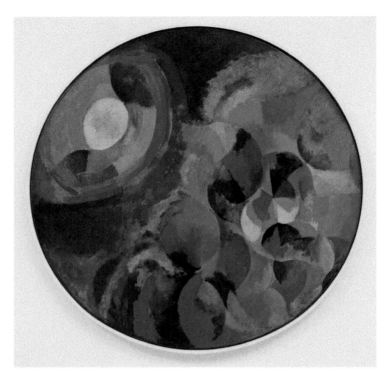

FIGURE 4.25: Robert Delaunay, *Simultaneous Contrasts, Sun and Moon*, 1912–13, oil on canvas, diameter: 134.5 cm. Museum of Modern Art, New York. Photo: © SCALA, Florence.

The ambiguous status of Delaunay's iconography was highlighted by the poet Guillaume Apollinaire, a friend of the artist, who was himself achieving for poetry what Delaunay was achieving for painting; that is to say, liberating the formal properties of his materials – in Apollinaire's case, words – from their traditional role as descriptive mediators of meaning, such that the typefaces and the very organisation of the letters on a page – and not just the meanings of the words – could be invested with expressive potential. In 1912, for instance, he described how in Delaunay's work 'coloured planes are the structure of the painting and nature is no longer a subject to be described, but a pretext, a poetic evocation of expression by coloured planes which order themselves by simultaneous contrasts. Their coloured orchestration creates an architecture which unrolls as phrases of colour and ends in a new form of expression in painting, Pure Painting.'[24] The fact that Apollinaire used a musical metaphor here ('orchestration') was no accident. As painting became less dependent on the poetic associations of its subject matter and more dependent on its purely formal effects, so analogies with the inherently abstract medium of instrumental music became increasingly applicable and common. Indeed, to define what he considered to be a new 'post-Cubist' phase in the history of painting, epitomised by Delaunay's *Fenêtres* of 1912, Apollinaire coined the musical term 'Orphism', from the god Orpheus, whose songs charmed all of nature. Although the figure of Orpheus had strong romantic and esoteric associations, Apollinaire used the term to refer to 'the art of painting new totalities with elements that the artist does not take from visual reality, but creates entirely by himself'. In so doing, he was helping to establish and institutionalise non-objective painting as a cultural convention and thereby to create a cultural form for the possibility of non-objective (and non-subjective) experience.

Delaunay did occasionally use musical metaphors to refer to his own work. For instance, he compared the movements implicit in the relationships between colours to sequences of musical notes or to the schematic progressions of fugues. But on the whole he was more interested in the experience of seeing on its own terms, using musical models as analogies to help explain what he was doing, rather than as revelations of natural law to be translated into visual media. Indeed, he often highlighted the differences between the two arts, stressing how relationships between the objects of sight, ranging from a painting to the visible universe itself, can be experienced simultaneously and in their totality, whereas heard relationships, including those of music, can only be experienced partially and in time. Furthermore, in 1913 he rejected the label 'Orphism' on the grounds that it was too imaginative and poetic, undermining the claims of his work to be technical rather than suggestive, and rooted in optical experience.

Another artist, also called an Orphist by Apollinaire on account of the luminous, neo-Cubist abstraction of his work, was the Czech painter Frantisek Kupka (1871–1957), who lived and worked in Paris from 1895. Although some of the work that Kupka produced at the crucial transitional period of 1911–12 bears some resemblance to that of Delaunay (whom he appears not to have known personally), he arrived at the threshold of non-objectivity by a very different route – indeed, by the very opposite route: he rejected the label 'Orphism' (and all labels) accordingly. Delaunay had been inspired by Seurat and Chevreul to take a quasi-scientific approach to the technicalities of optical experience, eventually focusing on the effects of light regardless of the objects it falls upon. Kupka, by contrast, trained (in Prague and Vienna) in the milieu of late Romantic symbolist art, which revolved around the subjectivity of visionary and imaginative experience, showing no great interest in the 'factual' appearance of physical objects for its own sake. Having spent many years painting from his imagination, he eventually arrived at non-figurative painting by striving to visualise the experience of subjectivity itself, prior to its projection into symbolic narratives. It is a testimony to the interdependence of objectivity and subjectivity that these two polarised approaches, seeking to distil objectivity and subjectivity to their respective essences, should have given rise to such comparable results.

The symbolists, who influenced Kupka, were a disparate group of artists and writers united by their rejection of worldly realism in all its manifestations – the historical literalism of history painters, the social realism of Courbet and the 'technical' realism of the Impressionists and their followers. For them, the essence of life was not to be found in 'this' world; nor could it be perceived by the senses or understood by reason. It was only accessible by means of insight into higher realms of nature, which presupposed altered states of subjectivity and awareness. The images through which its revelations were communicated were, therefore, mysterious and obscure. Although the symbolists were hugely influenced by traditions of religious and esoteric symbolism, they did not subscribe to any particular creed and were happy to synthesise their impressions into an exotic and sometimes irreverent mixture. Moreover, despite the debt of symbolist art to world religions and despite its name, its *modus operandi* was not principally symbolic. Indeed, although symbolist artists did make abundant use of symbols, loading their images with arcane references, their work was often vague and evocative, affecting their viewers as much by its suggestive associations as by its specific meanings (Fig. 4.26). To this end they capitalised on the 'formal' aesthetic advances of the Post-Impressionists. Rather than convey the depth of their experience as a series of symbolic narratives, realistically narrated (like Flandrin), and rather than simply isolate and develop the expressive potential of the medium of painting for its own sake (like Monet or Cézanne), the symbolists attempted to fuse the two. On the one hand, they sought to transmute the spiritual significance of their iconography, including its symbolic meanings, into the physiological impact of their work, thereby magically transforming the physiological experience of the work into a form of spiritual communion. On the other hand, they attempted to infuse their subject matter not merely with

FIGURE 4.26: Odilon Redon, *The Chariot of Apollo*, around 1905–16, oil on canvas, 66 × 81.3 cm. Metropolitan Museum of Art, New York.

decipherable meaning, derived from its exotic references and associations, but also with a powerfully felt presence, derived from the physiological experience of the work (as well as by a rich but often understated eroticism). These quasi-sacramental aspirations were enhanced by their abundant use of ritualistic iconography (especially female cult figures: goddesses, priestesses and prophetesses), the hieratic formality of their compositions and the subtle and mysterious quality of their colours and lighting.

In the tradition of the symbolists, Kupka's early work made use of exotic imagery, such as demons, spectres and mythical beings from ancient Egyptian and classical mythology, in order to evoke a sense of the invisible 'inner life' of the soul (Fig. 4.27). He had, however, also worked as a spiritual medium in Vienna and Paris in the 1890s and therefore had first-hand experience of spiritualism – belief in the possibility of psychic communication with the spirits of the deceased. It is not surprising, therefore, that he eventually abandoned the mere suggestiveness of symbolism in search of more 'scientific' evidence for the existence of inner worlds. In 1905, he began attending lectures on physics, physiology and biology at the

FIGURE 4.27: Frantisek Kupka, *The Beginning of Life/The Lilies*, 1900, aquatint on paper, 34.5 × 34.7 cm. Musée National d'Art Moderne, Centre Pompidou, Paris. Photo © Centre Pompidou, MNAM-CCI, Dist. RMN-Grand Palais/Philippe Migeat. © ADAGP, Paris and DACS, London 2018.

Sorbonne, and by 1910, he was also studying neurology.[25] It was these experiences that introduced him to new scientific methods for investigating the nature of mind and matter, inspiring him to develop his own visual language with which to visualise the inner 'spiritual' world of human beings – for instance, X-rays (discovered by W. C. Rontgen in 1895), which several spiritualists considered to be related to clairvoyance, spirit photography and the photography of thought forms. Following this shift, Kupka produced a number of impersonal depictions of people (alongside a series of more focused self-portraits) in which the figures are outlined by contours of brightly coloured paint that liken the works both to clairvoyant images of auras and to X-rays, in which the areas of flesh surrounding the skeleton are suggestively pale, ethereal and luminous. One series of images (*Woman Picking Flowers*, 1909, Fig. 4.28) appears to have been inspired by the time-lapse chronophotography of Jules-Étienne Marey in its attempt to capture several stages of a simple action – in this instance, a woman leaning forward to pick flowers – as a staggered sequence of superimposed positions. The translucence of each of the positions, which enables them all to be seen at the same time, gives the impression that the woman is an immaterial, ghostly presence and that one can actually see through the surface of her body 'into her'. In another work, representing a bather in a pond (1906–9, Fig. 4.29), ripples of clear water contribute towards the apparent dematerialisation of the body by bending its light rays, while also giving the impression that the body

FIGURE 4.28: Frantisek Kupka, *Woman Picking Flowers*, 1909, pastel on paper, 48 × 52 cm. Musée National d'Art Moderne, Centre Pompidou. Paris. Photo: © SCALA, Florence. © ADAGP, Paris and DACS, London 2018.

FIGURE 4.29: Frantisek Kupka, *Water/The Bather*, around 1906, oil on canvas, 63 × 79 cm. Musée de Beaux Arts, Nancy. Photo: © Service de la documentation photographique du MNAM-Centre Pompidou, MNAM-CCI/Dist. RMN-GP. © ADAGP, Paris. © ADAGP, Paris and DACS, London 2018.

is itself emitting vibrations; the image recalls the views of the sociologist and amateur physicist Gustave le Bon, whose reflections on the discovery of radioactivity in 1896 led him to propose, in his *Evolution of Matter* (1905), that matter is merely 'a stable form of inter-atomic energy'.[26]

For several years, Kupka was interested in new imaging techniques, developed in a scientific context, that enabled people to see phenomena that could not ordinarily be seen by the human eye. To some extent, these techniques and the images they yielded functioned for him as metaphors for seeing into the immaterial, psychic world of the soul or self and, in so doing, they provided him with a visual language with which he could resonate. Moreover, precisely because they presented the world in a way in which it is not conventionally seen, they also enabled him to depart from the tradition of naturalism in which he had been trained. It soon became clear to him, however, that although the world that can be accessed by X-rays and chronophotography cannot be seen without the aid of technology, it is still a physical outer world and it still operates, as far as its poetic and psychological effects are concerned, according to the symbolist principles of suggestion and association. As such, it still involves the projection or objectification of narratives, which acquire their meaning from extraneous considerations just as the iconography of symbolism acquires its meaning from the extraneous contexts of religion and mythology. This ambiguity between the inner world of the soul or self and the merely unfamiliar sights of modern science began to resolve itself when Kupka ceased to refer to science and spiritualism as models of enquiry and turned to music, using it as a model of 'contentless' art around which to develop an equivalent visual language by analogy. This was an important point in his career as it was the first time he became able to conceive of his work as being – like most instrumental music – entirely without subject matter. This development was captured in *Piano Keys/Lake* (1909), which documents the very moment at which Kupka's representational language was translated, with the help of music, into the non-representational language of pattern and colour (Fig. 4.30). The painting depicts a boat in a lake above the keys of a piano. The piano keys are used not only to suggest music in a typically Romantic, 'associationist' way, but also to provide the visual motif – the vertical stripes of the keys themselves – by means of which the ripples of the lake are transformed, before the viewer's eyes, into rippling patterns of vertical black and white lines. These lines rise up above the piano, as if the piano not only makes music but also becomes music, and fill the central area of the painting. Here, they begin to transform the

FIGURE 4.30: Frantisek Kupka, *Piano Keys/Lake*, 1909, oil on canvas, 79 × 72 cm. National Gallery, Prague. Photo: © National Gallery in Prague 2018. © ADAGP, Paris and DACS, London 2018.

descriptive brushstrokes that are used to define the trees around the lake and their reflection in it into their own abstracted form. For the first time, there is no suggestion that these areas of pattern actually represent anything. On the contrary, they constitute Kupka's first attempts to explore the realm of subjective experience on its own terms, without recourse to iconographic associations. In order to articulate this intention, he made use of music as an analogy, expressing his wish to 'produce a fugue in colours, as Bach has done in music'.

The organic links between music and painting had long been recognised, at least since the time of Aristotle.[27] Since the Romantic period, writers had maintained that music offered a more suitable parallel to painting than poetry – its traditional 'sister' art – as music revolved around feeling and sensation, rather than intellect and meaning. In 1859, for instance, the writer Louis Viardot, a friend of Delacroix, proposed that the recent flowering of instrumental music corresponded to the growing popularity of landscape painting, both of which were primarily about communicating mood; vocal music, he claimed, corresponded to history painting. Correspondences of this kind – between rhythm and pictorial composition, melody and line, harmony and colour – were upheld throughout the nineteenth century. In 1854, however, the music critic Eduard Hanslick published his influential claim that music was the only truly 'pure' art – superior to painting – because its impact depended entirely on its own form and not on any extraneous referential subject matter. Although not all artists agreed – Delacroix (like Delaunay) maintained that the simultaneity of painting gave it a superiority over the temporal extension of music – a majority of those in search of 'purity' accepted the ideal, summarised by Walter Pater in 1877, that 'all art constantly aspires towards the condition of music'.[28] And, certainly, many artists attempted to nuance their work – especially if they valued its formal effect independently of its subject matter – by attaching the conventions of music to it. James McNeill Whistler, for instance, named several of his works 'symphonies', 'harmonies' or 'nocturnes', and Paul Signac, a disciple of Seurat, gave his works opus numbers. Indeed, by the 1870s, the status of music as a model of 'pure' self-referential art had become so established that the writer and preacher Reverend H. R. Haweis could abstract it as a concept and transfer it imaginatively to the visual arts, as he did in his *Music and Morals* of 1871:

> Colour now stands in the same kind of relation to the painter's art as Sound amongst the Greeks did to the gymnast. Just as we speak of the classical age as a time long before the era of real music, so posterity may allude to the present age as an age before the colour-art was known – an age in which colour had not yet been developed into a language of pure emotion, but simply used as an accessory to drawing, as music once was to bodily exercise and rhythmic recitation. And here I will express my conviction that a Colour-art exactly analogous to the Sound-art of music is possible, and is amongst the arts which have to be traversed in the future, as Sculpture, Architecture, Painting and Music have been in the past.[29]

As if waiting for it to evolve, Haweis speculated about what a visual 'language of pure emotion' might look like. For instance, he provided a graphic equivalent for each of what he considered to be the five key characteristics of emotional experience (Fig. 4.31). Although he attached a story to these graphic elements to make them

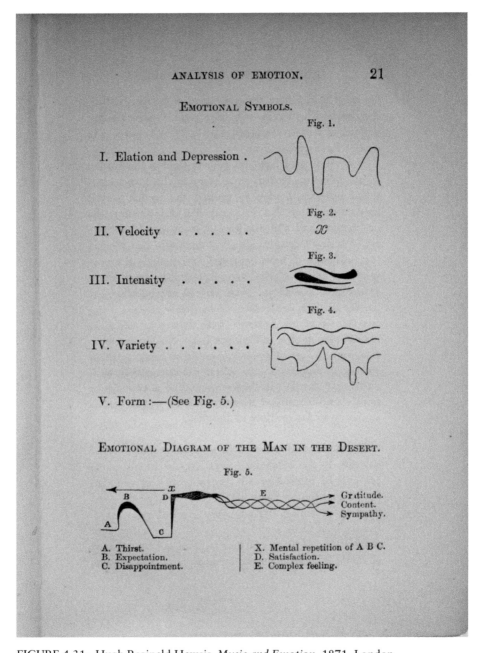

FIGURE 4.31: Hugh Reginald Haweis, *Music and Emotion*, 1871, London.

more accessible and comprehensible, he was keen to point out that they did not actually need a narrative as they were 'capable of indicating the progression and the qualities of emotion without the aid of a definite single idea'. Indeed, he added that 'although the emotional region is constantly traversed by thoughts of every possible description, it has a life of its own, and is distinct from them even as water is distinct from the various reflections that float across its surface'.[30] Even so, while his graphic signs may (with the benefit of hindsight) seem prophetic to us, in their own day they were too ahead of their time to be able to be of value. Haweis added: 'It must also be observed that although I have expressed by symbols the properties of emotion, simple and complex, no art-medium of emotion has as yet been arrived at; nothing but barren symbols are before us, incapable of awakening any feeling at all, however well they may suffice to indicate its nature and properties.'[31] Haweis was also convinced, from his own experiences of natural beauty, that colour was as capable as sound of mediating emotion. He maintained, however, that if colour was to become communicative of artistic value, it had to show 'evidences of human design', reflecting the unique capacity of art to translate the beauty of nature into a human language, thereby making it meaningful and usable:

> The reader whose eye is passionately responsive to colour, may gain some faint anticipation of the Colour-art of the future, if he will try to recall the kind of impression made upon him by the exquisite tints painted upon the dark curtain of the night at a display of fireworks. I select fireworks as an illustration in preference to the most gorgeous sunset, because I am not speaking of Nature, but Art – that is to say, something into the composition of which the mind of man has entered and whose very meaning depends upon its bearing the evidences of human design.[32]

It is arguable that the reason for this dependence is that an object that 'bears evidence of human design' is not merely an extant object; it is also an embodiment of a mode of human experience, and of the model of personal identity on which that mode is based. As a result, an individual that experiences it is not experiencing an object per se; he is also experiencing that degree of personal identity – i.e. that degree of himself – that it is able to reflect to him and that he is able to see reflected in it.[33] It therefore acquires inordinate significance for him. Because nature was not created subject to human modes of experience, the experience of it is not innately informed by, and reflective of, a principle of personal identity (until it is subjected to the humanising conventions of the picturesque or art).

Appreciating this important condition, Haweis stated that, before the full potential of 'Colour-art' could be experienced, it 'must first be constituted, its symbols and phraseology be discovered, its instruments invented, and it composers born. Up to that time, music will have no rival as an Art-medium of emotion'. One of the first practical steps in this direction was taken by the British artist and composer/performer of 'colour music' A. W. Rimington, who, in 1895, was also imagining an art 'in which there is neither form nor subject but only pure colour . . . trusting solely to all the subtle and marvellous changes and combinations of which colour is capable as the means of its expression'.[34] In order to bring the dimension of time and movement within the range of the art of colour co-ordination, he invented a colour organ, 'the object of which . . . was to lay the first stone towards the building up of such an art in the future' (Fig. 4.32). In the following year, the philosopher George Santayana suggested, in *The Sense of Beauty*, that abstract art would remain impossible and unrealised until the cultural fabric of the time became able to accommodate it, giving it meaning and currency: 'There are certain effects of colour that give all men pleasure, and others which jar, almost like a musical discord. A more general development of this sensibility would make possible a new abstract art, an art that should deal with colour as music does with sound.' But while music could certainly set a precedent for painting, the question remained: is colour *actually* subject to natural laws in the way that music is subject to the natural laws of harmony, or is it simply stimulating to imagine what the equivalent manifestations of natural law might be in the case of the visual arts?

Many enthusiasts were intent on proving that music and painting were subject to the very same natural laws – and were therefore, in some sense, aspects of each other. Some, for instance, maintained that objective proportions in space, such as the 'golden section', had the same effects on the mind as did musical harmonies and rhythms, based on the same numerical relationships. Reflecting their sensitivity to the power of natural proportions, the group of painters whose style Apollinaire described as 'Orphism' called themselves the *Section d'Or*, or Golden Section. In the eighteenth

FIGURE 4.32: Alexander Wallace Rimington, *Colour Music: The Art of Mobile Colour*. London, 1912, facing page 44.

century, Louis Bertrand Castel, the builder of an 'ocular harpsichord', went so far as to suggest that harmonious relationships between the colours of fabrics could be achieved if the amount of time that each fabric spent in the vat of dye was determined by numerical proportions.[35] The subject had acquired respectability when Newton's inability to resist modelling his theory of colours on the laws of harmony, and seeing the rainbow as a visual scale of seven 'notes', initiated a tradition of belief that there must at least be *some* objective correspondence between the experience of sight and the experience of sound. His colour wheel set a precedent for innumerable variations, despite the fact that its circularity is based on the repetitive cycle of octaves and is, therefore, a musical characteristic; it is not immediately applicable to the colour spectrum, which – at least as far as it is visible – does not repeat. In 1910, Kupka paid homage to Newton, acknowledging his establishment of the correspondence between musical notes and colours, by creating his own colour wheel, although his inclusion of ten colours (inherited from the physicist Hermann von Helmholtz) was not directly compatible with any musical scale. His appreciation of the musical potential of Newton's theory was explicitly reflected in his painting *Disks of Newton*, which are subtitled *Study for Fugue in Two Colours* (Fig. 4.33). The overlapping and

FIGURE 4.33: Frantisek Kupka, *Disks of Newton: Study for Fugue in Two Colours*, 1912, oil on canvas, 100.3 × 73.7 cm. Philadelphia Museum of Art, The Louise and Walter Arensberg Collection. © ADAGP, Paris and DACS, London 2018.

tonal grading of the discs in these works recalls the structured layering of forms in *Woman Picking Flowers* (Fig. 4.28), as well as Delaunay's earliest non-figurative 'disc' paintings (Fig. 4.25), although the explicit association of these later works with Newton's colour wheel clearly reorientates them towards the possibility of a musical development. Indeed, the fact that Kupka called them 'fugues', rather than the more atmospheric but imprecise terms 'symphonies' or 'nocturnes', highlights the fact that their development was based on purely formal considerations, just as the musical motifs in a fugue are subjected to structured sequences of repetitions, inversions and modifications. The important point here is not only that Kupka's images of discs and fugues are among the very first works to be completely non-figurative, but also that, in order both to develop them in his own imagination and to ensure that the cultural context into which they were born could comprehend and accommodate them, he had to adapt the possibilities of total abstraction that had already been formulated in the context of music. Having used the analogy of music to help him graft the notion of non-figurative painting on to the stock of contemporary culture, he was able to dispense with it. Indeed, when the idea of non-figurative painting was firmly established in his mind, he distanced himself from the analogy of music, writing:

> It would be better to treat with greater circumspection than hitherto the analogies that certain people would have us establish between colours and sounds, and not take as gospel all these theses put forward with regard to this subject . . . The fact is that a piece of music suggests different images to each of its listeners, an accompaniment that each one creates from the reserves of his own visual memory. In other words, chromaticism in music and the musicality of colours are of values only as metaphors. Such a shame . . . yet another illusion goes up in smoke.[36]

The dream of transposing music into a visual medium was engaged as a way to transfer music's capacity for abstraction to the visual arts. It was engaged as a way of articulating the desire to develop a visual medium that was informed by its own internal rationale, but which did not need to have a narrative to legitimise it. It is surely significant in this context that, when mid-eighteenth-century thinkers were striving to define a model of knowledge that was independent of religious belief, and indeed of any source other than experience itself, they too substantiated it by developing an alternative discourse of pure sensation – interdependent sensations (bordering on synaesthesia) and the notion of a 'common sense'. This discourse gave rise to the amorphous and proto-abstract rococo style, the first style to be wilfully 'meaningless' and significant of nothing. The fact that Kupka made reference to the baroque form of the fugue (the most abstract and mathematical of musical forms) and that he appears to have composed his paintings 'in a fugal manner' rather than 'as complete pieces of music' suggests that he too was using the *idea* of music – principally the idea of relating abstract forms to each other in an illuminating and affecting way – as an experimental tool, rather than attempting to write 'visual music' as such.

The Russian painter Wassily Kandinsky (1866–1944) was working along the same lines as Kupka, but he took a very different approach. The 'musicality' of Kandinsky's work was not simply based on the abstraction of instrumental music, epitomised by the highly abstract but harmonious music of Bach; it was also inspired by the *atonality* of contemporary music, particularly as pioneered by the Austrian composer Arnold Schoenberg, with whom Kandinsky maintained a lengthy correspondence from 1911. Significantly, music was also undergoing a process of abstraction in these years – challenging the conventions of harmonic and melodic coherence (and the coherence of the self-sense that identified with it) in exactly the same way that visual artists were challenging the conventions that supported coherent subject matter. Kandinsky wrote to Schoenberg in 1911, acknowledging that 'in your works, you have realised what I, albeit in uncertain form, have so greatly longed for, in music. The independent progress through their own destinies, the independent life of the individual voices in your compositions, is exactly what I am trying to find in my paintings.'[37] Kandinsky's first fully abstract works – his musically named *Improvisations* and *Compositions* – did not simply use the idea of music as a model on which to base a parallel concept of non-objective art; in some cases, they actually *worked* like pieces of music, aspiring to acquire a temporal and even sonic dimension. While Kupka's compositions resemble the impact of a single musical motif, suggesting a duration of a few seconds – in the manner, for instance, of ripples in a pond, a firework exploding or a rising plume of smoke – Kandinsky's abstract works matured into complex combinations of a wide range of different ideas, enabling the viewer's eye to traverse the surface of the painting in numerous different ways, endlessly plunging back into its centre to pursue new sequences of motifs (Fig. 4.34). In this way, viewers were encouraged to experience the works as

FIGURE 4.34: Wassily Kandinsky, *Improvisation 28 (Second Version)*, 1912, oil on canvas, 111.4 × 162.1 cm. Solomon R. Guggenheim Museum, New York. Solomon R. Guggenheim Founding Collection, by gift. 37.239.

complex developments and variations of forms, extended indefinitely in time like elaborate musical compositions. Indeed, in 1912, Kandinsky wrote in a letter to Schoenberg that he sometimes increased the dimensions of his work 'to prevent them being taken in at one glance'[38] (in contrast, say, to Delaunay, who aimed at a simultaneity of impression). In the following year, he described how he was attempting:

> to infuse into every part [of his pictures] an 'endless' series of initially concealed colour-tones. They had to lie in such a way that they were completely hidden at first (especially in the darker parts), revealing themselves only in the course of time to the engrossed, attentive viewer. Indistinct and at the same time tentative, quizzical at first, and then sounding forth more and more, with increasing 'uncanny' power.[39]

Kandinsky's desire not just to create abstract art in parallel with abstract music but to create 'visual music' was made explicit in his efforts to create 'total works of art' in the tradition of Wagner's *gesamtkunstwerk*, in which all the arts – theatre, music, dance, painting, sculpture and poetry – were brought together and fused into a universal medium that transcended the individual arts in the fullness of its effect. Only one of Kandinsky's theatrical projects ever materialised (though the music, by Thomas de Hartmann, may never have been completed) and plans to perform it were interrupted by the outbreak of the First World War. The work, called *Der Gelbe Klang* (*The Yellow Sound*, 1911), was intended to combine music, sound, light effects and choreography. Regarding its content, it revolves around a highly ambiguous sense of situation, involving shapeless giants and indeterminate people, although it has no narrative as such. In *Der Gelbe Klang*, Kandinsky created an artificial scenario in which it was as natural and meaningful to follow a sequence of notes with a flash of colour as with another note. He was not looking for equivalents or parallels between sounds and colours, as if to translate a motif from one sensory language into another; on the contrary, he was creating a context in which all sounds and colours were equal, unique and untranslatable parts of a single higher language of sensory impressions, a context in which there was no greater similarity of function between the colour red and the colour yellow as there was between the colour red and the sound of a trumpet; the sound of a trumpet could, therefore, serve the same function as the colour yellow and could, therefore, be, to all intents and purposes, a 'yellow sound'. Part of Kandinsky's aim in developing this higher unified language was precisely to strip colour of its purely optical aspect – the very aspect of it that enables it to define objects – and to invest it with a new capacity to represent a higher realm of invisible inner experience.

Kandinsky strove to represent the invisible world from his earliest days as an artist, though, significantly, he did not decide to embark on the profession of painting until 1896, when he was thirty years old, having originally trained as a lawyer. Several experiences inspired him to make this late decision. Firstly, his researches into the pagan culture of rural Russia, where he travelled as a student in 1889, exposed him to the psychosocial dynamics of peasant law. This experience presented him with an integrated vision of the world that was rooted in the intuition or belief that the material realm is thoroughly pervaded in its every fibre by a spiritual dimension; it was simply meaningless to look at the physical world as if it was an independent realm of existence. This vision of the metaphysical nature of things was reinforced by new scientific evidence from within the western tradition, which led to Kandinsky's second revelation: his world was genuinely changed by Becquerel's discovery of radioactivity in 1896 (as Kupka's had been). He later recollected:

> The disintegration of the atom was equal in my soul to the disintegration of the whole world. Suddenly the thickest walls fell. Everything became uncertain, wobbly and soft . . . Science seemed to me destroyed: its most important basis was only madness, a mistake of scholars, who were not building a divine structure stone for stone but rather were groping around randomly in darkness for truths, and blindly mistaking one object for another.[40]

This interpretation of the instability of the material world as a sign of disintegration and destruction was transformed into a liberating opportunity for growth and creativity by a third experience that Kandinsky had, also in 1896, of one of Monet's paintings of haystacks on display in Moscow (Fig. 4.16) through which he realised the possibility of non-objectivity:

> Previously I had known only realistic art, in fact only the Russians, and had often remained standing for a long time before the hand of Franz Liszt in the portrait by Repin, etc. And suddenly, for the first time, I saw a *picture*. That it was a haystack, the catalogue informed me. I didn't recognise it . . . I had a dull feeling that the object was lacking in this picture. And I noticed with surprise and confusion that the picture not only gripped me, but that it impressed itself ineradicably on my memory, always hovering quite unexpectedly before my eyes, down to the last detail . . . Painting took on a fairy-tale power and splendour. And, albeit unconsciously, objects were discredited as an essential element within the picture.[41]

The impulse to realise contentless art was further nurtured in Kandinsky by the innovations he encountered in Munich when he went to study painting there in 1896. In that year, the *Jugendstil* designers Hermann Obrist and August Endell were producing designs that they specifically considered to be non-representational. Indeed, Endell asserted that 'we not only stand at the start of a new period style, but also at the beginning of a whole new art, an art with forms that mean nothing and represent nothing and remind of nothing, yet excite our souls as deeply, as strongly, as only music before could'.[42] But nor, however, were their designs purely decorative. Although they were conceived to be applied in a functional context (for textiles, furniture and architecture), thereby mitigating their claims to be 'fine art', they also evolved as expressions of the interests of both designers in scientific phenomena, which provided them with meaningful origins, if not with meaning as such. Indeed, both designers originally trained in a scientific discipline – Obrist in botany and medicine, Endell in psychology and aesthetics – and 'converted' to design not because of the inherent potential of the design process, but because the *experiential* component in the perception and appreciation of visual imagery – absent from conventional scientific enquiry – enabled them to deepen their own understanding of their scientific interests. Partly inspired by Goethe's investigations into plant morphology (and the British Arts and Crafts Movement), Obrist developed a language of organic *artistic* forms in order to render the hidden principles of *natural* formation visible in the world (Fig. 4.35). Endell took his lead from Obrist but was more interested in the psychology of perception than the processes of nature, and his designs were therefore less inclined to resemble natural forms (Fig. 4.36).

Kandinsky clearly appreciated Obrist and Endell's understanding of abstraction as a spontaneous function of the natural world and, sensing the possibility of abstraction without knowing how to realise it, he too sought to allow it to evolve organically in his work. It was many years, however – from 1896, when he began painting, until 1913, when he completed his first totally abstract work – before this seed of intuition finally blossomed. During those years, Kandinsky was aware that a process of germination was taking place. It was as if he was waiting, in a state of Aristotelian 'entelechy', for a possibility – both in himself and in the language of art as a whole – to evolve into an actuality. But he was also an observant instrument of that change. In 1904, for instance, when he was still working in a painterly Post-Impressionist style, he could reflect: 'Without exaggerating, I can say that, should I succeed in this task, I will be showing [a] new, beautiful path for painting susceptible to infinite development. I am on a new track which some masters, just here and there, suspected, and which will be recognised, sooner or later'.[43] And when the moment finally seemed to arrive, he expressed an awareness of how the process had contained its own logic, which he had to discover, so to speak, rather than invent. He wrote, in 1913:

FIGURE 4.35: Hermann Obrist, *Whiplash*, 1895, embroidered silk on linen, 119 × 183 cm. Munich City Museum.

FIGURE 4.36: August Endell, *Atelier Elvira*, Munich, 1896–8 (destroyed in 1937 and later).

A terrifying abyss of all kinds of questions, a wealth of responsibilities stretched before me. And most important of all: what is to replace the missing object? The danger of ornament revealed itself clearly to me; the dead semblance of stylised forms I found merely repugnant . . . It took a very long time before I arrived at the correct answer to the question: What is to replace the object? I sometimes look back at the past and despair at how long this solution took me.[44]

The question 'what is to replace the object?' is one that preoccupied Kandinsky deeply. He was strongly averse to the notion of decorative art, or 'art for art's sake', which, in his view, expressed nothing and was, therefore, soulless. And yet how could he create a totally abstract art without it becoming merely decorative? How could he produce art that was significant and of value, despite the fact that it had no meaning or associations? Kandinsky's solution to this problem was his 'principle of inner necessity', according to which artistic forms were created as a natural and spontaneous function of the soul. On the one hand, art was an expression of the interior and immaterial essence of an individual and was, therefore, in some sense subjective; it was this psychic depth that gave it value. But on the other hand, it was also objective because it was generated as a natural function of that essence, necessarily determined by its laws, rather than as an arbitrary product of its will. That is to say, its rationale and organisational principles were provided from within itself, rather than from any external frame of reference. Thus, paradoxical though it may seem, the art of inner necessity was both subjective (because it was 'of the soul') and objective (because it was determined by objective laws); and yet, from a more conventional point of view, it was neither subjective (because it did not express the freedom of the self to exercise its personal will) nor objective (because it was independent of all determinants external to itself). With this thoroughly 'moebial' concept – in which apparent opposites are seen to become each other, without ever losing their points of difference – Kandinsky attempted to 'objectify subjectivity' and to find a form for its formlessness.

Kandinsky accommodated the paradox of the 'formless form' in his paintings by maximising the impression of movement within them; this impression was substantiated by its association with music, as we have seen. By incorporating an experience of temporality into his paintings, he was able to ensure that, despite representing forms, they were perpetually undermining their own finality; they were perpetually reconfiguring themselves, not as static, iconic images of a truth, but as the spontaneously generated signs of a 'state of becoming', whose unknowable source and destiny were powerfully implied (and even necessitated, according to Kandinsky's way of thinking) but never actually represented.

The notion of seeing or representing invisible realms became further established as a possibility for Kandinsky by virtue of its association with the theosophists. The Theosophical Society, founded by the Russian occultist Helena Petrovna Blavatsky in New York in 1875, brought together a circle of spiritualists who claimed that thought forms, auras and spirit bodies, which are normally invisible, could be seen by psychically awakened or 'clairvoyant' seers. Despite showing the highest respect for religious traditions, and indeed attempting to synthesise them (in keeping with the aims of symbolist artists), the theosophists also attempted to underpin their theories with scientific evidence. Indeed, some of their theories were articulated as extensions of, or at least by analogy with, the scientific conventions of the time. For instance, C. W. Leadbeater, one of the leaders of the Theosophical Society in London, maintained that the spiritual worlds (existing on astral, mental and causal planes) are not fundamentally distinct from the physical 'material' world. They are simply manifestations of more refined states of matter which, Leadbeater maintained, could exist not only in the solid, liquid and gaseous states in which matter is normally visible to ordinary human beings, but also in higher ethereal and spiritual states only visible to clairvoyants. As Kandinsky himself asked: 'Is everything material? or is everything spiritual? Can the distinctions we make between matter and spirit be nothing but relative modifications of one or the other?'[45] It was on account of the fundamental 'material' unity of the universe (dispensing with traditional mind–body dualism) that vibrations could be organically transmitted from one level of existence to another, and that individuals in whom the appropriate higher faculties had been developed could 'see' the matter of psychic phenomena in its higher states of refinement. A clairvoyant colleague of Leadbeater, Annie Besant, who later became president of the Theosophical Society in London, described the appearance of thought forms in terms that call Kandinsky's first fully abstract works to mind:

These vibrations, which shape the matter of the plane into thought-forms, give rise also – from their swiftness and subtlety – to the most exquisite and constantly changing colours, waves of varying shades like the rainbow hues in mother-of-pearl, etherealised and brightened to an indescribable extent, sweeping over and through every form, so that each presents a harmony of rippling, living, luminous, delicate colours, including many not even known to earth.[46]

The first occasions on which experiences of such phenomena were actually depicted and reproduced were Leadbeater's books: *Thought-Forms* (1901), co-written with Annie Besant, and *Man Invisible and Visible* (1902). Both books provided images of the thought forms or auras of individuals undergoing a variety of experiences. The images, Leadbeater stressed, were drawn from life and not from the imagination. In *Thought-Forms*, the scientific pretensions of theosophy were established by association with other recent discoveries in the field of psychic research. The fact that vibrations could be directly correlated to images, without the subjective intervention of human beings, was firmly established by reference to the experiments of the musician-physician Ernst Chladni (1756–1827), who as early as 1787 had demonstrated how grains of sand placed on a vibrating plate will naturally arrange themselves into regular patterns, in keeping with the source and intensity of the vibration; Leadbeater illustrated his experiment (Fig. 4.37).[47] The hypnotism of

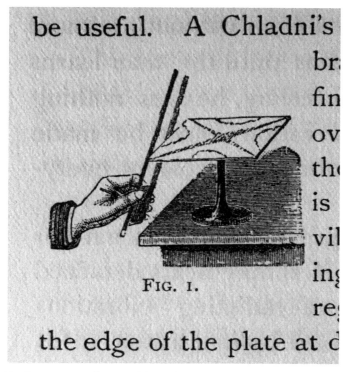

FIGURE 4.37: Experiment of Ernst Chladni showing how sand on a vibrating sound plate naturally forms patterns according to the strength and location of the vibration, from Annie Besant and C. W. Leadbeater, *Thought-Forms*, 1905 edition, London, 1905, p. 28.

Mesmer, the electro-magnetic 'odic' force of Carl von Reichenbach, the X-rays of Rontgen and the radioactivity of Becquerel were also cited as proof that science was being led 'beyond the borderland of ether into the astral world'. The development of 'psychic photography' provided further evidence. Dr. Hippolyte Baraduc's pioneering use of the camera as a scientific instrument with which to record the otherwise invisible 'effects that the vibrations of thoughts made on etheric matter' was presented as a clear precedent for the visualisation of thought forms. When his wife, Nadine, died in 1907, he claimed to capture some aspect of her departing spirit on film. In the same vein, Louis Darget claimed to be able to make cameraless photographs of a person's dreams by placing a photographic plate against their forehead while they were sleeping (Fig. 4.38).

Having established a scientific foundation for the visualisation of all kinds of psychic phenomena, Leadbeater and Besant proceeded to describe and illustrate the appearance of the individual thought forms that arise in conjunction with a wide

FIGURE 4.38: Louis Darget, 'Photograph of the Dream. The Eagle. Obtained by placing a photographic plate on the forehead of Madame Darget during her sleep', 1896. Photo: Institut für Grenzgebiete der Psychologie und Psychohygiene (IGPP, Institute for Frontier Areas of Psychology and Mental Health).

range of emotional experiences – affection, devotion, anger, fear – and in relation to a variety of emotional situations, including 'at a shipwreck', 'at a street accident', 'on meeting a friend' and 'appreciation of a picture'. They also described and illustrated examples of the complex thought forms that are generated by music – in this case, by monumental compositions by Mendelssohn, Gounod and Wagner, played on a church organ – adding a psychic dimension to the close parallels that already existed between the two arts (Fig. 4.39). Kandinsky was fascinated by these developments. He attended at least one lecture by Rudolf Steiner (an Austrian protégé of Madame Blavatsky) in 1908, and referred to the work of Madame Blavatsky in his *Concerning the Spiritual in Art*, published in 1911. He also had a significant collection of books on occult matters in his personal library, including *Thought-Forms* (in a German translation published in 1908). The ideas and images that he found in this work were surely influential on his work, on a number of fronts. Firstly, they set a unique precedent for the representation of invisible phenomena in visible form. Secondly, they seemed – at least by the standards of ordinary people – to create a visual language of abstraction, even though the theosophists considered them to be naturalistic representations of psychic phenomena. Thirdly, they established grounds on which abstract forms could be convincingly invested with spiritual value. And fourthly, they described and illustrated a form of experience – a psychic vibration of a kind – that he intended his own work to activate in its viewers. Adopting the theosophical view that 'vibration is the formative agent behind all material shapes, which are but the manifestation of life concealed by matter', he maintained that 'words, musical tones and colours possess the psychical power of calling forth soul vibrations . . . they create identical vibrations, ultimately bringing about the attainment of knowledge'.[48] Moreover, the possibility of such experience was only now evolving, following a stressful age of materialism, and the role of the artist was to magnify and transmit it:

> Shapeless emotions such as fear, joy, grief etc., which belonged to this time of effort, will no longer greatly attract the artist. He will endeavour to awake subtler emotions, as yet unnamed . . . His work will give to those observers capable of feeling them lofty emotions beyond the reach of words . . . Such works of art at least preserve the soul from coarseness; they 'key it up', so to speak, to a certain height, as a tuning-key [keys up] the strings of a musical instrument.[49]

Of course, the experiences described in *Thought-Forms* that were most relevant to Kandinsky's own case were those activated by works of art – that is, the appreciation of music and especially of 'a picture', as mentioned above (Fig. 4.40, right). Although the picture being appreciated was evidently very different to a painting by Kandinsky, the psychic dimension of the individual's response to it anticipates the quasi-psychic experience of 'inner necessity' that Kandinsky expected his own work to induce in its viewers. The description of the thought form in question, which bears a strong resemblance to Kandinsky's own description of the feeling associations of colours in *Concerning the Spiritual in Art*, is as follows:

> a somewhat complex thought-form representing the delighted appreciation of a beautiful picture upon a religious subject. The strong pure yellow marks the

FIGURE 4.39: Annie Besant and C. W. Leadbeater, 'The Music of Gounod', *Thought-Forms*, 1905 edition, London, 1905, facing p. 80.

 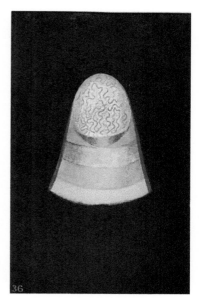

FIGURE 4.40: Annie Besant and C. W. Leadbeater, 'On Meeting a Friend' (left) and 'The Appreciation of a Picture' (right), *Thought-Forms*, 1905 edition, London, 1905, facing p. 64.

beholder's enthusiastic recognition of the technical skill of the artist, while all the other colours are expressions of the various emotions evoked within him by the examination of so glorious a work of art. Green shows his sympathy with the central figure in the picture, deep devotion appears not only in the broad band of blue, but also in the outline of the entire figure, while the violet tells us that the picture has raised the man's thought to the contemplation of a lofty ideal and made him, at least for the time, capable of responding to it.[50]

Kandinsky's own interest in metaphysics pre-dated his knowledge of theosophy and is reflected in his earliest works, several of which use the mystique of ancient pagan Russia, which he had known as a student, as a pretext for exploring the realm of myth and imagination. Many of the themes that he developed at this time reappear in his later work; these include traditional symbols such as trees, ancient churches, boats and horses, but also apocalyptic imagery and a range of shamanic spirit figures and Christian saints (whose abundant haloes anticipate the auras of the theosophists). Indeed, Kandinsky's evolution towards total abstraction was so gradual, and the disintegration of his symbols into mere marks and patches of colour was so slow and indefinite, that there is a case for wondering whether the artist did actually ever fully relinquish them; they may equally well have become so diluted that they simply ceased to be noticeable. Even in his most abstract works, when he used the analogy of music to highlight the absence of subject matter, naming them *Improvisations* (as if they were spontaneous manifestations of 'soul content') and *Compositions*, there is enough visual continuity with the clearly semi-figurative images of a few years earlier to suggest that the same subject matter is still being addressed. The image of the horse and rider, for instance, preoccupied him throughout his career. While it first appeared as a mythical knight at the edge of the ancient forests of Russia, from around 1902, it soon became associated with the figure of St. George killing the dragon, as depicted in innumerable Russian icons. In the earliest images of this subject, all the narrative elements of the story are clearly visible (i.e. the saint; his horse, cloak, shield and lance; the dragon and the dragon's cave). By slow degrees, however, these objects become increasingly ambiguous until, in around 1911, they become so abstracted that it would be impossible for the viewer to recognise them unless he or she knew what to look for. For instance, if viewers were not aware in advance that the red patch in *Improvisation No. 20* (1911) could be traced directly back to the cloak of St. George, or that the mushroom-like shapes at the top of *Composition V* (also 1911)[51] were based on the domes of Russian Orthodox churches, these references would be completely lost on them. And if these ambiguous motifs can be traced back to recognisable sources, maybe some of the other ones – even the apparently most abstracted ones of 1913 – can be too? Are all motifs tinged with the associations of their sources? Should the motif of the zigzag, for instance, always be associated with the wing of the dragon, as it is in some contemporary representations of the scene, or is it a truly non-objective mark? And what about the forms that have not (yet?) been traced back to known sources? Despite the fact that Kandinsky claimed to have divested his work of all objects, it is highly unlikely that, having taken so much time and care to evolve his iconographic language step by step into a language of colours, shapes and lines, he would have denied the survival of its 'vibration' in them. Moreover, the fact that his references to identifiable symbols become more explicit again from around 1916 suggests that the thread linking them to his pre-war works was never completely broken, further raising the possibility that, although his *Improvisations* and *Compositions* may look non-objective, in the strictest and most absolute sense of the term, they may not be.

Kandinsky moved towards abstraction not for its own sake, but because it enabled him to bypass the interpretative function of the brain and stimulate a direct, psychic experience of his work. Thus, although he was highly appreciative of 'natural geometry' – the spontaneous presence of geometrical forms in nature – he was dismissive of any attempts to reduce the visual language of nature to its fundamental component parts – its geometrical units – which he considered to be *conceptual* and based on theory rather than experience. The Dutch artist Piet Mondrian (1872–1944), who was advancing towards abstraction at exactly the same time as Kandinsky, represented a very different view. Mondrian maintained that, in order to capture the essence of visual experience, it was necessary to purify it of any contingent and particular elements, in favour of fundamental and universal ones. By this he meant that it was necessary to reduce nature to the very principles that give it coherence, without any hidden references to its particular manifestations. With regard to the visual world, these principles are manifest as line and colour: that is to say, there is no visual experience of nature that is not ultimately an experience of these two elements. In contrast to Kandinsky, who delighted in the 'particularities of nature', seeking objectivity or 'inner necessity' in the infinitely varied experience of *subjectivity* that they stimulated, Mondrian attempted to find the same objectivity in the unified consistency of the *objective* world by reducing that world to its immutable essence. Thus, one could say that the two artists complemented each other: whereas Kandinsky was seeking objectivity in 'the subjective experience of the world', Mondrian was seeking it in 'the objective world that is experienced'. Both of them arrived at solutions that were necessarily determined from within themselves (rather than in keeping with an external frame of reference) and which, therefore, took them to the threshold of non-objective art.

Significantly, both artists underwent 'apprenticeships' in Post-Impressionism and the art of the Parisian avant-garde, and both artists were interested in theosophy. While Kandinsky was especially indebted to the colourism of the Fauves (who he experienced while staying in Paris in 1906–7), Mondrian was inspired by his compatriot Van Gogh, who had his first major exhibition in Amsterdam in 1905, and the Cubists, whose work became known in Holland from around 1908 and which he experienced more directly while living in Paris from 1912 to 1914. Moreover, in 1909, Mondrian became a member of the Theosophical Society. These two influences – Paris and theosophy – were instrumental in the development of his own style. As with Kandinsky, theosophy provided him with a spiritual context for his work; this association was important to him as a contextualising source of depth and meaning, especially as his work became less dependent on the poetic associations of iconography. It is most evident in a series of portraits of individuals, mostly women, in which the sitters appear to transcend their ordinary social personas and personal idiosyncrasies and become impersonal initiates into a luminous, contemplative state of being (Fig. 4.41). These works, dating from 1908 to 1911, give a clear impression of Mondrian's wider preoccupations and aspirations at the time. Although the figures in question are conceived as static, iconic structures that seem to exist on a higher plane and could be said to anticipate his later abstractions, their quasi-visionary character does not provide a particularly natural link between his earlier Post-Impressionist paintings and the later work, suggesting that the artist had not yet fully integrated his feelings for theosophy into his artistic style. The influence of Cubism, on the other hand, catalysed a thoroughly organic transition between these two phases of his career, enabling him to progressively dismantle the structures of the external world, to the extent that his work became entirely independent of them, organising itself instead according to the purely pictorial values of line and colour. However, for several years (including the disorientating early years of the First World War, which Mondrian spent in Holland), elements of the visible world – especially trees, church towers, sand dunes and the sea – remained identifiable or implicit in his work. For instance, his *Composition* of 1916 (Fig. 4.42), which consists of fields of colour loosely contained by a broken network of vertical and horizontal bars, looks entirely abstract; however, it is known from drawings to be have been based on the church at Domburg, which, over the years, Mondrian had already painted many times (Fig. 4.43). It was not until 1917 that the principle of representation was first truly replaced by an independent rational principle, according to which images were constructed around the internal logic of

FIGURE 4.41: Piet Mondrian, *Devotie*, 1908, oil on canvas, 94 × 61 cms.
Gemeentemuseum Den Haag.

FIGURE 4.42: Piet Mondrian, *Composition*, 1916, oil on canvas with wood, 120 × 75.6 cm.
Solomon R. Guggenheim Museum, New York. Solomon R. Guggenheim Founding
Collection, 49.1229.

FIGURE 4.43: Piet Mondrian, *The Church at Domburg*, 1914, pencil, charcoal and ink on paper, 63.0 × 50.3 cm. Gemeentemuseum Den Haag.

their own language. This shift was precipitated by contact with two other Dutch artists, Theo van Doesburg and Bart van der Leck, who together with Mondrian formed the *De Stijl* group. Throughout 1917, Mondrian experimented with the constructive potential of line and colour, both in conjunction with each other and independently. In 1918, he began painting rigorous chequerboard works in which the picture surface is conceived as a uniform grid divided into regular units. These works are significant because they represent the first examples of designs that were clearly and explicitly based on mathematical calculation rather than abstraction from nature; that is to say, they were not based on the observation of objects. This shift of orientation is reflected in the fact that it was at around this time that Mondrian ceased to produce preparatory drawings, which he had previously used to work out the 'process' of abstraction. In the following year, Mondrian began painting the coloured grids for which he is best known (Fig. 4.44). These definitive works consist of nothing more than the fundamental constituent parts of the language of visual experience itself: lines (reduced to the horizontal and vertical axes) and colours (black, white and the primary colours: red, blue and yellow). They are no longer extreme abstractions, in which subject matter may still exist, albeit abstracted beyond recognition; they are truly non-objective; they have *no* subject matter. Moreover, by consisting of nothing but the raw materials of visual art, they also

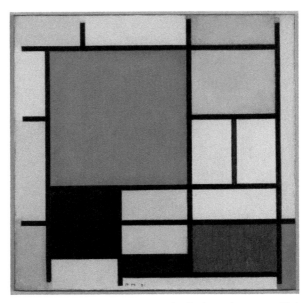

FIGURE 4.44: Piet Mondrian, *Composition with Black, Red, Gray, Yellow, and Blue*, 1921, oil on canvas, 59.5 × 59.5 cm. Gemeentemuseum Den Haag.

constituted the very principle and possibility of all such art; there was no possible visual art, and no possible experience of visual art, that was not implicit in them.

Mondrian attempted to reduce the language of visual art to its 'atomic' or indivisible essence, to a state of essentiality beyond which it cannot be taken. As such, it was conceived by him to be the purest possible form of art, accommodating the purest possible experience. By limiting himself to the basic materials of vision, he aimed to isolate that which is universal in art and to relieve it of all that is inessential, superfluous or incidental to it: namely, any references to, or associations with, sources of meaning or value outside itself. More important in the present context is the fact that, by divesting art of all iconographic references and associations, he was also implicitly ceasing to support the elaborate structures of meaning that such references depend on and generate. And most important of all, he was ceasing to support the *principle* of those structures, which is the sense of personal self or identity. Indeed, partly influenced by theosophy, he felt that it was the role of the artist to create cultural forms of a universal nature that would enable people to evolve beyond their egotistical identification with their individuality towards a transpersonal realm of being.

Having said this, although Mondrian claimed to reduce the language of art to its most fundamental level by eliminating all illusory references to extraneous sources of meaning and value, his work did retain some elements of illusion and reference, which did, therefore, limit its existential purity. Most significant of these was the illusion of *space*, which is partly created by the differences between the pictorial elements (its colours and lines). To some degree, for instance, the black lines seem to be 'on' or 'against' the white 'background'. Because the impression of depth belies the factuality of the flatness of the canvas, it does in effect presuppose an act of imagination on the part of the viewer, undermining the ideal of *formless* subjectivity (as the 'experience of space' thereby becomes a *form* of subjectivity). The reduction of the language of art to its basic component parts is not, therefore, as ultimate as it seems to be, because these component parts can also become a source of illusion, in which space is represented like an object, as if it were subject matter. Moreover, if the differentiated elements that create the illusion of relative depth were to be eliminated, the problem would still not be entirely solved because, as is clear from Mondrian's paintings, different colours give different impressions of projection or depth, thereby also creating illusions of space. Therefore, for the fundamental essence and universal potential of art to be truly realised, both internal differentiation and colour would have to be eliminated, leaving . . . *nothing*.

This giant step into nothingness was taken by the Russian painter Kasimir Malevich (1878–1935). Malevich's journey towards abstraction was as painstaking as Kandinsky's and Mondrian's. Like them (and like almost every other aspiring artist of the period), he began painting in a loosely impressionistic style. He then moved through forms of pointillism, symbolism, Fauvism, Cubism and Futurism, appropriating their possibilities before digesting and discarding them; he even went through a proto-Dadaist phase of antagonism in which he dissociated from traditional art (in a way that Picasso and Matisse never did) by violating classical ideals – for instance, in 1914, by including a crossed-out print of the *Mona Lisa* in one of his works (Fig. 4.45).[52] Indeed, his passage through the styles of contemporary art was so predictable that one cannot help but sympathise with his Hegelian view that his development was as much due to the inexorable logic of art history using him as an instrument or prophet through which to realise itself, as it was to the artist 'making history'. It was not until 1913 that Malevich began to develop his own truly unprecedented style, Suprematism, so called because he considered it to be the supreme and unsurpassable perfection of art. The first signs of this development appeared in his quasi-Cubist works, in which the typically rhomboid, tilted and shaded facets of classic Cubism (Fig. 4.23) are complemented, and eventually replaced by, rectilinear shapes of a single unmodulated colour (Fig. 4.45). The regularity of these new shapes, and their lack of foreshortening and shading, suggest that they are parallel to, and sometimes flat up against, the picture surface. By 1915, Malevich raised Suprematism to a new level by realising that even the simplest differentiation between forms on a surface creates an illusion of depth and, therefore, that paintings that rely on such forms are not entirely free of extraneous references. The same was true of fields of colour, both in relation to other colours and alone. In order to remedy this situation, Malevich removed both limitations (forms and colours), creating his celebrated *Black Square* (1915) in which there is no content whatsoever, not even pictorial space (Fig. 4.46). With this work, he went further than Mondrian (whose explorations of comparable territory were independent of Malevich's and took place a few years later), challenging the very notion of art.

The *Black Square* is truly non-objective in that it has no objects or subject matter whatsoever; unlike Mondrian's work, it includes no 'form', 'space', 'colour' or

FIGURE 4.45: Kasimir Malevich, *Composition with Mona Lisa*, 1914, collage, 62.5 × 49.3 cm. Russian State Museum, St. Petersburg. Photo: © SCALA, Florence.

FIGURE 4.46: Kasimir Malevich, *Black Square*, 1915, oil on canvas, 79.5 × 79.5 cm. Tretyakov Gallery, Moscow. Photo: © SCALA, Florence.

'relationships'. By taking this step, Malevich minimised the extent to which his art represented, or even related to, reality. In fact, by removing all *mediation* between reality and the viewer, his art became transparent to reality, allowing and enabling it to communicate itself *immediately* and directly. Indeed, by eliminating all manifest characteristics from *Black Square*, Malevich was removing those qualities that differentiated it from reality itself. To all intents and purposes, therefore, it became indistinguishable from reality; that is to say, by ceasing to *relate* to reality as if reality was 'other', it *became* reality. It became a form of 'absolute art' in the sense that its value did not reside in its references, meanings, associations or effects. On the contrary, it resided in its mere existence, in the simple experience of it as an existential phenomenon, in keeping with the artist's own statement that his Suprematist works 'will not be copies of living things in life, but will themselves be a living thing'.[53]

In order to underline his conception of the work as an absolute and substantial realisation of the fullest value of art in itself – in its mere existence, rather than in meanings – Malevich presented *Black Square* as a modern icon. In contrast to western medieval art, which revolves around the didactic or emotive power of iconography, Russian icons were believed not just to represent, but to actually *incarnate*, their sacred subject matter. That is to say, they were believed to be an absolute and sacramental form of art – indeed, an extension of the incarnation of Christ – in which the physical substance of the object, and not just the figures represented on it, is considered to be sacred. Thus, like an icon, *Black Square* did not merely represent reality; it *was* reality. Despite – as a discrete object – dispensing with all references to external sources of meaning, its iconic status was clearly proposed at its first exhibition by the way in which it was displayed; it was hung it across the corner of the room like a Russian icon, which is typically hung in this position in all Russian homes (Fig. 4.47).

The *Black Square* was intended to incarnate the very essence of art. By reducing the *actual*, manifest characteristics of the painting to an absolute minimum – *prior* to form, line and colour – Malevich not only maximised its potential to contain all possible works of art within itself in seed form, and thereby to accommodate and reflect all possibilities of *artistic* experience (like Mondrian); he also realised its potential to accommodate all possible visual experience, *beyond* art. As a result, *Black Square* represented the consummation of the entire tradition of art, reducing it to a primordial state of potential beyond which it was not possible to go. Indeed, one of his other 'black' works of the period – *Black Circle* – was wittily dubbed by one contemporary critic 'the full stop in the history of art'.

While the *Black Square* succeeded in eliminating all extraneous sources of meaning, thereby denying the personal self an opportunity to exercise, and thereby validate, its self-affirming and self-enhancing powers of interpretation, Malevich did not transcend the self-sense altogether with this work. On the contrary, he left the self with one final object, enabling it, for the last time, to identify itself therein as the subject: the work of art itself. Even though *Black Square* reduced the language of art to nothing – to the point at which it has no artistic qualities – the fact remains that it exists *as a work of art*. And therefore, even if it does not invite the individual self to elaborate narratives of personal experience around it (in relation to its qualities, references, etc.), it does allow it – by virtue of its own existence and visibility – to

FIGURE 4.47: The Last Futurist Exhibition of Paintings 0.10, Petrograd, 1915.

exist. Indeed, it reduces a circumstance that had been implicit in western European culture since the Renaissance, and explicit since the Romantic era, down to its very principle: namely, the fact that the notion of the personal 'self' and the notion of 'art' are fundamentally correspondent to each other and are even functions of each other. That is to say, art is a discourse, spontaneously generated by the self for the sake of its own self-awareness and self-propagation, and as a medium of communication with other selves; it is an imaginative realm in which the world is translated into the currency of personal identity and experienced, mostly unwittingly, as a function of the self. Moreover, as the rationale of art became less and less dependent on legitimising references to iconography (which had given it a social and psychological dimension that had hitherto enabled the sense of self to become lost in the fantasy of personal narratives), it now became ever more able to accommodate the self in the purest and most essential state of subjectivity. Although Malevich's suprematist art ceased to accommodate the cultural, social and psychological manifestations of the self, it continued to function as a mirror of its existence. Despite having no content with which to differentiate itself from reality, *Black Square* did differentiate itself by virtue of its distinctive existence as an object or work of 'art'. For it to become truly transparent to the totality of reality, even this distinguishing feature would have to be relinquished; his art would have to cease to exist as such.

It was for this reason that, in 1918, Malevich painted a series of white paintings, in which a number of vestigial forms, including a white square, are seen to sink

FIGURE 4.48: Kasimir Malevich, *White on White*, 1918, oil on canvas, 79 × 79 cm.
Museum of Modern Art, New York. Photo: © SCALA, Florence.

and dissolve into their white backgrounds, and to lose their distinctiveness in the
infinite field of whiteness (Fig. 4.48). These radical works took him to – and beyond
– the very limits of art as an expressive medium. As he said himself, he wanted to
go 'beyond zero'. Through his *White on White* paintings, Malevich sacrificed the
language of art to the ineffable and unknowable state of non-objectivity that
precedes it:

> The familiar recedes ever further and further into the background . . . The
> contours of the objective world fade more and more and so it goes, step by step,
> until finally the world . . . becomes lost to sight. No more likenesses of reality, no
> idealistic images – nothing but a desert! But, this desert is filled with the spirit of
> non-objective sensation which pervades everything.[54]

While producing his *White on White* works, Malevich came to realise that not only the forms of art, but also the very concept of art, imposed a limitation on his freedom to experience reality *as it is*, in its immediate, unmediated state. He realised that just as a visual form imposed a limitation on the absolute potential of a work of art to accommodate the totality of artistic experience, so the concept of art was itself a distinctive form – a thought form – that imposed a limitation on the absolute potential of consciousness to experience reality. For reality, whatever it might be, was no longer being created, or even revealed, by art; it could now be recognised as an innate and self-evident quality of existence. Tautological though it may sound, it became clear that whatever is real simply is real, whether it was comprehended by the mind or not. It no longer needed human agency to express it or make it real; indeed, it no longer needed human agency at all. The possibility of mediating the totality of experience to society was no longer the privilege or property of art; it was found to be naturally present in life itself. It spoke for itself. The phenomenon of art, therefore, became redundant; it became defunct as a social and cultural convention and died.

The 'death of art' inevitably implied the death of the artist. Malevich acknowledged that just as art was consummated in its own dissolution, so the sense of self, to which art was made to correspond, was consummated in self-sacrifice or self-transcendence. Indeed, speaking of the numerous examples of his Suprematist work in which the form of the cross appears, albeit without explicitly Christian associations, he stated: 'the cross is my cross'. Accepting this fate, he gave up painting in 1918 and devoted himself to teaching and utilitarian design. Moreover, the death of the subject was as necessary for the public as it was for the artist. To understand the non-objectivity of his works, the viewer would also need to transcend him- or herself, for the sense of self presupposed a corresponding object and, by maintaining an object, it was obviating the possibility of understanding non-objective art.

Malevich maintained that the social and cultural convention of 'art' had run its course. Apart from the purposes of individual works, one of the key functions of art had been, over several centuries, to bring cultural value to the *content* and *modes* of human experience. With regard to the *content* of human experience, this had been achieved by including ordinary people, places and things in the subject matter that artists considered to be worthy of artistic representation – firstly at the expense of religious meaning (in the sixteenth century) and later at the expense of secular but moralising meaning (in favour of pure pleasure and sensation, in the eighteenth century). In the nineteenth century, aspects of psychological experience that had hitherto been suppressed, or projected into legitimising narratives, were brought into the field of consciousness via the medium of art and validated for the first time.

With regard to the *modes* of personal experience – sensing, feeling, thinking – the experience of optical seeing had been legitimised by the evolution of pictorial realism in the fifteenth century. During the seventeenth century, refinements in the accurate measurement – and experience – of time coincided with a greater awareness of fleeting changes in the experience of personal feeling; these changes were ascribed cultural value by new artistic conventions (animated portraits, dramatic history painting) that evolved to accommodate them. In the eighteenth century, this development came to a head with the proliferation of 'sensibilities' that institutionalised the possibility of entirely new forms of subjectivity. Most significant among these was a sensitivity to aesthetic experience which created and sacralised parameters of personal identity that continue to prevail today. This institutionalisation of legitimate pleasure liberated personal identity from the traditional shackles of belief and obligation, enabling it to crystallise into the notion of the 'absolute self' in conjunction with the corresponding, polarised ideal of 'pure art'.

But as soon as the ideal of the 'absolute self' seemed to be achieved at the beginning of the nineteenth century, so the cultural forms on which it depended started to become less coherent and rational, and less able to reflect a coherent and consistent sense of identity back to its consumers. Just as the self had been inducted into a sense of its own coherence by the evolution of cultural forms towards the reflective ideal of pure art, so it was now being inducted into its own formlessness and indeterminacy by the disintegration of those cultural forms. In the late nineteenth and early twentieth centuries, the growing capacity for complex 'psychological' experience coincided with a less literal approach to the physical integrity of material objects, and it was accommodated in various forms of artistic stylisation accordingly. Picasso's Cubist works, for instance, not only offered their viewers immediate opportunities to feel new depths of irrational energy and feeling – in response to the works themselves – but, perhaps more significantly, also awakened in them an abiding capacity to appreciate the creative potential of the irrational dimensions of their own minds that would have otherwise remained inaccessible to them; it also enabled them to appreciate all kinds of traditional, indigenous arts that would have otherwise seemed 'uncivilised' and 'primitive'. As art became ever more stylised, progressively sacrificing its objects and evolving towards its own dissolution, so its capacity to accommodate unmediated self-awareness increased to the point at which the purest possible art – which only existed, for Malevich and his followers at least, *beyond* art – reflected and accommodated the purest possible realisation of the self, which also only existed in self-transcendence.

Just as the ideal of art had been developed over many centuries to function as the purest and highest form of 'cultural object', so its apparent death or disintegration corresponded to the death or dissolution of the 'cultural subject' – that is, the sense of identity that defined itself in terms of cultural and linguistic conventions. While this sense of personal identity had been newly accommodated in Renaissance art, and had been propagated in states of ever-greater complexity in the cultural forms of subsequent centuries, so those cultural forms were now being dismantled to the extent that they no longer supported it. Artistic conventions developed to such a state of purity and refinement that they evaporated altogether, consummating themselves in self-transcendence and thereby enabling consciousness to arise without being mediated through the prism of personal subjectivity – that is to say, without seeming to arise as a function of the self, or of the sense of 'I'. Conversely, the sense of personal self evolved to such a state of independence from cultural conventions that it ceased to need art as a medium through which to reflect itself to itself and, as a result, it ceased to be identifiable as such. Or so it seemed.

CHAPTER FIVE

The Democratisation of the Self: the Integration of Creative Endeavour into the Fabric of Daily Life and the Death of Art

While Malevich and others drove art towards its own consummation in non-objectivity on the basis of its *internal* logic, the dissolution of art was also precipitated by changes to the *external* contexts – especially the social and political contexts – in which the concept of art arose and acquired meaning. Although by the end of the eighteenth century the subjectivity of artistic experience had been raised to the level of an autonomous absolute, it also functioned in a more relative manner in that it compensated for the sublimation of the sense of personal identity (on the part of non-elite consumers of culture) into the impersonal notion of the 'public'. As we have seen, the notion of the public was institutionalised for the first time in conventions – such as Salon exhibitions and state museums – that promoted the 'public' appreciation and consumption of cultural products. These new conventions conferred cultural value on the bourgeois public as an identifiable group of individuals – in contrast to the uncultivated 'masses', who were largely considered to be disengaged from the cultural process. By the beginning of the nineteenth century, the romantic ideals of 'art' (as a projected medium of self-expressive individuality) and of the 'artist' (as an archetype of the individual self) had been crystallised to complement the impersonal equalising effect of being a member of the 'public' – and arguably, it continues to serve this purpose today, in the sense that people continue to seek experiences that they consider to be more profound or insightful than ordinary everyday experiences via the cultural media of film, music, visual art, theatre, etc.. Indeed, by slow degrees there developed an interdependent relationship between artists and the public that encouraged the two parties to define themselves in relation to each other; they became two sides of the same coin. Artists became increasingly aware that they were working for the benefit of a public audience and sought approval from them, and the public expected artists to realise and express their ideals and feelings more exquisitely than they could express them themselves.

It is no accident that, in Britain, the status of the artist as poet, intellectual and prophet was institutionalised – in the Royal Academy of Arts, founded in 1768 – precisely when its corresponding public was being formed; they functioned co-operatively as source and receptacle respectively. The elevation of the notion of 'fine art' – painting and sculpture – to the level of high culture was also complemented by the relegation of applied art – the manufacture of utilitarian objects – to the other end of the spectrum, where it scarcely had cultural value at all. This circumstance originated in the sixteenth century but was only now acquiring 'critical mass'. It was effected, on the one hand, by the mechanisation of the processes of production culminating in the Industrial Revolution, which erased the element of individuality currently being lionised in the fine arts; and on the other hand, by the production of abundant, cheap, uniform goods which were specifically aimed at a larger, less affluent and less individuated body of consumers. These phenomena did not coincide by chance; they were organically related to each other. Indeed, the notions of the 'individual artist' and 'art' *depended* on their opposites: a group of people who had no significant personal identity, and products which had no significant cultural value. The identity of group members was realised in two ways: firstly, as we have seen, they constituted an 'audience', whereby they aspired to realise themselves at an elevated level by projecting their capacity for personal identity into the archetype of the artist; they did this by imaginatively entering into the artist's creative experience as presented in his work. Secondly, they were 'consumers', whereby they sought to realise themselves, at a more mundane level, by acquiring and owning commodities. These developments constituted ways in which the possibility of personal identity was extended to a vastly increased proportion of the population – not just theoretically, but as a key aspect of their lives; but they also show how access to this possibility was facilitated by public institutions: museums and exhibitions on the one hand, and factories and department stores on the other. It was as members of the public that the majority of individuals were able to express themselves.

With regard to the production of useful everyday objects, the identification of a new 'consumership' was acknowledged in two principal stages. In the first stage, it was reflected in *industrialisation*, which related especially to how objects were made. This development, which led to the mass production of designed, if homogenous goods, was initially directed at the growing bourgeoisie, enabling them to 'fashion' themselves for the first time. Products were designed in traditional decorative styles, often making educated references to historical or cultural sources that retained associations with the nobility. In its second phase, which came to a head at the end of the nineteenth century, the acknowledgement of the public – now widened to include the working class as well as the bourgeoisie – was reflected in the development of the ideal of *functionalism*, which related to how objects were used. Supporters of this trend argued that historicist decoration was applied to objects arbitrarily and meaninglessly, only serving to indulge the vanity of the bourgeoisie and exclude the uneducated lower classes. They maintained that products should be designed in keeping with their function, which is innately accessible to all people, and that decoration for its own sake should be moderated and even eschewed. Just as the coherence of the high-art object, as the manifestation of a transcendental aesthetic ideal, began to dissolve at the end of the nineteenth century (as we have seen in the last chapter), so the desire to enhance mass-produced utilitarian objects by applying aesthetically self-conscious decoration to them was also widely challenged. As the 'forms of art' had evaporated in order to allow the essence of art – life itself – to communicate itself immediately, so, for many progressive commentators, the aesthetic dimension of utilitarian objects became so deeply submitted to, and infused into, their functionality, as reflected in the naturalness and economy of their structures, that it too ceased to operate as an independent phenomenon. In the eyes of those idealists that associated aestheticism with subjective individualism and efficient functionality with social service, this sublimation of the sense of the 'aesthetic' within the 'functional' constituted the ultimate naturalisation of the identity of society as a whole, beyond the aestheticist sense of personal selfhood. It was these changes – partly in the products themselves, but above all in the demography of the people who consumed them – that constituted the greatest cultural and commercial achievement of the nineteenth century. On the one hand, styled commodities became more available to a larger percentage of society, facilitating their self-fashioning; on the other hand, those commodities were increasingly homogenised, limiting it. The painstaking development of the infrastructure of industrial design as an index of collective identity, and the sublimation of aesthetic agendas within that infrastructure – in service to the *public*, but at the expense of *personal* identity – is the subject of this chapter.

The transformation of the rural 'peasantry' into the urban 'working class' was largely brought about by the Industrial Revolution. This change was especially rapid in Britain. Various reasons have been proposed for this precociousness. It has been suggested, for instance, that the insularity of the country necessitated the development of naval skills, which in turn led to travel, trade, colonisation and prosperity. In the same way, the Protestant abolition of 'holy days' (saints' days) in favour of a morally edifying work ethic may have led to increased productivity, wealth and capitalism. The earliest industrial installations were located in rural places of great natural beauty, as they depended on natural sources of power, such as water from waterfalls, and new natural resources – especially coal, often mined in rolling landscapes (Fig. 5.1). They coincided with the development of the notion of the 'picturesque' and were thought by some contemporaries to enhance the sublime appeal of their settings by highlighting and harnessing the elemental power of the land. But, following improvements in the quality of roads and canals, and especially following James Watt's invention of the steam engine (1775), which enabled sources of power to be established away from natural resources, industrial centres began to develop in more tractable land, leading to changes in the material environment of daily life that would alter the parameters of identity definitively. Most noticeably, cities began to grow rapidly. The contribution of industrial enterprises to the romanticisation and objectification of natural beauty now ceased to be due to the way they seemed to enhance the forces of nature by using them in service to mankind. It was increasingly because they seemed to generate the very opposite of nature – goods that were formed by neither man nor nature, but by machine – that they served this role.

Where the possibility of earning a living for most peasants had traditionally been determined by their rural environments – the changing seasons, the weather, the times of day, the availability of local materials – thereby requiring them to interact

FIGURE 5.1: Wilson Lowry, *An Iron Work for Casting of Cannon*, 1788, engraving, 34.6 × 51.8 cm. Yale Center for British Art, Paul Mellon Collection.

very directly and immediately with the natural world, the industrialisation of work in 'manufactories' had the effect of abstracting the conditions of work to the extent that they were no longer affected by the vagaries of nature. All of a sudden, the same work could begin at the same time at the same place every day and, especially when mechanisation became widespread, the daily (and sometimes nightly) programmes of work were increasingly dictated by the operability of machines. Many of these machines were activated at specific times of day, submitting workers to the factory infrastructure and requiring punctual routine behaviour from them. Inevitably, as the factories grew, traditional cottage industries became unsupportable. The traditional method of spinning fibres into thread on a distaff (as seen in numerous medieval images of Eve at work following the expulsion from paradise) could be done anywhere at any time, indoors or out; single-thread spinning wheels were also relatively portable (Fig. 5.2). However, the 'spinning jenny', invented by James Hargreaves in 1765 to accelerate the process by accommodating eight (and eventually many more) spindles at a time, was a more substantial structure (Fig. 5.3). All of these processes used human power and could be used at home for piecework in the evenings and in winter; therefore they did not necessarily disturb traditional patterns of work. But the more productive 'water frame', patented by Richard Arkwright in 1768, relied on water for power and could, therefore, only be used in a factory (Fig. 5.4). Work became increasingly concentrated in factories, and housing was

FIGURE 5.2: Geertruydt Roghman, *Spinning Woman*, 1648–50, engraving, 21.3 × 11.7 cm. Rijksmuseum, Amsterdam.

FIGURE 5.3: Spinning jenny (invented by James Hargreaves, 1764), woodcut, around 1880, Britain.

FIGURE 5.4: Water-frame spinning machine (patented by Richard Arkwright in 1768), early nineteenth century.

accordingly built in the vicinity of the workplace, eventually giving rise to industrial towns (for instance, Manchester and Oldham) and an urban working class. As manufacturing processes became more ambitious and complex, individuals were increasingly required to take responsibility for ever-smaller parts of the overall process of making an object. Different parts of a product or different stages in its production came to be associated with different parts of a factory building, offering workers minimal opportunity to develop a relationship to the product as a whole. As a result, the working class became increasingly disengaged both from the natural environment and from the material culture of everyday life (now divested of the 'individual touch' that had for centuries been an innate feature of the production and use of handcrafted objects). Their role became homogenised in relation to the mass production of uniform goods and, as far as their profile in society was concerned, they were identified as part of the productive masses rather than as individuals.

It is significant that, even though the guilds had relatively little power in Protestant countries, which had stripped them of their religious responsibilities in the sixteenth century, industrial towns in Britain were established in areas that had no traditions of guild power – for instance, Sheffield, Birmingham, Manchester and Leeds. By contrast, medieval towns with histories of guild activity – Salisbury, Gloucester, Lincoln, Canterbury – began to fall into decline. The traditional role of the guilds was superseded by the new role of the 'entrepreneur', a middleman or businessman, who managed workshops or manufactories, mediating between makers and consumers. Richard Arkwright (1733–92), for instance, was just one of several individuals whose inventions, over many years, led to the radical transformation of the textiles industry.

The enormous success of his 'water-frame' spinning machine required him to open a mill (in Cromford, Derbyshire) that not only resulted in an improved product – strong cotton thread – but also led to radically changed lifestyles for both its producers and consumers. The production processes of furniture, metalwork and pottery were similarly revolutionised, by Thomas Chippendale (1718–79), Matthew Boulton (1728–1809) and Josiah Wedgwood (1730–95) respectively, each of whom manufactured an abundance of products in the fashionable neoclassical style. Significantly, the regularity and restraint of neoclassical ornament – especially its narrow bands of repeated motifs – lent themselves well to mechanical production. Although this style was grand, the use of new materials (creamware in place of porcelain, Sheffield plate in place of solid silver) enabled producers to keep the prices down (Fig. 5.5).

In France, efforts had been made since the middle of the eighteenth century to improve the dire economic condition of the country by reconfiguring the social status of manufacture and commerce. While the traditional elite – the nobility – considered it demeaning to be involved in trade (typically preferring to engage in military and courtly pursuits), a growing number of writers attempted to recontextualise commercial activity as a 'noble' practice on the grounds that it was patriotic, requiring makers and traders to place the economic interests of the country before their own interests, in keeping with the neoclassical ideal of self-sacrifice. This perspective extended the possibility of nobility to a new sector in society, thereby challenging the aristocracy's traditional monopoly of the determinants of honourable status. However, although British acceptance of this point of view was cited as one of the factors that accounted for the commercial superiority of Great Britain, French politicians continued to seek personal dignity in aloof superiority, and the scope for commercial expansion, therefore, remained limited. An effort to

FIGURE 5.5: Fly-pressed Sheffield plate salt cellar, revealing a copper body beneath the silver plating, 1785–90, Sheffield, length: 9.1 cm. Victoria and Albert Museum, London, M.147-1912.

break this deadlock was made in 1776 when the controller general of finance (and prophet of progress) Anne-Robert-Jacques Turgot attempted to abolish the all-powerful craft guilds, which monopolised every aspect of the production and distribution of commodities in France and had tight control over their members. He failed, however, for while the guilds protected craftsmen against competition and maintained high standards of quality control, they also had vested interests in maintaining the status quo and they therefore stifled innovation, expansion and free trade. Indeed, as a significant source of revenue for the crown, they were integrally involved in the power structures of the *ancien régime*. It was not, therefore, until the French Revolution in 1789, when the regime itself collapsed, that the guild system in France was finally abolished, abandoning craftsmen to their fate and opening up the French market to progressive innovations that had been developed elsewhere. This shift also undermined the monopoly that the guilds had over the teaching of technical craft skills, by means of the system of apprenticeships. While the guilds were usually family based and highly nepotistic, post-revolutionary regulations relocated such teaching to new technical schools that were developed to serve the education of the public as a whole.

Although the Industrial Revolution is called a 'revolution', it was only revolutionary in its impact, not in its focused purposefulness, nor in its temporal intensity or suddenness. In fact, it unfolded over many decades – from the 1730s onwards – as an innovation in one area (e.g. an increased rate of production) required innovations in others (e.g. an improved supply of materials, or improved quality of roads), until every stage in the process of production and consumption had been transformed. As the various links in the chain were gradually subjected to industrialisation, the material culture of daily life began to change. By slow degrees, objects came to be made more quickly, more cheaply, more precisely and in greater abundance. The consequences of these changes were vast. The increased speed and reduced cost of producing objects in vast quantities meant that more commodities could be made, and that they could be sold more cheaply. Both of these outcomes implicitly empowered a larger number of less affluent people to become consumers of cultural commodities and, therefore, to participate in the cultural process of identity formation through self-styling. The very possibility of choosing commodities made new space for the exercising of free will and the feeling of personal power. In such circumstances, conspicuous consumption could no longer be monopolised by the affluent elite, who had traditionally used it to differentiate themselves from the rest of society; it now became one of the primary media through which members of the public strove to define themselves.

But while mechanical production increased the scope for personal self-expression, it also subjected individuals to conditions that developed in relation to the group as a whole. For although it led to an increased number of commodities, it also made them more uniform. The technical perfection and repeatability of machine-made products erased the tactile signature of individuality, concealing all signs of the source of their production and thereby rendering them impersonal. Partly as a result of this shift, the status and livelihood of craftsmen (unprotected in France from 1789, as we have seen) declined; but the identities of the users of objects were also affected. By eliminating all visible traces of difference from products, users were implicitly identified not

FIGURE 5.6: Wedgwood and Byerley showroom, York Street, St James's Square, from Ackermann's Repository of the Arts, 1809. Private collection.

as individuals engaging with unique objects, but as a homogenous, uniform group engaging with standardised objects. Both factory workers and consumers were constructed as instruments of collective social forces, rather than as individuals to be identified by the uniqueness of their sensations. The experience of consumption was further generalised by the development of showrooms, shops and department stores, which replaced transient, seasonal markets (Fig. 5.6). That commodities could be predictably standardised made it viable to produce accurate printed design books and catalogues from which they could be preordered (Fig. 5.7). As the members of the public became increasingly involved in the consumption of machine-made products, so they became less and less able and inclined to construct their identities, as projected into their possessions and personal environments, without surrendering to the dictates of public taste. Thus, although the Industrial Revolution nurtured the impulse in individuals to articulate a personal sense of self in relation to society as a whole – by providing an increased number and range of affordable styled commodities – it also frustrated this impulse by homogenising those commodities.

Especially in Britain, the mechanisation of the processes of producing domestic commodities was frequently cited as the cause of a drastic decline in the quality of their design and manufacture, which was visible in the objects themselves. This view would eventually lead to calls for design reform, but in the meantime, what it overlooked was the fact that – invisible in the individual objects – mechanical production made culturally charged commodities available to a vastly increased number of consumers for the first time. People whose families had, one hundred years earlier, worn indistinct, undyed clothes of linen and wool, and used uniform utensils made of earthenware, base metal and wood, could now afford to wear styled, colour-printed cottons and eat from handsome silver and porcelain substitutes

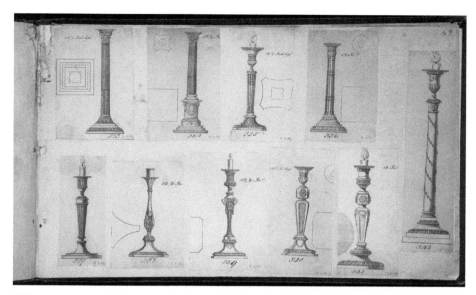

FIGURE 5.7: Book of designs for silver items, including etchings of designs for candlesticks published by Matthew Boulton, c. 1790, engravings on paper, bound in cloth, 23 × 37.5 cm. Victoria and Albert Museum, London, E.2060-1952.

(Fig. 5.8). However, what was gained in the quantity of styled goods was seen by many to be lost in quality. Notwithstanding the ecological and health-related fallout of the Industrial Revolution, which was not fully appreciated until well into the nineteenth century, it was argued that social and economic progress was made at the expense of aesthetic progress. The reason for this perceived decline was not entirely commercial; it also reflected changes in taste. Because middle-class consumers had little history of visual education behind them, they were not in a position to indulge the theatre of discriminating connoisseurship that the nobility traditionally considered to be their birthright. Thus, although several established styles of decoration continued to be popular, they were often enjoyed with little understanding of their original associations. Indeed, the eclecticism of the later nineteenth century may have owed something to the bourgeoisie's relative lack of knowledge of, and interest in, the specific associations of historical styles, in favour of their purely aesthetic, economic and status-related associations. The classical style, for instance, had been used by the aristocracy throughout the seventeenth and eighteenth centuries due to its associations with antiquity, dignity, rationalism, grandeur and education. Rococo, chinoiserie and 'Gothick', by contrast, were promoted in the mid-eighteenth century as evocative and irrational *alternatives* to rational classicism. Reacting in turn against the unprincipled triviality of the rococo, neoclassicism attempted to reinstate some the dignity of the classical style. However, as 'grand tourists' began to venture beyond classical Italy to the lands of other ancient civilisations – for instance, Egypt and Mesopotamia – their erudition was shrouded in the atmosphere of esoteric and hieratic cults that resonated as much with the

FIGURE 5.8: François David Soiron, *A Tea Garden*, 1790, stipple engraving, printed in colour, 47 × 54.3 cm. Yale Centre for British Art, Paul Mellon Collection.

romantic imagination as it did with classical antiquarianism. Each of these styles expressed a distinct sensibility, clearly reflecting the personal taste and character of its patron. But as they became common in the nineteenth century, their particular associations were diluted and they came to be used indiscriminately. Household items could be ordered in any or all of these styles and more. Indeed, as the middle classes became ever more psychologically inclined (and financially able) to fashion their identities, so the significance of the various different styles was lost on them, and the choice of style became more whimsical than knowledgeable, to the point at which eclecticism became a style in itself.

By the 1820s, the downside of industrial progress began to reveal itself – the inhumane working conditions and the impoverished quality of factory-made products – and measures were taken to reform it. Efforts to introduce formal education to ever-broader sections of society created 'cultural space' for a phase of life between childhood and adulthood – the 'teenage' years – and all the signs of individuation associated with it. This development brought to an end an era in which children had been made to work as soon as they were able to. Attention was also put on the aesthetic environment, not least because it was increasingly believed to have a morally improving effect on people. These changes were part of a wide range of social reforms (relating to education, voting, legal rights, sanitation, etc.) that were introduced in all industrialising countries to improve the lot of the underprivileged majority of working people. In Britain, concern for the aesthetic environment was also prompted by the perception that French and German factory products were of a higher quality than British ones, due to the training of factory workers in the rudiments of design. As a result, the design and manufacture of mass-produced goods was slowly invested with new cultural potential, paving the way for the radical challenge to the elevated notion of 'fine art' that the vision of a fully 'integrated creativity' would unleash towards the end of the century. This shift was directly reflected in changing attitudes towards education. Indeed, it was primarily through developments on this front – to the extent that, by the end of the century, state-funded education was universally available in industrialised countries – that the possibility of participation in the cultural process ceased to be an exclusive privilege and became available to all.

Educational reforms were based on the romantic ideal of the individual as an independent subject of experience – born innocent and free, rather than guilty and fatally flawed on account of original sin. It was in the light of this ideal, originally promoted by John Locke in the seventeenth century, that all individuals – not just the hereditary nobility – were believed to be worthy and capable of education, both for their own sakes and to maximise their value to society as a whole through work. In the nineteenth century, especially as industrial processes became established and the traditional system of guild apprenticeships fell into abeyance, a new type of practical education, conceived to meet the new demands of mechanical engineering, became necessary. At first, local working men's societies and 'Mechanics Institutes' were created, providing lectures on technical subjects for working people; in 1823, a Mechanics Institute was set up in London by the pioneer of a national movement, George Birkbeck, after whom the London institution was later renamed. Besides empowering an entirely new sector of society, the development of practical training schemes reflected a new ascription of cultural value to technical knowledge, at the expense of the intellectual curriculum on which the traditional structures of authority were based. It was rooted in the practical possibilities of nature and reason, rather than the high-minded idealism of the classical tradition, and as such it made steps towards reducing the polarisation that had existed since the Renaissance between the poetic status of fine art and the perceived banality of utilitarian production. Because industrial processes were orientated towards the design and production of functional objects rather than the artistic representation of objective phenomena for its own sake, they also led to the development of a new visual language that revolved around the technical relationships between the component parts of an image rather than its potential as fodder for the imagination. This initiative put a new premium on precision, and gave rise to a vocabulary of functional, rather than aesthetic, forms (Fig. 5.9). It is arguable that, over many years, such forms habituated viewers to the visual vocabulary of abstraction – long before the notion of abstraction was conceived and formed into its own language – and, as such, they constitute a key but much neglected part of the prehistory of abstract art and modernism.

Especially in early nineteenth-century France and Germany, new schools were set up specifically to train individuals to work in industry. Besides aiming to improve the

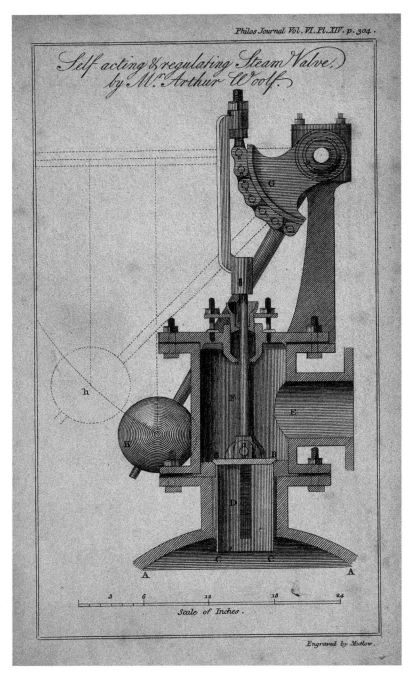

FIGURE 5.9: A self-acting and regulating steam valve, by Mr. Arthur Woolf. Engraved by Mutlow (active 1808–40), plate to *The Philosophical Journal*, Vol. VI. Pl. XIV. p. 304, Wellcome Collection.

quality of products, these institutions contributed to the development of an aesthetic sensibility among the manufacturing classes that enabled them to participate more self-consciously in the cultural process. The institutions also ensured that the aesthetic dimension of everyday life was, by slow degrees, reinvested with the possibility of cultural value that had hitherto been monopolised by 'high art'. In France, where the tradition of academic painting was especially strong, schools that taught drawing to limited numbers of artisans had existed since the middle of the eighteenth century (often in manufacturing towns such as Dijon and Lyon), but their programmes stressed the importance of artistic values and usually included significant amounts of academic drawing.[1] In the Royal Free Drawing School in Paris, founded in 1766, classes in technical, rather than academic, drawing were introduced for the first time in 1810.[2] Moreover, reflecting the growing need for a new kind of workforce – too large to be supplied from within the family tradition – there also developed a drive to teach the rudiments of technical knowledge, not just as professional training but as part of the mainstream curriculum of elementary schools, where it would be able to become a part of the mentality of every pupil. Both in principle and method, this drive paralleled the educational programmes that Victor Cousin was introducing across France at the very same time, to instil a sense of *moi* in the bourgeosie (see page 75). In 1819, the mathematician and engineer Louis-Benjamin Francoeur (1773–1849) published a manual of 'lineal drawing' (*Le dessin linéaire d'après la méthode de l'enseignement mutuel*) that aimed to teach all middle- and lower-class children in France how to make accurate freehand drawings of geometrical figures, partly with a view to applying them in the context of a practical trade (Fig. 5.10). In the manual, Francoeur stated that:

> the Art of Lineal Drawing, the faculty of estimating proportions by the eye alone, and of tracing them on paper, would be a useful acquirement in most of the occupations of the middling and lower classes of society, but its direct advantages are perhaps not so important as the habit it encourages of accuracy and precision, which, when acquired in youth, in any one instance, usually extends its influence over the general character.

He also acknowledged that 'the art of Lineal Drawing may not contribute as much as the power of reading and writing, to improve the moral sense; but it is perhaps more conducive than these to the prosperity of industry, to the practical success of each individual in his trade'.[3]

Francoeur's system advocated that, following the example of a teacher at the front of a classroom, pupils should copy a prescribed sequence of geometrical models, progressing from simple lines to flat shapes, eventually culminating in complex three-dimensional forms (Fig. 5.11). In German-speaking lands, by contrast, a more liberal and morally orientated tradition was developed. This was partly due to the influence of the poet and writer Friedrich Schiller, who advocated in 1794 that the only remedy for the social ills that caused the idealism of the French Revolution to collapse into anarchy and terror was the 'aesthetic education' of man – that is to say, the cultivation of his instinct for 'play' that balanced his sensual and intellectual instincts. Schiller's identification of the moral potential of aesthetic experience was important in that it set a precedent for cultivating visual awareness,

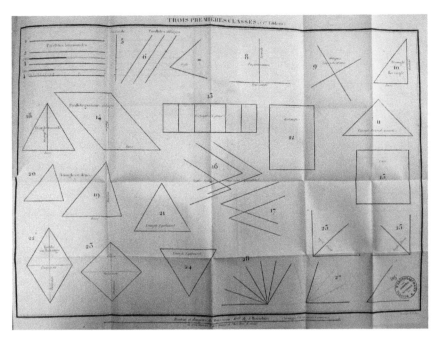

FIGURE 5.10: Straight lines and simple geometrical shapes from *Le dessin linéaire* by Louis-Benjamin Francoeur, 1839, third edition. Bibliothèque de la Société d'encouragement.

FIGURE 5.11: Winslow Homer, *Blackboard* (exercise in linear drawing after Francoeur), 1877, watercolour on woven paper, 50.2 × 32.4 cm. National Gallery of Art, Washington, gift of Jo Ann and Julian Ganz, Jr., in honour of the fiftieth anniversary of the National Gallery of Art.

not only among the privileged consumers of fine art, but among all members of society, whether they were destined to work in industry or not, on the grounds that it would lead to social cohesion and personal fulfilment.

In a practical educational context, this morally orientated view was espoused by the Swiss educational reformer Johann Heinrich Pestalozzi (1746–1827), who is often considered to be the father of modern education. Pestalozzi was inspired by Rousseau's *Emile, or On Education* of 1762 to advocate that children of all classes could and should be educated naturally and organically by 'guided play' rooted in sense perception. Each child was to be nurtured, in keeping with his or her varying capacities, rather than indoctrinated with preconceived ideas from books, as in traditional schools; the memorisation and recitation of moralising texts, enforced by the threat of punishment, was abolished. As an extension of this view, advocates of vocational training maintained that students, including those preparing to work in industry, did not need to be trained in academic life drawing, as prescribed in French design schools and at academies of painting; they needed to be trained in the practical skills of measurement, mathematics, perspective, etc.. Independent 'trade schools' were established expressly for this purpose. This approach was partly inspired by the romantic belief that nature itself was spontaneously and inherently disposed to produce coherent, rational structures, as demonstrated throughout the natural world, and that it was, therefore, unnecessary to contrive them on the basis of a classical ideal; on the contrary, it was simply necessary to be as aligned to nature as possible and thereby to function as an extension of nature.

It was in direct response to the example of nature that one of the most lasting benefits of the educational reforms – the kindergarten – came into being. The kindergarten system was conceived in Germany by one of Pestalozzi's followers, Friedrich Froebel (1782–1852), who in the 1820s designed a series of basic educational object-toys to facilitate the process of organic exploratory learning (Fig. 5.12). These objects, which Froebel called 'gifts', were conceived to help very young children develop their faculties on the basis of their natural curiosity and as a direct result of their physical sensations, perceptions and observations. While the 'gifts' were designed as simple geometrical forms and shapes to enable children to develop empirical knowledge of such simple properties as unity and difference, motion and stability (Fig. 5.13), they also reflected Froebel's five years of work as a crystallographer in the Museum of Mineralogy at the University in Berlin (Fig. 5.14). This training had convinced Froebel that all developmental processes – from those of abstract crystalline forms to those of human beings – occur as organic functions of nature, subject to the capacities of the materials involved, rather than as the outcome of pursuing artificial, abstracted ideals. Moreover, besides enabling children to develop natural and practical foundations of knowledge, they were also used to help children develop a sensitivity to beauty, especially as manifest in the intelligence of natural forms, and to become instruments of natural beauty through their own creativity (Fig. 5.15). After many years of experimentation, in 1837, Froebel opened his first school for very young children in Bad Blankenburg, near Weimar; in 1840, he coined the term 'kindergarten', reflecting his vision of the school both as a garden *for* children and as a garden *of* children, allowing children to 'grow' in a natural and naturally structured way, like flowers.[4]

FIGURE 5.12: Friedrich Froebel's 'second gift': a cube, cylinder and sphere, conceived in 1836, produced by J. W. Schermerhorn & Co., New York, around 1890, Norman Brosterman Collection.

Pestalozzi first applied his principles in a school context in 1799; six years later, he opened his own school at Yverdon, near Lausanne, from where his ideas were disseminated all over Europe. The first state to take full advantage of this initiative was Prussia. Sorely stung by its defeat by Napoleon at the Battle of Jena in 1806, Prussia was intent on rebuilding its national dignity from the ground upwards. In 1808, the Prussian Department of Public Instruction sent seventeen teachers to study for three years with Pestalozzi in Switzerland, with a view to revolutionising and nationalising its educational system. By 1840 there were an estimated 30,000 elementary schools in Prussia, feeding the vocational 'trade schools' that were also opening all over the country to serve German industry.

In early nineteenth-century Britain, the influence of progressive ideas from the continent, both about the education of children and about the training of designers, was impeded by the Napoleonic Wars, which limited travel in Europe, and by the overall resistance of the British ruling class to social change. Although Pestalozzi's vision of education as an organic process was introduced to Britain by 1820,[5] it was not until the mid-1830s, when the threat of competition from France and Germany began to loom large, that the government first took steps to promote training in technical design on a national scale. Britain had led the world in industrial production for many years, but the actual quality of its products was increasingly perceived to be inferior to that of continental wares. In 1837, therefore, the first state-run design school, the Government School of Design, was founded. William Dyce, the first superintendent of the school, was commissioned to travel to Europe to research

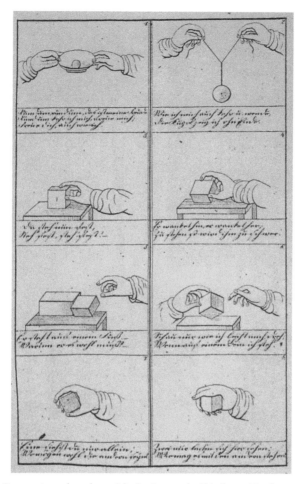

FIGURE 5.13: Suggestions for play with the 'second gift', from *Ein Sonntagsblatt . . . von Friedrich Fröbel*. No. 9, 25 February 1838. Norman Brosterman Collection.

French and German schools with a view to implementing their methods in Britain. Dyce's experience directed his attention towards the technical rather than the aesthetic dimension of design and gave rise to his *Drawing Book of the Government School of Design; or, Elementary Outlines of Ornament*, published in 1843. Like Francoeur, whose book of 'lineal drawing' was translated into English in 1824, Dyce encouraged students not to attempt to draw objects in a representational way, with a view to transferring such designs, as decorative motifs, on to independently conceived forms, but to copy flat geometrical shapes of increasing complexity, with a view to learning the fundamental language of graphics (Fig. 5.16). But, unlike Francoeur, he did not recommend that they progress to three-dimensional forms. On the contrary, he insisted that they continue working on flat forms, but develop

FIGURE 5.14: Wooden models of twinned feldspar crystals, Gustaf Eduard Kayser, 1834, Berlin, 18.5 × 10.1 × 1.6 cm. Presented by Kayser to his teacher, Christian Samuel Weiss (who was also Froebel's teacher). Photo with permission: Virtual Museum of the History of Mineralogy. www.mineralogy.eu.

them to ever-greater levels of interest by abstracting new designs from historical models (which had already reduced nature to regular ornamental motifs). His reason for this was his belief that artefacts should not be decorated with naturalistic representations of objects, independently conceived like works of art and applied to the artefacts in question regardless of their particular character, but that they should be conceived in direct relation to those artefacts, and indeed that they should, at least to some extent, be a function of them, as they had been among ancient civilisations. The aesthetic principle that informed such objects was not a product of *artistic* inspiration (to which a variety of irrelevant privileges and preconceptions could be attached); on the contrary, it was organically and objectively determined by their form, function and materials. As such, it challenged the hegemony of artistic genius (which was predicated on aesthetic excellence). In this respect, Dyce's views reflected the pragmatic and organic orientation of the German system, which was geared towards producing designs for manufacture at the expense of naturalistic figure drawing. They also embodied an ethical dimension, maintaining that designers were morally obliged to submit to the objective conditions of the

FIGURE 5.15: Friedrich Froebel's designs for 'beauty and knowledge forms' of the 'fifth gift', from *Ein Sonntagsblatt . . . von Friedrci Fröbel* (*A Sunday Paper for the Like-Minded*), Vol II, 1838–40. Norman Brosterman Collection.

artefacts they were designing – their form, function and materials – on the grounds that such 'truth to materials' signified a kind of moral transparency and honesty. To apply decoration to an object without paying attention to its form or function, or to apply ornament that concealed the techniques used to produce it, was considered deceitful; carpets, for instance, should be decorated with geometrical ornament to convey a sense of the hard flatness of the floor beneath them.[6] The extent to which 'aesthetic dishonesty' in the domestic interior was believed to be capable of inducing

FIGURE 5.16: William Dyce, *Elementary Outlines of Ornament*, 1842–3, London, lithograph, ink on paper, mounted on card, 31 × 37.2 cm. Victoria and Albert Museum, London.

immoral thoughts and actions in people was expressed by Sir Robert William Edis in 1883:

> If you are content to teach a lie in your belongings, you can hardly wonder at petty deceits being practised in other ways . . . All this carrying into everyday life of 'the shadow of unreality' must exercise a bad and prejudicial influence on the younger members of the house, who are thus brought up to see no wrong in the shams and deceits which are continually before them.[7]

Dyce's insistence on submission to classical precedents (no matter how abstracted he allowed them to become) eventually hardened into a turgid and unforgiving formula, devoid of the 'natural morality' that he had hoped his system would embody; it was much disliked by students and bitterly opposed by advocates of more 'artistic' methods which eventually replaced it. Nevertheless, his impulse to improve the design of household goods on moral grounds was taken up by William Morris and pioneers of the Arts and Crafts Movement in England, in reaction to what they considered to be the meaningless and self-indulgent eclecticism and ornamentalism of High Victorian taste – a lack of principle which, at the other extreme from Dyce, resulted from an excessive tolerance of 'artistry' in the design education process. In 1849, Henry Cole, later director of the South Kensington Museum, expressed a degree of sympathy for Dyce's systematic approach when he described a dessert plate that he particularly disliked as being 'from the design of a pupil taught at the School of Design, where it is evident he could not have learned even the ABC of his profession – the rim is pure Louis Quatorze, the ornament of an Alhambra character, and the centre of the Italian school – forcible evidence of imperfect education in the designer'.[8]

In place of the fussy, undiscriminating juxtaposition of Egyptian, classical, Chinese, rococo and other historic and exotic styles that were so proudly but tastelessly exhibited to all the world at the Great Exhibition (the first International Trade Fair, held in Hyde Park in London in 1851), Morris advocated a new simplicity and integrity in the design of the domestic environment. He rejected the application of random ornament to randomly decorative but often impractical forms – not least because such forms served to cover a seething mass of social injustices with a thin veneer of cultured respectability – calling instead for a return to a simple functionality, and 'truth to materials'. He rejected the use of exotic imported materials, such as lacquer and mahogany, which were both unecological (wasting energy and depleting natural resources) and antisocial (using remote, anonymous labourers for demeaning work), in favour of indigenous materials, such as oak and elm, worked by local craftsmen. And by refusing to conceal how an object was constructed – indeed, by making a feature of its construction rather than hiding it behind irrelevant, 'deceitful' ornamentation – he promoted what he believed to be a more 'honest' and morally transparent approach to cultural and social life (Fig. 5.17). Objects were not to be mass produced by machines, a circumstance that he considered to be degrading to both workers and consumers alike because it depersonalised and automated them. They were to be handcrafted by skilled individuals, who would be involved in every part of the creative process, thereby restoring to manual work the dignity and cultural value that it had begun to lose in the Renaissance, when painting was elevated from the level of a technical craft to the level of a poetic, 'liberal' art at its expense. Morris articulated this ideal as a revival of the indigenous traditions of craftsmanship that had fallen foul of the Industrial Revolution. Indeed, his original source of inspiration was the tradition of medieval craftsmanship, and many of the earliest objects that were made to serve the Arts and Crafts cause were, therefore,

FIGURE 5.17: Table, designed by Philip Webb, made by Morris, Marshall and Faulkner, owned by Edward Burne-Jones, around 1865, oak, 73.7 × 165 × 59.8 cm. Victoria and Albert Museum, London.

designed in a neo-medieval Gothic style. This was largely because the Gothic style was considered to be a morally upright style on account of the perceived piety of medieval art, most of which seemed to have been executed, and patronised, by the Church. This piety, therefore, was considered to have been integral to the practice of true craftsmanship until it was sullied by the sophisticated rationalising effect of Renaissance secularity. The Gothic style had not had this association when it was first revived in the middle of the eighteenth century. At that time, it was associated – somewhat playfully – with mystery, imagination and sublimity (not to mention national identity).[9] But in the 1820s, its moral implications were fervently promoted. This was largely due to the efforts of the Gothic revivalist architect A. W. N. Pugin, whose observation of the fact that the Gothic style was originally an expression of Catholic rather than Protestant culture was so strong that he felt compelled, in 1834, to convert to Roman Catholicism. It was as if religious conversion was the natural and necessary outcome of his appreciation of the style. In doing this, he was participating in the rehabilitation of Catholicism, which had been destigmatised or 'emancipated' in Britain five years earlier – three centuries after its suppression in the Reformation. Because, in Protestant Britain, Catholicism was associated with the medieval *past* (as it was not in Catholic Italy, France and Spain), it seemed desirable and even obligatory to Pugin to promote use of the Gothic style, not merely as a change of taste, but as the *revival* – after three hundred years of deprivation – of a cultural orientation that he considered to be morally upright, inspired and accessible to all.

Although the medieval style was revived to herald a return to a mode of working that was relevant to the present day, it was, of course, an exotic, historic style, like the styles it challenged, and it was not long, therefore, before it too was eventually rejected as a form of derivative eclecticism. Moreover, Morris's insistence on time-consuming craftsmanship had the ironic effect of raising the prices of simple handmade goods beyond the reach of the ordinary householder. The medieval revival did, however, leave a powerful legacy: principally that there is an ethical dimension to the manufacture and consumption of household goods, and that products should be conceived to empower and ennoble the whole of society, rather than alienate and humiliate a majority of them. It was this conviction that motivated progressive designers to pursue further reforms in the latter part of the nineteenth century. Such reforms were not manifestly articulated as an expression of religious belief. What replaced the moralising rationale provided by the romanticised ideal of medieval integrity was the notion that human creativity is *natural* and, following Darwin, evolutionary. Indeed, in the most advanced cases, human creativity was considered to be an extension of natural processes, in exactly the same way that a cobweb or a honeycomb is created by natural processes (as we have also seen in relation to contemporary theories of history). To some extent, the Arts and Crafts concept of 'truth to materials' – working materials in keeping with their own capacities, rather than imposing preconceived designs on them – already invested nature with some power to determine the outcome of human productivity; but the movement's continued use of images as ornament – for instance, stylised depictions of plant forms (Fig. 5.18) – gave it a representational dimension that differentiated its products from natural phenomena.

FIGURE 5.18: Dish, John Pearson, 1890, copper, 61.5 cm. Victoria and Albert Museum, London.

The notion that the most 'truthful' form and decoration of an artefact is naturally and objectively determined by the artefact itself, rather than by a random preconceived idea, became one of the most strongly held ideals of the design reform movement in Britain. It was supported theoretically on the grounds that nature is objectively true, in the sense that it pre-exists human intervention; it constitutes what is spontaneously 'born' (*natus*, in Latin) into the world, rather than what is 'made' by man. And it was supported morally on the grounds that, because it was implicitly created by God, it must also be good. Above all, by being subjected to the laws of nature – including both the 'natural world' (as manifest in the materials used in the production of objects) and the 'nature' of the objects themselves (as manifest in their functions) – such designs were believed to be derived from an inherently 'true' principle. Some reformers took a moderate view of this principle, advocating that objects should be decorated with motifs that were simply *related* to their function or materials. For instance, it was acceptable to decorate a vase with water lilies or bulrushes, but not sunflowers, because water lilies and bulrushes were naturally related to water (Fig. 5.19). With regard to the domestic interior, it was unacceptable to decorate a carpet with flowers because it was unacceptable, in

FIGURE 5.19: 'Well Spring' carafe, Richard Redgrave, designed and conceived in 1847, made in 1851 for Felix Summerly's Art Manufactures, glass, painted in enamel, 26 × 13 cm. Victoria and Albert Museum, London.

nature, to tread on flowers. Plants could be used on wallpaper because, in that medium, they could at least grow upwards; irrelevant iconography, ranging from exotic flowers that do not grow in Britain to battle scenes and railway stations, should not be used, though the latter (Fig. 5.20) were, lamentably, popular in boys' bedrooms. Indeed, it was more appropriate and natural for the decoration of wallpapers to be flat, because walls are flat; to give wallpaper designs undue depth was to detract from the spatial coherence and integrity of the interior as a whole.

The interest in the flatness of picture surfaces had originally developed in tandem with the revival of medieval and early Renaissance art. As we have seen, it both inspired and was inspired by the mid-nineteenth-century reappraisal of the painting of this period (as promoted by Pugin in Britain and Flandrin in France). But it was also precipitated by the revival of interest in medieval craft techniques. The stylisation of medieval imagery had to some degree been determined by the media in which it was realised (none of which could achieve the degree of realism that was later made possible by oil painting). Accordingly, it was now reinvested with appeal by the rehabilitation of those media, such as champlevé enamel, woodcut printing, embroidery and stained glass (common in bourgeois houses of the period), which had largely been forgotten in the intervening years on account of their stiffness (Fig. 5.21). Significantly, the working circumstances in which these crafts were traditionally taught and practised were also revived, indicating the extent to which

FIGURE 5.20: Wallpaper design decorated with perspective views of a railway station, around 1853, made by Potters of Darwen, Lancashire, colour woodblock print on paper, 50.5 × 53 cm. Victoria and Albert Museum, London.

the ethos that was projected into the products was equally projected into the lifestyle (of making and using) that they presupposed. Craftsmen assembled and worked together in 'guilds' – for instance, John Ruskin's Guild of St. George (1871), Arthur Mackmurdo's Century Guild (1882) and Charles Robert Ashbee's Guild of Handicraft (1888). 'Sororities' of Christian women formed to produce medieval-style embroideries, harking back to the communities of devotional laywomen that thrived in the late Middle Ages.

Despite the legitimising association of flatness and stylisation with the religiosity of medieval art, efforts were also made to justify these features on their own terms. One of the first people to make a case for flatness in design was the designer and architect Owen Jones (1809–74). Jones was initially inspired, in the eclectic manner characteristic of his time, by Islamic art, which he celebrated in his *Plans, Elevations, Sections and Details of the Alhambra* of 1836–45. He was attracted to this source partly because, as Islam is an iconoclastic religion (avoiding the use of figurative

FIGURE 5.21: 'Music', from the series *King René's Honeymoon*, designed by Dante Gabriel Rossetti, for Morris and Co, around 1863, stained glass, 64.2 × 54.7 cm. Victoria and Albert Museum, London.

imagery), its art was an abundant source of flat, ornamental motifs, and partly because it was not, in his time, laden with ideological associations (unlike classical or medieval art). However, in his *Grammar of Ornament* of 1856, in which he attempted to propagate his ideas among a wide range of manufacturers, Owen downplayed the authority of traditional cultures such as Islam, prioritising the example of 'Leaves and Flowers from Nature' as the most important source. In fact, although *Grammar of Ornament* is a compendium of historical styles of ornamentation – from ancient Egyptian and Roman to Islamic, Indian, medieval and Renaissance – these styles were not offered as models to be imitated for their own sakes (Fig. 5.22). They were given as demonstrations of the ways in which all great cultures have developed their ornamental languages by adapting the forms of *nature*, albeit in ways that have been uniquely appropriate to their own climate and cultural needs. Jones was hoping that,

FIGURE 5.22: Owen Jones, original drawing for *Grammar of Ornament* (Moresque No. 5), published 1856, 54.1 × 36.0 cm. Victoria and Albert Museum, London.

inspired by these eminent precedents, a new era of distinctly British contemporary design, primarily based on natural sources, might be inaugurated.

Jones's views were taken a step further by his greatest protégé, Christopher Dresser (1834–1904). Dresser was a student and then a teacher at the Government School of Design, and he produced one of the illustrations, examining the botanical structures of plants, for Jones's *Grammar of Ornament* (Fig. 5.23). While inheriting his teacher's insistence that ornamentation should be naturally appropriate both to the form and function of the objects it adorned and to the environment to which it contributed, Dresser also advocated that naturalness did not consist in *representing* natural phenomena, realistically or otherwise – because such an act of representation was in itself unnatural – but that it consisted of *behaving in a natural way*. Thus, for a designer to work as naturally as, for instance, a spider did not involve making or representing a spider's web; it simply involved acting spontaneously in an equivalent

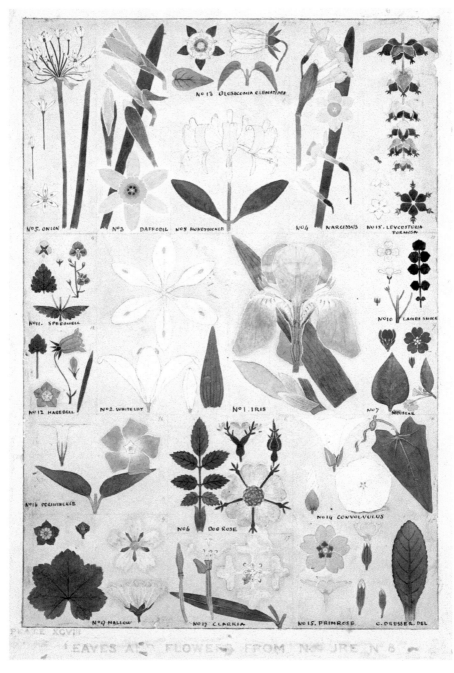

FIGURE 5.23: Christopher Dresser, original drawing for *Grammar of Ornament* ('Leaves & Flowers No. 8'), published 1856, 52.8 × 36.5 cm. Victoria and Albert Museum, London.

way – in keeping with his own nature. The designed outcome of this naturalness was no more required to resemble or represent a cobweb – or anything at all – than a cobweb is required to resemble or represent anything. In order to substantiate this notion, Dresser sought to abstract the natural principles of botany and apply them to the process of product design. As a young man, he had studied botany at the Government School under Richard Redgrave,[10] and in 1860 he was awarded a doctorate from the University of Jena, a leading university for the study of natural sciences, for his work on Goethe's studies of plant morphology. In his pioneering work *An Attempt to Explain the Metamorphosis of Plants* (1790), Goethe had attempted to identify the principles that govern the development of form in plants, establishing not only that the forms of plants were coherently structured, but also that they developed in ways that were themselves invested with cohesive and constructive principles that implicitly linked all plants to each other.[11] Especially following the publication of Darwin's *On the Origin of Species* in 1859, when the notion of evolution became mainstream, Dresser developed the view that the very process of design was itself a natural 'evolutionary' process and that, just as the structures of plants were spontaneous manifestations of the hidden principles of plant formation, so the most elevated and 'purely ideal' kind of ornament was 'wholly a creation of the soul . . . an offspring of the inner man'.[12] In his book *The Art of Decorative Design*, published in 1862, he argued that the highest form of ornament did not imitate or reproduce works of nature (the first and lowest grade of ornament); nor did it stylise them in accordance with a perfect ideal (the second grade); nor indeed was it required to be symbolic in any way. On the contrary, it was 'utterly an embodiment of mind in form', 'embodying in form a mental idea which has been suggested by nature, and yet the form neither represents any actually existing object nor any intention of nature'.

As an example of the way in which the design of an object should be determined by its materials and function, rather than an abstracted idea, Dresser paid special attention to the centre of gravity in objects. For instance, he observed how traditional water vessels designed to be carried on the head (as in ancient Greece) were made wider at the top than at the base because their high centres of gravity made them easier to balance (Fig. 5.24, right). For equivalent reasons, vessels designed to hang down from a handle held in the hand were wider at the bottom (Fig. 5.24, left). He then abstracted this principle and applied it to his own work. For instance, he placed the handle and spout on a jug in relation to its centre of gravity – rather than in imitation of, say, a Roman ewer (a popular form in the early nineteenth century) – to ensure that it poured well (Fig. 5.25). In connection with a characteristic soup tureen that he designed in 1880, he explained that the moulding around its circumference was not simply an ornamental detail with historical associations; it was intended to add strength to the bowl of the tureen to prevent it from buckling (just as a sharp fold in a flimsy piece of paper gives it an axis of stiffness), while also allowing it to remain thin, thereby keeping the quantity and cost of the metal down (Fig. 5.26). By seeking the design rationale for an object within its materials and function in this way, Dresser was subtly devaluing ornamental associations in favour of technical efficiency. Indeed, some of his designs are almost entirely undecorated (Fig. 5.27). Despite the fact that these precocious pieces are rooted in natural principles rather than mathematical

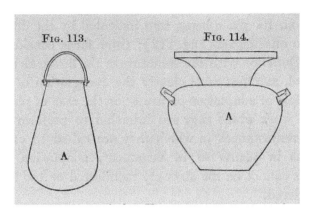

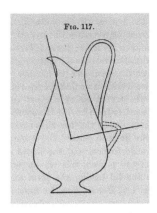

FIGURE 5.24: Christopher Dresser, *The Art of Decorative Design*, London, 1862, p. 130.

FIGURE 5.25: Christopher Dresser, *The Art of Decorative Design*, London, 1862, p. 136.

FIGURE 5.26: Bowl, designed by Christopher Dresser, 1879. Victoria and Albert Museum, London.

calculation, and despite their subtle references to Japanese art, it is impossible to trace them back to a source of inspiration in plant forms or in an earlier design.

Dresser's sensitivity to the materials, function and context of objects was clearly derived from the ethical orientation of Pugin and Jones, and it was consistent with the socialist ideals of the Arts and Crafts Movement. But, in some crucial respects, it went further than both. On the one hand, his most radical and uncompromising designs eschewed non-functional ornament to such an extent that they remained incomprehensible, and were therefore ignored, for fifty years. On the other hand, he sacrificed the ideal of hand craftsmanship on the grounds that it required too much time and too many highly trained individuals to be feasible on a large scale, and that it therefore perpetuated the social hierarchy that it was intended to overcome. In its place he was committed to the use of industrially produced materials – for instance,

FIGURE 5.27: Teapot, designed by Christopher Dresser, manufactured by James Dixon
& Sons, 1879, electroplated nickel silver with ebony handle, 13 × 23 cm. Victoria and
Albert Museum, London.

electroplated metals instead of silver – and industrial techniques. For this reason –
and because the objects he designed are sometimes stamped with *his* name, together
with that of the manufacturer – he is often considered to be the first 'industrial
designer'.

Dresser's commitment to mechanical production was important because it ensured
for the first time that the fruits of fully trained and conscientious designers were
potentially available to all sectors of society at affordable prices. Prior to his initiative,
the quality and quantity of domestic wares were perceived to be mutually exclusive
and, as a result, the cultural status associated with the possibility of aesthetic self-
determination was withheld from much of the population. By producing educated
designs for mass production, Dresser challenged these trends. He contributed towards
the aestheticisation of the domestic environment at all levels of the social scale and,
in so doing, played a key part in the depolarisation of the extremes of 'high' and
'applied' art. A part of this shift involved the replacement of all forms of ornament
that derived their value from their associations with elite phenomena (such as the
dignity of antiquity), with ornament that was dictated by the materials and function
of the object in question. As a result, Dresser was also instrumental in developing a
language of design in which the ideal of utility was raised to the level of an 'absolute
truth' at the expense of mere decoration. Although he only rarely realised this ideal
in his own designs – chiefly for electroplated tablewares (Fig. 5.27) – this ideal
established a precedent for the sublimation of creative endeavour in the production
of utilitarian goods that would resound in the future.

The challenge by Dresser (and by like-minded contemporaries, such as E. W.
Godwin) to what they considered to be the demoralising pointlessness of randomly
applied ornament gave rise to several design solutions. At one end of the scale, there

was the idea that ornamentation should be so fundamentally determined by the purpose and materials of an object that, to all intents and purposes, it becomes a function of that object, arising out of it, rather than being applied to it; this idea was developed by *Jugendstil* designers in Munich, such as Hermann Obrist and August Endell, as we have seen (Figs 4.35, 4.36). In such a context, ornament is so natural and organic that it is entirely non-representational, in exactly the way that natural forms are non-representational. At the other end of the scale, there was the view that applied ornament is entirely superfluous to the function of utilitarian objects and should, therefore, be abolished altogether. This view was most vociferously promoted by the Viennese architect Adolf Loos, who maintained in his celebrated essay 'Ornament and Crime' of 1908, that 'the evolution of culture is synonymous with the removal of ornament from objects of daily use'. Loos claimed that, after centuries of ornamentation – a sign of the infancy and immaturity of human culture – society had now 'outgrown' the need to decorate objects and buildings. The absence of ornament became a sign for him of a new level of intellectual self-awareness and self-sufficiency (Fig. 5.28). Moreover, because the decoration of utilitarian objects caused them to go out of date and be discarded long before they actually ceased to function, it was also a waste of a worker's time and energy, and of the materials used, to decorate them. In fact, reflecting his debt to the moralising agenda of the Arts and Crafts Movement, Loos claimed that it was so anachronistic to perpetuate the conventions attached to the production and appreciation of ornament that to do so amounted to a pathological obstruction to social and cultural change, and a denial

FIGURE 5.28: The Loos House, Vienna, designed by Adolf Loos, 1910.

of the moral obligation to respond to society's needs. It was, therefore, a 'crime' against society.

The significance of both of these approaches – to absolutely fuse ornament with function or to absolutely remove it – was that they provided a radical challenge to the tendency to apply random decoration to utilitarian objects. Neither of them made an allowance for *independently conceived* ornament. For much of the nineteenth century, utilitarian objects had been decorated with ornament that drew its appeal from its independent associations with a diverse range of sources: the antiquity of ancient Rome, Greece and Egypt, the exoticism of India, China and Japan and the fulsome blooms of Victorian gardens, among others. Decoration of this kind bore no direct relation to the form or function of the objects in question and, therefore, the aesthetic and utilitarian agendas of such objects remained disconnected from each other. As long as this paradigm prevailed, the cultural value of such objects continued to be determined by aesthetic considerations at the expense of their utility. The appreciation of these styles presupposed a degree of education and social breeding, and their use, therefore, subtly reinforced the existing status quo. As the century progressed, however, there was an increasing call for the design and decoration of objects to be subjected to their function, through which all people had equal access to them. As a result of this demand, an entire grammar of non-representational ornament, designed to enhance the form and function of objects, was conceived. In the most extreme cases, parallels can be drawn here with the realisation of total abstraction in 'fine art'. In both cases, purely aesthetic contingencies were rigorously sacrificed for the sake of 'essence'. While 'fine art' was reduced, in some quarters, to the non-existence of total transparency – becoming so absolutely transparent as a medium of life experience that it ceased to exist as such – so the most radical 'applied art' was reduced to the ideal of pure functionality, determined by the materials and use of objects, but with no *independent* aesthetic dimension.

The ordinary functionality of everyday life became infused with cultural value when culturally validated design principles were fully integrated into the fabric of the environment. What differentiated the total functionality of objects designed in keeping with the principles of design reform from the merely sufficient functionality of decorated objects was the fact that, in the latter, function was buried under layers of ornament and was, therefore, denied cultural value, whereas in the former, the sense of the 'aesthetic' was sublimated within the 'utilitarian', thereby conferring cultural value on the functionality of everyday life, while also sacrificing itself as an independent phenomenon. By reconciling these two aspects of objects in this way – functionality and lack of an *independent* decorative agenda – the impulse to reform the process of product design challenged the Renaissance hierarchy of artistic values and restored a degree of parity between all fields of visual culture in a way that recalled the parity of medieval crafts before the elevation of painting to the level of a liberal 'art'.

This integration of the 'aesthetic' into the 'utilitarian' was further reflected in the fact that, towards the end of the nineteenth century, several artists began to feel that, following Post-Impressionism, which seemed to take representation as far as it could go, there was no future for fine art. As a result, a significant number of them gave up painting in order to dedicate themselves to architecture and the design of utilitarian

FIGURE 5.29: Henry van de Velde, *Reaper*, 1891–2, lime-watercolour on canvas,
75 × 95 cm. Private collection. © DACS 2018.

objects. Several of these artists eventually became key players in the early history of
industrial design. The Belgian designer and architect Henry van de Velde, for
instance, was trained as a painter, pushing the formal properties of the Post-
Impressionists – the pointillism of Seurat, the amorphous colour fields of Gauguin
and the feverish brushstrokes of Van Gogh – to the threshold of abstraction (Fig.
5.29). But, in 1892, he abandoned painting and committed himself to architecture
and product design, precisely in order to bring the benefits of aesthetic experience
to a wider audience. Much inspired and influenced by William Morris, he produced
designs for a wide range of everyday media, including advertisements, wallpaper,
fabrics, ceramics, light fittings and cutlery (Fig. 5.30). In 1902, van de Velde was
invited to Weimar to found an Arts and Crafts college, where he advocated that
ornament should not be used simply to adorn objects; it should be suffused into the
form of objects, in keeping with the latter's function and materials, to the extent that
the forms themselves become ornamental. Many of his own designs, from around
1895 onwards, suggest the liquid strength of bone forms, as if they had been pared
back to their skeletons (Fig. 5.31). The structural dynamics that makes them
coherent, stable and functional can be seen in their shapes, as if they had been
formed by the flow of forces within them. There is nothing visible in them that does
not serve a structural function and yet, although they have not 'been decorated' as
such, they are charged with aesthetic appeal.

In 1907, van de Velde was closely associated with the foundation of the *Deutscher
Werkbund* (German Work Federation), set up in Munich to forge links between
product designers and manufacturers with a view to promoting German trade and
economy on an international scale (though he was not admitted as a 'member'

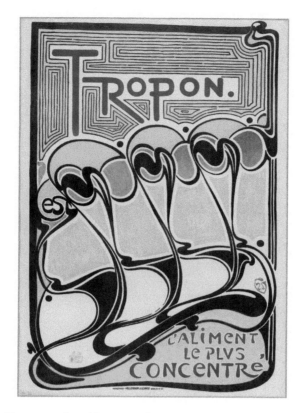

FIGURE 5.30: Henry van de Velde, poster for the Tropon Factory, Mulheim, 1898, colour lithograph on paper, 36.7 × 27.9 cm. © DACS 2018.

FIGURE 5.31: Henry van de Velde, candlestand, 1899, silvered bronze. Private collection. © DACS 2018.

himself because he was a foreigner). One of the key purposes of the *Werkbund* was to reintegrate the intelligent, life-enhancing properties of consciously and organically conceived design principles into the fabric of everyday life, in order to reinvigorate it from within. This was a dimension of existence that had been sadly neglected by the insensitive, formulaic application of industrial manufacturing techniques to object production. The definitive moment in the *Werkbund*'s history took place in June 1914, when disagreements over the relative importance of creative individuality and product standardisation erupted into conflict. Van de Velde maintained that artistic freedom and individuality were necessary if the objective principles of function and material were to be understood and processed at a high level, whereas Hermann Muthesius prioritised the standardisation of design at the expense of artistic self-expression, in order to facilitate mass production. Although the two views were not necessarily as polarised as they were made to seem by this confrontation, they highlighted the crucial question: should objects designed for mass production and consumption express the aesthetic preferences of the individual that designed them or should they sacrifice this possibility for the sake of society as a whole? The question was critical in the present context because it impacted on the extent to which the designed environment was empowered to embody the vibration of personal identity. It remained unanswered for several years due to the outbreak of war in August 1914, a calamity that led van de Velde to withdraw from the *Werkbund* and resign from his posts in Germany.

The initiative to cross over wholeheartedly into industrial design, at the expense of self-expression, was taken by one of van de Velde's colleagues at the *Deutscher Werkbund*, Peter Behrens, who also trained as an artist but gave up painting for the sake of product design in 1897. Behrens's first designs were mostly two-dimensional (for graphics, posters, carpets, wallpaper, etc.), reflecting his experience as a painter. They revolved around the sensuous potential of line, unfolding in a sinuous and smoky *Jugendstil* style (Fig. 5.32). From 1898, he began producing designs for three-dimensional media (glass, ceramics and furniture) and the lines in his designs stiffened and became more articulated, in keeping with their new role as structural elements, somewhat in the manner of van de Velde. His work took on a new significance in 1907, when he began working as a consultant designer for the *Allgemeine Elektricitäts Gesellschaft* (AEG) – the General Electricity Company, founded in Berlin in 1887 – for which he designed a range of electrical goods such as lights, fans, kettles and clocks, using mass-produced standardised parts. The adaptation of the design of utilitarian objects to electricity all but completed their entry into the realm of industrial production. Some of the earliest designs that Behrens produced for AEG show lingering signs of an artisanal aesthetic – for instance, the hammering effect on the surface of his kettles (Fig. 5.33), a conventional Arts and Crafts sign that objects had (or seemed to have) been worked by hand (Fig. 5.18) – but this lingering nostalgia did not last (Fig. 5.34). On the contrary, Behrens also designed buildings, advertising, stationery and even logos for the company – creating the first ever corporate identity – and, in this capacity, he was instrumental in establishing the possibility of affordable, mass-produced designer goods, beyond the realm of the personal, at a fully institutional level. On the one hand, he integrated aesthetic principles into the design of utilitarian objects, transmitting the possibility of aesthetic self-awareness quasi-

FIGURE 5.32: Peter Behrens, *The Kiss*, 1898, lithograph, 27.2 × 21.6 cm. Private collection.

FIGURE 5.33: Electric kettle, designed by Peter Behrens for AEG (*Allgemeine Elektricitäts Gesellschaft*), Berlin, around 1908, nickel-plated brass with wicker-covered handle, 22.5 × 15.5 cm. Victoria and Albert Museum, London.

FIGURE 5.34: Electric kettle, designed by Peter Behrens for AEG (*Allgemeine Elektricitäts Gesellschaft*), Berlin, 1909, nickel-plated brass with wicker-handle. Private collection.

'intravenously' to the public; on the other hand, he erased the suggestion of individuality from such objects. While the pursuit of pure art had led the sense of personal self to its essence, to the point at which it transcended itself, so the sublimation of aesthetic principles in mass-produced utilitarian objects also served to immerse the self-sense into the collective to the point at which it was no longer distinguishable and supported on its own terms.

The erasure of personality from industrial design, and the suggestion by the most avant-garde provocateurs that 'art is dead', stimulated a wide range of reactions: it was embraced, diluted, rejected and ignored. In Germany, belief in the progressive nature of industry was badly shaken by the First World War. Thus, when the Bauhaus School of Design opened in Weimar in 1919 (absorbing the remains of the School of Arts and Crafts there), it made concessions to the self-expressive 'needs' of individuals that van de Velde had advocated before the war and, for the first few years of its existence, it went through an 'expressionistic' phase. Indeed, in many ways – particularly in the way it encouraged students to experiment with forms and materials – it was a natural heir to the kindergarten, developed by Froebel almost a hundred years earlier. According to its first director, the architect Walter Gropius, the aim of the Bauhaus was to 'create a new guild of craftsmen, without the class distinctions which raise an arrogant barrier between craftsman and artist';[13] and certainly one of its definitive characteristics was its use of accomplished artists (most notably Wassily Kandinsky and Paul Klee) to teach principles of colour and form – a further sign of the attempt to integrate aesthetic values into the production of utilitarian goods. The aim to integrate art and life was also implicit in the self-conscious association of the school with medieval traditions that pre-dated the invention of 'art' – from the use of medieval nomenclature for teachers and students ('masters' and 'apprentices') to the prefacing of the opening manifesto with a neo-primitivist woodcut of a medieval cathedral. However, especially following its move to purpose-built premises in Dessau in 1925, the school became increasingly orientated towards designing objects for mass production, for the benefit of an egalitarian society. In 1933, it was closed down on the grounds that it was 'culturally Bolshevik', and many of its protégés emigrated, especially to America, taking their ideas with them. In this respect, the school again recalled the kindergarten concept. Kindergartens had been banned in the German provinces between 1851 and 1860 on the grounds that they were hotbeds of democratic values, also causing their advocates to develop the kindergarten idea abroad.

In Russia, where Malevich worked (and from where Kandinsky had fled in 1921), the implications of the 'death of art' were taken to the extreme, as we have seen. The shift coincided, not insignificantly, with the Russian Revolution of 1917, in which diverse dreams of political, cultural and spiritual change came to a head. The notion of the death of art and of subjective identity was adapted by the Bolsheviks to serve their communist ideals. Subjectivity, for instance, was identified with personal selfishness and came to be seen as a form of antisocial separatism.[14] Individuals were not simply forced into collectives by new circumstances; they were encouraged to activate a collective spirit, consciously conformed to Soviet ideals that transcended self-interest.[15] Efforts to realise a society in which the thoughtless wastefulness and inefficiency of individualism were erased were made by the industrialist and one-time Futurist poet Alexei Gastev (1882–1939), who believed that human productivity could be accelerated and rendered more cost-effective, in service to the state, by rigorous analysis and standardisation. Inspired by the reforms of the American engineer and management consultant Frederick Winslow Taylor, Gastev founded the Central Institute of Labour in Moscow in 1920 to instigate a process of industrial reform across the Soviet Union. First of all, he reduced the repetitive actions of factory workers to their most essential and economic gestures, abstracted from selected specimen workers with the help of long-exposure photography (Fig. 5.35). He then created imitative body-frame contraptions that performed these gestures in their purified form and attempted to reinstil them in the workforce by subjecting workers to long courses of mechanical body programming. The regulated movements of machines conformed the physical movements of individuals to themselves, thereby 'improving' them and raising them to a higher level of functionality, at the expense of their personal interests and mentalities:

> The world of the machine, the world of the mechanism, the world of industrial urbanism is creating its own collective bonds, is giving birth to its own types of people . . . History urgently demands . . . us to pose, not these small problems [regarding] the protection of personality by society, but rather a bold design of human psychology in reliance upon such an historical factor as machine production.[16]

Gastev also believed that his initiatives could be introduced to the life of communist society as a whole:

FIGURE 5.35: Alexei Gastev, 'Analysis of an Action', Central Institute of Labour, 1923.

The mechanization, not only of gestures, not only of production methods, but of everyday thinking, coupled with extreme rationality, normalizes in a striking degree the psychology of the proletariat . . . It is this that lends proletarian psychology such surprising anonymity, which permits the qualification of separate proletarian units A, B, C, or as 325,075, or as O and the like . . . In this psychology, from one end of the world to the other, flow potent massive streams, making for one world head in place of millions of heads. This tendency will next imperceptibly render individual thinking impossible, and thought will become the objective psychic process of the whole class, with systems of psychological switches and locks.[17]

To the same end, language could be purged of its anachronistic confusions and rendered direct and unambiguous, facilitating super-functional, transpersonal clarity of mind in its users.[18] Time-saving acronyms and abbreviations were highly recommended. Several proletarian poets attempted to abolish the word 'I'. According to Mayakovsky, 'the proletcultists never speak of "I" or of the personality. They consider the pronoun "I" a kind of rascality.'[19] In 1921, Yevgeny Zamyatin responded to Gastev's ideas with a satirical dystopian novel called *We*, in which the notions of 'soul' and 'dreaming' are so 'historical' that they are almost incomprehensible; people are named by numbers. Declaring that the word '*We* comes from God, *I* from the Devil', the protagonist D-503 maintains that 'self-consciousness is just a disease . . . It's only the eye with a lash in it, the swollen finger, the infected tooth that feels itself, is conscious of its own individual being. The healthy eye or finger or tooth doesn't seem to exist.'[20] The novel is set in the distant future in an imaginary city in which the walls of all the buildings are made of glass in order to prevent privacy.

Soviet interiors of the 1920s strove to undermine the individualist aestheticism of the pre-war era. Rooms were designed around objective principles of functionality, which were believed to be socially uniform, rather than the subjective possibility of pleasure. Kitchens began to resemble clinics or laboratories; hygiene was pursued scientifically. Some Soviet idealists maintained that private residences per se were bastions of bourgeois self-indulgence, and they promoted the development of communal apartments in their place (Fig. 5.36). Thousands of apartment blocks in which families were confined to a single room, sharing bathroom and kitchen facilities with other families, were built all over the Soviet Union. Against this background, private bedrooms were considered to be pernicious havens of solitude and subjectivity, in which individuals could retreat into their own spaces and even into their own minds, and they therefore met with stern disapproval. In a further attempt to undermine the material culture of personal identity, the ex-artist Alexander Rodchenko advocated the suppression of beds and bedrooms altogether; perhaps some aspect of this inclination was presaged by the fact that, when he was still an impecunious painter, he used bedsheets as canvases. As a teacher at the VKhUTEMAS school of design in Moscow (the Russian equivalent of the Bauhaus), founded in 1920, he encouraged his students to design multifunctional, metamorphic furniture that could be used as a table or armchair in the daytime, but be converted into a bed at night and set up anywhere in the apartment – for instance in the kitchen or a corridor. Examples

FIGURE 5.36: The western facade of the communal apartment, Narkomfin, Moscow, designed by Moisei Ginzburg, 1928–32. Photo: Alexey Ginzburg.

by Petr Galaktianov and Nikolai Sobolev were published in the journal *LEF* in 1923 (Fig. 5.37).[21] Similar ideas were developed, albeit less extremely, all over Europe. In the Rietveld-Shroder House in Utrecht (conceived by the De Stijl designer Gerrit Rietveld for Truus Shroder in 1924), mobile partitions were used to transform the open first-floor living space into compartments for sleeping at night; couches were converted into beds. As with much of the most rigorous design of the period, comfort – one of the mainstays of late nineteenth-century bourgeois domesticity – took second place to the 'look' of impersonal universality and functionality, on the grounds that it was stuffy and stifling, sapping individuals of their energy to strive for higher ideals and serve society.

By eliminating permanent bedrooms from their domestic interiors in this way, Rodchenko and Rietveld were frustrating the appetite for private, personal identity. Just as the early twentieth-century development of artistic abstraction from classical naturalism reversed the development of Renaissance naturalism from medieval

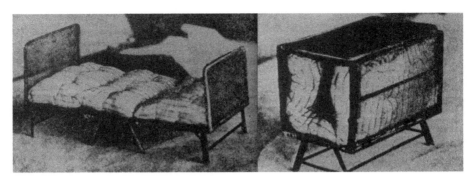

FIGURE 5.37: Convertible bed, designed by Aleksei Galaktionov, VKhUTEMAS, *LEF* (Moscow), No. 3 (1923), 54. David King Collection.

stylisation, so this initiative also moved in the very opposite direction to a corresponding impulse that emerged in elite households of the late Middle Ages: namely the elaboration of beds and bedchambers as signs of privacy, status and selfhood. Rodchenko and his colleagues applied their hyper-functional approach to design to all aspects of daily life. With regard to clothing which, in the pre-communist era, had become increasingly expressive of the personal taste of the individual consumer, he advocated the use of uniforms, for uniforms expressed the social function of the wearer rather than his or her personality and proclivity for private time spent 'at leisure'. To express his own role as a designer, working for the benefit of society, he designed a working outfit for himself that likened him more to an engineer or pilot than a poet or artist. With his wife, Varvara Stepanova, he also designed sportswear. Team sports were much promoted in the Soviet Union because, with the help of team 'uniforms', they socialised and 'deprivatised' leisure time (Fig. 5.38).

Besides believing that the notion of personal identity was superfluous, Rodchenko also followed Malevich in maintaining that art was dead. Like Malevich, he gave up 'easel painting' in 1918 on the grounds that it was a redundant bourgeois convention designed to safeguard the privileges of the elite at the expense of the working class. Because easel painting required not only wealth with which to acquire it, but also, more subtly, aesthetic and social education with which to appreciate it, he believed it to be secretly supportive of a system of social values – and of the hierarchy of political power attached to those values – from which the non-elite were fundamentally excluded. Thus, although it was promoted in the name of inspiration, beauty and pleasure, 'high art' was in fact seen to be deviously informed by a political agenda. It was, therefore, time to dispense with it. In its place, Rodchenko advocated that *all* creative endeavour should be channelled into the design and production of utilitarian objects or political propaganda (which was utilitarian in the sense that it served a practical social function). Personal creativity should be integrated into the fabric of daily life for the benefit of all society without discrimination. Although Rodchenko championed the death of high art as Malevich had done, his attempt to infuse all artistic endeavour into the impersonal

РАБОТЫ СТЕПАНОВОЙ

Проэкты спорт-одежды

FIGURE 5.38: Design for sportswear, Varvara Stepanova, Moscow, 1923. David King Collection.

stream of political life differed greatly from Malevich's attempt to transcend it altogether.

The Industrial Revolution facilitated the evolution of parameters for a new model of identity that was socially inclusive and transpersonal. On the one hand, industrialisation brought the possibility of consumership to the entirety of the population, thereby granting all individuals unprecedented access to the possibility of aesthetic self-awareness and undermining the association of 'taste' with an elite model of selfhood. On the other hand, it complemented the demise and death of 'art' by progressively sublimating the aesthetic component of design within the functionality of utilitarian objects, minimising its explicit distinctiveness to the point of non-existence (in the most extreme cases), while maximising its implicit accessibility to the point of universality. Significantly, it also usurped the function of 'visual communication' that had hitherto been monopolised by the crafts of painting, drawing and handwriting, further threatening to challenge the hegemony of 'art'. This shift was reflected particularly clearly in the development of commercial printing and telecommunications. As with the production of utilitarian objects – the stuff of everyday life – these media were subjected to the process of industrialisation in the nineteenth century, facilitating mass communication both to and between vast communities of people, over and above the personal circumstances of individuals. The evolution of new 'infrastructures of communication' and the collective models of identity which these infrastructures progressively realised is the subject of the following chapter.

CHAPTER SIX

The Transpersonalisation of the Self: the Material Culture of Communication and the Communalisation of Identity

In the last two chapters, we saw how, at the time of the First World War, the notions of 'art' and the sense of the 'aesthetic' were superseded as independent and autonomous embodiments of cultural value. At one extreme, the concept of art consummated itself in self-transcendence as the necessary outcome of its own internal logic. At the other, the notion of the aesthetic was fully integrated into the realm of the 'utilitarian', by mechanical means, for moral and social reasons. In both contexts, art and the realm of the aesthetic ceased to exist and function as independent phenomena. This state was reached most absolutely and explicitly in Soviet Russia, where, for several years, 'art for art's sake' was banned altogether. Most significant, from the present point of view, is the way that the demise of art put pressure on the notion of the personal self, which identified with the concept of art as the perfect medium for its self-reflective experience – the very function for which it had originally evolved in the sixteenth century. The challenge to the concept of art was paralleled by the attempt to provide universal access to the discourse of cultural value, and thereby to substantiate the self-conscious identity of society as a whole. Besides mechanising the processes of producing utilitarian objects and homogenising their use, this shift was also precipitated by the development of new, technologically based means of communication. By appropriating some of the communicative functions of art, these inclusive media – especially print technology and film – threatened to usurp the role of art as a key co-ordinate of the self-sense; indeed, they worked to render *public* the sense of selfhood that the elite conditions of art appreciation had kept *private* for three centuries. This shift occurred in two distinctive ways. On the one hand, the mechanisation of *mass* communication – from the 'authorities' to the 'people' – contributed towards the concretisation of its audience; we have already seen how, with regard to art appreciation, the notion of the 'public' was institutionalised through the development of national museums and galleries. On the other hand, the processes of *personal* communication – between individuals – were systematised, such that the networks of communicants that used them increased in size, realising ever-larger scales of community. The construction and expansion of collectivised forms of identity through the mechanisation of publicity and communication are the subject of this chapter.

Given the high rate of illiteracy in medieval Europe and the scarcity of texts among the laity, it should come as no surprise that, for a majority of people at this time, the most common means of mediated communication – organised communication that depended on a medium of exchange – were oral and visual. Having said that, while popular access to text was in many cases non-existent, even images were relatively scarce, especially in the home; not all churches were decorated, and popular prints did not emerge until the fifteenth century. Most such communications, therefore, will have taken the form of 'live' gatherings, services, ceremonies and festivals, which, despite being regular and abundant (Christian rituals were performed daily, weekly and annually), were also transient. Although they could be lavish, they left few permanent material traces other than those rare exceptions recorded in descriptive text and images. Notwithstanding the growing sophistication of courtly life that was reserved for the few, a large majority of these communications were organised by the Church. They were designed to communicate the values of the Church in all its roles, and people will have seen any objects or images associated with them as sources of religious value, rather than as 'works of art'.

During the Renaissance, religious ceremonies were increasingly supplemented by theatrical displays of secular political propaganda. Because people did not necessarily know what their rulers looked like, celebrations and processions were regularly staged to communicate hierarchies of values, and to consolidate memories of those values. Inspired both by ancient accounts of Roman triumphal marches and by images of Christ's entry into Jerusalem, the entry of a prince into a city for the first time was often celebrated with ostentatious pageantry and music, conceived by the most eminent artists and composers of the day (Fig. 6.1). Such occasions often included a procession of the city's relics, enabling secular powers to adapt the semantic conventions of religious rituals and objects to their own purposes, and thereby to sacralise their authority. Prevailing structures of power were also conspicuously communicated further down the social scale. For instance, marriages between notable families and the holy days of the patron saints of guilds were also broadcast to the whole community by means of memorable, attention-seeking celebrations.

These declarations of political and religious power and legitimacy reached a peak of ostentatious grandeur in the baroque period. Indeed, it is arguable that what we now think of as the political or religious 'art' of the time – and approach with a post-Romantic appetite for aesthetic appeal and self-expressive depth – was, in its own day, a form of media or advertising. Although such images often involved extraordinary artistry, it is, in some ways, anachronistic to think of them as 'art' in the modern sense of the word and to expect them to behave as 'art' (as a means of self-expression or as a source of beauty or inspiration). Indeed, it is arguable that it was not until the eighteenth and early nineteenth centuries, when the political and

FIGURE 6.1: Denys van Alsloot, *The Ommegang in Brussels on 31 May 1615: The Triumph of Archduchess Isabella*, 1616, Brussels, oil on canvas, 117 × 381 cm. Victoria and Albert Museum, London.

ideological functions of baroque painting were taken over by other techniques of image production – initially new forms of print – that the concept of 'pure art' was able to emerge. This shift coincided with the growing independence of painting and sculpture from the dictates of patrons, in favour of direct inspiration on the part of the artist, thereby allowing these ennobled media either to strive freely towards a consummate state of perfection (as 'fine art') or to become socially redundant (unless subjected to functionality), as we have seen. Of course, the concept of 'art' as an autonomous cultural convention had been evolving since the Renaissance. However, as the many secular paintings and sculptures that were produced at this period were mostly luxuries, they cannot be said to have functioned as a *popular* medium of communication. On the contrary, these objects were largely created for a very small elite and they will have remained completely unknown to the majority of people, in whose own homes luxuries were non-existent and imagery was comparatively rare.

As a result of this relative lack of access, a majority of the population was unable to use the communicative medium of imagery as an instrument of identity formation until well into the eighteenth century, when new technologies began to facilitate the mass production of images. In fact, although cheap woodblock prints – mostly of devotional, but also of topical subjects – began to circulate in the fifteenth century, and although the collecting of prints, including hand-engraved copies of paintings, was avidly pursued by the middle classes throughout the eighteenth century, it was not until the nineteenth century that images became a staple and ubiquitous component of *popular* culture. The fact that images could now be endlessly and exactly duplicated enabled them to be seen by infinitely more people than could have ever viewed a unique, hand-worked painting, and as such, they implicitly accommodated the identity not only of the bourgeois public but also of society as a whole. Particularly following the application of steam power to the printing press, and the replacement of flatbed printing with continuous roller printing, introduced together in 1814, printed matter could be reproduced mechanically and cheaply in vast quantities.

The earliest mass-produced images were published in popular newspapers and periodicals. The editors of the first of these in Britain – *The Penny Magazine*, produced from 1832 to 1845 by the Society for the Diffusion of Useful Knowledge – stated that 'what the stage-coach has become to the middle classes, we hope our Penny Magazine will be to *all* classes'; indeed, in its first year, the magazine's circulation reached 200,000. Both in this magazine and in the more enduring *Illustrated London News*, produced from 1842, the images were made from handmade woodcuts, leading to a revival of that craft. Even after the invention of photography, woodcuts continued to be used in newspapers because they were easier to reproduce. The National Gallery's acquisition of Van Eyck's *Portrait of a Gentleman* (1433) in 1852 was announced with a handsome woodcut (Fig. 6.2), and three years later Roger Fenton's celebrated photographs of the Crimean War were

FIGURE 6.2: *Illustrated London News* (announcing the National Gallery's acquisition of Jan Van Eyck's *Portrait of a Gentleman*, 1433), 10 January 1852. Photo: 1853 Collection, Southern New Hampshire University Archives.

published in the same medium. But in the 1890s, woodcuts were increasingly overshadowed by photography. As a result, the craft of drawing became less and less patronised by this outlet. The documentary potential of photography also put pressure on contemporary history painting, thereby making a further contribution to the reduction and relativisation of the usefulness of fine art in the world of visual communication. Paintings that aspired to record contemporary events – such as Benjamin West's *The Death of Nelson, 21 October 1805*, painted in 1806 and widely disseminated through engravings, or Henry Nelson O'Neil's *The Landing of HRH The Princess Alexandra at Gravesend, 7th March 1863*, painted in 1864 though the event itself was reported live in the *Illustrated London News* the year before – were neither sufficiently accurate nor quickly enough produced to hold their ground, and they ceased to play a primary role in the process of reportage.[1]

This process of dilution was taken a step further by the production of lifelike reproductions of historical paintings, which was facilitated by developments in the technology of colour printing. Ironically, it was the mechanical reproduction of works of art that first caused the unique quality of 'authenticity' to be ascribed to 'original' works, from which copies could then be made. Prior to this development, all works of art had, in effect, been unique and authentic embodiments of themselves (with the exception of relatively few easily distinguishable hand-painted 'copies'); the quality of 'authenticity' had been universal and innate, and therefore unworthy of attention. But following the development of techniques of mechanical reproduction, the difference between 'unique, authentic originals' and 'common, inauthentic copies' became a significant phenomenon, cementing the association of the unique work of art with the uniqueness of personal identity, and common reproductions with the more levelled identity of the community. It was only under these conditions that 'authentic' objects could be seen to have an 'aura'. With regard to Walter Benjamin's theory that mechanical reproduction diminishes the aura of an 'authentic' work of art by debasing it, it is equally arguable that it has the opposite effect: consolidating its status, by contrast, as 'authentic', firstly by considering it to be worth copying, and secondly by differentiating it from its copies. The extent to which the mechanical duplication of objects is disjunctive with the fully embodied experience of individuality in its most simple and immediate state – but presupposes instead the impersonal, preprocessed experience (and therefore identity) of members of industrialised societies – is highlighted in a story told by the American sociologist Margaret Mead (1901–78). Mead once showed a book to an Indonesian tribe that had never seen a book before. Not knowing what the object was, the tribespeople were naturally curious – but only curious. When Mead showed them an identical copy of the same book, they were truly mystified, wondering how the same object could be 'in two places at the same time'. They had never seen identical objects before, as they do not exist in nature. Moreover, unlike their western observers, the tribespeople had not systematised and perfected the processes of production to the extent that their products showed no sign of the idiosyncrasies that are inevitable in handmade artefacts. Consequently, the ability and inclination to abstract the design of an object and conceive it in the mind as an *idea* – of which *actual* objects were identical materialisations – was alien to them; and the generalised sense of self that identified itself in relation to such abstraction and uniformity remained unevoked in them accordingly.

One of the most important media in which to produce high-quality images in significant numbers was lithography. This new technique, which was invented by the German playwright Alois Senefelder in 1796 (but not published until 1818), was innovative because it depended on the *chemical* reactions that occurred between the printing materials used, rather than on the *physical* processes of woodcutting or copper engraving, and in this respect it anticipated photography. The technique involved drawing an image using a greasy, water-rejecting crayon on to a flat surface of water-accepting stone (*lithos* in Greek). Oily ink was then applied to the surface, sticking to the crayoned areas but not to the water-saturated areas, from which it could then be transferred, in a printing press, to paper. The technique was used by several artists in the first half of the nineteenth century (e.g. Daumier, Gericault, Delacroix), mostly working in black and white. In the 1830s, colour lithography (chromolithography) was developed, using a different stone for each colour. Realistic, 'painting-like' lithographs and convincing reproductions of original works

FIGURE 6.3: *Bubbles, painted by Sir J. E. Millais, Bart. R.A. 1886. From the celebrated picture the property of Messrs. A. & F. Pears of London*, chromolithograph after Sir J. E. Millais, 42.8 × 31.2 cm. Wellcome Collection.

of art might use as many as thirty or forty different colours and therefore, despite intending to democratise the appreciation of art by bringing it into the bourgeois home, they were time-consuming and expensive to make. The medium did not come into its own until it joined forces with advertising, which, alongside reportage and reproduction, represented yet another challenge to the traditional domination of

FIGURE 6.4: Facsimile chromolithographed presentation print from a poster for Pears Soap, featuring a child playing with bubbles, from a painting by Sir John Everett Millais, adapted by the addition of a bar of Pears Soap in the lower right corner, 1889, 22 × 13.1 cm. Victoria and Albert Museum, London.

visual culture by fine art (Fig. 4.13). Indeed, the best lithographed posters were of such high quality that they were sometimes stolen from public hoardings at night. Conversely, while letterpress advertisements had appeared in newspapers since the seventeenth century, commercial advertising did not begin to occupy a powerful position in the image world until it began to make use of chromolithography, capitalising on the leaning of that medium towards the use of limited numbers of strong fields of unified colour for dramatic effect (which, as we have seen, was also one of the precedents for abstract art). But on the whole, while needing to be attractive, advertisements did not aspire to having independent artistic value. On the contrary, they were above all intended to stimulate a subtle sense of deficiency in their viewers by presenting them with an image of an ideal, and to awaken a desire in them to improve their lot by realising that ideal in their own lives by consuming a product.

The sense that advertising had invaded the sanctified territory of fine art and stolen some of its privileges was clearly reflected in the controversy that developed around the use of a painting, *A Child's World* (1886), by the one-time Pre-Raphaelite painter John Everett Millais, in an advertisement for Pears soap. The painting, which shows a five-year-old boy, seated on a stone between a flowering plant and a broken terracotta pot, blowing a bubble, was intended to convey a sense of the fragile beauty and transience of life, in the spirit of a seventeenth-century Dutch *vanitas* painting. It was originally bought by Sir William Ingram to be reproduced in lithographic form and offered as a presentation plate in the *Illustrated London News*, of which Ingram was the proprietor (Fig. 6.3). But the painting was then bought by Thomas J. Barratt, managing director of Pears soap, who asked Millais for permission to add a bar of soap to lithographic reproductions of the painting – thereby suggesting that the boy had blown his bubble from Pears soap – with a view to using it as an advertisement for the company. Despite expressing some reservations about using the image commercially, Millais eventually granted permission. Sacrificing its transcendent status as 'art for art's sake', the painting was retitled *Bubbles* and quickly became one of the best-known images of the Victorian age (Fig. 6.4). While Barratt used the image to elevate the reputation of his product and of the company, he also succeeded, according to some commentators, in debasing the currency of art.

By the end of the nineteenth century, public and private environments alike were awash with mechanically produced images – in newspapers and magazines, on posters, pamphlets and packaging. Although many of them made use of the pictorial conventions of academic painting in one way or another, their purpose was very different. Unlike unique works of art, they were not focused 'sites' at which an individual was invited to enter into a state of communion with artistic creativity or to gain insight into the nature of experience. On the contrary, they were instruments of homogenisation, inducing a generalised, one-size-fits-all mentality and appetite in as many people as possible. To ensure maximum effectiveness, ambiguities and inscrutable subtleties that left scope for subjective interpretation were minimised. As a result, the sense of identity that they increasingly generated and maintained became less and less personal (despite often strategically seeming to be personal) and more and more determined by broad patterns of social behaviour. Moreover, as reproductions of works of art became increasingly common and accurate – first of all in engravings, then in colour lithographs, then in black-and-white photographs, and eventually in colour photographs – so people began to experience works of art *more* through reproductions than through the originals. Exactly the same became true of music, which – following Thomas Edison's invention of the phonograph, or gramophone, in 1877 (commercialised from around 1890) – eventually came to be experienced more through recordings than live performances, as it is today. It even came to be conceived to be consumed in this way. Each of the four movements of Igor Stravinsky's *Serenade for Piano*, composed in 1925, was limited to three minutes in order to fit on to one side of a ten-inch 78 rpm gramophone record.[2] Thus, in this era of art reproduction and sound recording, which only became widespread at the beginning of the twentieth century, even the precious experience of *art*, once so exquisitely and intimately connected to the personal touch of an artist, was now mediated by the technology of mass production and thereby reconfigured to act as much as a reflector of collective, as of personal identity.

The degree of collectivity that was projected on to, and into, consumers of mass-produced objects and images was qualified by the fact that, although such objects were designed to induce a uniform experience in their consumers, the circumstances in which this experience occurred could be very different – i.e. not necessarily in a prescribed place. However, in the case of one new medium, which was destined to overcome all the others, even this minute pocket of difference was hard to protect. With regard to the viewers of 'motion pictures', which were first publicly broadcast in 1895 and were of course conceived to be viewed by people in groups, the presumption of collectivity was present as much in the circumstance of experience as it was in the object of experience. In Germany, the first audiences of films were frequently referred to as a homogenous mass.[3] Some critics were anxious that people were being lured by the suggestive power of the film medium from a state of individual self-consciousness into a state of hypnotic unconsciousness, leaving them vulnerable to manipulation. For better or worse, this power could either be exploited positively – by harnessing the nationalistic potential of the masses (considered to be a positive motive) – or it could be abused, by manipulating them to act unconsciously and even atrociously. This view was partly stimulated by the theories of the French sociologist Gustave le Bon, who wrote in his pioneering study *The Psychology of Crowds*, also written in 1895: 'Organised crowds have always played an important part in the life of peoples, but this part has never been of such moment as at present. The substitution of the unconscious action of crowds for the conscious activity of individuals is one of the principal characteristics of the present age.'[4] In post-revolutionary Russia, many Bolsheviks regarded film not only as a sign of the times but as the ideal medium through which to actively collectivise the people. Firstly, its production was heavily dependent on impersonal technology, erasing the possibility of personal self-expression, and secondly, it was specifically conceived to be experienced by groups of people, rather than by individuals (Fig. 6.5).

While, at its most extreme, the mechanisation of the processes of *mass* communication (*to* the masses *by* people in authority) transformed its audience into a homogenous collective, infusing it with its own identity over and above that of the individual, so the systematisation and mechanisation of *personal* communication

FIGURE 6.5: *USSR in Construction*, Moscow, 1 January 1938, pp. 5–6: '52,000,000 people viewed [the film] Chapayev'. 'Possessing exceptional potentialities for spiritually influencing the masses, the cinema helps the working class and its party to train the working population in the spirit of Socialism . . .' (Stalin). David King Collection.

(between individuals) gave rise to expanded networks of communicants, which also contributed towards the evolution of ever-larger denominations of identity. With regard to personal communication, it needs to be remembered that the majority of the inhabitants of medieval Europe were illiterate and, for these individuals, communication was primarily vocal. Reading and writing were the privilege of the clergy and a new breed of secular scholars. When, during the Renaissance, the concept of honour was reconfigured to presuppose a degree of education (alongside military prowess or inherited status), these practices also became more common among the nobility. However, for most of the population, verbal communication between individuals was *spoken* and *heard*. Even when text was transmitted to the community, it was read out loud and received aurally. One of the implications of this lack of literacy and literature is that an individual's possibilities of knowledge were limited to his or her *memories*; people could only 'know' what they could *remember*. Individuals had no access to 'offshore' repositories of information such as books – which constituted additional *possibilities* of knowledge – and it was, therefore, in their interest to develop a prodigious memory. Much information was conveyed in verse, or as songs, specifically to make it easier to memorise.

In the absence of external repositories of information, an illiterate individual's knowledge could be said to have resided, at any given time, in and as his body; it was available to him as an immediate function of his body, just as his physical strength or eyesight were available to him as functions of his body. In the absence of photographs, diaries, letters, school reports, etc., even his knowledge of himself – unsophisticated though it may have been – was remembered, and it too, therefore, was only available *actually*, in the present moment or not at all. At the same time, the range of his verbal communication was also limited to the vicinity of his physical presence. Because his verbal communication was oral, he could not communicate without engaging with his communicants *as* his body. His immediate community, therefore – the people with whom he communicated – were the people he met personally. Given that a majority of individuals lived in the countryside and travelled infrequently – indeed, peasants were not permitted to travel without permission from their lords – many of these people would have been local and familiar. But even if an individual engaged in the expensive and dangerous business of travel – for trade, pilgrimage or war – he would have communicated bodily.

For much of the population in Europe, this situation remained in place until the sixteenth century; for most peasants it lasted until much later. The key cause of change to this situation was the increase in rates of literacy. In Northern Europe, where literacy spread most quickly, this development was prompted by the Protestants' rejection of what they considered to be Catholic idolatry (the veneration of cult images) and their return to the founding 'truth' of the biblical word. The requirement that Protestants at all social levels should engage with biblical sources necessitated the translation of the scriptures into indigenous languages. This process capitalised on the invention of movable type (for Gutenberg's printing press in around 1440), which enabled such texts to be published in printed form. Printed text was not only cheaper and quicker to produce than manuscripts and therefore more abundant; it was also easier to standardise and control. These initiatives encouraged Protestants to learn to read, giving them unprecedented access to what they believed to be a unique and necessary source of salvation.

The spread of literacy had a direct impact on the possibilities of knowledge and communication among those touched by it. Above all, it ensured that knowledge among ordinary people was no longer dependent on, and limited to, memory; it could also be accommodated abstractly in documents and books, and 'sourced' accordingly. This meant that the sense of personal self was also no longer dependent on memory and present experience. It could now project itself beyond the immediate vicinity of the physical body into an imaginary virtual realm where its range and capacity were newly determined by the conditions imposed on it by the new media of communication that it used. With regard to personal communication, it was the sending of *messages* – especially the writing of letters (which of course presupposed literacy, unless they were dictated) – that first enabled the self-sense to be projected beyond the physical body into imagined networks of relationships that existed in times and spaces other than that which was experienced by the body immediately. The expanded network of communicants that this new mode of communication made possible constituted a new community, participation in which involved acts of communication and imagination that presupposed a modified sense of identity – one that was both more abstracted and more complicated than that which was coterminous with the body. In 1569, a French merchant called Gaspar de Saillans published a collection of letters that he had written to his wife, in order 'to create a place where my name might survive my body'.[5]

The most basic form of message was a simple oral communication between two people by means of a third party. When this everyday occurrence became institutionalised in the role of a professional 'messenger' or 'nuncio' (as, for instance, illustrated and identified with inscriptions on the eleventh-century Bayeux Tapestry), it began to suggest more complex structures of identity and power. The fact that the sending – or 'announcement' – of oral messages was common among the elite is reflected in the explanation, in several thirteenth-century letter-writing manuals, that one of the reasons for writing letters was that, after long and arduous journeys, messengers might not be able to remember their sender's messages accurately enough to convey them orally (under Edward I, messengers walked so much – up to thirty miles a day – that they were granted extra allowances for shoes).[6] Having said this, while medieval letters were sometimes intended to supplement oral messages, it is also clear that they were often designed to be supplemented by spoken comments from their messengers, who were, therefore, well chosen for the purpose. This was especially important if secrets were to be conveyed – another of the avowed purposes of medieval letters; the purveyors of such messages were their senders' 'secretaries'. Some letter-writers specifically asked the reader to destroy the letter once he or she had read it. Combining the two forms of messages – written and spoken – many letters of the period were dictated to professional scribes and were specifically intended to be read out loud to their recipients. In such minuscule ways, each of these conditions subtly determined the possibility of communication.

Throughout the Middle Ages, the practice of sending and receiving letters – whether dictated and heard, or written and read – was restricted to the ruling powers, clergymen and scholars. It was not until the sixteenth century that personal letters between members of the gentry also became common. The fact that such letters were transported by dedicated carriers reflects the absence of a general infrastructure with which to process mail (Fig. 6.6). The development of organised 'postal services' did not occur until the end of the fifteenth century. In 1490, the North Italian Taxis family was employed by Maximilian I, Holy Roman Emperor, to establish a system of 'posts' throughout the Empire. These were to be placed at regular intervals and were to be equipped with a relay of fresh horses and couriers, with a view to ensuring a rapid, non-stop service according to a fixed timetable. In England, the first systematic postal service of this kind originated in 1512, when Henry VIII appointed Sir Brian Tuke as his first 'Master of the Posts'.[7] Both of these services were originally conceived to transport royal mail, but, partly in order to raise revenue and partly in order to keep an eye on private communications, they also began to carry the personal mail of members of the public. In Britain, the Royal Mail was made formally available for public use in 1635, institutionalising the phenomenon of letter-writing at an unprecedented level, though many letter-writers, suspicious of censorship, continued to use private letter-carriers. Either way, the delivery of letters within England could take several days and, if they were going abroad, several weeks or even months to arrive. And many, of course, never arrived at all, as the many publications of letters that – credibly, if not always actually – 'fell' out of postbags and were 'found' on the roadside testify.

In the ensuing years, improvements to the postal service were introduced, increasing the range of its reach across the country, as well as the speed and safety of delivery. The invention of postmarks in Britain in 1661, requiring mail to be stamped with the date on which it was received at a post office, enabled the prompt delivery

FIGURE 6.6: Thomas Trevelyon, *1608 Miscellany Book*, Folger Shakespeare Library V.B.232, f. 193r, Folger Shakespeare Library, Washington.

of letters to be monitored. In around 1720, the postmaster in Bath, Ralph Allen, developed a system of 'cross and bye posts', which made it possible, for the first time, to transport mail from one locality to another without having to pass through London. In 1784, John Palmer proposed to adapt the use of stagecoaches, which he had been using to ferry actors and sets between two theatres that he owned in Bath and Bristol, to the delivery of mail (Fig. 6.7). This change revolutionised the postal service (reducing the time required for a letter to travel from Bristol to London from three days to sixteen hours overnight) and remained in place until the development of the first rail train in 1830. Ten years later, Rowland Hill's proposals to reform the postal service, thereby opening it up to the poor, were accepted (even though illiteracy still prevented many of them from using it). His reforms replaced an expensive and inefficient system in which the cost of sending a letter was variable, depending on the distance covered, the mode of transport used and the number of sheets of paper sent (Fig. 6.8). The latter factor had motivated some letter-writers to keep the cost down by writing on the same sheet of paper both horizontally and vertically (Fig. 6.9). Moreover, because the cost of postage was charged to the recipient, ingenious ways were sometimes found to enable an addressee to see a coded message on the envelope, before refusing to pay for it. In the new system,

FIGURE 6.7: James Fittler, *Mail Coach* (after George Robertson), around 1787, etching and stipple engraving, 25 × 28.7 cm. Yale Center for British Art, Paul Mellon Collection.

implemented in 1840, the rate was fixed at a penny, prepaid by the sender in exchange for a postage stamp – initially the 'penny black'.

The significance of these developments was that, as the possibilities of communication increased, so the networks of relationships into which letter-writing individuals were able to project themselves also grew, expanding the parameters of their identities beyond the confines of their physical bodies and beyond the confines of the present moment in time into an imaginary realm. As people's 'communities of communicants' – the communities of people with whom they maintained communication – became ever more dispersed, so the frames of reference from which they derived their sense of self became more virtual and their self-sense more abstracted. For instance, throughout the seventeenth century, natural philosophers shared their work with each other by letter. Their letters were not simply an informal means of maintaining personal contact with colleagues and sharing ideas; on the contrary, until specialist journals and periodicals became widespread at the end of the century, they functioned as a primary means for the publication of work in progress and new discoveries.[8] By the middle of the century, this international network had become sufficiently coherent to be identified as a community. In 1646, Robert Boyle called it an 'invisible college'. Others referred to it as a 'Republic of Letters'.

In relation to more intimate, emotional types of letter, the impact of the mode of communication both on the character of the relationship that it facilitated and on the identities of the writers was equally strong, albeit in a different way. It is

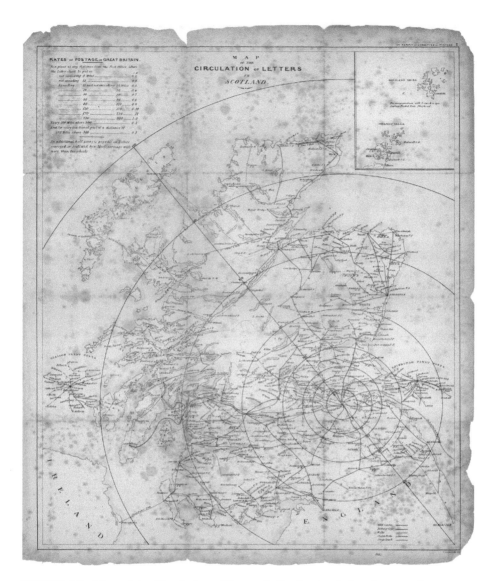

FIGURE 6.8: Map of the Circulation of Letters in Scotland, relating the cost of postage to the distance and mode of delivery, printed by S. Arrowsmith, 1838.

noticeable, for instance, that because letters to distant correspondents could sometimes take several days, weeks and even months to deliver, expressions of feeling were often related to the perception of time and space: impatience, longing, expectation, regret, relief, distance. This was nowhere more evident than in the case of Madame de Sévigné, a Parisian aristocrat and prolific letter-writer, whose identity as a loving and affectionate mother was forged by the 1120 letters she wrote to her

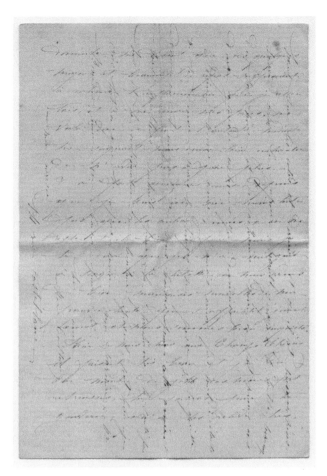

FIGURE 6.9: A cross-written or 'cross-hatched' letter, nineteenth century.

daughter in the South of France over a twenty-five-year period (1671–96). It was the timely transformation of the French postal system into a centralised public service in the late 1660s that enabled and even encouraged her to do this; how would she have been able to do it under any other circumstance? As a reflection of the extent to which her identity was shaped by the mode of communication she was using, she expressed some of her feelings in terms of the delight or frustration that the postal system inspired in her (on account of its efficiency or inefficiency respectively). The service enabled her to be in a constant state of communion with her daughter:

> I am bent on admiring the goodness and decency of these postal messengers, who are incessantly on the roads, carrying our letters about. Not a day goes by that they are not carrying one letter or another to you and to me; they are out and about at all times, at all hours . . . what a lovely invention the postal system is.

Indeed, it became a part of her extended metabolism: 'as soon as I have received a letter, I'd like another one right away; they are my life's breath'.[9] Thus, while the postal service radically increased the scope for maintaining relationships with absentees, it also structured the possibilities of experience and identity that such correspondence offered, institutionalising a disembodied sense of personal self by diffusing it into a virtual network of imaginative relationships with people in other times (the past and future) and other places.

This impulse to propagate the sense of self along new routes of communication was minutely regulated by the innumerable new practicalities and conventions that punctuated the process, rather as cogs regulate the rate at which the driving force in a clock is spent. As a result, each of these phenomena – which ranged from the improvement of roads and the introduction of tolls with which to pay for them, to the refinement of paper, ink, quills and sealing wax – made a subtle but significant contribution towards the co-ordination of a sense of personal identity. 'Where is my pen taking me?' Madame de Sévigné wrote on several occasions.[10] In the mid-eighteenth century, a new breed of extreme materialists – most notoriously Julien Offray de La Mettrie – believed the communication and communicable intelligence of human beings to be entirely determined by the material infrastructures of life, as if they were machines. La Mettrie was inspired by the Dutch physician Herman Boerhaave, whose observations he translated into French – for instance, Boerhaave's 'certainty' that 'Joy depends much upon a free Circulation of the Blood through all the Viscera and Vessels of the Body, which being obstructed, produce Anxieties, and an uneasy Sense to the Mind'; and, conversely, that 'Sadness will follow if the Spleen is obstructed, since itself will be invaded with an obtuse Pain or Anguish, and will not attenuate the Blood as usual, and as is necessary to perfect Health'.[11] In his own *Man a Machine* of 1748, La Mettrie asserted that, during sleep, 'the movement of the blood calms, and a sweet feeling of peace and tranquillity spreads through the entire machine'.[12] The expression of feeling was determined as much by the free circulation of blood in the veins for La Mettrie as it was by the free circulation of letters along the country roads of France for Sévigné. Consistent with his view of the materialistic determination of feeling, the Jaquet-Droz family of watchmakers produced a series of sophisticated automata that could play a keyboard instrument, make a drawing or write a text. The fact that *The Writer* automaton, made in around 1770, could be programmed to write any text of up to forty characters, follow his hand with his eyes and occasionally dip his quill pen in ink resonates with La Mettrie's belief that a performance of the conventional actions associated with intimacy and sensitivity is not necessarily a sign of intimacy and sensitivity; it could equally well be the product of conditioning or programming (Fig. 6.10). The invention of the typewriter in the nineteenth century represented a further step in the prescription of the possibilities of writing and thinking. Typing on his new Hansen Writing Ball – the first commercial typewriter to be able to create text more quickly than handwriting – the philosopher Friedrich Nietzsche observed in 1882: 'our writing instruments contribute to our thoughts' (Fig. 6.11).[13]

While the postal service facilitated long-distance communication between communicants, inducing them to extend their sense of themselves beyond their bodies, it still took place at the speed of the body, because it was effected by human intermediaries. When initiatives were taken to communicate more quickly than it is

FIGURE 6.10: *The Writer*, automaton made by Pierre Jaquet-Droz, 1768–4. Musée d'Art et d'Histoire, Neûchatel.

possible for the human body to travel, whether by foot, carriage or train, communication transcended the limitations of embodiment altogether and entered a new phase. The first systematic development of telecommunication occurred in the eighteenth century and took the form of semaphores. Semaphores (literally the 'carriers of signs') involved chains of beacons, placed at high points in the landscape or on unused church towers at intervals of up to twenty miles, between which messages could be relayed using flags, pallets, smoke or mirrors (Fig. 6.12). These messages were composed of sequences of abstract signals, operated manually and viewed with a telescope. In the 1790s, the Chappe brothers established a network of over five hundred semaphore points all over France, almost entirely for military and political use by the state, enabling brief messages to cross the country in a matter of minutes rather than hours or days. Originally tempted to call their system 'tachygraphy' (fast writing), which had been used in the 1640s for shorthand, they were eventually persuaded to call it 'telegraphy' (far writing). Although the actual time it took to transmit a message was nil, because it was seen rather than delivered, there were, of course, all kinds of logistical issues – for instance, the time it took to receive and dispatch a message, poor weather, maintenance of the stations and the scope for human error and unreliability. To address the latter problem, operators were threatened with fines if they failed to acknowledge receipt of a message, with a return message, within a minute. The whole process generated a complex series of practical and graphic conventions which formed part of the extended infrastructure of communication and, therefore, of identity formation.

FIGURE 6.11: The Hansen Writing Ball typewriter, made in 1878 and used by Nietzsche in 1882. Photo: Dieter Eberwein. © The Goethe and Schiller Archive, Weimar, Germany.

FIGURE 6.12: Ignace Chappe, *L'Histoire de la Télégraphe* (showing the use of smoke signals), Paris, 1824.

By the middle of the nineteenth century, semaphore systems were in operation all over Europe – just in time to be superseded by *electrical* telegraphy, which, in effect, simply converted them to electricity and streamlined them. With this new technology, which communicated by transmitting intermittent electric currents along lengths of wire cable, the conveyance of messages became even more abstracted from the immediacy of bodily experience. After many important but inconclusive experiments undertaken by a range of independent inventors in Europe and America, the first commercially viable system of electric telegraphy was invented by the British partnership of Charles Wheatstone and William Cooke, who were motivated by the developmental needs of the new railways to find a way to communicate rapidly over long distances in all conditions: in the dark, in tunnels and round corners (which semaphore systems could not do). Their invention, which they patented in 1837, involved the transmission of electric currents along five wires, to a series of five electromagnets, each of which corresponded with a magnetic needle mounted on a plate marked with the letters of the alphabet (Fig. 6.13). The needles could be activated independently and could, therefore, be deflected in a variety of different combinations, from which individual letters could be duly identified on the marked plate by the receiver. The system was first used to transmit messages between Camden Town and Euston railway stations in London on 25 July 1837. That such

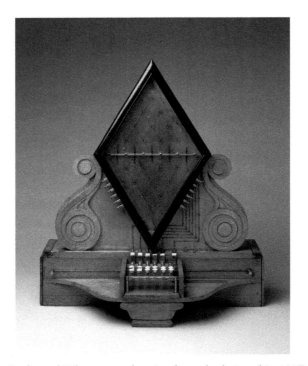

FIGURE 6.13: Cooke and Wheatstone electric telegraph, designed in 1837. The Science Museum, London. Photo: Science and Society Picture Library. Words that involved the six omitted letters used alternative spellings - for instance 'Kwaker' for 'Quaker'.

data could travel faster than, and independent of, a human courier was dramatically demonstrated on 1 January 1845, when a murderer escaping from Slough to London by train was overtaken by a telegraph message sent by the stationmaster at Slough, and identified as he got off the train at Paddington station; he was later arrested, tried and hanged. Despite its virtues, the Wheatstone and Cooke system was cumbersome due to the fact that it depended on the use of several cables at the same time and because it required the indicated letters to be recorded one by one by a human reader.

On the other side of the Atlantic Ocean, the artist Samuel Morse was also working on telegraphy. His independent system represented an advance on that of Wheatstone and Cooke because it was simpler, quicker and cheaper. Rather than linking each electrical signal to an individual letter of the alphabet, to be recorded manually by a receiver, it involved the use of a graphic code (Morse code, invented in 1837–8), which consisted of a series of dots and dashes, transmitted along a single cable as an interrupted current. This coded sequence of interruptions was then recorded at the receiving end as a series of dots and dashes drawn on strips of paper tape by a magnetised pencil before being translated back into letter forms. The first commercial application of this system took place in 1844 – the Baltimore–Washington Telegraph Line – and it was soon adopted as the international language of telegraphy.[14]

Morse gave up his career as an academic painter to pursue telegraphy, and his personal story therefore manifests a development in the possibility of human communication that was also taking place on a much greater scale at this time – from the individuality of handcrafted images and signs to the collectivity of mechanical processes. His early aspirations to become an artist came together in 1811, when he first travelled to Britain, aged 20, to study painting (under Benjamin West) at the Royal Academy, where he eventually exhibited his work to great acclaim. After three years in London, he returned to America, where he opened a studio and began to make a name for himself. He settled with his family in New Haven, but frequently travelled to Charleston, Washington and New York to execute commissions for paintings. On one of these occasions, in 1825, the delayed news of his wife's illness, transmitted by mail, prevented him from returning home in time to see her before she died – an experience that is said to have intensified his desire to develop an improved system of telecommunication. Between 1829 and 1832, Morse was in Europe again, studying old master paintings; while in France, he also witnessed the use of semaphores. It was on the return journey from France that he first conceived the dot-and-dash system that he would eventually develop into his famous code – no doubt partly in response to this experience.

Back in New York, Morse completed one of his best-known paintings, *Gallery of the Louvre*, which he had begun in Paris (Fig. 6.14). The work represents the *salon carré* (the gallery in which public Salons had been held since the eighteenth century), densely hung with a fanciful mixture of paintings from the Louvre's collection, including the *Mona Lisa* and works by Titian and Tintoretto, in the manner of a seventeenth-century 'gallery painting'. The picture was intended to convey a sense of the morally uplifting dignity of art that Morse was keen to promote at home, and as such, it was didactic and informative, rather than narrative (though it is does also depict a man, probably the artist himself, with a number of his friends at ease in the

FIGURE 6.14: Samuel F. B. Morse, *Gallery of the Louvre*, 1831–3, oil on canvas, 187.3 × 274.3 cm. Terra Foundation for American Art, Daniel J. Terra Collection, 1992.51. Photography © Terra Foundation for American Art, Chicago.

company of the European masters). Indeed, it is so schematically organised that, at one level, it amounts to little more than a visual inventory of masterpieces from the history of art, presented as codified references to their originals, to be deciphered by their viewers. In line with this view of the picture, Morse provided an accompanying catalogue of the paintings represented. Indeed, with the benefit of hindsight, the picture could be read as a series of 'zipped compressions' of images that Morse wished to transmit to America in manageably sized 'bytes', where they could be 'decompressed'. This was not the first time that Morse had demonstrated an interest in the technology of data storage. Although he was clearly ambitious as an artist, his many experiments with the recording, duplication and translation of images also reveal a fundamental interest in the mechanical transmission of data for its own sake, over and above the significance of its content. For instance, in 1823, he had co-created a machine that could carve marble replicas of sculptures (a project he abandoned when he discovered that a British patent for the technique already existed). The collection of paintings that he gathered together in his *Gallery of the Louvre* was copied using a camera obscura. And in the 1830s he experimented – albeit unsuccessfully – with a proto-photographic way of transferring images directly to paper. On a later trip to Paris in 1839, he met Daguerre and mastered his new photographic technique. In 1840, he opened a daguerreotype studio in New York. Significantly, while Morse's quest to improve the technology of communication was stimulated by the death of his wife, his interest in the subject continued to pervade

FIGURE 6.15: Sheldon, *Samuel Morse with his first telegraphy apparatus, 1835.*
Wellcome Collection.

his private life. His second wife, Sarah Griswold, whom he married in 1848, was a deaf-mute. He claimed that 'her misfortune of not hearing and her defective speech only excited the more my love and pity for her' and he took the opportunity to communicate with her by tapping her hand in Morse code.[15]

It was partly due to the failure of *Gallery of the Louvre* to communicate the meanings that he had invested in it that Morse gave up painting in 1837, aged forty-six, to devote his time to telegraphy. Poignantly underlining the continuity between these two means of communication, his first telegraphic apparatus was partly made of an old picture frame and stretcher (Fig. 6.15). Although he was largely motivated to take this step by his failure as a painter, his decision also reflects the way that electrical telecommunication was beginning to challenge and eclipse the importance of fine art as a primary means of communicating information, and eventually to utterly transform the possibilities of human communication and community. In the 1840s, he dreamed of a transatlantic cable and, indeed, the first submarine telegraph cables were laid – between Dover and Calais – in 1850. Messages that had been telegraphed to the British coast, shipped across the sea and then retelegraphed to their destination from the French coast could now be telegraphed the whole way in a fraction of the time. After several heroic attempts to accomplish the same between Britain and America, the goal was finally achieved in July 1866. It involved the laying of 6000 tons of cable, coiled up in the bowels of a single ship, over a distance of 2600 miles, sometimes to a depth of two miles (Fig. 6.16).

FIGURE 6.16: *Landing the Cable at Porthcurnew Bay*, Illustrated London News, 25 June 1870. Wellcome Collection.

The scale and accessibility of communication networks were further increased by the invention of the telephone by Alexander Graham Bell in 1876. This device was initially stimulated by both the perceived limitations of current technology – the electric telegraph was thirty years old at the time – and Bell's personal experience, like Morse's, of deafness in his family; both his mother and his wife were deaf. The ability of the telegraph to transmit *speech* was originally developed as an afterthought. Noticing that different strengths of current caused telegraphic receivers to vibrate at different pitches, Bell speculated that sound could be converted into electrical currents and transmitted along wire cables, and vice versa (using what he called a 'harmonic telegraph'). If messages in Morse code could be transmitted at different wavelengths, like a bundle of distinct notes in a musical chord, then several messages could be sent at the same time, and separated out at the receiving end. But when it was realised that these sounds could consist of not just a bundle of different pitches to be decoded but a coherent voice, the technology developed in a completely new direction, facilitating the transmission of speech. Firstly, it removed the time and space that seemed to separate people in distant parts of the world by enabling them to engage in live conversation in real time. The world became smaller; indeed, to the extent that it was the physical distance between people that had hitherto prevented them from communicating with each other directly (if at all), the telephone created a scenario whereby distant people were – at least while they were talking to each other – *in the same place*. And, secondly, it made it possible to use telegraphic appliances in the office or at home, rather than in telegraphic stations, from where printed telegrams still had to be delivered to their recipients in the medieval way, by 'runners'.

Having said this, although the *possibility* of live telecommunication now existed, the reality of it took many years to achieve on a large scale. First of all, there was a certain amount of resistance to the telephone for social and cultural reasons. Some people feared it would promote idle chit-chat or criminal scheming. Others felt it amounted to an invasion of privacy, allowing strangers into the home; for this reason, domestic telephones were frequently mounted in the 'public' hallway near the front door. Even the pioneers of telephony were conscious of its disruptive potential. Bell restricted use of the telephone in his house, and William Preece, who introduced the telephone to Britain in 1877 and was engineer-in-chief at the Post Office until 1899, is said to have commented: 'The absence of servants has compelled the Americans to adapt communications systems for domestic purposes. I have a telephone in my office, but just for show. If I want to send a message I use a sounder, or employ a boy to take it.'[16] Some such boys were upgraded from 'telegram runner' to 'telephone exchange operator'; however, their manners left much to be desired and they were soon replaced by trained 'hello girls', who, according to one journalist, had voices 'like summer streams trickling through a forest glade'.[17] This, in its turn, was a source of concern in some quarters, as it left vulnerable young ladies alone talking to strange men (Fig. 6.17). Moreover, many people were confused about what the telephone was actually for, and how it worked. Did it work for all languages? Could germs be spread over the phone? Confusing the device with an

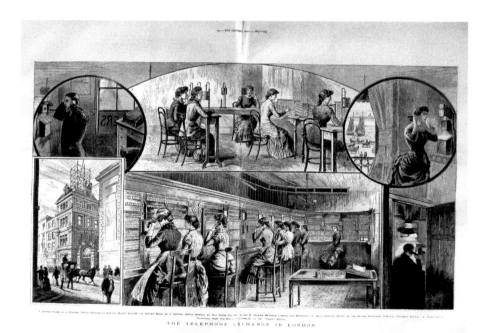

FIGURE 6.17: 'The Telephone exchange in London', from *The Graphic*, 1 September 1883.

oracle, one visitor to a public demonstration asked it: 'Who will be the next president?' Until its practical potential was understood, it remained a source of entertainment, wonder or anxiety.

Secondly, telephony presented enormous technical challenges that took time to surmount. The first ever telephonic communication (between Bell and his assistant) took place between two adjacent rooms. Enlarging on this model, the first working telephone lines were dedicated to specific connections, linking a single transmitter and a single receiver – for instance, between an office and a bank, or a clinic and a pharmacy. Anticipating the function of radio, they were also used by telephone companies for one-way broadcasts of news or entertainment. Telegraph exchanges, facilitating the development of *networks* of telephones, were not established until the number of users warranted it. Subscriptions were initially slow. In 1878, the District Telephone Company of New Haven printed what amounted to the first telephone book: a list of the names of its fifty subscribers (only eleven of whom were residential), but without numbers; to contact a fellow subscriber, a caller had to give their name to the operator, who would then make the connection.[18] But under this elaborate system, it could take five minutes or more to make a connection. The delay was partly solved when automatic exchange companies began to operate in the 1890s. While manual exchange continued well into the twentieth century, the first automatic exchange mechanism was designed in 1889 by an undertaker from Kansas City, Almon Strowger, when he discovered that one of the operators was directing business intended for him towards her own husband, also an undertaker;[19] thus, not all the 'hello girls' were what they seemed to be. By slow degrees, the range of the networks grew – the first intercity line, between New York and Boston, was established in 1884 – but the quality of the sound was often poor. As the length of cables increased, so signals lost power and needed to be refreshed and amplified at periodic intervals by automated 'repeaters' (just as signals had been retransmitted by the operators of semaphores). Furthermore, the growing *quantity* of cables darkened the skies and filled the air with humming and buzzing sounds (Fig. 6.17, bottom left frame).

A third reason for the slow take-up of the telephone was that the system was expensive, both to establish and to use. As in previous eras, efficient communication, such as the use of messengers or the sending and receiving of letters, was a luxury and was initially restricted to businesses and the elite. Before the provision of coin-operated telephone booths, patented in the USA in 1889, members of the public could in principle use telephones at the premises of exchange companies, though they had little cause to do so as few of their peers had phones. This need for *both* communicants to subscribe to the technology of telephony retarded its expansion, but eventually strengthened it, enabling it to become entrenched; unlike earlier forms of media, through which it was possible to receive communications without buying into the infrastructure that supported them, the necessarily two-way technology of telephony ensured that it developed as an even network rather than as a constellation of independent centres, emanating communications. In most European countries, the slow adoption of the telephone in the home was also due to the fact that national monopolies of telecommunications services resulted in uncompetitive subscription prices that enabled anxious governments both to control the process of communication by limiting it and to protect government-run telegraph and mail systems.[20] But, following energetic advertising campaigns in the 1930s, domestic use of the telephone began to gather momentum. By the end of the century, it was almost ubiquitous in developed countries.

While the installation of a telephone in every home was an ideal in the 1930s, it was soon perceived to have limitations because it was *fixed*: people could only use the telephone when they were at home, where they usually had to share it, or at a public kiosk. Significantly, the idea of the *mobile* phone was not, at first, conceived abstractly as a 'good idea' in itself (though it did appear as an object of fantasy in some futuristic contexts); on the contrary, it emerged in the 1940s, out of pre-existing technology. Because telephone technology was so bulky and heavy, the first mobile telephones were not originally designed for the pocket or handbag; they were conceived for the automobile, which was both strong enough to support them and innately suited to take advantage of their capacities. But the power and the range of these devices was extremely limited. It was only when it became possible to concentrate them into a manageable size, increase their power and range and reduce their cost, that they began to resemble today's mobile phones, orientated around each individual rather than each household. This mobility not only changed the actual experience of communication; it also changed the wider demography of communication. For while the technology of the mobile phone may have *emerged* organically from a historical infrastructure – battling against a plethora of cultural, technical and economic constraints for over a century (as reflected in the limited but growing access that people had to the technology of telephony, even in the countries that developed it) – it was no longer *dependent* on that infrastructure for its use. New users could bypass the telegraphic and landline phase, and the costs and complexity associated with them. As a result, the number of mobile phone users increased exponentially, spreading beyond the parameters of the developed world, to the point at which they became almost universally available.

Not surprisingly, these advances in the technology of communication led to new configurations of personal identity. Indeed, by enabling more people to communicate more widely than ever before, the telephone created new possibilities of self-expression and became a key instrument of identity formation. This relationship – between personal identity and the possibilities of self-expression that the technology of communication offered it – took a leap forward with the development of the mobile phone.[21] Firstly, the mobility and size of the mobile phone enabled it to become a permanent extension of the individual person; it no longer needed to be only intermittently available because fixed in place or shared. Secondly, when mobile phones were packed with the data-processing capabilities of computers, in smartphones – enabling them to 'see', 'remember' and 'analyse' the world on behalf of their users – they appropriated functions that are usually ascribed to the conscious individual. By analysing previous choices, they became able to identify an individual's personal preferences. Moreover, some of the functions of smartphones are *specifically* conceived as instruments of self-expression. The possibility of communicating by sharing images, for instance, via Instagram or Pinterest, is *created* by the technology. Role-playing computer and phone games have also been instrumental in this shift. Virtual 'avatars' were conceived in the 1970s as quasi-realistic surrogate selves to be activated, performed or lived online.[22] They constitute representations of the self of the user as a completely imaginary, technology-dependent being, corresponding, to a greater or lesser extent, with the embodied version. The extent to which individuals can become identified with their phones is also reflected in the fact that *loss* of a phone can lead to a personal 'crisis', in which the user is deprived of certain key abilities – not only the ability to stay in touch with his or her community, but also the ability to navigate his or her world (for instance, through the phone's 'schedule' and 'reminder' functions). In 1975, a devastating fire at the New York Telephone Exchange disabled the telephone connections of 170,000 people for three weeks, causing widespread anxiety and stress in the affected community.[23] Nevertheless, the feeling of being incomplete without one's phone is a largely twenty-first-century experience. While the positive value of phones cannot be doubted – are they not miracles of modern technology? – it is arguable that one of their key attractions – the feature which, in fact, stands to make them addictive – is the very high rate of 'cause and effect' that they offer; for besides facilitating communication, the process of browsing one's phone is a process in which the 'will to make things happen' is being exercised and gratified from moment to moment, more so perhaps than in any other activity. And in so doing, it reflects the self to itself in an irresistible continuum of miniature satisfactions.

But while giving space to the self-sense on the one hand, the mobile phone has also had the opposite effect: of depersonalising the user. The text-only medium of the first messaging services was so utilitarian that it made messages seem generic and *impersonal*. In subsequent designs, this impression has been reinforced by 'predictive text', which anticipates what the user intends to write, implying that he or she is merely a manifestation of conventions that are latent in the culture and that his or her thoughts and feelings can be identified probabilistically. The same can be said of the selfie stick, which has, since 2014, institutionalised the self's inclination to reflect on itself, just as mirrors had done in the sixteenth and seventeenth centuries. Although the selfie stick seems to express a craving for individuality in the contemporary world, it can also be seen as an instrument of mass conformity. It promotes a ritual act, performed by millions, that uses commercialised technology to confer value on a diverse range of experiences, to the extent that those experiences are replaced by artificial representations that transform them into 'functions of the self'; indeed, to this end, it seems that experiences are often contrived *in order to be documented* in selfies. Thus, while smartphones can be highly personal objects, expressing and extending the self, they can also be seen to manifest a *loss* of self. For while they facilitate experience of the world, they also offer standardised *alternatives* to experience – filming and photographing the world instead of observing it, recording it instead of remembering it, processing data instead of reflecting on it. Moreover, the knowledge of the individual that they seem to acquire is based not on intimate sensitivity to his or her character, but on statistical analysis of behavioural patterns. In this respect, smartphones and the behaviour they generate *virtualise* the self; they make it merely *seem* to exist, by deduction. Indeed, the ability of smartphones to relay information about their users to third parties without their knowledge and, reputedly, to film and record them even when they are switched off, reflects the extent to which the definitive 'characteristics' or 'attributes' of the self can seem to function, or be made to function, independently of a 'conscious subject'.

From its earliest days, many people berated the destructive effects that the telephone would have on local communities, as individuals withdrew into their own semi-simulated worlds. However, some idealists capitalised on the potential for objectivity that they found in its mechanical processes, using it to transcend what they considered to be the arbitrariness and self-indulgence of subjectivity. In his 'telephone works' of 1923, for instance, the Hungarian artist Laszlo Moholy-Nagy used the levelling effect of the telephone to erase all personal touches from his work; he specifically conceived these works with such geometrical precision that they could be described over the telephone to technicians who could then execute them purely from the data given, leaving no trace whatsoever of the 'artist's hand' and no grounds, therefore, for a *personal* response on the viewer's part (Fig. 6.18).

The ability of technology to suppress the particularities of individual embodiment – deliberately or otherwise – was paralleled by the way that people's personal 'communities of communicants' became increasingly virtual and dispersed during the course of the twentieth century. With the exception of the people with whom an individual actually lived or worked, personal communities – consisting mostly of friends and extended families – became ever more supported by mail and telephone contact, in place of physical contact; they could stay 'in touch', while in fact being untouchable. The obverse of this development has been that the sense of community in physical neighbourhoods – in the vicinity of an individual's physical home – has in many ways weakened.[24] This trend has taken root to such an extent that, at least in cities and large towns which grew in tandem with industrialisation, people

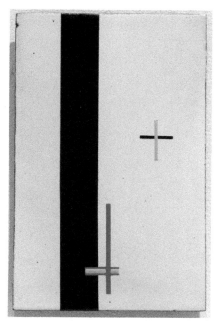

FIGURE 6.18: Laszlo Moholy-Nagy, *EM2 (Telephone picture)*, 1923, porcelain enamel on steel, 47.5 × 30.1 cm. Museum of Modern Art, New York. © Photo SCALA, Florence.

scarcely know their neighbours. Already during the Industrial Revolution, when thousands of rural peasants were made to seek work in factories in cities, some of which developed especially to accommodate them, local communities began to consist more and more of people who did not know each other (Fig. 6.19). In ancient communities, strangers had been relatively rare. In the most primitive societies, they were so unusual that, when they did appear, they were sometimes invested with magical, auspicious or dangerous powers; in extreme cases they could be worshipped or sacrificed. But in an urban context, in which it became less and less possible for inhabitants to maintain personal relationships with all the people they encountered, the experience of strangers (and related experiences, such as loneliness) became increasingly common.

As the number and populations of cities in the developed world grew, escalating dramatically throughout the nineteenth and twentieth centuries, it became increasingly important, for the sake of social cohesion, for alternative sources of common ground to be found. One of the key conventions that evolved to serve this purpose was *celebrity*. Ironically, celebrity was a by-product of the development of printed and electronic media, for whatever the media covered necessarily became known to a wide range of people. Especially pertinent in the present context is the way in which the cult of celebrity became a 'currency of strangers' among the urban populations of the nineteenth and twentieth centuries (rather as civility had become a 'currency of strangers' in the sixteenth century, albeit on a much smaller scale). While the modern obsession of the media and its audiences with celebrity is frequently trivialised and ridiculed on the grounds that it is superficial, vain and exploitative, the shared awareness of widely mediated phenomena such as celebrities, news and sport created a medium of common knowledge and values between strangers that contextualised them as members of the same community. It gave them something to talk about, thereby enabling them to identify with and relate to each other. Just as it was the technology of mass production and telecommunications that created the social chasm between local people in the first place, so it was, in this instance, the same technology that attempted to fill it (Fig. 6.20).

In some areas, the obverse of the challenge to personal selfhood was the imagining of a sense of *communal* identity, to which the dynamics of personal identity were subjected. The sense of a depersonalised, collective identity was most intensely visualised following the application of wireless telegraphy, discovered in the 1880s, to the broadcasting of news, advertising and entertainment – by radio, popularised in the 1920s, television in the 1940s and 50s, and the internet in the 1990s. Above all, the 'wireless' breakthrough made it possible to communicate a wider range of data types to a vastly increased number of people in more diverse places, at a far greater speed than previous technologies – ultimately to the extent that, notwithstanding technical, cultural and economic constraints, its scope has embraced the vast majority of the human race. But, to some observers, it also promised to unify human beings, not merely as a concept or an ideal, but as an *actuality* – i.e. as single user groups, audiences and readerships, identified as such by their use of common networks of communication. Indeed, from this perspective, wireless telecommunications could be said to have acquired a degree of autonomy, reflecting the collective identity of their users, by virtue of the fact that the technology by which that identity now

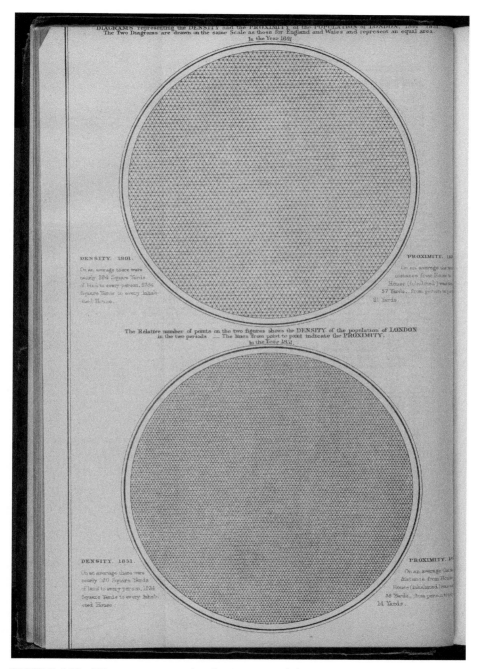

FIGURE 6.19: 'Diagrams representing the Density and the Proximity of the Population of London, 1801–1851', Census of Great Britain, 1851. Wellcome Collection.

FIGURE 6.20: 'The Language of the Walls', John Orlando Parry, *A London Street Scene*, 1835, watercolour. Celebrity, cultivated in advertisements and newspapers, became a 'currency of strangers'.

communicates with itself has become uncontrollable. It has become so complex and incomprehensible to its users that the latter have become dependent as a group – rather than independent as individuals – on a system that has itself become sufficiently ingrained in the modern world to be beyond the control of any one individual or group of individuals. As a result, it has become imaginable – to some – that, in so far as the identity of humanity is registered and realised by its capacity for, and means of, communicating with itself, it is more than the sum of its parts; it could become, in some sense, a self-reflective whole. Indeed, it has been argued that the notion of 'global identity' (inhabiting a 'global village') has been, or is being, generated by the technology of electronic telecommunications, which actualises and substantiates it by providing it with a medium of conscious self-reference (Fig. 6.21). This co-causal relationship between technology and global identity, partly forged in service to the cult of celebrity, was demonstrated in July 1985, when an estimated two billion people from all over the globe – just under half the entire population of humanity at the time – 'came together' in an unprecedented and hitherto impossible way to watch the Live Aid rock festival live on TV. In our own time, the threat of a pandemic virus has precipitated the development of new types and intensities of global internet connectivity, no longer in conjunction with physical travel but in place of it.

The technology of telecommunications has facilitated the realisation of innumerable new forms of virtual community – from radio and TV audiences to online subscriber groups and beyond – thereby invoking new principles of communal identity. However, the notion that history is progressing towards higher denominations of identity or self-consciousness is not a new one. Its origins lie in traditional visions of sacred history, as in the biblical books of prophecies and the millennial philosophies of medieval thinkers such as Joachim of Fiore, according to whom history was the process of God's self-revelation in the world. It was not until the eighteenth century, when this notion was purged of its visionary status and aligned to the emerging theory of evolution, that it was first theorised in a quasi-modern 'rationalist' form. Most significantly, the philosopher

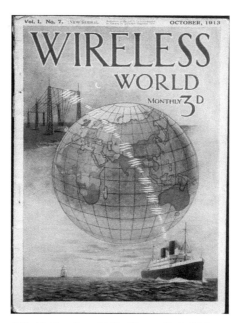

FIGURE 6.21: *Wireless World*, October 1913. Photo: Jack Weber.

Hegel proposed, in the 1820s, that the process of universal history consisted of the evolution of the matter of the world – at all levels, from physical matter to the raw, indeterminate substance of human culture and psychology – towards ever-greater levels of internal coherence. It accomplished this to the extent that transcendental 'spirit' or consciousness, otherwise residing in an unrealised state of infinite potential, could become self-conscious in it, and could thereby be realised in it as the principle of its self-determination, or self-consciousness. Conversely, while the evolution of the world enabled spirit to become self-conscious in it, so the impulse of spirit to become self-conscious caused the world to evolve. Thus, the self-realisation of spirit as 'I' enabled the world to evolve towards ever more comprehensive levels of internal consistency; and, conversely, the evolution of the world towards ever more comprehensive levels of internal consistency enabled spirit to realise itself self-consciously as 'I', at ever-higher levels of inclusivity. To the extent that the evolution of the matter of the world occurred both in response to the influence of spirit and in keeping with its own nature and laws, it constituted the parameters of human cultural history.

In the context of world history, Hegel theorised that the personal identity of individual human beings was only fully validated when it achieved objectivity. It accomplished this by freely conforming not to the subjective whims of its own inclination (which constituted selfishness), but to the objective principles underpinning the society in which it functioned. The impulse to conform to these principles, from which its society derived its own unity and coherence, was experienced as its sense of morality and was processed as its religion. It was this evolution – and struggle – towards ever-higher levels of conscious community, perfected in the nation state, that constituted human history. Hegel theorised that the first human communities evolved from arbitrary gatherings of individuals, living lives of spontaneous and intuitive creativity that bore no relation to the notion of a higher nation state, and, therefore, afforded spirit (the substance of the self) little opportunity to realise itself at a transhuman level; from his point of view, this 'childish' level of life was still manifest in oriental cultures. The ancient Greeks represented a second 'youthful' stage of evolution, in that the personal inclinations of individuals revolved around an objective principle of beauty, even though that principle was not yet self-consciously realised as 'national statehood'. At the third, 'manly' stage, as realised in ancient Rome, the notion of the state – with its laws and constitutions – became self-conscious, but its pagan agenda conflicted with that of its citizens, whose submission it demanded as a matter of principle, regardless of their own preferences. At the final, 'senior' stage, currently realised in the Christian nations of the Germanic world, the state had become a fully self-conscious and self-determining unity, in that its laws, morally perfected by virtue of their Christian source, are freely supported by its citizens, who consciously sacrifice themselves into these laws at the expense of their own personal inclinations, and embrace them as the form of their religion. Hegel's philosophy of history – fusing nationalism, Romanticist subjectivity and historical determinism – seemed to some of his followers to find confirmation in the fact that the ancient city states of the Italian peninsular were unified into the kingdom of Italy in 1861, and the multiple disparate states of the German Federation (formed at the Congress of Vienna in 1815) became reconfigured into a unified German Empire in 1871, when smaller units of identity, revolving around their own principles and princes, sacrificed their sovereignty for the sake of the higher state of national identity. Although knowledge of its subsequent abuse at the hands of the Nazis gives Hegel's philosophy of history an ominous resonance, and despite its evident ignorance of oriental cultures, it is anachronistic to consider it out of context. In their own time, his ideas were considered to be liberal and progressive; they represented a visionary departure from the static abstractions of Enlightenment idealism, and entitled the 'common people' to a form of ideological power (rooted in national rather than classical history) that eventually gave rise to liberal social reforms.

In Germany, the possibility of national unity was precipitated by the development of networks of transportation and communication – a growing nationwide railway system – which established a degree of practical unity in the country before the concept of national unity was actually realised and ratified. Practical connections precipitated psychological ones. Elsewhere in the industrialising world, the possibilities of electronic telecommunication stimulated a similar vision of a paradigm shift on an even greater scale: from the identity of the individual brain to the identity of a global brain. This vision contextualised individuals not merely as social, cultural beings – as parts of society or mankind – but, more materially and impersonally, as psychophysical constituents of the earth itself. One British observer, looking back from the 1890s, commented that, at the time of Queen Victoria's accession to the throne in 1837, when electronic communication and photography had barely got off the ground, 'the masses were almost as restricted to oral communication and local commerce as their ancestors were under the Stuarts'.[25] But by 1851, the American novelist Nathaniel Hawthorne could speculate:

Is it a fact – or have I dreamed it – that, by means of electricity, the world of matter has become a great nerve, vibrating thousands of miles in a breathless point of time? Rather the round globe is a vast head, a brain, instinct with intelligence! Or, shall we say, it is itself a thought, nothing but thought, and no longer the substance which we deemed it![26]

According to this global vision, the surface of the earth was no longer compartmentalised by the dynamics of several different, self-referential communities. It was unified by the web of communications that at any given time encircled it, thereby realising it as a single being or even a single intelligence. In such circumstances, human beings would be the equivalents of the brain cells of the earth, spread over its surface like the cerebral cortex, such that, when their level of connectivity reached a point of saturation, their different minds would be reconceived as a transpersonal unity, as 'more than the sum of their parts' – as a tree rather than leaves, a day rather than hours, a book rather than pages; that is to say, as a self-conscious global brain.

The notion that the earth is a conscious whole, comprising the consciousness of its parts, emerged from the theory of evolution, which, as we have seen, shifted the motive force in history from God, providence, fortune and reason towards nature. According to this new vision, all of matter is necessarily pervaded by the force and intelligence of nature. But if this is the case, in what kind of subject or subjects does the intelligence of matter inhere? The experimental psychologist and philosopher Gustav Fechner (1801–87) answered this question by conflating the idea of the personal self – or, putting a mystical spin on it, the human soul – with the great 'chain of being'. The great chain of being was a hierarchical classification of the universe, derived from texts by Plato and Aristotle, that reached down from the highest cosmic level of life (sometimes, but not always, associated with God) to the lowest formation of matter, via the solar system, planets, earth, animals, plants and minerals, each of which corresponded to the others by proportion and analogy. According to Fechner, the natural intelligence that pervades matter manifests in all creatures as a soul appropriate to their level of life. Moreover, the consciousness of individual souls coheres with that of others to form orders of collective consciousness higher up the scale.[27] The psychologist William James (1842–1910), one of the first to promote Fechner's philosophy in English, summarised his view in 1909:

In ourselves, visual consciousness goes with our eyes, tactile consciousness with our skin. But altho[ugh] neither skin nor eye knows aught of the sensations of the other, they come together and figure in some sort of relation and combination in the more inclusive consciousness which each of us names his *self*. Quite similarly, then, says Fechner, we must suppose that my consciousness of myself and yours of yourself, altho[ugh] in their immediacy they keep separate and know nothing of each other, are yet known and used together in a higher consciousness, that of the human race, say, into which they enter as constituent parts. Similarly, the whole human and animal kingdoms come together as conditions of a consciousness of still wider scope. This combines in the soul of the earth with the consciousness of the vegetable kingdom, which in turn contributes its share of experience to that of the whole solar system, and so on from synthesis to synthesis and height to height, till an absolutely universal consciousness is reached.[28]

Fechner also proposed that, by virtue of its correspondence to the structure of man, the soul of the earth has its own distinctive operations that are the equivalent to, but different from, human brain activity (its orbit and vibrations, the polarisation of electrical forces, the refraction of light). In the words of the Russian philosopher P. D. Ouspensky, who also championed Fechner: 'In *electrical charges*, in lightning, in thunder, in the gusts and howling of the wind are felt flashes of sensory-nervous tremors of some gigantic organism.'[29] Fechner maintained that human thought and experience also form part of the inner life of the earth. Just as optical and aural signals are transmitted to the brain by networks of nerve fibres, so the earth has 'pathways' along which the movement of human interactions becomes its mental activity. The mind of the earth subsumes the minds of men; 'our [human] individuality is sustained by the greater individuality':

> Has not the earth [got more than enough pathways], by which you and I are physically continuous, to do for our two minds what the brain-fibres do for the sounds and sights in a single mind? Must every higher means of unification between things be a literal brain-fibre, and go by that name? Cannot the earth-mind know otherwise the contents of our minds together? . . . [Just] as our mind is not the bare sum of our sights plus our sounds plus our pains, but in adding these terms together it also finds relations among them and weaves them into schemes and forms and objects of which no one sense in its separate estate knows anything, so the earth-soul traces relations between the contents of my mind and the contents of yours of which neither of our separate minds is conscious.[30]

That is to say, unbeknown to individual people, human communication constitutes the synaptic activity of the earth's brain. The role of communication in the development of higher denominations of subjectivity was highlighted by the philosopher Eduard von Hartmann, who speculated, in his pioneering *Philosophy of the Unconscious* of 1869, that, just as neurons in the brain are connected to each other by nerve fibres, so the consciousness of two individuals could be connected to each other by communication:

> Only because the one part of my brain has a direct communication with the other is the consciousness of the two parts unified; and could we unite the brains of two human beings by a path of communication equivalent to the cerebral fibres, both would no longer have two, but one consciousness.[31]

While individuals may be unaware of the porosity of their minds, their condition might also result in changing states of consciousness that could, despite their foundation in 'natural science', be compared to experiences of higher, collective realms of existence traditionally described as 'mystical' or 'religious'. William James speculated that such insights into the 'collective unconscious' of mankind might only be experienced by extraordinary individuals:

> For my own part I find in some of these abnormal or supernormal facts the strongest suggestions in favor of a superior co-consciousness being possible. I doubt whether we shall ever understand some of them without using the very letter of Fechner's conception of a great reservoir in which the memories of

earth's inhabitants are pooled and preserved, and from which, when the threshold lowers or the valve opens, information ordinarily shut out leaks into the mind of *exceptional individuals among us*. But those regions of inquiry are perhaps too spook-haunted to interest an academic audience, and the only evidence I feel it now decorous to bring to the support of Fechner is drawn from ordinary religious experience. I think it may be asserted that there are religious experiences of a specific nature, not deducible by analogy or psychological reasoning from our other sorts of experience. I think that they point with reasonable probability to the continuity of our consciousness with a wider spiritual environment from which the ordinary prudential man (who is the only man that scientific psychology, so called, takes cognizance of) is shut off.[32]

But such experiences could also be known to ordinary people, albeit in the extraordinary circumstance of self-sacrifice. Such experiences, James suggested, became especially pertinent and prevalent at the time of the Reformation, when individuals became newly preoccupied with their own moral predicament:

> There are resources in us that naturalism with its literal and legal virtues never recks of, possibilities that take our breath away, of another kind of happiness and power, based on giving up our own will and letting something higher work for us, and these seem to show a world wider than either physics or philistine ethics can imagine. Here is a world in which all is well, in spite of certain forms of death, indeed because of certain forms of death – death of hope, death of strength, death of responsibility, of fear and worry, competency and desert, death of everything that paganism, naturalism, and legalism pin their faith on and tie their trust to.[33]

Such experiences do not simply lead to philosophical conclusions; they are life changing:

> Those who have such experiences distinctly enough and often enough to live in the light of them remain quite unmoved by criticism, from whatever quarter it may come, be it academic or scientific, or be it merely the voice of logical common sense. They have had their vision and they know – that is enough – that we inhabit an invisible spiritual environment from which help comes, our soul being mysteriously one with a larger soul whose instruments we are.[34]

Notions about human identity were partly prompted by – and then 'proven' by analogy with – recent developments in technology. Just as telegraph cables encircling the earth had suggested the unity of mankind and of the world, so electromagnetism (predicted on theoretical grounds by James Clerk Maxwell in the 1860s and proven to exist by Heinrich Hertz in 1886) prompted the thought that human beings may be able to communicate with each other *psychically* – sharing mind content, or transmitting it to each other, without any external medium of exchange. Communication of this kind was traditionally ascribed to angels (believed to be bodiless and placeless) and – according to Gregory the Great, writing in the sixth century – it would be experienced by humanity after the Resurrection of the Dead; but it now seemed plausible to find it among living human beings. The notion of 'telepathy' – a term coined in 1882 – gained credibility by comparison to X-rays, which were discovered by Wilhelm Rontgen in 1895, and wireless telegraphy, which was applied to radio communication by Guglielmo Marconi in the same year. In 1893, the evangelist Henry Drummond had argued that 'however little we know of it, however remote we are from it, whether it ever be realised or not, telepathy is theoretically the next stage in the Evolution of Language'.[35] In 1906, the poet Edward Carpenter speculated that:

> [just] as modern science shows us that the air, the sea, and the solid frame of the earth itself may be the vehicle of waves which, without wire or definite channel, may yet convey our thoughts safely to one another through intervening leagues of distance, so surely we must believe that the countless vibrations ever going on around, and ever radiating from and impinging on every known object, are messengers too of endless meaning and feeling.[36]

And, as we saw in chapter 5, in 1920 the Russian visionary Alexei Gastev dreamed of a single 'world head' superseding 'millions of heads', such that thought would become 'the objective psychic process of the whole class, with systems of psychological switches and locks'.[37] Throughout this period, many experiments on the possibility of psychic communication were undertaken (Fig. 6.22). Indeed, it has been surmised that the fact

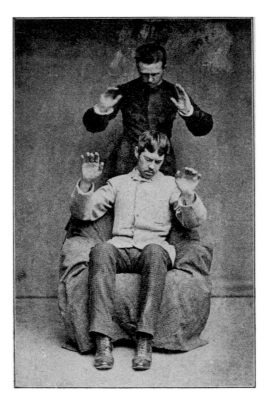

FIGURE 6.22: 'The direct transfer of thoughts, by mental suggestion', from Wilhelm Gustav Gessmann, *Magnetismus und Hypnotismus*, Vienna, 1895, plate XVIII, opposite p. 198.

that human beings cannot easily identify the source of their thoughts (despite being quick to appropriate them as 'our own') may indicate that we are already much more telepathic *spontaneously*, and therefore less independent as individuals, than we realise.[38]

While several writers contemplated the sublimation of personal identity in the identity of the earth, some went further, exploring the evolution of identity in relation to the cosmos as a whole. In such a context, human self-consciousness was the consummation of the development of the universe over millions of years – from a state of chaotic energy (manifest as the prevalence of atoms), to a state of cohesive matter (prevalent as molecules), to animate life (prevalent in organisms), to self-conscious mind (prevalent in human beings). This sense of the realisation of self-consciousness and self-determination at ever-higher levels of manifestation was anticipated by the thirteenth-century mystic Meister Eckhart, who, by stating that 'even God can only say "I" in so far as I am one with him', suggested that, while God is consciousness, *self*-consciousness is only possible at the level at which the manifest universe is sufficiently integrated and organised to accommodate it – which, at his time, was that of the human individual – giving rise to a personal sense of self.[39] The scope of God's influence was complicated by the thought that there may be life on other planets. If other planets were inhabited, would those inhabitants be corrupt (having not been descended from Adam) and could Christ redeem them?[40] This possibility of extraterrestrial life had been contemplated in antiquity and, having been deemed preposterous by many medieval philosophers, was revived with vigour in the Renaissance. When the earth was dislodged from its position at the centre of the universe, it ceased to be inherently unique, whereupon the possibility that there may be others like it arose. Giordano Bruno (1548–1600) was burned at the stake for suggesting that there might exist an infinite number of other 'worlds'. In 1638, the English clergyman and natural philosopher John Wilkins hypothesised that there are mountains, valleys, plains and seas on the moon, as on the earth, and that 'tis probable there may be inhabitants in this other World, but of what kinde they are is uncertaine'. In sympathy with these speculations, the evolutionary model of identity formation suggested that not only mankind and the earth but *all* the planets would eventually become self-conscious, and indeed that the self-conscious identities of the planets will eventually evolve to such levels of refinement that they too will fuse into a collective form of identity that is self-conscious at an even higher level of self-determination: that of the solar system; and that the self-conscious identities of the solar systems will in turn coalesce and evolve into the higher self-conscious identity of the galaxy; and so on, until eventually spirit – in the Hegelian sense – becomes conscious of itself as the totality of the universe. In 1851, Gustav Fechner proposed that:

> The vaster orders of mind go with the vaster orders of body. The entire earth on which we live must have . . . its own collective consciousness. So must each sun, moon, and planet; so must the whole solar system have its own wider consciousness, in which the consciousness of our earth plays one part. So has the entire starry system as such its consciousness; and if that starry system be not the sum of all that is, materially considered, then that whole system, along with whatever else may be, is the body of that absolutely totalised consciousness of the universe to which men give the name of God.[41]

From the creation of the postal service to the globalisation of the internet, the development of the technology of communication has precipitated – or been seen to precipitate – the formation of ever-larger denominations of 'virtual community'. As we have seen, these communities have ranged from peasants who rarely left their villages to dispersed families and networks of officials; from the citizens of nations to the whole of humanity; and from the earth to the totality of the universe itself. Under the spell of evolutionary theory, optimists imagined and hoped that the obsessive sacrosanctity of national identity would yield to a more inclusive and harmonious form of world community; that wars would no longer happen. In the same way, the philosophy of humanism, which originally promoted human interests in relation to the medieval church, but now indulged them at the expense of other creatures, would be superseded by a more holistic and ecological view of the conscious, living earth.[42] The Russian geochemist Vladimir Vernadsky (1863–1945) speculated that the evolution of the earth towards ever-higher levels of intelligence was a *geological* process, determined by the continuous, progressive reconfiguration of the atoms of which the planet is composed. He maintained that it was the photosynthetic processing of solar radiation that enabled the realm of inanimate matter – the 'geosphere' – to release pure oxygen and thereby support a thin film of animate life covering, and constituting, the surface of the earth – the 'biosphere'. Subject to the same evolutionary logic, the redistribution of calcium in the earth's surface was one of many shifts that enabled the biosphere to become fully established; for by migrating from the shells of primitive molluscs to the skeletons and skulls of mammals, it facilitated the development of brains and intelligence. The self-reflective use of intelligence, uniquely possible in human minds, has given rise to the pervasive infrastructures of human civilisation – languages, cultures, technologies, institutions, etc. – but on account of their *geological* determinants, these infrastructures should be seen as a function of the *earth* – amounting to a film of intelligence on its surface (the 'noosphere') – rather than of human ingenuity.

The notion of the earth as a whole remained a figment of the imagination until 1968. Although the wholeness and rotundity of the earth had been *visualised* since antiquity, and was frequently represented in globes from the sixteenth century, it is arguable the earth could not be *realised* as a self-conscious unity until it was actually experienced as such, self-consciously. On the grounds that earth is covered by billions of eyes, ears and other sense faculties, this experience could be said to have occurred as the first human sighting of the earth as a unified whole, during which the earth – via a human 'part' of itself – actually saw itself as a discrete object for the first time. This moment of self-recognition was powerfully disseminated throughout the world by the celebrated *Earthrise* photograph taken in December 1968, and the publication of the first ever photograph in which the entire planet is visible, taken in 1972 (Fig. 6.23). In the same years, the scientist and environmentalist James Lovelock conceived his 'Gaia hypothesis', which aimed to put the notion of the living earth on to a scientific footing without recourse to analogy or reference to the supposed 'purpose of evolution'. This controversial theory proposed that the earth is a unified, 'homeostatic' system which, not unlike the human body, is able to maintain a consistent temperature and chemical composition, as well as other conditions necessary for life, despite millions of years of inconsistency in the

FIGURE 6.23: The Earth seen from Apollo 17, 7 December 1972. Photo: NASA.

chemical and atmospheric environment in which it exists. Many of these views were highly speculative and even visionary and it has not been the purpose here to evaluate them. More to the point is the way that new possibilities of communication have facilitated the formation of ever-larger forms of community, which have in their own way qualified and relativised the status of personal identity. On the one hand, personal identity has become thoroughly fragmented and inconsistent; on the other, it has been relegated to the level of an 'expedient illusion'. Certainly it is no longer presumed to be absolute or whole; nor is it securely supported by the social, cultural and material infrastructures of the contemporary world.

CHAPTER SEVEN

The Psychological Self: the Pathology of Art and Cinematographic Modes of Self-remembering

The intuition that the nature of personal identity was provisional rather than absolute was reflected in several developments that occurred in the opening decades of the twentieth century. As we have seen, the coherence of the concept of art as a primary instrument of self-reflection was being deconstructed at this time. Einstein's claim that time was not an absolute and objective truth, but was relative to space, radically challenged what was conceivably the most fundamental condition for the existence of a sense of personal self – the space–time frame of reference. His theories of special relativity (1905) and general relativity (1915) demonstrated that the consistency and coherence of objects, and the space–time in which they seem to appear, were innately relative to the conditions in which they were perceived. By undermining the possibility of absolute objectivity in this way, he was also undermining the possibility of absolute subjectivity. At the same time, Sigmund Freud (1856–1939) was questioning the nature of subjectivity from the point of view of the 'science' of psychology. Although he acknowledged the existence of a subjective self, the definitive boundaries of that self were impossible to pin down. By inventing the language and conventions of psychoanalysis, he (and his supporters and detractors) transformed the way in which selfhood was understood and experienced in the twentieth century. Its coherence was certainly under threat; that it was a mental convention – a short circuit within the maelstrom of thoughts – became a possibility. More to the point in the present context is the fact that, while the psychological models of selfhood articulated by psychoanalysis have undoubtedly had an extremely profound impact on the ways in which the self is currently conceived, it is also arguable that the language and conventions of psychoanalysis were themselves determined and even precipitated by the cultural conventions of their time. It explored the fragmentary nature of the self by analysing it directly, but also *demonstrated* its existence as a convention of mind, institutionalised as such in the fabric of the culture, by virtue of its emergence as a discipline and discourse. It is the latter aspect of its significance that is the subject of the present chapter.

The significance of psychology was that it attempted to address the personal self-sense not just by conceptualising it – for instance, as a principle of religion or philosophy – but by scrutinising it as an experiential phenomenon in itself. When it first evolved in the eighteenth century, the study of psychology was considered to be a branch of philosophy; it presupposed a metaphysical principle at the source of human experience and was, therefore, presented as a subject for speculation. Following the example of Maine de Biran and Victor Cousin in the early nineteenth century (see chapter 2), it now came to be seen as an independent science. Moving beyond the unpredictability of introspective 'associationism', according to which phenomena were allowed to acquire significance from the other phenomena with which they were associated in experience (rather than from an abstract code of meaning), a new genre of research now aimed to establish it on an analytical, experimental footing.[1] One of the key characteristics of psychology that enabled it to be differentiated from philosophy was its ability and willingness to make practical use of mental abnormalities, rather than to limit itself, on theoretical grounds, to the abstract pursuit of 'healthy' ideals. Indeed, especially in France, the science of psychology developed in the context of pathology. Its research focused on examples of 'abnormal' psychology (hysteria, hypnosis, amnesia, somnambulism, etc.) with a view to offsetting these conditions against a sense of 'normal' psychology, which, on its own, was difficult to characterise, and which, therefore, quickly fell back on the logic and analogies of philosophical speculation. One of the chief significances of these abnormal phenomena was the innumerable ways in which they demonstrated how a person could perform actions that were clearly *motivated* or *caused*, without consciously identifying with their cause or subject. For instance, from the middle of the nineteenth century, it had been observed that a sleepwalker might perform an apparently normal act (like getting dressed) while asleep, but have no knowledge of it when in the waking state; they might even commit a crime (Fig. 7.1).[2] Or a person might remember an event from the past while under hypnosis, but would have no recollection of it when his or her 'normal' state of self-consciousness returned. In cases of this kind, it was unclear who the subject of the experience was, or what the cause of the effect was – for in what sense could a person with no awareness of his or her actions be said to be their subject? Two important outcomes followed from the observation of this inconsistency. The first was the realisation that the traditional model of the coherent and unified subjective self, upheld by the logic of philosophy since the time of Descartes, could no longer stand up to the simple evidence of experimentation and observation. Descartes had challenged the credulous and uninspected presumption that all motivation that originated outside of his own consciousness must be caused by an external agent or god figure, concluding instead that it must be mechanical – in effect, 'unwilled'; but it now seemed equally implausible and unsatisfactory that such unwilled effects as somnambulism could simply be mechanical. The crucial question, therefore, was: how could human actions be deliberate without being conscious, and to what source could the causation of such actions be ascribed? The second outcome of the observation of discrepancies between behaviour and volition was that innumerable new theories and counter-theories about the nature of the self were developed. Religious authorities seeking to preserve the 'unity of the soul' claimed that anomalous psychological phenomena,

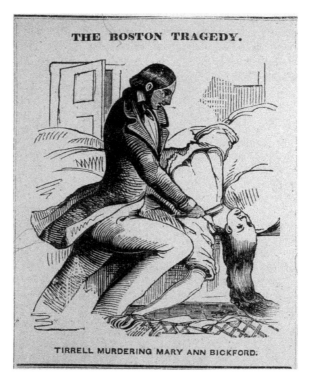

FIGURE 7.1: The Boston Tragedy': Albert Tirrel murdering Mary Ann Bickford, from the *National Police Gazette*, 1846, Library of Congress, Washington. Tirrel also started three fires at the crime site, but he was known to be a sleepwalker and was acquitted due to the fact that he was said to be sleepwalking at the time of the murder.

such as amnesia, were negligible mechanical functions of the brain. At the other end of the scale, extreme materialists attempted to annihilate the traditional mind–body distinction by subjecting all mental phenomena (not just anomalous phenomena) to a process of observation and measurement, as if they were material functions of the body with no 'transcendent' principle of their own. Others took – or created – a middle ground. Philosophers in the German idealist tradition (for instance, Schelling and Carus) developed the notion of the 'unconscious mind' as a logical necessity. On a more empirical basis, Pierre Janet proposed a syndrome of 'dissociation' or 'co-consciousness' in which, during altered states of mind or following traumatic experience, a person's consciousness could become splintered into different centres of subjectivity, and that those centres could then coexist or alternate with each other without awareness of each other, within the same individual. His hypothesis that there exist centres of identity or selfhood that are somehow causal, without being conscious, gave impetus to the closely related notions of the 'subconscious' and 'unconscious' mind. Even though these notions are thoroughly paradoxical and hypothetical – for the subconscious and unconscious mind can never truly be known to exist without ceasing to be themselves – they became two of the most definitive and influential theories of the twentieth century, not least due to the characteristic ways in which they were adapted by Sigmund Freud.

Freud appropriated and adapted the theory of the unconscious mind in two key ways. Firstly, he supplemented the 'abnormal' states of consciousness that were typically excavated for evidence of the unconscious mind with *dreams*, thereby bringing the experience of 'normal' people into the orbit of psychoanalytical research and locating the unconscious within the boundaries of 'normal' psychology. Of course, dreams had been understood as symbolic or prophetic signs in antiquity, inviting interpretation from soothsayers, but they were mostly seen, at that time, as auspicious messages sent by external agents (the gods) from on high; indeed, people would sleep in temples especially in order to receive them. Similarly, throughout the Middle Ages and the Renaissance, dreams were usually considered to be 'visions of the night', imparted from a divine source, often with auspicious significations (Fig. 7.2). In later, more secular times, when belief in spiritual communications was being discredited, psychologists tended to regard dreams as the insignificant detritus of the mind; such experiences were not regarded as constructive functions of the psyche that revealed the dynamics and disposition of the self in complex acculturated forms, as Freud

FIGURE 7.2: The three kings are told in a dream not to return to the land of Herod (from the Gospel of St. Matthew, chapter 2, verse 12), late sixteenth century, engraving, 20.9 × 25.4 cm. Wellcome Collection.

proposed. His *Psychopathology of Everyday Life*, published in 1901, further established the 'normality' of unconscious psychological activity.

Secondly, besides reconceiving the status of dreams, Freud reconfigured the unconscious as a repository of repressed and distorted memories of proto-sexual encounters experienced during infancy. His division of the psyche or self into a self-conscious personality – the *ego* – uncomfortably cushioned between an unconscious quagmire of repressed desires – the *id* – and an unconscious regiment of repressed rationalisations – the *superego* – became a paradigmatic expression of the dynamics of the self, despite the fact that the model was ultimately unable to provide it with definitive parameters (Fig. 7.3). On the basis of this view, it became possible that, because individuals were no longer believed to be entirely conscious of themselves – or rather, to be conscious of their 'entire selves' (whatever those selves might be) – they were no longer able to have truly 'detached' and 'objective' views about things. Even in the 'sanest' cases, their views – indeed, all their thoughts and actions – were as much a reflection or manifestation of their own subconscious inclinations as they were free reflections on the external phenomena to which they were intended to relate. Moreover, the inherently elusive nature of the self led one-time associate

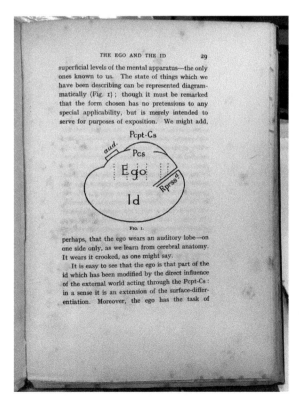

FIGURE 7.3: Sigmund Freud, *The Ego and the Id* (translation of *Das Ich und das Es*, first published in 1923), London, 1927.

of Freud, Carl Jung, to further challenge its independence and autonomy by positing the existence of a '*collective* unconscious'. For Jung, the 'collective unconscious' constituted a common pool of intelligence that pre-exists the process of human individuation, but which is naturally coextensive with the unconscious minds of individuals. As a result, its effects could manifest in human experience and culture, but it did not thereby presuppose a principle of personal identity in the way that the 'personal unconscious' of Janet and Freud did; indeed, it could not be directly known by an individual without ceasing to be collective. In this respect, it could be said to relate to 'instinct', which operates as a spontaneously intelligent regulatory principle in the body of every individual, without presupposing personal volition.

Freud's significance lies in the way he attempted to liberate the individual self from its entanglement with social and cultural conventions acquired during and since infancy. He also aimed to define the self on its own terms, thereby restoring its primary naturalness and freedom to it (though, significantly, it was only following the popularisation of Rousseau's revolutionary ideas about children at the end of the eighteenth century that infancy had come to represent an archetypal state of naturalness and freedom). In order to achieve this, he rejected both the redundant morality of organised religion, which he considered to be an anachronism based on neurotic fantasies about an absent father figure, and the secular conventions of social etiquette. The conventions of social etiquette had been developing since the late Middle Ages, when they appeared at court both to increase hygiene (especially at table) and to promote the use of diplomacy, civility and politeness as a means of maintaining order and resolving conflict; these customs were intended to take the place of warfare and duelling, as encouraged by earlier medieval chivalric codes of honour. As these conventions became ever more complex and sophisticated, they developed into a highly elastic medium through which the personal self came to articulate itself, especially in relation to others. However, as they became established and began to filter down through the ranks of society, they ceased merely to facilitate the 'civilising process', but hardened into a carapace of conventions within which the secret promise of personal identity seemed to be imprisoned. Access to a socially legitimate state of personal identity depended on conformity to these conventions, at the expense of the 'naturalness and freedom' that lay at its root. Freud attempted to reverse this trend. Thus, what was once seen to be 'wild', 'uncouth' and needing to be civilised was now seen as 'natural' and 'free', needing to be liberated. The historical timing of this shift was by no means random. Indeed, Freud later made a direct connection between the relentlessly repressive attempts to 'civilise' the primal instincts that came to a head in his time and the outbreak of the First World War, as if the parameters of the personal self had become so fixed as cultural and social conventions that they could only explode. Significantly, this nightmarish eventuality also coincided with the development of his own work, which was precisely conceived to dismantle these conventions and resolve the conflicts they generated, using more organic and self-aware methods.[3] It also coincided with the dissolution of many other 'forms of personal identity' – especially the discourse of art – as hypothesised elsewhere in this book.

It is significant that, from Freud's perspective, the development of psychoanalysis to some extent presupposed the superseding of art. As most clearly reflected in his analytical essay 'Leonardo da Vinci' (1910), Freud generally considered the production of artistic imagery to be a quasi-neurotic practice that was engaged in order to process, and compensate for, subconscious and unresolved childhood memories, typically of a sexual nature, though he did also concede that art could have a therapeutic effect on both artist and viewer. At a time when the work of contemporary avant-garde artists (such as the Fauvists, Cubists and Expressionists) was being compared to images produced by the inmates of lunatic asylums, this 'pathographic' view of art was highly topical (Fig. 7.4). Freud's theory, which overlaps with the Romantic notion that artistic inspiration involves a degree of spontaneity, sometimes bordering on madness, seemed to find confirmation in the case of Vincent Van Gogh, whose artistic urgency and freedom were currently setting a precedent for the avant-garde; indeed, Van Gogh, who spent several of the last months of his life in an asylum before committing suicide, stated that painting was a 'lightning conductor for his madness'. Freud considered psychoanalysis to be a means with which to cure people of neuroses that they might otherwise attempt to process through the creation or appreciation of art (besides numerous other means). Having said this, while the pathological sources of artistic inspiration were accepted by many people, not all artists wanted to be 'cured'. Some, like the poet Rainer Maria Rilke, who rejected the offer of psychoanalysis on the grounds that it might impede his creativity, preferred the beautiful poetry of their anxiety to the perceived inertia of psychological stability, recalling Nietzsche's famous comment that 'we need art lest we perish of the truth'.

Freud idealised the primitive state of awareness that prevailed before patricidal guilt and taboos about incest crystallised into a mindset of sexual repression – an ancient mindset that he believed later became objectified and codified as religious morality and the strictures of social conventions. It is, therefore, ironic that, despite 'pathologising' art, he shared some of the concerns of avant-garde artists (especially the primitivists) in the sense that he too was using the notion of the 'primitive' as a metaphor for a purified mental state. Indeed, the fact that two of his most important concepts – narcissism and the Oedipus complex – are based on classical myths could be said to exemplify the kind of poetic revivalism that is usually associated with the history of artistic culture, rather than the history of science.

Although Freud strove to develop a new understanding of the human psyche as an objective and autonomous phenomenon, developing an idiosyncratic vocabulary that was relatively free of poetic associations, his model of the self was nevertheless dependent on the suggestive potential and momentum of several pre-existent conventions. For instance, with the benefit of hindsight, it is arguable that his theory of the Oedipus complex, which was integral to his concept of the self, was as much *suggested* by the classical narrative of Sophocles' *Oedipus Rex* as it was *demonstrated* by it. The figure of Oedipus became increasingly familiar in the nineteenth century. While Ingres painted him as a crisp classical nude in 1808, in keeping with the antiquarian interests of his time, in 1864, Gustave Moreau infused him with an atmospheric mystique that invited a more ambiguous psychological interpretation (Fig. 7.5). Freud knew Sophocles' drama well as a student, and saw it on stage in Paris and possibly Vienna in 1885 and 1886 – long before he began to use Oedipus metaphorically – and again in 1911; indeed, it was the play's popularity among modern theatre audiences, conferring celebrity on its actors, that persuaded him to

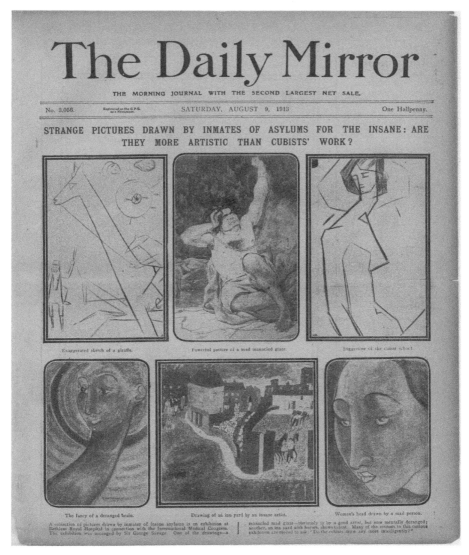

FIGURE 7.4: 'Strange Pictures Drawn by Inmates of Asylums for the Insane: Are They More Artistic than Cubists' Work?', *The Daily Mirror*, London, 9 August 1913.

ascribe universality to it (Fig. 7.6). In the light of this background, it is conceivable that, in slightly different circumstances, other fatalistic stories – such as that of Salome and John the Baptist, which inhabited the same psychological territory as Oedipus (love, lust, power, murder) and was equally popular in the final 'symbolist' decades of the nineteenth century – might just as easily have provided an effective blueprint for a 'universal neurosis' (though, in this case, the fact that the story was Christian and John the Baptist was a Jew would have required artful interpretation).

FIGURE 7.5: Gustave Moreau, *Oedipus and the Sphinx*, 1864, oil on canvas, 206.4 ×
104.8 cm. Metropolitan Museum of Art, New York, bequest of William H. Herriman.

It is equally intriguing to observe that Freud's preoccupation with dreams,
culminating in his *Interpretation of Dreams* – begun in 1895, but not published until
1899 – crystallised in exactly the same year as the first public screening of a motion
picture – by the Lumière brothers in 1895 – raising the question as to whether the
methods and processes of psychoanalysis were in any sense 'filmic' or predicated by
cinematographic thinking. Certainly some of the predecessors of cinema combined
subversive content with the experience of private introspection. For instance,
Thomas Edison's kinetoscope, commercialised in April 1894 and witnessed by the
Lumière brothers in Paris two months later, involved peering into a closed cabinet
and viewing a rapidly passing strip of sequential images *against* a light source, rather
than having them projected on to an external screen *by* the light source (Fig. 7.7).
The fact that the spectacle could only be viewed by one person at a time, and often
showed racy peep show subjects such as vaudeville dancers, made the contraption
the perfect prefiguration of psychoanalysis, which also made allowances for an
introspective state of mind, in which material that was usually deemed illicit and was
therefore repressed could legitimately rise to the surface of consciousness and be
seen. Although there is no evidence to suggest that Freud's interest in dreams was

FIGURE 7.6: Jean Mounet-Sully as Oedipus in Sophocles' *L'Oedipe roi*, performed in Paris in 1881.

influenced by film (he was, in fact, rather disparaging about the new medium, which he considered to be a perpetrator of trivial, populist spectacles), the two developments do appear to have been exploring the same new territory – the potential and possible significance of moving images, remembered, imagined or seen – at exactly the same time. Moreover, the potential of the two practices for mutual clarification was expounded explicitly from the outset, albeit by psychoanalysts other than Freud, and it was reflected, very directly, in the plethora of early films that included elements of psychic or psychological experience in their narratives. Indeed, Freud himself commented on the fact that his colleague Otto Rank's book *The Double* (1914), which uses the theory of a kind of 'alter ego' to analyse artistic inspiration and personality development, was directly inspired by seeing the film *The Student of Prague* (1913), in which the protagonist's 'double' is persuaded by a demonic magician to turn against him. Capitalising on the characteristic ability of film to splice strips of images from different reels together, both roles in this film (the protagonist and his double) are performed by the same actor and appear on screen

FIGURE 7.7: Publicity photograph of a man using an Edison Kinetophone, around 1895. Clients could listen to a soundtrack through earphones linked to a cylinder phonograph within the cabinet.

at the same time (Fig. 7.8). In the same way, the possibilities of animating inanimate objects in film – for instance, as in *The Thieving Hand* (1908), in which a detached prosthetic arm comes to life and steals things – may have facilitated the conceptualisation both of a kind of 'automatic consciousness' or 'unconscious will' and of the fetish object, charged with its own psychic intensity. As Rank himself suggested: 'It may turn out that cinematography, which in numerous ways reminds us of the dream-work, can also express certain psychological facts and relationships – which the writer often is unable to describe with verbal clarity – in such clear and conspicuous imagery that it facilitates of understanding of them.'[4]

A fascination with the technical potential of film had, of course, been characteristic of early cinema from the outset. Indeed, initially, when films were very short – not more than a few minutes long – there was little scope for complex narrative and, alongside realistic vignettes, directors contented themselves with scenarios that enabled them to explore and exploit the medium, often using special effects for their own sake. The French film-maker Georges Méliès adapted the antics and trickery of pantomime and magic theatre (in which he had been employed for many years) to film, using special effects to create comic worlds of spectacle and illusion. In several

FIGURE 7.8: A still from *The Student of Prague*, showing the protagonist, Balduin, shooting his exteriorised double and thereby killing himself, 1913. Directed by Stellan Rye and Paul Wegener, who acted both of the protagonist's 'selves', using double exposure.

of his works – for instance, *Un Homme de Têtes* (1898), *L'Evocation Spirite* (1899) and *L'Homme Orchestre* (1900) – Méliès used a range of stop-action camerawork and double exposures to enable himself to appear on the set several times simultaneously (as a series of bodiless heads, as a spectre and as all the players in the orchestra respectively), thereby unwittingly giving form to the idea of multiple selves (Fig. 7.9). These brief films, which last for approximately a minute each, have no particular narrative. Other works by Méliès, however, did have micronarratives, most of which were fantastical; in examples such as *Le Manoir du Diable* (1896) and *Le Voyage de la Lune* (1902), which run for three and eleven minutes respectively, special effects were used not for their own sake, but to represent the unreal and otherworldly dimensions of the narrative. Just as the exploration and exploitation of photographic techniques (for instance, using double exposures to capture ghosts or thought forms) had encouraged belief in paranormal phenomena from the 1840s, so these films capitalised on the technical potential of film-making to explore visionary or psychic phenomena. As a result, they have, despite their absurdity, come to be seen as the earliest horror and science-fiction films. Similar observations could be made about the fantasy films of the British film-maker George Albert Smith, whose *Haunted Castle* (1898), *Photographing a Ghost* (1899) and *Let me Dream Again* (1900) used a range of special effects to depict ghosts and dream states. Having worked as a magic lantern projectionist and performing hypnotist, and as a member of the Society for Psychical Research in London, Smith was presumably partly

FIGURE 7.9: A still from *Un Homme de Têtes*, by Georges Méliès, Paris, 1898.

attracted to the medium by its apparent ability to capture psychic phenomena. It was not until around 1906, when it became possible to produce lengthy, multireel films of an hour or more, enabling film-makers to develop plots with psychological depth, complexity and suspense for the first time, that the full 'artistic' potential of film was seriously recognised and applied. *The Student of Prague*, which lasts for approximately one hour, was one of the earliest films of this type. It epitomises how uniquely cinematographic effects – in this case, double exposure – were not only integral to the psychological character and dramatic impact of the new narratives; they also helped to shape the mentality that generated such narratives, with a view to finding new aspects of itself reflected in them.

As film-making techniques became increasingly sophisticated, the potential of cinema to capture and explore the provisional nature of the self was not only reflected in irrational narratives worthy of psychoanalysis; it was also reflected in a more subtle and 'artistic' exploitation of the technical effects of which the medium was capable, with a view to simulating the discombobulation of abnormal experience, or visualising the content of the subconscious mind. As an indication of the extent to which this unique relationship between the techniques of cinematography and psychoanalysis was increasingly being recognised and explored at this time, the psychologist Hugo Munsterberg devoted an entire book to the subject – *The Photoplay: A Psychological Study (1916)* – in which he drew direct parallels between the cuts, dissolves and flashbacks of the new medium and the psychological processes of attention, memory and imagination. Reflecting on the possibility of cutting short strips of film into minute fragments and then reassembling them out of sequence in order to create a sense of 'trembling', or mounting the camera 'on a slightly rocking support' to ensure that what it captures 'moves in strange curves' and takes on 'an uncanny whirling character', he commented that 'the content still remains the same as under normal conditions, but the changes in the formal presentation give to the mind of the spectator unusual sensations which produce a new shading of the emotional background'. He continued:

> Of course, impressions which come to our eye can at first awaken only sensations, and a sensation is not an emotion. But, it is well known that in the view of modern physiological psychology our consciousness of the emotion itself is shaped and marked by the sensations which arise from our bodily organs. As soon as such abnormal visual impressions stream into our consciousness, our whole background of fusing bodily sensations becomes altered and new emotions seem to take hold of us.

It may, therefore, be the case that, just as telegraphy had precipitated the conception of a global brain, so many of the earliest pictorial devices of cinema, as specifically determined by the unique technical properties and potential of the medium, were also integrated into the language and thinking of psychoanalysis, providing models for 'modes of experience' and 'forms of identity' that became central to the understanding of human psychology in the twentieth century. This raises the questions: what modes of experience or forms of identity are implicit in the fragmented narratives of film? And to what extent do the examples of filmic modes of experience inform the ways in which dreams came not just to be remembered but to be *reviewed*?

While the notion of 'projecting' some aspect of one's unconscious narrative *on to* one's analyst or the 'outside world' may have been based on the example of the magic lantern, it was greatly substantiated by the breadth of analogous possibilities that film projection offered. Munsterberg commented that even the impressions of movement and space that are conveyed by films are products of the viewer's mind, for they are synthesised from rapid sequences of static configurations of light projected on a screen (unlike theatre, in which at least the movement and space are 'real'). In this respect, films immediately resemble dreams which also only *seem* to have been seen by the eyes, when they are, of course, constructed in the brain. Moreover, in film there is no *real* human relationship between the viewers and the actors in the narrative; the viewer cannot participate in what he or she sees. This unsocial condition gives the viewing experience the quality of a vision that is only experienced inwardly and in solitude (despite the paradoxical fact that the earliest films were watched *collectively*). Here, again, film differed significantly from theatre, in which there is always a live relationship between the audience and the actors, even if it remains extraneous to the narrative being dramatised. In psychoanalysis, this 'fantasy mode' is positively encouraged by the way in which analysts purposefully place themselves out of the view of the analysand – behind the famous couch, in Freud's case – thereby minimising the possibility of a manifest relationship; like the cinema-goer, the analysand is encouraged to feel that they are alone in their imagination, albeit thinking out loud.

The fact that films could be replayed and reviewed (the short ones were sometimes shown as loops) subtly overlaid them and charged them with the associations of memories (rehearsable in the mind time and time again), implicitly contextualising the stories that they told as secondary, remembered or 'memorable' experiences, rather than as primary experiences of 'reality'. Significantly, when an analysand is attempting to understand the potential impact of a dream on the state of his or her identity, it is a *memory* of the dream, rather than the dream experience itself, that is reviewed or 'rewatched'. Moreover, the fact that the earliest examples of films were silent, and in black and white, also differentiated them from the experience of 'reality', further allying them with fantasy and the inwardness of silent thought. This highly suggestive quality in films is reinforced by the possibility they offer of assembling disparate fragments of experience from random sources, thereby giving cultural value to the comparable processes of daydreaming, distraction and the random association of images in the mind more effectively than any other medium.

These filmic effects were uniquely facilitated by the technology of film-making. What makes them significant in the present context is the new dimensions of experience they stood to evoke in their viewers. But while they engaged with their viewers' psychology, reflecting their subjectivity back to them very directly, they also projected a characteristically fantasised and fragmented *mode* of existence on to them, complicating the notion of the self and undermining its stability. On the one hand, film revealed to them sights that could not be experienced by the conventional self (the self that already seemed to exist and flourish in the 'real' outer world) because they were not real; and on the other hand, it reflected states of mind that were thoroughly multifaceted and indeterminate, in keeping with the fragmented models of identity that were being newly articulated by psychoanalytical theory. On both fronts, the habitual coherence of the self-sense was undermined and rendered provisional. For instance, the fact that the protagonists in films never, or rarely, addressed the viewer directly by looking at or speaking to the camera subtly enforced the impression that he or she was 'not really there', or was certainly not there in any meaningful way (in contrast, for instance, to TV, in which the viewer is frequently addressed, as if personally, by presenters). In the same way, because the rememberer of an episode in life is never addressed from within the memory (the content of which is in the past) – even if they featured in the *original* episode – their *current* existence is not accommodated by the remembered narrative and therefore remains virtual in relation to it. Moreover, the increasing complexity of viewpoints and cuts in film narratives interrupts the impression of continuity that had been considered to be characteristic of the unified self since the time of John Locke. As a result, the viewer is not present as the self-conscious 'me' that he and other people 'know' him to be in the 'real' world, but only as a virtual presence; he is never acknowledged as such by the film and is therefore virtualised by the imaginative space it creates.

The notion that, since the invention of psychoanalysis, the conventions of film-making have impacted on the way we remember, process and interpret out dreams is highly speculative. It nevertheless remains significant that the parallel discourses of dream analysis and film production both reflected the fragmentation and displacement of the sense of personal identity that increasingly took place at the beginning of the twentieth century; in both contexts, the indetermination and discontinuity of the narratives they highlight reflect an increasingly indeterminate and discontinuous experience of subjectivity. In conjunction with other contemporary trends, such as the development of telecommunication and globalisation, which, as we saw in the previous chapter, expanded the parameters of identity beyond the personal, both developments undercut the stability of the personal self by creating space for alternative models of identity formation. Indeed, over a century later, the status of personal identity has become so provisional and so contingent on the acceptance of other provisional truths that, although it continues to function as an ideal and an archetype – preserved by the material culture and conventions that accommodate it – there is a case for questioning its existence. This will be the task of the next and final chapter.

CHAPTER EIGHT

The Linguistic Self: the Deverberation of the Self and the End of Meaning

The notion of personal identity came to a head in the seventeenth century, when, freed at last from long years of credulity, it became able to prove its own existence to itself from within its own experience: I think, therefore I am. The circularity of this position ensured that, to the extent that the self-sense looked for itself, it found itself and knew itself to exist. Moreover, to the extent that it knew itself to exist, it *had to* exist; according to its own evaluation, it could not *not* exist. On the one hand, it *exercised* and *manifested* its new autonomy by engaging in philosophical enquiry without recourse to belief; on the other hand, it *described* itself as newly autonomous by recording its characteristics. While this insight was originally so radical that even Descartes could not bring himself to accept all its implications (e.g. that the idea of God is inessential), it was, by the beginning of the nineteenth century, being mediated to the public by a new type of 'artist-prophet' and, more generally, by the increasingly institutionalised discourse of art, whereupon it became *currency* throughout the western world. But what the self-sense could not see was that, while it seemed to be self-authenticating, it was also tautological – a kind of 'optical illusion' – for when the self-sense 'looked in the mirror' (so to speak), it was inevitable that it should see, or seem to see, itself. What it was unable to take on board (just as we are unable to take it on board in our own time) was that the conventions of self-expression that it used were themselves *mirrors* of a kind, spontaneously generated to act as mechanisms of self-reference; over and above their social, political or aesthetic functions, they served as perfect materialisations and reflections of the mindset that created them. The self was not therefore seeing *itself*, as an objective truth that existed independently of the act of looking; it was seeing a reflective mirage, generated by the conventions to which it subscribed, and which it had, in previous ages, created as instruments of self-reference. In an endless corridor of reflections, it experienced the self-perpetuating illusion of its own necessity, accelerated, like audio feedback, to the point at which it became autonomous and self-representational – and sometimes isolated.

The idea of the self-authenticating self, and its contract with the discourse of art, persisted throughout the nineteenth century. Indeed, the period was one in which individuality was celebrated and even glorified – with a surfeit of great art to account for it. But conditions changed rapidly throughout the century and the significance of even the most resilient mental abstractions was forced to change with them. The theory of evolution removed the 'agency in history' from human beings and placed it in nature. New institutions were conceived to address the needs of the new 'public' and, even when they celebrated the exemplary individuality of a few, they generalised the individuality of the many. The mass production of utilitarian goods improved the quality of life for vast numbers of people, but it standardised the experience of both manufacturers and consumers. Telecommunication systems empowered people to project themselves beyond their traditional confines, but it imposed modes of behaviour and even thought on them. And the discipline of psychology radically threatened the metaphysical coherence of the self-sense on purely practical grounds, finding purely physiological explanations for it. In the meantime, the mainstay of the self – the discourse of art, which was the primary medium of its self-expression – went through its own cataclysmic changes to the point at which its internal coherence seemed to disintegrate, leaving the self mirrorless and profoundly unsure of itself – lonely in the internal conviction it had about its own existence, but with ever-diminishing support from nature, society and history. This conflict precipitated an existential crisis. On the one hand, the self *had* to exist, on the basis of its own logic; on the other hand, its self-concern seemed increasingly to alienate it from the wider world.

How could this problem be solved? The answer is that it could not be solved; the self-sense could never surrender its attachment to itself without reinforcing itself, through the very *intention* to surrender. But the problem could be discovered *not to exist*. What is often overlooked is the fact that *the verbal language in which the problem is articulated is itself a cultural construction and that, therefore, it too is subject to cultural determination*. The implication of this conjecture is that the duality of the subject/object polarisation that lies at the root of the 'self predicament' is not absolute, but is a function of the language in which it is described and propagated. Not only is the self-sense deeply vested in myriad cultural conventions that pervade our social and cultural lives – from objects and spaces to gestures, behaviours and rituals – but it pervades the very medium of our thinking. It is crucial to observe in this context that the principle of verbal language is itself dualistic, in that its very building blocks revolve around the fundamentally dualising notion of the *subject* of a sentence and its various relationships to *objects* (nouns and pronouns) – as elaborated in ever more complex structures of verbs, prepositions, conjunctions, adverbs, etc.. Indeed, the logic of dualism pervades the grammar and syntax of language so thoroughly that it has become completely invisible, and the dualist mode of experience – 'I' and 'not I' – has come to seem entirely natural. It necessarily follows from this condition that any understanding that is formulated in words is *inherently* refracted into a dualistic mode of experience, whether the consciousness that underpins that mode of experience is itself dualistic or not. It is, therefore, impossible to use verbal language without subscribing to the dualistic values that inform and structure it. The significance of this point is that, while dualism is implicit in the notion of the subjective self (inherently complemented by its objects), it is especially implicit in verbal language – the most fundamental medium through which the self reflects itself to itself. This raises the question as to whether an individual's consciousness of his or her own identity – and the subject/object dualism that arises from it – might not also be a function of the dualism of language, which innately informs the process of self-reflection, rather than of consciousness itself.

Significantly, the ability to explore the extent to which the possibilities of knowledge are determined by language, and by the capacity of language to accommodate them, is itself determined by cultural conventions. The very concept that language is not an absolute phenomenon, created by God in paradise, could not emerge until the medieval edifice of religious belief (especially with regard to language) had been challenged by the empiricism of natural science; for medieval notions of language were themselves subject to the conditions of religious belief. For most medieval thinkers, words – especially names – were believed to be the properties of objects, not the products of human culture. Before the study of languages began to be objectified and secularised in the seventeenth century, it seemed entirely reasonable to suppose that the language that Adam used – for instance, to name the animals, as described in the book of Genesis – was directly revealed to him by God. Unlike modern languages, which consist of words that are arbitrarily connected to the objects to which they refer, this natural 'Adamic' language was believed to have used words that emanated directly from their referents – which were, in their turn, believed to be direct manifestations of God's wisdom. Thus, by virtue of his prelapsarian state of innocence, Adam was able to know the names of animals simply by *seeing* them, whereupon their inner natures were revealed to him (Fig. 8.1).

FIGURE 8.1: 'Adam names the animals in the Garden of Eden', around 1800, etching with engraving, 23.1 × 38.8 cm. Wellcome Collection.

Conversely, a true understanding of the names of things constituted a mystical insight into their inner significance as manifestations of God's wisdom. It was only when man angered God by arrogantly building the Tower of Babel that he was made to speak in diverse tongues, falling out of a paradisiacal state of harmony with his fellow beings into a state of spiritual blindness and mutual incomprehension. This explanation of language was largely developed by occultists, such as Paracelsus (1493–1541), John Dee (1527–1608/9) and Jacob Boehme (1575–1624), who sought to recover the mystical language of natural man and its ability to reveal the inner nature of things accordingly. They rejected the rational, textual approach to philosophy, as espoused by Renaissance humanists, maintaining instead that the signature of God was directly inscribed in the fabric of nature and that his wisdom could be read in its laws, with the 'inner eye'. In 1527, Paracelsus, an empirically minded physician at the University of Basel, scandalously demonstrated his disrespect for the coldly rational and unmagical use of words by humanists, as well as their excessive respect for authority, by burning texts by the ancient physicians Avicenna (c. 980–1037) and Galen (129–c. 200) in public. Others went even further. One radical Protestant group, founded by Nicholas Storch at Zwickau in Saxony in 1520, was so committed to direct communion with God that they outlawed literacy altogether. They refused to teach their children the alphabet on the grounds that verbal knowledge was an obstruction to divine illumination, preventing things from revealing their inner natures to them *immediately*. To have taught them the alphabet would have been to install an 'infrastructure of illusion' in them – hence the name of the group, the 'Abecedarians'.

The Abecedarians were in the minority. Throughout the seventeenth century, efforts were made to create a language of perfect clarity, in which meanings were not merely represented by words, as they are today; they were to be *revealed* by words, in the Adamic manner. This was attempted in a number of ways. Some writers claimed that the Adamic language had partially survived – either in the Hebrew language (in which the book of Genesis was written) or scattered among all the languages of the world (since Babel) – and they spent years attempting to reconstruct its lexicon from what they perceived to be its fragments. Because such original words were believed to be magically empowered embodiments of the essence of their referents (like mantras in the Vedic tradition or the Jewish Tetragrammaton), they were also believed to carry tremendous power; this power could be used benevolently, for prayer and healing, or malevolently, for curses and spells. One English physician, John Bulwer, suggested that the Adamic language also incorporated gestures, enabling Adam and Eve to communicate with God and the animals in silence. In his *Chirologia* of 1644, Bulwer explained how the 'natural language of the hand . . . had the happiness to escape the curse at the confusion of Babel' and how it continued, therefore, to be a universally comprehensible language, as reflected by the fact that foreign merchants and deaf people can easily understand others by using gestures (Fig. 8.2).

The concept of an Adamic language was based on the medieval mode of Christian belief – accepting that God had created language at the beginning of time – and its subscribers, therefore, were ultimately traditional believers. Other philosophers took a more rationalist approach, abandoning the belief that God created language,

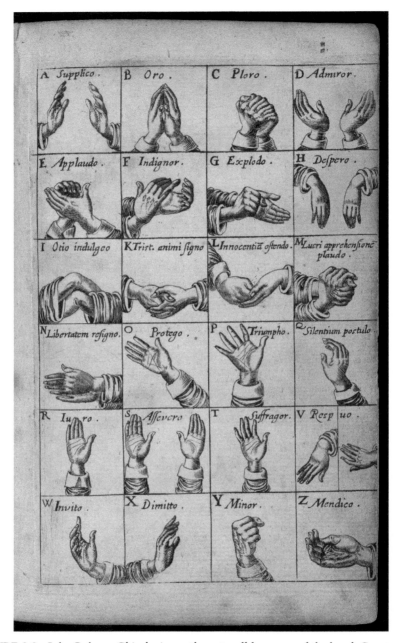

FIGURE 8.2: John Bulwer, *Chirologia: or the naturall language of the hand. Composed of the speaking motions, and discoursing gestures thereof. Whereunto is added Chironomia: or, the art of manuall rhetoricke. Consisting of the naturall expressions, digested by art in the hand, as the chiefest instrument of eloquence, by historicall manifesto's, exemplified out of the authentique registers of common life, and civill conversation*, 1644, London, p. 151. Wellcome Collection.

but upholding the notion that a universal philosophical language could nevertheless be artificially created. This universal language would be constructed from rational, rather than arbitrary or mystical elements and it would, therefore, be immediately comprehensible to its users; moreover, because it was rational, it could – theoretically, at least – be used by all of mankind. Advocates of such a language implicitly presupposed that all human ideas were interrelated and could be organised into a single interlocking system or hierarchy of known phenomena, which could be represented by a correspondingly systematic and interlocking arrangement of letters and words. Presupposing that the possibilities of knowledge are determined by the capacity of language to accommodate and express it, the French philosopher Marin Mersenne contemplated the maximum number of statements that could be made in a language of twenty-four letters, when organised into the maximum number of possible combinations. In his *Harmonie Universelle* of 1636, he speculated about what the object of such maximum possible knowledge could be. What would the 'totality of truths' amount to? Moreover, should unpronounceable combinations of letters, and combinations of letters that were pronounceable but for which there was (as yet) no referent or meaning, be taken into consideration? Mersenne also ruefully appreciated the prohibitive amount of time it would take to consider each of these combinations, in relation to an average human lifespan. In 1651, the Nuremberg poet Georg Philipp Harsdörffer explored the possibility of increasing knowledge systematically by creating a combinatorial device with which to generate a plethora of new words from a given structural template (Fig. 8.3). Narrowing down the scope of the enquiry, the Bohemian pioneer of education Jan Amos Comenius contemplated the possibility of a language that was so closely linked to the sensible realities to which it referred that it would be technically impossible to express a falsehood in it, just as it is impossible to 'break' the laws of physics; in his *Via Lucis*, written in 1641–2, he upheld that groundless fictions of the imagination, detached from 'real' objects, were not to be accommodated by it. By these means he aimed to eradicate the possibility of religious conflict. In other cases, individual words, many of which constituted complex ideas in themselves, were to be composed of elementary particles, each with its own independent form and signification, structured hierarchically. According to John Wilkins's scheme, elaborated in his *Essay Towards a Real Character and a Philosophical Language* (1668), every letter in a word would carry its own signification, commencing with a general categorisation – for instance, 'animal' – before proceeding letter by letter to 'mammal', 'wild cat' and 'lion', etc. – like numbers (1, 10, 100, 1000) or different-coloured beads threaded on to a piece of string in a particular order.[1] In contrast to Wilkins, Gottfried Leibniz was inspired by the example of the Chinese language to propose that the elemental ingredients of words should be pictographic, constituting a representational 'alphabet of fundamental thoughts'.[2] Even if abstractions themselves could not be represented as such in a language of this kind, he saw no reason why the individual component parts of the words used to denote them should not be. Like Wilkins, Leibniz believed that such elemental particles of meaning could be systematically combined into syntheses of meanings – individual words – which could then be arranged, subject to rationalised systems of grammar and syntax, into complex statements and propositions. Indeed, he imagined that the perfectly rational

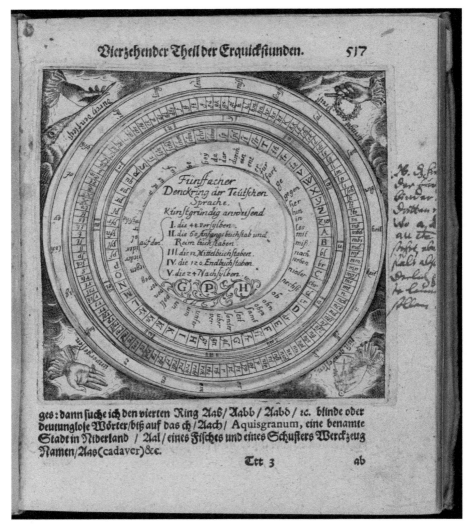

FIGURE 8.3: Georg Philipp Harsdörffer, *Fünffacher Denckring der Teutschen Sprache* (*The Five-fold Thought-ring of the German Language*), 1651. Photo: Beinecke Rare Book and Manuscript Library, Yale University.

system of grammar and syntax would be so precisely rooted in logic (rather than the accidents of history) that, by understanding the component parts of a sentence, one could *calculate* its meaning.

   Although the idea of a universal philosophical language was rationalist in its methods, it was also based on belief, in its underlying principle. It implicitly presumed that the world consisted of a range of determinate phenomena that simply needed to be identified, categorised correctly, according to rational criteria, and named. Thus, although the names of objects may not pre-exist, the objects themselves do. The subtext of this position was that, if phenomena can be known to exist beyond a mystical Christian frame of reference – i.e. objectively – and can subsequently be identified as such with the help of a rational system of names that is believed to be transparent to their 'truth', then the subject of their knowing – the subjective self – must also implicitly be known to exist, as an equally objective truth; the two polarities complemented and depended on each other, and, indeed, brought each other into existence. But while this system managed, in its own way, to develop a rational and secular theory of knowledge and language, it did not question the grounds on which the indeterminacy of experience was divided into subject and object, and it showed little awareness of the complexity of human psychology – as the discourse of psychology had not yet evolved – and it was therefore doomed to fail.

It was not until the end of the seventeenth century that philosophers began to take a more pragmatic approach to language, based on observation and experience rather than belief. Where language had habitually been seen as a function of the objective world – directly determined by that world or serving as a coded key to understanding it – it increasingly came to be seen as a function of the mind that created it, incarnating the self-sense and reflecting the 'structures of ideas' that inform it. This tradition was initiated by John Locke, who rejected the notion of innate ideas (that some objective truths are innately present in the human mind from conception) and indeed that 'absolute meanings' exist at all. The idea, for instance, that the names of the animals in the Garden of Eden were created by God and could be known mystically seemed totally absurd to him, and completely unfounded in experienced evidence. On the contrary, language was a cultural construction. In his celebrated *Essay Concerning Human Understanding* (1690), Locke expounded the view that, from the moment of conception, the mind was a *tabula rasa* and that it acquired all its knowledge from experience (including *in utero*). This is evident from the experience of infants, who are clearly not born knowing 'fundamental truths'. On the contrary, their earliest knowledge is associated with the experience of sensations. Moreover, the earliest cognitive processes are only activated in them in response to *present* sensations. That is to say, they are not even able to *abstract* from their sensations; their attention revolves around sensible objects, as presently experienced. At this stage, they are still unable to deduce that two similar objects are indeed 'similar' to each other – by abstracting or *identifying* that which they have in common – for to do this would require a reflective, comparative capacity that is not yet developed in them. As this reflective faculty develops, so infants become able to conceive abstractions; they become able to develop *notions* – for instance, the notion of a 'spoon' as a general category – by comparing presently experienced sensations to memories of past sensations. As a result, they become able to use the notion of 'spoon' as an *idea* by which to link specific spoons that would not otherwise appear connected. Thereafter, the idea of 'spoons' could be linked to the idea of 'food' or 'bowls', etc.. Having learned to identify not just objects but *ideas* of objects, children soon begin to use language as a means with which to refer to abstractions that have no tangible referent, often by analogy with sensations. Eventually they become able to use it as a medium through which to reflect on their own mental processes and states and to identify that aspect of them that recurs and endures. The fact that many of the words people use to refer to their diverse 'modes of thinking' are adapted from descriptors of sensation reflects the extent to which the interpretation of human experience is itself determined and precipitated by the experience of sensation. In Locke's own words:

> It may also lead us a little towards the original of all our notions and knowledge, if we remark how great a dependence our words have on common sensible ideas; and how those which are made use of to stand for actions and notions quite removed from sense, have their rise from thence, and from obvious sensible ideas are transferred to more abstruse significations, and made to stand for ideas that come not under the cognizance of our senses; v.g. to 'imagine', 'apprehend', 'comprehend', 'adhere', 'conceive', 'instill', 'disgust', 'disturbance', 'tranquillity' &c., are all words taken from the operations of sensible things, and applied to certain modes of thinking. 'Spirit', in its primary signification, is breath; 'angel', a messenger: and I doubt not but, if we could trace them to their sources, we should find, in all languages, the names which stand for things that fall not under our senses to have had their first rise from sensible ideas. By which we may give some kind of guess what kind of notions they were, and whence derived, which filled their minds who were the first beginners of languages, and how nature, even in the naming of things, unawares suggested to men the originals and principles of all their knowledge.[3]

Locke's theory of language was innovative in two key ways. On the one hand, he maintained that language was not miraculously created by God but evolved organically and expediently as a means of communication and understanding; and, on the other hand, he maintained that the words commonly used to denote abstractions were adapted from experiences of sensation. Thus, the optical experience of 'seeing' provided vocabulary for the experience of 'understanding'; indeed, the word 'idea' – the archetypal object of understanding – is thought to derive from a Proto-Indo-European root for 'seeing'. Similarly, the tactile experiences of 'feeling' and 'being touched' were adapted to the experience of emotion, as was the perception of motion and 'being moved'. Moreover, of all the adjectives that were originally conceived to describe the sensible qualities of objects – hot, cold, bright, dark, shallow, deep, rough, smooth, etc. – there are few that have not subsequently been adapted to serve as metaphors for some mental state or disposition – and, therefore, to subtly precondition the human identification and understanding of those states. In the same way, the words 'silence', 'stillness', 'fullness' and 'emptiness', which are derived from the physical states of objects (the absence of sound, the absence of movement, etc.), are frequently used as metaphors to describe spiritual states. These influential ideas were explored and extended by several eighteenth-century philosophers, most significantly the French abbé Étienne Bonnot de Condillac, whose *Essay on the Origin of Human Knowledge* (1746) was – when first published in English in 1756 – subtitled *Being a Supplement to Mr. Locke's Essay on Human Understanding*. Adapting Locke's association of 'spirit' with 'respiration', Condillac even maintained that the concept of the 'mind' (*esprit* in French) was derived, by analogy, from an experience of sensation:

The imagination endeavoured to find, in objects that struck the senses, images of what occurred inside the mind. People have always perceived motion and rest in matter; they have observed the leaning or inclination of bodies; they have seen the air become agitated, darkened and clear; that plants grow, mature, decay – with all these things before their senses, they began to speak of the 'movement', the 'rest', the 'inclination' and the 'leaning' of the soul; they spoke of the mind becoming 'agitated', 'darkened', 'enlightened, of its 'growing', 'maturing' and 'decaying'. In short, they were happy to find some relation between a mental and a physical action in order to give the same name to both. For where does the word *esprit* come from if not from the idea of very rarified matter, of a vapor, of a breath that cannot be seen?[4]

Because the original needs of human beings were related primarily to the body, it follows that:

the first names that were given to what we are capable of feeling signified sensible actions alone. Later, as mankind gradually became familiar with abstract terms, we became capable of distinguishing mind from body, and of considering the operations of these two substances separately. They then perceived not only what the action of the body is when we say for example 'I see', but they separately observed the perception of the mind and began to regard the term 'I see' as being appropriate for both kinds of actions. It is even plausible that this practice came about so naturally that they did not notice the extension of the word's meaning. This shows how a sign which initially was limited to an action of the body, became the name of an operation of mind.[5]

Condillac's reflections throw light on a process that is otherwise impossible to imagine: the origination of such words, seminal to the notion of personal identity, as 'consciousness', 'experience', 'subjectivity', 'identity', 'existence', 'intelligence' and 'emotion'. It is inconceivable that the phenomena denominated by such words could, once upon a time, have been noticed as independently existing phenomena (like the animals in the Garden of Eden), simply waiting to be named – for if they had no names, on what grounds would they have been identified as objects? On the contrary, it is arguable that these words developed, progressively and over very many years, as practical terms to facilitate the apprehension, conceptualisation and communication of aspects of what is, fundamentally and primarily, an indeterminate and ineffable 'experience of existence' (notwithstanding the fact, of course, that the notions 'experience' and 'existence' are themselves only verbalised concepts). How these aspects of experience first came to be differentiated and deemed worthy of naming will forever remain elusive. Certainly their advent suggests a crucial shift away from a magical and mythologised relationship to the world, characteristic of ancient peoples, towards a more abstracted and conceptualised mode, to which an embryonic concept of personal identity was integral. But while the identification of new phenomena and the evaluation of them as 'nameworthy' clearly reflects changes in the content of experience, generating new vocabulary, it is also inevitable that it was to some degree determined by the capacity of language, as it stood at any given time, to accommodate new significations. It did this, as it still does, by providing scope for making analogies between new experiences and experiences that had already been identified and named. Without pre-existent points of reference already accommodated in language, these concepts, and the differentiated experiences which they represent and embody, would be inconceivable. It is arguable, therefore, that not only are the 'self'-related words derived from experiences of tangible, sensible processes, but also, more significantly in the present context, the mental infrastructure of personal identity *and indeed the very notion of personal identity* are culturally constructed.

The derivation of linguistic abstractions from the experience of sensation and the generally linguistic construction of selfhood is reflected in the English language. This is especially clear in relation to words that were imported 'ready-made' into Britain from Latin, initially during the Roman period (the first to the fifth century). Subsequent influxes of Latin words into the English language occurred in the eighth century, when the Latin alphabet began to replace runes for the writing of texts in 'Old English' and missionaries were actively disseminating the Christian scriptures in Latin, and in the fifteenth century, when the English language began to replace Latin altogether, absorbing many words in the process. With regard to such anglicised Latin words, the original source and meaning can be deduced from their etymology (giving a pale impression of how a universal language, based on strings of meaningful units, might have worked). The word 'congregation', for instance, comes from the Latin words *con* ('with' or 'together'), *grex* ('sheep') and *-ation* (derived from the past participle of Latin verbs ending in *-are*). The origin of the word *grex*, however, cannot be traced back to a solid source. More significantly, nor can many other single-syllable words that are key to the notion of personal identity and experience, such as 'mind', 'soul', 'self', 'mean', 'know', 'feel' and 'think' and all the personal pronouns and possessive adjectives that refer to individuals, e.g. 'I', 'me', 'my' and 'mine'. These words derive from Old English, which flourished in Britain from the fifth century onwards, and they can be traced back to the languages of the ancient Germanic tribes that invaded Britain at that time; but as one pursues them to an even earlier source, they become lost in the mists of the ancient Proto-Indo-European language, the hypothetical source language from which the languages of about half of the current population of the world appear to have evolved, and it is therefore impossible to account for their origination. The word 'I', for instance, is an abbreviation of the Old English word *ic*, which was derived from the proto-Germanic *ek*; its earliest material survival – as a written word in a form of English – appears to date from the seventh or eighth century (Fig. 8.4). Before being adopted and adapted by most Northern European peoples, *ek* originated in the Proto-Indo-European *eg*, which, through an independent route (via Greek), also led to the Latin *ego*. In English, *ic* was abbreviated to *i* in the twelfth century, and *i* was capitalised in the thirteenth. The crucial moment – or period – at which the utterance was transformed from an 'indicative sound' into a 'meaningful word' with an independent, conceptual referent in the mind is impossible to identify (and, indeed, is inherently unknowable).

Significantly, in the English language, it was not until *writing* took root in around the fifth century, with the introduction of Old English, that the meanings of words could begin to become established and semi-permanent, maintained in their own 'perpetual' forms – just as it was only when printed dictionaries were published in the eighteenth century that spelling could begin to be standardised. Although the Romans

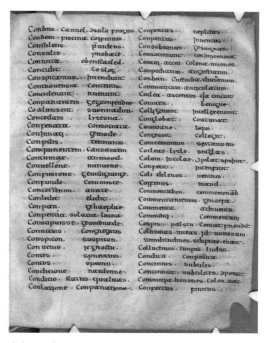

FIGURE 8.4: One of the earliest surviving forms of the word *ic* (Old English equivalent of 'I') in the 'Corpus Glossary', Parker Library, Cambridge, CCCC MS. 144, eighth century, vellum, 31.7 × 24.1 cm. Corpus Christi College, Cambridge. In this wordlist, 'Ic groetu' - 'I greet' (in the second column from the left, sixth row up) - corresponds to the Latin word 'convenio'.

in Britain produced inscriptions and writing tablets for their own use, the language of the indigenous Celts was primarily oral and the meaning of their words, therefore, was mostly actualised when those words were spoken. Thus, if a community of speakers was destroyed – as surely happened during the turbulent invasions of the Germanic Angles, Saxons and Jutes – so its version of the language, and the meanings it contained, would have been destroyed with it. Over the years, many words and dialects must have become extinct without leaving a trace. But when ideas began to be written down, whether in ideograms, letters or runes, the possibility that a people's language and meanings might outlive them was also created. Evidence of several obsolete languages has survived this way; even Latin mostly survives in its written and engraved texts. In Britain, language began to outlive its speakers in the fifth century, when an alphabet of runes first came into use – just as had happened with cuneiform and hieroglyphic scripts in ancient Mesopotamia and Egypt in the third millennium BCE. Having originated among Germanic peoples in the first or second century CE – initially for inscriptions on objects, rather than for writing on parchment – runes continued to be used in Britain until the ninth century, when they were replaced by the Latin alphabet, introduced to the country by Irish missionaries bearing the Christian message.

The introduction of the Latin language and alphabet to Britain (and throughout Europe) was instrumental in the evolution of abstract knowledge and of the sense of a 'knowing subject'. In contrast to written languages – in which meanings can be 'deposited' or 'stored' in written words, and spread and elaborated thereafter – oral language is direct and present; it is only current when being used by people in live conversation, announcements, etc.. The development and change of the meaning of words must therefore have been relatively gradual as, despite being highly organic and liquid, it could have only occurred within the process of speaking. Moreover, unlike sensible phenomena, such as 'trees', which continue to manifest as objects even when they are not being mentioned, abstract notions, such as 'honesty' or 'friendliness', do not exist per se in autonomous, independent forms. They only exist to the extent that they are made to exist, and are 'mentioned' (literally 'called to mind', from the Latin *mens*), by the speakers and thinkers who refer to them; they are only preserved by frequent use and memory. Indeed, one of the reasons for enacting *rituals* (besides their magical function) was to give form to emergent configurations of ideas that otherwise had no form, and to reinforce those ideas – as 'objects' of a kind – in the memory. It is partly because ancient oral cultures made so little use of *enduring* cultural expressions that we know so little about them. Nevertheless, a certain amount can be surmised. It seems reasonable to assume, for instance, that because Old Germanic words originated in a largely *oral* culture, they evolved to be *spoken* rather than *written*. As a result, the earliest ones can originally have had no spelling. Under such circumstances, it would have been difficult to deliberately *invent* new words; indeed, it may not have even been clear what exactly a 'word' was, or how many 'words' there were in a given sequence of spoken sounds. Thus, because words were not typically abstracted from their practical function as speech, they are more likely to have evolved organically from the inchoate vocalisations or interjections that were first uttered in direct response to phenomena than to have been 'coined'; some such 'words' may have been onomatopoeic.[6] The important point was the one at which vocalisations ceased to be 'significant' on account of their habitual associations or physiological character (their volume, pitch, timbre, etc.), but became 'meaningful' on account of their reference to *concepts* maintained *abstractly* in the mind. The crucial question is: when did the capacity to conceptualise and form abstractions evolve? And, from another angle, when did it first become possible for the human mind to reflect on its own contents, and to identify them as objects, or 'ideas'? Efforts have been made to find clues to the date of this shift in the parallel use of tools by early hominids, the changing form of the human larynx and brain over millennia, and the process of language acquisition in infants, but because the first spoken words left no trace, the answer to these questions can, of course, never finally be known. Even so, it is not inconceivable that, although 'meaningful speech' is thought to have replaced 'indicative signs' somewhere between and 50,000 and 100,000 years ago, some of the single-syllable words that are still in use in English today, and which can be traced, via Old English, to a Proto-Indo-European precedent – 'meat', 'drink', 'hearth', 'home', 'land', 'field', 'wood', 'stream', 'birth', 'life', 'death' – may have evolved at an even earlier date from a primal sound.

When a word is written down, its meaning, unlike that of spoken words, is preserved independently of its users and it can, therefore, acquire its own value as an independent phenomenon, albeit a conceptual one. In this way, writing enables concepts to become 'perpetual objects'. Such conceptual objects are no longer necessarily rooted in present experience, nor are they dependent on vocalisation. On the contrary, they become available as timeless repositories of abstracted meanings, embodied in enduring, sensible forms that subsequent users (both speakers and writers) are free to employ, develop, adapt, etc.. It was precisely this possibility of development that the Latin alphabet and vocabulary offered the English language. Unlike words that evolve within purely oral cultures, which originate in immediate responses to experiences, words that are created in literate cultures can also be based much more widely on other words, using them as an independent, ready-made resource, ripe for adaptation or imitation. The advantage of this shift is that it enables language users to develop complex concepts by referring to and adapting pre-existent meanings. Not only do written words offer 'prototypes' for new meanings (what kind of meanings already exist?), they also provide the very building blocks from which new words and new meanings can be created (using prefixes and suffixes, etc.), and a template to which they might conform (prefix-root-suffix). It is arguably for this reason that so many of the English words that were derived from Latin – especially those referring to conceptual or abstract phenomena – consist of more than one syllable: for unlike so many words inherited from Germanic sources, they are constructed out of pre-existent meanings, with meaningful prefixes such as *in-*, *ex-*, *sub-*, *con-*, etc. and suffixes such as *-ity*, *-itude*, *-ify*, *-ence* and *-ment*. In this respect, they reflect how the capacity to develop complex ideas is not only rooted in the experience of sensation; it is also dependent on *writing* and on the capacity of a language, at any given time, to inspire and accommodate new significations. Some key examples should suffice to show how new meanings and new possibilities of experience, or new interpretations of experience, were created in this way. Indeed, much of the mental and conceptual infrastructure that we use to articulate a sense of self and its various functions can be seen to derive from, and depend on, the vicissitudes of language:

- 'Identity' is derived from the Latin words *idem* (the same) and possibly *ens* (being), and denotes that part of an entity that renders it the same as, or identical to, another entity. It was not until the seventeenth century that the word was applied to the part of a person that remains the same *over time*, despite incidental changes, such that the person that appears one day could be the *same person* as the one that appeared two days or two decades earlier. But while identity denotes that part of an entity that renders it the same as another entity (in space or in time), it also refers to that characteristic in an entity that renders it different from another entity when it might have been expected to be the same. In this respect, while it relates phenomena to each other, it also distinguishes them. *Personal* identity, which was identified with – and seen to be the same as – continuity of consciousness by John Locke in the 1690s, rendered an individual both the 'same as himself' from one minute to the next, and different from other individuals. The word 'individual' originally referred to that which could not, or should not, be divided – for instance, the indivisible authority of the Church, or an 'individual' couple, made inseparable by marriage - and which acquired the status of an integrated whole accordingly; it only later came to refer to any distinctive phenomenon or person, whether dividable or not. Sadly, the word 'ipseity', which also means identity or selfhood ('being-itselfness', from the Latin *ipse* – itself), has fallen out of fashion.

- 'Subject' derives from the Latin words *sub* (under) and *iacere* (to throw), indicating both a person who is 'under, or subject to, the rule of a leader or a law', and the basic, fundamental or underlying content or substance of a phenomenon (its base or foundation) that is essential to it and inalienable. The latter use survives in modern references to the 'subject matter' of a painting or the 'subject' of a book, though, curiously, by today's standards, we would regard these fixed aspects of an artwork as *objective*. With the exception of this anomaly, the meanings of the words 'subject' and 'object' have migrated since the Middle Ages to the point at which they seem to have changed places. Where a 'subject' was traditionally a phenomenon that was fundamental and therefore unchanging (*objective* by modern standards), an 'object' was 'thrown across' (*ob* + *iacere*) the path of perception and therefore constituted a phenomenon *as it was experienced* (*subjective* by modern standards), rather than as it was 'in itself'. The shift away from this understanding took place in the seventeenth century, when it was mooted, most influentially by Descartes and Locke, that the fundamental condition of all phenomena was inextricably associated with the fact that they were *experienced* (and, indeed, could not be realised if they were not experienced), and therefore that their fundamental substance or subject was the *condition* of being experienced, or apprehended in consciousness, rather than an innate *property*. This fundamental condition of 'being experienced' corresponded to the formulation of the 'experiencer', 'I', which subsequently pervaded metaphysical discourse, implicitly and otherwise. Conversely, although it was accepted that the actual perception of phenomena was limited by the human capacity to perceive them, it was also hypothesised that such phenomena may nevertheless have some qualities that are not determined in this way – existing beyond consciousness – and which might therefore be considered to be 'objective' in the modern sense of the word. This shift may also have been facilitated by the use of the words 'subject' and 'object' in a grammatical context. The popularity of autobiographies and confessions in the seventeenth century provided plenty of opportunities for 'I' to become the 'subject matter' (as well as the grammatical subject) of a sentence by enabling the writer to use himself as both the source and content of his work. The polarisation of the meanings of 'subject' and 'object' into a 'conscious I' and 'that of which "I" is conscious' was completed by Kant and his followers, just as psychology – in some senses, the systematic (or 'objective') study of subjectivity – was emerging as a discipline.

- 'Person', 'personal' and 'personality' derive from the Latin *persona*, referring to the role of an actor performing in a play. Their association with a mask – 'through' (*per*) which to project 'sounds' (*son*) – gives a strong sense of their provisional, contingent nature. Precisely because *persona* was a contingent quality, formed in relation to its context (unlike human nature, which is deemed common to all people, prior to context), it also constituted that aspect of an individual that made him unique, differentiating him from other examples of his species – namely his personal identity. Significantly, early Christians referred to the three aspects of the Holy Trinity as 'persons' in order to express both how they relate to each other (through their shared 'personhood'), but also how they are differentiated from each other (as if by their 'personalities').

- 'Consciousness' derives from the Latin *con* (with or together) and *scire* (to know); *scire* may be associated with the Latin word *scindere*, which means 'to divide' or 'to separate' (as also in 'scissors' and 'schism'),[7] suggesting 'knowing by differentiation'. In antiquity, the Latin word *conscire* referred to sharing knowledge 'with' other people – first openly, then exclusively and even secretly (or 'privily'), and, finally, personally 'with oneself' – as in 'conscience'.[8] This situation must have been especially pertinent in societies in which knowledge was transmitted orally. As we have seen, it was not until the seventeenth century that the 'identity' of a person was considered to reside in his subjective *consciousness* of himself – his consciousness of being the same person over time (the same now as in a previous moment) – rather than in an objective entity, such as a body or a rational soul. The notion of a ubiquitous consciousness that exists prior to the dualistic mind or self-sense, and independent, therefore, of the polarisation of experience into objects and subjects, was articulated (albeit theoretically) by the German idealist philosophers of the late eighteenth and early nineteenth centuries, most explicitly by Johann Gottlieb Fichte (1762–1814); needless to say, such a phenomenon would unexperienceable by a 'subject'. In 1890, the monist philosopher and psychologist William James coined the word 'sciousness' in order to circumvent the implication – suggested by the prefix *con-* – that the word 'consciousness' presupposes one entity *with* another and is therefore inadvertently dualistic.[9]

- 'Perception' and 'concept' are both based on the word *capere*, meaning 'to capture' or 'to take', as in 'to take possession of' (an association that survives in the related word 'reception'), but also 'to take notice of'. This association is reflected in the phrases 'to grasp the meaning of something' or 'take it in'. The word 'conception' was derived from the notion of 'taking in seed and becoming pregnant', as in the 'immaculate conception' or the 'conception of a child', as if a concept was a kind of foetus. 'Apprehension' and 'comprehension' are also derived from a word (*prehendere*) meaning 'to take' or 'to grasp'. The root word retains its original meaning in 'prehensile' (able to grasp) and the French word for 'to take' (*prendre*). 'Understanding', by contrast, is clearly rooted in a perception of spatial relations.

- 'Experience' shares a source with 'experiment' and 'expert' and is derived from the Latin word *experiri* (*ex-* and *per*), meaning 'to try something out', itself ultimately based on the Greek word *peira*, meaning a 'trial' or 'test'. It originated as a specific temporal phenomenon (as in 'experiencing the coldness of ice'), before becoming abstracted ('my experiences at school'), and eventually generalised as an abiding function of self-consciousness.

- 'Intelligence' and 'intellect' derive from the Latin words *inter*, meaning 'between' or 'within', and *legere*, meaning 'to gather' or 'to pick out' – just as to 'collect' means to 'gather together', and to 'select' means to 'pick out' or 'choose'. 'Lection' (reading) signifies 'picking out words from a text' or 'gathering up meanings from words'.

- 'Exist' derives from the Latin prefix *ex-* (out) and *sistere* (to stand), indicating to 'stand out' or 'be perceptible'. It shares a root with a group of related words: 'assist' – to 'stand by', support or help; 'resist' – to 'withstand' or 'take a stand against'; 'insist' – to 'stand (on)' one's ground; and 'consist' – to 'hold together', both in the stability of a 'consistent' person's nature, and in the binding texture or 'consistency' of a substance that 'consists' of that which holds it together.

- 'Attention' derives from the word *tendere*, to 'stretch' (as in 'tension') and *a-*, meaning 'to' or 'towards'. The use of the word to refer to an independent quality of mind dilutes the original implication that attention is applied, or extended, to something, as retained in the French word *attendre*, meaning to 'wait for' or 'expect' (literally, 'look out for') which suggests a frame of mind. The same implication is present in the French word *entendre*, meaning to 'hear', sometimes used (as in English) as a metaphor for understanding.

Having described how the words used to refer to abstract phenomena were derived from the experience of sensation, Condillac went on to point out how language not only *creates* the possibility of self-awareness – by providing a reflective medium though which the self can know itself – but also *limits* it, by providing a limited and pre-nuanced range of analogies with which to refer to it and express it. Although the possibility of human knowledge is facilitated by the existence of language, it is also determined by the capacity of language to accommodate it:

> If we recall that the exercise of the imagination and memory depends entirely on the connection of ideas and that it is formed by the relation and analogy of signs, we will also understand that the poorer a language is in analogous expressions, the less assistance it gives to memory and imagination, which means that it is ill suited to foster talent. It is with languages as with geometrical signs; they give new insights and enlarge the mind in proportion to their degree of perfection. Newton's success was prepared by the choice of signs that had been made before his time and by methods of calculation already contrived . . . The success of the most gifted geniuses depends altogether on the progress of the language in regard to the age in which they live . . . In a language short of words or without sufficiently convenient constructions, we should, therefore, expect to meet the same obstacles as they faced in geometry before the invention of algebra. The French language was for a long time so unfavourable to the progress of mind that if we could imagine Corneille successively at different times during the monarchy, we would gradually find less genius in him as we moved away from the century in which he lived, and in the end we would come to a Corneille who could not give any proof of his talent . . . On these grounds, it is demonstrable that that

superior geniuses cannot arise in nations until their languages have already made considerable progress.[10]

Conversely, just as language determines the possibilities of knowledge in individuals, so the imaginations of precocious individuals (artists, writers, scientists, etc.) give rise to new language:

> If great talents owe their growth to the evident progress of language before their time, the language in turn is indebted to men of talent for the further progress which raises it to its ultimate phase . . . [for although talented writers are] bound by rules which constrain them, their imagination strives with increased effort, thus of necessity creating new expressions.[11]

Of course, people are unaware of the way in which their possibilities of experience are determined by their language, precisely because their knowledge of their possibilities is itself determined by their language. Indeed, their expectations of life as a whole are subject to the possibilities that language is able to support: 'having been accustomed to conceive of things in the same way as they were expressed in the language they had grown up with, their minds were naturally constrained. The lack of precision and correctness would not shock them, because it had become habitual with them.'[12] That is to say, because the language of any given period is always perfectly suited to the prevailing parameters and aspirations of the self-sense at any given time – precisely because the self-sense itself arises from those parameters and changes with them – it is difficult for an individual to notice the way in which his or her possibilities of experience are determined by it. This position was even more vigorously advocated by the German philosopher Johann Gottfried Herder, who argued that people's capacity to conceptualise phenomena, and thereby to *think*, was determined by their language, which evolved historically, and, conversely, that the component parts of their language offered a vision of their mental and cultural capacity. Ideas were not, therefore, formed abstractly in, and in relation to, a transcendental mind or subject; they were generated in conjunction with, and as a sign of, cultural processes. Accordingly, individuals were taught to think *when* and *as* they were taught language. Writing in 1767–8, Herder maintained:

> [Language] is . . . the form of cognition, not merely in which but in accordance with which thoughts take shape, where in all parts of literature thought sticks to expression, and forms itself in accordance with this . . . In being brought up we learn thoughts through words, and the nurses who form our tongue are hence our first teachers of logic; with all sensible concepts in the whole language of common life the thought sticks to the expression . . . Language sets limits and contour for all human cognition.[13]

Because the language that 'I' use is a perfect product and embodiment of my self-sense, it is impossible for me to see how my self-sense is determined by it. Indeed, to the extent that my self-sense is determined by language, it *is* language; it is a linguistic convention that pervades the culture in which it is involved and becomes a norm. But when a historical civilisation encounters a civilisation that is culturally remote from itself, the culturally specific character of its values and practices, and the extent to which those values are supported by linguistic and other conventions, immediately become apparent. Assumptions that once seemed entirely 'natural' and 'habitual' suddenly reveal themselves as being localised and culturally constructed. Of course, degrees of difference can also be found between neighbouring cultures (and within a single culture). For instance, exact translations of the key English words 'mind', 'awareness' and 'conscience' do not exist in French. This is especially striking when one takes into consideration the fact that a rational understanding of philosophy and metaphysics (not least between English and French philosophers) depends on a high degree of intellectual clarity and precision. On this basis, it could be argued that, while an understanding of the ideas to which these words refer is implicit in the English-speaking view of the world, it is ultimately impossible for a French speaker who speaks no English to have a truly accurate understanding of them; indeed, how could they even exist for him? Needless to say, in this example, the sources and underlying values of the two cultures are sufficiently close for alternative, equivalent ways of articulating (or approximating) these ideas to be found; and the fact that they are cultural constructions is, therefore, not sufficiently manifest to expose their limitations and become excessively obstructive. But in more disparate cases, in which cultural backgrounds are not shared, it is not just the vocabularies that differ; it is also the frames of reference that they implicitly sustain. Over time, ways to bridge these gaps can evolve; but especially when such civilisations first encounter each other, the incommensurability of their frames of reference – and the proof, therefore, that these frames of reference are not universal – becomes abundantly clear.

This is precisely what the Jesuit missionaries experienced when they attempted to introduce their Christian world view to China in the sixteenth and seventeenth centuries. In South America, Christian missionaries (mostly uncompromising Dominicans and Franciscans) had imposed their beliefs and practices on the local people, partly by forcing them to adopt the Spanish or Portuguese language in which those beliefs were enshrined. In the same way, in Macao, the first port in China in which westerners were allowed to settle (in 1557), Portuguese missionaries required Christian converts to take Portuguese names, wear Portuguese clothes and follow Portuguese customs, thereby inducing them to appropriate the European mindset that was implicit in those forms. However, in the latter case, because the strategy was not supported by force, it was unsuccessful. As a result, when a new supervisor of Jesuit missions, Alessandro Valignano, arrived in Macao in 1578, the Jesuits took a more flexible and accommodating approach to their work by trying to minimise the appearance of difference between Christianity and the local traditions, and to husband any common ground they found between them towards a Christian interpretation. To this end, some Jesuits (the 'figurists') even proposed that Noah's son Shem had travelled to China after the Deluge, taking knowledge of the Adamic language with him, and that the *I Ching* preserved elements of ancient biblical wisdom. Some of them speculated that the Chinese language might provide vital clues as to how to create a 'universal language'. More practically, many Jesuit missionaries to China committed themselves to living and dying in the country, learning to speak and read the Chinese language, adopting local customs, donning the appropriate robes and altogether getting to know the land, its people and its ways (Fig. 8.5). Capitalising on their knowledge of the Chinese people's down-to-

FIGURE 8.5: Matteo Ricci and Li Paul (Li Yingshi, a Chinese convert to Christianity), from Athanasius Kircher, *China Illustrata*, 1667.

earth appreciation of technical ingenuity (reflected in their ancient inventions or developments of paper, printing, metallurgy, horology, gunpowder, porcelain and many other materials and processes), the Jesuits further improved their credentials by introducing their hosts to the new wonders of European technology: cartography, astronomy, clocks, pictorial perspective, harpsichords and automata, among others. Nevertheless, despite these impressive and persuasive distractions, designed to reflect well on Catholic Christianity, there was simply not enough real overlap between Christianity and the traditional beliefs of the Chinese – whether Confucian, Buddhist or Taoist – for the Jesuits' strategy of 'accommodation' to work. It was for this reason that Matteo Ricci (1552–1610), pioneer of the Jesuit missions in China, began to modify the changes that Chinese converts to Christianity were required to make, allowing them to continue their traditional practices, such as venerating Confucius and their ancestors, despite the fact that these practices were un-Christian.

It was here that the differences between the two paradigms led to conflict. For, despite having prudently recontextualised traditional practices as social and cultural, rather than religious, in order to avoid religious disputes, Ricci was accused of moral laxity, by other Christians, for allowing them. More significant in the present context is the fact that the Chinese did not have words for the Christian concepts of 'God', 'angels' and the 'rational soul', because these concepts simply did not exist for them.[14] Thus, even these concepts, which are considered to be so fundamental to the European vision of the world, are revealed to be localised cultural constructions. Ricci took an artful, flexible approach to this problem, but, needless to say, when he adapted the Chinese concepts of 'heaven', 'spirits' and 'life force' to make them refer to these Christian concepts, he was accused of compromising the Christian faith – again, not by the Chinese, who did not understand the implications of the Latin words, but by missionaries from other Christian orders.[15] The latter, for instance, objected to the Chinese words that the Jesuits used for 'God' – *Shang-di* and *Tian-zhu,* meaning 'emperor from above' and 'lord of heaven' – because they were ambiguously tolerant of veneration of the emperor, who was traditionally considered by the Chinese to be the 'son of heaven'. This disagreement – between the practical compromises of the Jesuits and the unbending absolutism of the Dominicans and Franciscans – eventually became so vociferous that the reputation of the Jesuits became tarnished in the eyes both of the papacy in Rome and the Imperial Court in Beijing. Eventually, in 1704 and again in 1715 (in a formal papal bull), Pope Clement XI forbade both the use of the Jesuit names for God and the veneration of Confucius and family ancestors, whereupon, in 1721, the Christian missions were expelled from China. The conflict continued to flare up in Europe until 1773, when the Jesuit order was suppressed altogether.

The significance of this story lies in the way it exposes the relativity of the cultural paradigms that feature in it. It is arguable in this particular case that the personalisation of God and the implicit personalisation of the sense of identity that co-ordinated itself in relation to it is highlighted as a distinctive aspect of the European Christian (monotheistic) frame of reference. This stands in stark contrast to the Chinese frame of reference, in which the notion of the 'sacred' – for want of a better word – was more diffuse and, therefore, less well reflected in an extended pantheon of personalised entities. The notions that God has a will like a human being, that he created the world like a craftsman, that human beings were made in the image of God and that immortal souls may or may not be saved at the end of time did not resonate with the antipathy that the Chinese felt towards metaphysical abstractions, their impersonal view of heaven, their feeling for the pervasion of nature by *chi* energy and their belief in the dissolution of human beings into impersonal spirit and matter at death. Indeed, the Jesuits were so aware that the idea of God incarnating as an individual man, and suffering and dying on the cross, was alien to the Chinese feeling for the spirit of life in all things that they minimised the role it played in their propaganda. Interestingly, it was on the basis of exactly the same differences that, when mid-eighteenth-century European designers were looking for ways to dissociate from the ponderous, anthropocentric rationale of baroque classicism and move on to something more lively and fresh, they found a precedent in the Chinese tendency to blend individual human beings into the natural environment (as manifest, for instance, in their landscape painting). Capitalising on the same fundamental dissonance between the Chinese sensitivity to energies dispersed in nature and the mainstream rational individualism of the West, chinoiserie was developed to legitimise the whimsical spontaneity of rococo taste and the irrational waywardness of picturesque gardens.

While the relationship between Christian and Chinese cultures was being played out at the level of social and cultural interactions, what was occurring under the surface was an encounter between two totally different models of identity that, despite the Jesuits' strategy of accommodation, were unable to fuse with each other. While the European Christian model was predicated around an abstracted principle of personal identity, absolutised and sanctified by the vision of a personal deity, the Chinese model revolved around the more impersonal vision of family identity and the natural elements, sanctified by the vision of auspicious ancestry and natural *chi* energy. It is arguable that, despite innumerable subsequent developments in the relationship between the two paradigms (such as the relaxation of the ban on ancestor veneration among Chinese Catholics by Pope Pius XII in 1939), the differences continue to manifest. Numerous recent studies in the cultural construction of emotion have used a comparison between the Chinese (and, more broadly speaking, Asian) prioritisation of duty and family honour, and the European (and American) valorisation of personal desire, pleasure and happiness to highlight the culturally constructed nature of westernised individualism today.[16]

The tendency of language to embody cultural frames of reference, and to accommodate the principles of selfhood that derive their parameters from those frames of references, is thrown into raking light when cultures with different histories and languages – to a greater or lesser extent – are juxtaposed; but it can also be deduced from the way in which language is used within a given culture. For, although the language of any given period will always seem to be perfectly suited to its self-awareness and cultural needs – precisely because it is generated by those needs, as we have seen – it can also be a source of perpetual confusion and misunderstanding that, according to Locke, amounts to a form of madness. The chief cause of this confusion is the chronic inclination to associate words with *objects*, rather than with the *ideas* of objects. According to Locke, most nouns – for instance, the word 'tree' – do not refer to particular objects; they refer to *types* of object (unless a definite article 'the', 'this' or 'that' is added to them, or unless they are names). In fact, the ideal tree does not exist in itself, for trees must acquire particular characteristics in order to exist (shape, form, colour, etc.). The effect of this error is of no great consequence in relation to material objects because people's understanding of such objects is tied to their sensations of them and, as these sensations appear to be similar for all people (in the sense that all people perceive oranges to be round), they leave little scope for divergence of opinion. But with regard to abstractions such as 'freedom' or 'identity', not to mention 'God', the 'soul' or the 'self', where the nature of the referent is far less clearly determined because it cannot be sensed, there can be a great variety of opinion, despite the fact that the same word is used. Thus, if several people are asked to visualise and depict a tree, each person would be able to recognise that all the depictions represent trees, despite whatever slight differences there might be between them, whereas, in the case of freedom or identity, God, the soul or self, this would not necessarily be the case; and therefore, particularly because people expect the same word to mean the same thing for all people (a legitimate but unrealistic condition that enabled language to develop in the first place), confusion easily arises.[17]

According to Locke and Condillac, this confusion occurs largely because children learn words before they become fully familiar with the ideas to which they refer. By becoming habituated to verbal discourse, they become so adept at using words and at subjecting themselves to the conventions of language, that they take their referents for granted without necessarily experiencing them or understanding them properly. This state of presumed familiarity and understanding may continue throughout their lives. Forgetting that words originally developed as practical tools of communication, often based on effective but imperfect analogies, people frequently mistake them for signs – or even proof – that the ideas to which they refer must actually exist as absolute realities. Because the principle that 'words refer to existing realities' is established at a very early stage in a child's development, it becomes ingrained in their way of relating to the world. It quickly acquires the status of a universal truth, and people become spontaneously inclined to extend it to the referents of all words. For instance, it is commonly taken for granted that a range of specific emotions (named by such words as 'anger', 'fear', 'joy', etc.) pre-exist as absolute forms or possibilities of experience. On the basis of this presumption, individuals are often inclined to identify and describe their feelings by selecting words from the preconceived repertoire of possibilities 'on offer' – taking them 'off the peg', as it were – without necessarily examining them as unique, present experiences. In the same way, it is frequently supposed that, because words and phrases such as 'free will', 'predestination' and 'the meaning of life' have been coined, those phenomena must somehow exist (to be affirmed or denied), and, therefore, that the questions 'does free will exist?' and 'what is the meaning of life?' must make sense and have answers. Just as naturalistic perspective in a painting or photograph can give utterly convincing impressions of pictorial space ('another' space that is apparently continuous with the space in which the viewer of the picture stands) and *promise* the other worlds that are represented in that space, so words seem to *promise* meaning, by virtue of the 'power of reference' invested in them – despite the fact that they evolved not as iconic embodiments of metaphysical truths, but in order to facilitate communication. As language becomes ever more articulate and elastic, adapting itself to every aspect of life (both real and imagined), so it increasingly becomes a self-sufficient medium not only of expression, but also of experience, parallel to, but independent of, the world of real objects in relation to which it originally evolved. And the more self-sufficient it becomes, the more it begins to revolve around its own self-referential logic and coherence, rather than its 'objectively real' referents. In such a state, the difference between objective realities and mere verbal constructions becomes increasingly difficult to ascertain; for it is arguable that the objects that language identifies, names and discusses (for instance, 'free will', 'predestination' and the 'meaning of life') are as much shaped by the capacities of language to articulate them as by any objective divisions or categories in the world per se. Meanings that are realised in language in this way are the perfect objects of the mind, for they correspond directly with its capacity for self-understanding (from which they evolve) and enable it to find itself perfectly reflected in them; unlike natural objects, on to which meanings are merely projected, verbal language is *specifically* created to embody meaning, and tacitly to support the frame of reference from which that meaning derives its value. Meaning, therefore, is the perfect currency of the self; it is the very medium of its self-awareness – though it too is itself a cultural construction, supported in language. Indeed, the Old English verb 'to mean' originally signified 'to intend' – as in 'I didn't mean to disturb you'. The development of the noun 'meaning' and the shift in its signification from the 'intentions of people' to the 'significance of people's actions or words', and ultimately to the 'significance of objects and ideas per se' – thereby institutionalising the notion 'that objects and ideas have significance' – was a subsequent one.

While language purports to represent the real world, it is also sufficiently elastic to express thoughts and states in words that are grammatically correct but which nevertheless cannot prevail in the world of 'real referents' (in so far as that world can be thought to exist as an object independently of reference to it). For instance, language has no trouble in accommodating *paradoxes* and *impossibilities*, and it is therefore the very breeding ground of confusion – the 'madness' to which John Locke referred. This can be clearly demonstrated by such self-undermining and yet self-perpetuating statements as 'this sentence is untrue', or by referring to 'that to which it is impossible to refer'. Such expressions embody principles that are fundamentally inconsistent with the logic of the 'real world', while retaining their own grammatical coherence and consistency. So long as they are perceived to be internally coherent, they can invent and accommodate their own unique truths and possibilities. Like images of 'impossible objects', such as the famous 'Penrose triangle' or the designs of M. C. Escher, which are also internally consistent but otherwise impossible to realise, they contain no particular point at which they can be seen to be incompatible with the objective world. In precisely the same way, language is solipsistic; it is like a hall of mirrors, organising itself not simply in relation to the complex world of objects to which it purports to refer, but in relation to the endless possibilities of meaning that it is able to extrapolate from within itself (reflected in the infinite possibilities of the mind, including its infinite capacity for self-deception). As such, it derives its coherence not from the objective world of referents, but from the mindset which creates, understands and uses it. That mindset is the provisional sense of a self that creates its objects in its own image and, despite having no independent existence, holds them in place around itself; though it contains nothing in itself, the whole world appears in it, contorted to its form, as in a crystal ball. Indeed, the self-sense is so identified with its abstractions, and *as* the sum of its abstractions, that it is impossible for it *not* to see the world through the lens of its own capacity; it is impossible for it not to submit its experience of the world to its capacity for self-understanding, to the extent, indeed, that its experience of the world becomes a *vision of its capacity for self-understanding*.

It was precisely in order to identify the moment at which the indeterminate unity of consciousness acquired the capacity to reflect on itself, thereby dividing itself into subject and object – 'I' and 'other' – that empirical philosophers such as Locke, Condillac, Rousseau and Herder speculated on the origins of language. Condillac suggested that the first words evolved from passionate cries associated with basic physical needs. In the most primitive societies, such cries were uttered spontaneously and unselfconsciously, until familiarity, sympathy for each other's suffering and a will to help each other led people to recognise, remember and repeat them. In his account of the origins of language, Condillac does not explain the source of the sympathy that first encouraged people to take this initiative. Rousseau proposed that the sense of personal identity first evolved as a corollary to the notion of property. He maintained that the first human beings had lived in solitary, silent bliss, owning nothing. As with Condillac, language and concepts only appeared in relation to other people, as a medium of sociability and communication, although in Rousseau's case, they developed as much as an expression of anxiety as of sympathy. For it was only when communities formed and began to compete with each other for resources that the instinct of the first people to defend their territory developed into the idea of land ownership. As groups of individuals began to build their own huts, rather than sleep under trees or in caves, so they began to be identified by and with their territory, to the extent that their property – in the sense of their possessions – became fused with their properties, in the sense of their definitive characteristics as people; that is to say, their identities acquired *properties* (characteristics, just as coldness is a 'property' of ice) by acquiring *property* (possessions). Among their first notions were the ideas 'mine' and 'yours', in respect for which conventions of courtesy evolved, requiring people – even savages – to act 'appropriately', 'properly' and with 'propriety' (i.e. according to the status of their identity).

Important clues regarding the natural prelinguistic state of human beings were also sought in feral children. In the seventeenth and eighteenth centuries, several abandoned children, believed to have been brought up in the wild by bears or wolves, were found in various parts of Europe (especially Lithuania, Poland, France and Germany). Until the eighteenth century, such rarities had simply been seen as objects of amazement or mockery, to no great avail. But with the advent of the Enlightenment, attitudes began to change and writers, including the French *philosophes*, became interested in them for the evidence that they hoped these children would yield about the essence of human nature and the origins of language. In the belief that they represented an early state of human development, lost in a later time, efforts were made to civilise and educate these 'savages', partly in order to observe how they acquired language and knowledge. Some hopefuls expected them to spontaneously develop the ability to speak Hebrew, proving their preconception that Hebrew was the 'natural' language that Adam had spoken in paradise. A more modern approach was taken by Daniel Defoe, whose novel *Robinson Crusoe* of 1719, about an English castaway shipwrecked on a remote island, already reflected the author's interest in the condition of humanity in a primitive state of nature. In 1726, Defoe wrote an essay, 'Mere Nature Delineated or A Body without a Soul', about Peter, the Wild Boy of Hamelin, who had been found living in the woods near Hanover in the previous year and brought to England to satisfy the curiosity of the Hanoverian king George I. When Peter was found, he was thought to be around twelve years old; he lived off mosses and grass, and used to move on all fours at great speed, climbing trees 'like a squirrel'. He could not speak and, despite living until 1785, never learned to do so. This mystified Defoe, prompting him to speculate:

My Enquiry then is, By what Images, and in what Manner, does he form the Conception of Objects in his Mind, whereby to consider of Things or Persons, which he sees about him, and of Sounds which he may be supposed to hear; as he understands no Language, so he can form no Words to himself, by which to think either of this or that. Words are to us, the Medium of Thought; we cannot conceive of Things, but by their Names, and in the very Use of their Names; we cannot conceive of God, or of the Attributes of God, of Heaven, and of the Inhabitants there, but by agitating the Word 'God', and the Words 'Infinite', 'Eternal', 'Holiness', 'Wisdom', 'Knowledge', 'Goodness' as Attributes; and even the Word 'Attribute'; we cannot conceive of Heaven, but in the very Use and Practice of the Word that signifies the Place, be it in what Language you will; we cannot muse, contrive, imagine, design, resolve, or reject; nay, we cannot love or hate, but in acting upon those Passions in the very Form of Words; nay, if we dream 'tis in Words, we speak every thing to ourselves, and we know not how to think, or act, or intend to act, but in the Form of Words; all our Passions and Affections are acted in Words, and we have no other Way for it: But, what do these silent People do? 'tis evident they act their Senses and Passions upon Things, both present, and to come, and, perhaps, upon Things past also; but in what Manner, and how, that we are entirely at a Loss about; it confounds our Understanding, nor could the most refined, or refining Naturalist that I ever met with, explain it to me.[18]

Similar meditations were stimulated by the wild Victor of Aveyron, who was discovered in 1797 in the South of France, also at the age of around twelve (Fig. 8.6). Typically, Victor was more sensitive to smell and taste than to sight and hearing, reflecting the undeveloped state of his cognitive faculties, which depended more on sight and hearing than on the other senses. He showed no signs of self-awareness when he was found and, when first shown a mirror, he looked behind it to see who was there. Intrigued by the fact that the boy had not been conditioned to construct an identity for himself in time, and indeed that he had no notion of the passing of time, Jean Marc Gaspard Itard, who strove to care for him and educate him into the realm of human feeling and communication (largely unsuccessfully, according to his own estimation), speculated:

Supposing in order to try every hypothesis, that he had likewise remembered the time when he lived in the forest, it would have been impossible for him to represent it to himself but by the perceptions which he would have recalled to mind. These perceptions could be very few; and as he had not remembrance of those which had preceded, followed, or interrupted them, he would never have recollected the succession of the parts of this time. The consequences of this must have been, that he would have never suspected it to have had any beginning, and yet he would only have considered it as an instant. In a word, the confused remembrance of his former state would have reduced him to the absurdity of imagining himself to have always existed, though he was as yet incapable of representing his pretended eternity to himself as but a moment. I do not question but that he would have been greatly surprised, as soon as he had been told that he had begun to exist; and still more so when he had been also told that he had passed through different degrees of growth.[19]

FIGURE 8.6: *The Young Savage, Found in the Forests of Aveyron in France in the Year 1798*, 1805, coloured engraving, London. Wellcome Collection.

What this passage suggests is that the experience of personal identity and the perception of time are organically related to each other. It reflects how – impossible though it is for the mind to grasp – the discourse of 'experience in time' is only sustainable in the mind with the help of words. Indeed, in keeping with this view, it is arguable that the reason that time cannot be experienced and known *in itself* is precisely because it does not exist *in itself*. The *measurement* of time was abstracted in the seventeenth and eighteenth centuries; it was at this date that timekeeping ceased to be determined by religious occasions, the seasons, the weather and the differing amounts of daylight occurring at different times of year, and came to be determined, on a more consistent basis, by mechanical clocks that kept the same regular time in all conditions. This change represented a shift away from a bodily sensation of time towards a more conceptual notion of time, corresponding to a shift of personal identity away from a sense of self that was, to some degree, determined by the vicissitudes of nature, towards a notion of the self that was increasingly abstracted in the mind. The fact is, however, that whether one refers to 'sunrise' or 'six o'clock in the morning', the concept of time is being sustained in words. Indeed, it is impossible to experience time without recourse to this referential medium. Even visual memories or expectations can only be interpreted as being 'of the past' or 'of the future' in this way. Without words with which to link memories and expectations to other experiences and thereby to establish them as part of a network of mutually substantiating associations, such experiences would simply exist as isolated phenomena arising and fading in consciousness – precisely as they appear to have done for Victor of Aveyron. Indeed, it would be difficult to articulate the differences between them (as it is for senile or demented – '*de*minded' – people who 'lose their minds' and seem to 'forget' what once seemed so familiar to them).

It is arguably for this reason – lack of a self-sense or mind – that people tend not to remember experiences from their early infancy. This is not because they have 'forgotten' those experiences, but because the capacity to abstract aspects of experience and fix them as psychological objects – i.e. to *remember* them – is not developed in them at this early stage of their lives. It is not until an infant becomes aware of himself as being different from the environment around him that it becomes possible for him to develop the sense of a unified spatio-temporal frame of reference within which to support memories and expectations. Indeed, the sense of a unified spatio-temporal frame of reference – and the accumulation of memories and expectations that it facilitates – is itself a direct function of the burgeoning sense of self or mind with which it co-evolves. For it is only when the mind begins to be formed that a person can begin to put their attention on distinct objects of experience – as the co-ordinates of their growing subjectivity; that is to say, to 'mind' them – and subsequently to be '*re*minded' of them or have them brought back to attention. Conversely, the sense of self or mind is itself progressively substantiated as the subject of remembered experiences. Indeed, to the extent that this is so, it could be argued that the mind or self has no independent existence of its own (despite the existence of the words 'mind' and 'self' with which to refer to it), and that it is in fact no more than a *state* of remembering/expecting, or 'minding', objects. The impression of its permanency arises as the obverse of the growing perception that the 'outside' world is a permanent realm of differentiated, nameable and remembered but transient objects. As the indeterminate realm that precedes the formation of the mind is increasingly differentiated into objects and subject, so the perceived *fragmentariness* of objects is polarised against the perceptive *unity* of the subject, on the grounds that fragmentation and transience cannot be recognised as such unless a standard of wholeness, continuity and permanency, against which to recognise them and relate them to each other, is not also tacitly acknowledged: in this instance, the subjective self or 'mind'.

The vocabulary in which the discourse of time is sustained is based on a bedrock of technical words that make direct reference to specific times – e.g. 'past', 'future', 'yesterday', 'tomorrow'. But it also consists of more passing references to time by the past and future tenses of verbs ('did', 'will', etc.), their past participles ('loved', 'shown') and their sophisticated derivatives, which make it possible, for instance, to imagine moments in the future when they will be in the past – 'I will have done it by the time you arrive' – and moments in the past when they were still in the future – 'I was about to do it when you arrived'. In conjunction with these explicit references, language is also pervaded by subtle associations with time by virtue of such words as 'memory', 'expectation', 'hope', 'regret', 'nostalgia' and 'history', as well as all words beginning with the prefixes *ante-* and *pre-* (both meaning 'before', as in 'anticipation' and 'premonition'), and *re-* (meaning 'again', as in 'repetition'). All of these words are saturated with a feeling for the passing of time that is deeply infused into the sensibility and identity of their users. The suggestion here is that it is only by means of the vocabulary of time that it is possible to experience (or seem to experience) a sense of the past or future. In fact, it is arguable that, because the vocabulary of time is a mental construct, it is ultimately impossible to truly *experience* the past or the future; on the contrary, both the past and the future are mere concepts. Despite appearances, both of them can only be experienced in the present moment – though, to the extent that the 'present moment' is defined as that 'period of time' that lies 'between the past and the future' (lasting a second, half a second, a tenth or a thousandth of a second?), it too is just a concept. Memories and expectations are illusionistic representations of 'other times', clothed in words and images, in exactly the same way that naturalistic photographs are illusionistic representations of 'other places', despite the fact that they can only ever be 'here', in the same place as the viewer.

Without the possibilities of illusion offered by words, the logic of time is altogether unsupportable. Time is a frame of reference facilitated by the existence of words, which are themselves functions of the self-sense. Therefore, to the extent that the illusion of time is experienced at all, it is not experienced *by* the self, as if the self was a detached and independent viewer; on the contrary, the illusion of time is experienced *as* the self. It *is* the self, in that the sense of self is the very frame of reference – the 'frame of mind' – through which the indeterminacy of existence appears to be refracted into spatio-temporal, object/subject components; that is to say, the self innately historiates itself (and writes its own histories). Conversely, just as the self does not stand apart from time, so time is not an abstracted frame of reference, like a stage on which the self can move; it is spontaneously generated by the self as its own form. It does not 'pre-exist' the self as an independent condition of life; on the contrary, it is a *function* of the self. Most significantly, the notion of time services the self's need to feel that it has *possibilities*. Without the concept of time, nothing is *possible* (because possibilities depend on a sense of the future); everything is only actual. Because nothing can be changed without invoking the 'future', everything that occurs appears, in the moment of occurrence, to be *necessary*. But because the self is fearful both of the selfless experience of timelessness and of the restrictions that appear to be imposed by the concept of necessity, it spontaneously generates the impression of time as the illusory medium through which it experiences the possibility of its own freedom; for its vision of itself as a centre of subjective freedom, and as the seat of identity, depends on the perception that it has possibilities, and possibilities only exist in time; its *potency* as an independent source of consciousness depends on its sense of its own *potential*. It therefore fabricates the illusion of time as a frame of mind in which the possibilities and freedom of personal identity seem convincing and real to it, further enshrining it in the vocabulary of conditionality – 'would', 'could' and 'might': 'I might go to the cinema this evening, therefore I exist'.

Because personal identity and the experience of time are arguably functions of each other, it is entirely natural, and to be expected, that Victor of Aveyron, in whom no conventions of personal identity had been developed, should have had no conception of his own birth or death. Indeed, absurd though it may it may seem, there is no *absolute* evidence, currently known to *us* in present experience, to prove that we too have not 'always existed'. Although there is, of course, plenty of circumstantial evidence to indicate that the body-mind will die, we have no *actual* and *present* knowledge of our own non-existence – just as we cannot watch ourselves fall asleep. It is arguable that our own births and deaths are only known to us as thoughts, abstracted from our observations of other people's lives, and that such thoughts are only accommodated in words, which are in turn culturally constructed; indeed, in the absence of perfect evidence, they are little more than beliefs. And if one looks into one's own mind, or present consciousness, one cannot trace the sense of a self back to its source at the moment of its birth. How then can one be *radically sure* – without submitting to the cultural conventions of language, in which time, thought and memory are enshrined – that it ever happened? And although we see other people's bodies die, how can we be *absolutely and consciously certain* that death will happen to us? We cannot. Of course, in so far as we are conventionally identified with, and as, our body-minds – to the extent that 'I am my body-mind' – we are destined to die. But on what basis is consciousness itself *known* to be identified with the body-mind? Subject to the dualistic conventions of language, which are innately invested with a sense of temporal extension, 'I' am sure to believe that 'I' am the body-mind (as distinct from that which is not the body-mind) and that 'I' was born in time and that 'I' will die in time – *because the conventions of timekeeping are functions of the body-based self*. But if consciousness itself, prior to conventional differentiation, conceptualisation and naming, is truly and presently examined – not as mediated by solipsistic thoughts and beliefs, but as it arises unmediated in experience – not only is no evidence of birth and death found there, but no sense of 'I' is found either. It is only because every thought and cognition that 'I' have is innately a reflection of 'my' capacity to have thoughts and cognitions – as embodied in, and determined by, cultural and psychological conventions – that they seem to reflect 'me' to myself, as an automatic and necessary function of 'my' existence.

Thus, while it may be entirely expedient in psychosomatic situations to subscribe to the convention of selfhood, and make use of the word 'I', there are no grounds for upholding them as absolutes. Indeed, it has been the purpose of this book to explore how the sense of personal self or 'I' is not an absolute truth, but a cultural and linguistic construction, supported by social, artistic, linguistic and other cultural conventions. A sense of personal self thrived between the Middle Ages, when the identities of individuals gradually ceased to consist of their selfless membership of the Christian community, and the beginning of the twentieth century, when the parameters of identity were again increasingly collectivised – potentially, some would claim, at a higher level of self-consciousness. The relationship between personal identity and its cultural forms was a dialectical one. Because cultural forms were directly shaped by their interactions with the self – determined by its self-reflective activity – they implicitly embodied the parameters and co-ordinates that defined and characterised it. As this symbiotic relationship evolved, new patterns of thought, feeling and action – determined by the capacities of the new cultural forms to accommodate them – also developed. Without such cultural accommodation, these new possibilities of experience would have remained inchoate and unborn – just as the experiences of future generations remain inconceivable to us today. In the fifteenth century, the notion of 'art' evolved as the perfect medium and reflector of personal identity. The subsequent history of art consisted of the generation of a swathe of ever-changing cultural forms, in which new possibilities of personal experience were made accessible to society as a whole, thereby facilitating a gradual process of mass individuation that enabled people to become increasingly conscious of themselves as independent selves. At the beginning of the twentieth century, the ability of individuals to be self-conscious without depending on the mediation of artistic culture arguably led to the demise and even death of art, and the dissolution of the personal self as the primary seat and subject of identity. When telecommunications exploded the parameters of identity well beyond the personal level – towards communal, national and even global levels – and the new science of psychology further relativised them to the point of disintegration, it was proposed that the notion of personal identity had become a redundant cultural construction – a persona, an illusion – and that higher, more collective units of identity were being formed. While the idea of 'global identity' offers the possibility of world peace, and 'planetary identity' is seen by some to represent an evolutionary step forward, the fantasies of 'religious identity' and 'national identity' – monsters of institutionalised selfishness – offer far less auspicious futures.

Although the parameters of identity have been reset in the outside world at *collective* levels of denomination that eclipse and usurp the power of *personal* identity, and although personal identity is innately undermined by the conditionality of language in which it is rooted, the fantasy of personal identity continued to arise throughout the twentieth century, as it does today, perpetuated by the momentum of psychological and cultural conventions. Especially since the perceived death of art at the beginning of the twentieth century, it has specifically sought to perpetuate its sense of itself, resisting its demise, by fabricating apparent reflections of its permanence in the world. This resistance constituted a radical crisis and turning point in western and, ultimately, world culture. Indeed, there is a case for arguing that it was linked to, and even contributed to, the outbreak of the First World War, with which it dramatically coincided; that the collapse of European culture was integrally connected to the illusory structures of self-representation on which the personal self depended and, above all, to its inability or refusal to relinquish those structures. Precisely on account of the supposed 'death of art', one of the ways in which the self resisted its own exposure was by perpetuating the concept of art, which it continued to use as the perfect self-reflector despite the fact that, according to some members of the avant-garde, it was an anachronism. As Nietzsche had said, prophetically: 'we need art lest we perish of the truth'. It is surely no coincidence, therefore, that as soon as Malevich applied the 'full stop in the history of art' in 1915, artists and art commentators became intent on identifying and defining the meaning of art, in order to objectify its claim to independent existence. In the very year in which Malevich realised the consummation of art with his *Black Circle* and *Black Square* (Fig. 4.46), the artist Marcel Duchamp announced the existence of his first 'readymades': found objects that became works of art simply by virtue of the fact that he identified them as such. These works – for instance, the *Bottle Rack* (Fig. 8.7) and the snow shovel (called *In Advance of the Broken Arm*) – resonated with the self-transcending aspirations of Malevich's work in the sense that, because they were not actually made or altered by an artist, there was no 'art' or 'artistic identity' in them. Indeed, like Malevich's self-transcending works, they claimed to have no artistic agenda whatsoever (and, like Malevich, Duchamp eventually felt compelled by his insight to give up painting, which he did in 1923, in favour of chess). But, despite making no contribution to the appearance of his selected objects, Duchamp's decision to identify them as works of art constituted an artistic choice, and they were, therefore, rooted in the presumption of artistic identity and authority. As a result, because their status as works of art lay not in any of their objective or visual properties, but simply in the conceptual, self-referential act of acknowledging them as works of art, they are the first objects that can be considered to be one hundred per cent 'conceptual' art (in contrast to what Duchamp disparagingly called 'retinal' art). In an entirely circular fashion, their artistic content is *their status as works of art*. As if to tacitly acknowledge that the role of 'high art' was no longer integral to the unfolding of cultural life and that it had in some sense become socially redundant, art attempted to invent its own rationale. Regardless of its relationship to any social context, it turned itself into a mechanism of self-authentication, constructing itself as an autonomous existential fact (rather as the Church had conceived itself in the thirteenth century, developing the doctrine of transubstantiation in order to *necessitate* itself). And more significantly in the present context, it further institutionalised the corresponding sense of the personal self on the same highly abstracted self-referential grounds.

A circular preoccupation with such unanswerable questions as 'what is art?', 'is it art?' and 'how is it art?' – through which the personal self finds itself permanently employed and reflected – has remained at the heart of avant-garde art ever since. Following Duchamp, a significant amount of twentieth-century art and art criticism has revolved around the nature of art per se. Many artists challenged the apparent superfluity of art by searching for objective principles within the artistic process that seemed to legitimise it from within itself. In many cases this was attempted by eliminating all traces of subjectivity from their work. Such work – which, somewhat

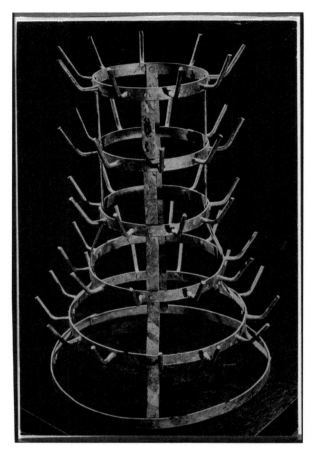

FIGURE 8.7: Marcel Duchamp, *Bottle Rack/Readymade, 1914*, photograph by Man Ray, 1936, 29.1 × 18.9 cm. Museum of Modern Art, New York. 1936. Photo: © SCALA, Florence. © Association Marcel Duchamp/ADAGP, Paris and DACS, London 2018.

ironically, aspired to reflect the 'personal non-being' of the artist – was justified on the grounds that it was determined by its own principles and was, therefore, self-authenticating. In the 1920s, for instance, the Surrealists attempted to minimise the subjectivity of their work by invoking objective, self-determining sources for their artistic creativity. Some of the *papiers collés* of Jean Arp were created by throwing pieces of paper at a sticky surface, appearing to undermine the ideal of artistic creativity by leaving the design to chance. In the same way, André Masson engaged in a process of 'automatic writing', executed in a hypnotic trance state in which the conscious mind played a minimal part (Fig. 8.8). Salvador Dalí transcribed his dreams and fantasies (of which he was as much the witness as the author), no matter how irrational, incongruous and whimsical they might be. And as we have seen, Moholy-Nagy's *Telephone Works* were designed to erase any sign of a personal touch

FIGURE 8.8: André Masson. *Automatic Drawing*, 1924, ink on paper, 23.5 × 20.6 cm. Museum of Modern Art, New York. Photo: © SCALA, Florence.

(Fig. 6.18). Although these artists did not conform to an abstract system or idea, making universal claims for their work, they did seek principles of creativity that were outside of themselves – subject to the objective laws of physics or psychology, rather than to the will of the individual subject – and that seemed thereby to be selfless. At the same time, however, the Surrealists were notorious for the meaningless randomness of their work, deliberately subverting the conventional notion that art should be coherent, consistent and comprehensible. In this respect, they minimised the extent to which their work conformed to a universally accepted 'objective' notion of art and, as such, it was highly unique and personal to them. At the other end of the spectrum were artists who attempted to create objective, self-determining art, in the very opposite way – by subjecting it as rigorously as possible to preconceived systems of geometrical organisation that allowed for a minimum of irrational subjective interference. In the 1960s, minimalists such as Donald Judd (1928–94) and Sol Lewitt (1928–2007) appeared to eliminate the random particularities of personal psychology from their work (Fig. 8.9). But it could equally well be argued that, by maintaining maximum control over every aspect of their art, they were subjecting it as absolutely as possible to their own wills at the expense of extraneous accidental effects for which they could not be responsible, and that their works were, therefore, the products of pure subjectivity. Whereas surrealism was objective in that it was

FIGURE 8.9: Donald Judd, *Untitled (DSS 120)*, 1968. Christie's Images, London/Scala, Florence. © Judd Foundation/ARS, NY and DACS, London 2018.

determined by the objective laws of external processes, and subjective in that it was uniquely associated with the idiosyncrasies of its individual agent-artists, geometrical minimalism was objective in that it conformed absolutely to the conditions of a preconceived idea, but subjective in that the leading idea was invented or selected by the individual will of the artist. Both forms of practice were intended to be based (at least to some extent) on an objective principle, in order to eradicate any invalidating traces of subjectivity. But, despite their efforts – in fact, *because* of their efforts – they necessarily undermined their own ideals. By perpetuating the fantasy of absolutely objective art, they institutionalised the polarity of 'objective truth' and 'subjective experience', thereby subscribing to the discourse of dualism and consolidating the dualistic paradigm in which the personal self-sense has currency.

To the same end, several 'structuralist' writers in the 1960s strove to downplay the role of individual artists, even in their own work, by investing the structures of cultural activity with their own principles and logic, and their own patterns of behaviour. Michel Foucault, for instance, imagined hidden political powers that oppressed or impeded the subject; Jacques Lacan and Pierre Bourdieu deflected the ability to influence one's life away from the individual, in whom such an ability was deemed to be an illusion, towards hidden psychological and social forces. From this perspective, artists were seen to be mere instruments or agents in developments that were beyond their personal control. In reaction to the excessively abstracted reductionism of this approach, 'post-structuralist' writers challenged the notion that there was *any* pre-existing frame of reference (including both the intentions of individual artists and the apparent inclinations of cultural conditions) in relation to which definitive meaning could be distilled from a text or work of art. In 1967, Roland Barthes announced *The Death of the Author*, in which he argued that the meaning of a text was by no means limited to the author's intentions; it could also be accidental, or provided by its readers, or both. Jacques Derrida credited the impossibility of creating meaning and value (including a sense of personal self) to the innately tangled and imperfect nature of communicative media. Inspired by the Surrealists' experimentation with automatic writing and other forms of random creativity, several writers not only theorised the ultimately unprincipled and indeterminate nature of works of art, and of the selves that engage with them, thereby undermining their claims to coherent objecthood; they also *demonstrated* this indeterminacy by making their own texts highly complex and difficult to understand – for instance, by using convoluted, ungrammatical sentences and modifying the meanings and spelling of words – to the point at which they themselves become more surreal and poetic in their impact than communicative of 'meaning'. But what many of these writers often seemed to overlook was the fact that, while striving to destroy the hierarchy of social and psychological values that seemed (to them) to stabilise itself around the production and appreciation of artistic culture, they also supported that hierarchy, by *producing* artistic culture; and they were, therefore, destined to fall into place in the ebb and flow of its history. In this respect they resembled the 'mannerist' artists of the sixteenth century, who regarded *difficultà* (the semblance of struggle) as an impressive virtue, or rococo designers two centuries later, both of which groups reacted against outmoded manifestations of classical rationalism by appearing to abandon formal principles. More to the point in the present context is the fact that, although both 'structuralist' and 'post-structuralist' writers attempted to undermine the notion that a work of art or text was a discrete, coherent entity that could be interpreted in relation to a pre-existent frame of reference, they did nevertheless continue to engage in forms of cultural activity and they were thereby implicitly reinforcing the principles that enable a work of literature or art to be identified as a distinctive cultural product. However much they may have aimed or claimed to dissociate themselves from the notion of the personal 'authorial' self, the very fact that they acknowledged the existence of cultural products by reading, writing, discussing and even noticing them indicates that they were tacitly giving them their approval: the 'author' was distracted, maybe absent-minded, but he was certainly not dead. Indeed, it could be argued that it is – paradoxically – impossible to 'kill the author', or even to 'allow the author to die', because even this act of killing, or allowance, is a form of authorial volition that affirms the vital reality of the author. However oblique or minimal or self-undermining they may seem to be, the self needs and subtly generates cultural objects (or translates natural phenomena into cultural objects by conferring cultural value on them) in order to see itself reflected in them, and thereby to perpetuate itself, to prove its existence to itself, to survive. The truly 'dead authors', on the other hand, leave no trace of themselves.

It is therefore arguable that, despite the avowed demise of the individual and the death of art, the sense of self is preserved, as if on a life-support system, by the conventions and paraphernalia of the art world that have outlived it – from habitual preconceptions about the nature of art and artistic inspiration, to patterns of consumption, cultural politics, domestic conventions, the existence of museums and galleries, networks of commercial commitments, etc. – not to mention deep-rooted habits of taste, and thoughts and feelings about oneself and others. In this respect, the cultural and conceptual infrastructure of the art world could be compared to a symphony orchestra, assembled to perform a genre of music that thrived especially between Haydn in the eighteenth century and Shostakovich in the twentieth. Because people still enjoy hearing historic symphonies performed live, and because the material infrastructure of symphony orchestras is so colossal and unwieldy – requiring substantial investment of many different kinds (instruments, people, auditoria, etc.) – the ensemble has been preserved into the twenty-first century. There is, however, a case for saying that it is partly because the symphony orchestra still exists, for these circumstantial reasons, that contemporary composers continue to write music for it, rather than because it is, in itself, the perfect medium for the expression of contemporary musical ideas. In exactly the same way, it is arguable that (regardless of the marvels of creativity it has generated) the western sense of a personal self has been preserved in the social, cultural and psychological conventions associated with traditional concepts of art and artistic culture, which are themselves preserved and perpetuated by their own momentum, and justified by their own internal, self-referential contracts.

It is also arguable that, taken to extremes, the impulse towards self-affirmation, and the aestheticist modes of identity formation on which it depends, are potentially pathological. Just as communism aimed to eradicate subjective aestheticism in the 1920s, so fascism attempted to politicise it by transforming it into a transpersonal social ideal. From the end of the eighteenth century onwards, the discourse of aesthetics strove to establish a mode of perception that was inherently free of moral preconceptions. The notion of beauty acquired the status of an objective truth and the experience of beauty became the epitome and proof of subjectivity, often mediated through the appreciation of art. To the extent that art was judged aesthetically – i.e. according to its own self-legitimising principle (initially its beauty, but from the beginning of the twentieth century, the circular fact that it was recognised as 'art') – it too aspired to be free of moral obligations and constraints. But, while aestheticism may originally have seemed to consummate the possibility of subjectivity, as it did throughout the nineteenth century, so it can also be seen to have justified and even beautified a culture of 'self-centredness' to the point at which it became a social malaise; the boundaries between the amoral and the immoral became blurred. In the 1930s, the philosopher Walter Benjamin argued that, as consumer products were mass produced, so the discourse of aesthetics was increasingly depersonalised and politicised – and politics, conversely, was aestheticised. From this perspective, Hitler was seen to have been inspired by what he perceived to be the *beauty* of his political ideal. Thus, especially when applied to political ideologies and processes, (apparently legitimised by efficient documentation), rather than to works of art – that is to say, to abstract ideals, such as the 'purification and perfection of the human race' – aestheticism can be truly de-moralising, anaesthetising society against the moral implications of its actions, precisely because the experience of 'beauty' (whatever form it may be made to take) is seen to be self-authenticating.

In the same way, but on a much smaller scale, the attribute of 'art' can provide any object, thought or action with artificial legitimising parameters that, despite nominally aspiring to realise, gratify or express the self, also alienate people from their moral and aesthetic instincts and undermine their capacity to make moral and aesthetic judgements (because they are deemed to be superfluous in this context). This possibility has been in place since the time of Duchamp, when the notion of 'art' became so self-authenticating that it became able to monopolise control over the 'determinants of aesthetic or artistic value' without having to subject itself to conventional standards of evaluation. Having liberated itself from the need to be morally uplifting or meaningful, it now also liberated itself from the need to be beautiful or well made – ironically, in the name of a higher artistic autonomy. It is, however, arguable that much of the subsequent art that indulges the licence to be ironic – using irony as a means with which to challenge the conventions of everyday life (including the parameters of art) for its own sake – allies itself to stand-up comedy as much as to traditional 'art', or even to a new genre of 'stand-up tragedy', offering momentary 'hits' like stand-up comedy, but without the humour. Many such works are like stunts, belonging as much in a fairground as in a museum or gallery of 'art'.

The 'art/self contract' can throw other shadows too. In so far as the label of 'art' places cultural value on phenomena that have been acknowledged and approved by the art establishment – even to the extent that they are recognised as 'art' – it tacitly withholds value from experiences that are not so recognised. We will stand in a long queue to see Vermeer's exquisite painting of a milkmaid pouring milk from a jug, but are we able to perceive the exquisite beauty of pouring milk when we do it ourselves or see it in the world? A modernist photograph of a stretch of pavement may attract attention as a source of cultural value, but the myriad shapes, textures and colours of the pavements themselves rarely do. As a result, to the extent that the notion of art is institutionalised, both in the world and as an idea, it monopolises access to creativity and tacitly contributes towards the alienation of people who do not perceive themselves to be artists or practising an art, from their *own* creativity; it subtly inhibits them from finding sufficient value in everyday experiences, even though there is no reason why such experiences should not grant as much access to the essence of life as any others. Moreover, as cultural value is invested in works of art and harvested through the *experience* of art objects (which tends initially to be a mental process, preceded by expectations, albeit with an emotional impact), it becomes an increasingly disembodied phenomenon. The body becomes an appendage of, or a vehicle for, the mind, reinforcing the identity of the mind as an autonomous subject, but tacitly relegating the body to a position of mere utility. To the extent that it is hyper-conceptualised, in the name of autonomy, art itself can promote this virtuality. Though this alienation may seem unexceptional – indeed, it has become conventional – it is arguable that it is profound, perpetuating a chronic lack of contentment in the modern world that, despite the occasional release, is becoming ever more unmanageable. Especially in times of uncertainty and radical change, there is much to be said for intensifying the appreciation of ordinary life experiences, beyond the accredited realm of culture. If our hidden agendas in maintaining the conventions of the art world could be recognised, creativity could become a way of life, realisable in every circumstance – not just by those enfranchised by society to do so, and not necessarily subject to the approval of an audience.

It is not the purpose here to identify the myriad ways in which postmodernist art and culture have implicitly sustained a posthumous discourse of personal identity – even when sometimes pretending to do the opposite. But there is scope for examining our reasons for investing energy and attention into this discourse, while at the same time seeming to acknowledge its purely contingent nature. One reason for doing this – arguably the most radical reason – may be our fear of having to apprehend our selves *directly* (unmediated by the world of objects), precisely because we tacitly know the self-sense to be provisional and even mortal, and ultimately non-existent. Despite the paradoxical proposition that the personal self cannot die because it does not exist as such, it responds to this deeply subconscious sense of its non-existence with fear of its own death; it prefers to believe in projected illusions (presumed knowledge, religious tradition and cultural truths) because they help it seem to locate itself, rather than to suffer the mere and sublime mystery of existence, which does not reflect it as such. As a result, despite having no *actual* experience of its own mortality, the fantasy of certain death becomes its ever-felt destiny, which it therefore chronically resists – as an illusion fleeing from itself; indeed, by seeming to invent itself in order to avoid dying, it becomes a very embodiment of the fear of death, nightmarishly trapped in the perception of its own demise. It was arguably in order to 'positivise' the deeply intuited 'transience of personal identity', thereby rendering it acceptable, that the discourse of aesthetics evolved, providing a frame of reference in which the vicissitudes of personal experience could be perceived to be sufficient in an otherwise incomprehensible world. Besides magnifying and celebrating the possibilities of personal identity, the perception of 'beauty', formally institutionalised in the concept of art, also constituted a mode of experience in which (in place of religion) the mystery of existence and the unimaginable fact of mortality could be made to feel meaningful. It provided a palliative set of values against which suffering could become tolerable, enabling the sense of self to endure it: 'we need art lest we perish of the truth'. Gustav Mahler's *Songs on the Death of Children* (1901–4) are one of the most symptomatic – and beautiful – outcomes of this impulse.

Having said this, the self-seeking action of the self consists of a double action. While striving to substantiate itself, by finding itself reflected in the world – in self-made reflectors, if necessary – the self-sense is also chronically motivated, like Narcissus, to *lose* itself in its reflections and, therefore, only to know itself indirectly or by implication – in its apparent 'qualities' or experiences, rather than its 'essence' – as it cannot know itself directly without recognising its non-existence, or dying. That is to say, although it seeks to confirm its existence by seeing itself reflected mentally in the world, its self-identification also separates it from the world, alienating it and making it feel lonely and insecure. From this position, it strives to reconnect with the world and become immersed in it, often via bodily sensation, to the point at which it seems to lose itself again – whereupon it seeks to reidentify itself, albeit without doing so directly or completely enough to expose its illusoriness. Thus, while it chronically avoids *direct* reflection on itself (which would reveal its non-existence) by losing itself in the sensations of the body and in the world, it also dissociates from the physical body, which it knows to be structurally potentiated towards death; for it intuits and fears that, to the extent that it is identified with the body, it too will die; it is therefore a no-win situation. It effects this dissociation by compulsively generating autonomous and self-authenticating 'mental' realms and furnishing them with self-perpetuating conventions of mind that seem to reflect it to itself at a transbodily level. It sustains these mental realms by animating them habitually – above all, by thinking, dreaming and mentating chronically. To the extent that it senses its own mortality (and even non-existence), it strives to perpetuate itself in an endless stream of thoughts, desires, ideas and fantasies – especially as abstracted and automated in the solipsistic, self-referential conventions of language (and now exacerbated by the technology of 'virtual reality'). This tendency has been chronically legitimised in the West by the dignification of intellectual knowledge – and, more recently, the cultification of data. But it also manifests, more questionably, as a widespread prejudice in favour of academic education over emotional wisdom and technical skill, and of fine art over craft (as reflected in their respective market values). Indeed, it could also be said to constitute a radical neurosis, for by inhabiting the virtual but often lonely world of thoughts, the self-sense strives to protect itself from both the selflessness of silence (in which it would see its non-existence) and the mortality of the body (in which it would see its death).

It is arguable that, by subscribing to the conventions of historical time, this book is just one more thought, dream and idea, rooted in the fantasy of personal identity; and so it is, at one level. But, while it presents a history of material culture, especially a history of art, as the manifest form of the history of the sense of personal identity, it also radically undermines itself by undermining the principle on which it appears to base itself: historical time, the very perception of which is directly subject to the conventions of language and mind. As a result, by unsubscribing from belief in the absolute reality of historical time in this way, the book also becomes an exploration of the way in which the notion of identity is *presently* experienced in consciousness, and of the roles that the imaginary discourses of art, history, culture and language play in that process. On the basis of this shift, it reconfigures itself as a mere meditation on the sublime complexity, beauty and intelligence of nature unfolding as the myth of history, in which the self-sense, like an exquisite eddy in a river, seems to create itself by chasing its own tail, before eventually relinquishing its shape and returning to its fundamental and formless state of being in consciousness and existence.

NOTES

1. INTRODUCTION

1. Izenberg, G., *Identity: The Necessity of a Modern Idea*, University of Pennsylvania, 2016.

2. For instance, Sorabji, R., *Self: Ancient and Modern Insights About Individuality, Life and Death*, Oxford University Press, 2006; Taylor, C., *Sources of the Self: The Making of the Modern Identity*, Harvard University Press, 1989; Seigel, J., *The Idea of the Self: Thought and Experience in Western Experience Since the Seventeenth Century*, Cambridge University Press, 2005; Martin, R. and Barresi, J., *An Intellectual History of Personal Identity*, Columbia University Press, 2006; Thiel, U., *The Early Modern Subject: Self-Consciousness and Personal Identity from Descartes to Hume*, Oxford University Press, 2011.

3. Morris, C., *The Discovery of the Individual, 1050–1200*, University of Toronto, 1972; Burckhardt, J., *The Civilisation of the Renaissance in Italy*, 1860; Heehs, P., *Writing the Self: Diaries, Memoirs and the History of the Self*, Bloomsbury, 2013.

2. THE NARRATED SELF

1. For a fuller consideration of this shift, see Spira, A., *The Invention of the Self: Personal Identity in the Age of Art*, Bloomsbury Academic, 2020, chapter 9.

2. Moller, A., 'Greek Chronographic Traditions About the First Olympic Games' in Rosen, R. M. (ed.), *Time and Temporality in the Ancient World*, University of Pennsylvania Museum of Archaeology and Anthropology, 2004, p. 173.

3. Bodleian Library, Oxford, MS. Auct. T.II.26.

4. Bede calculated the date of Easter for as many as 532 years into the future. Mosshammer, A. A., *The Easter Computus and the Origins of the Christian Era*, Oxford University Press, 2008, p. 30.

5. Mosshammer, A. A., *The Easter Computus and the Origins of the Christian Era*, Oxford University Press, 2008, p. 31.

6. For the years 794–803, each of the entries in the Lorsch Annals was written by a different anonymous scribe. McKitterick, R., *The Frankish Kingdoms Under the Carolingians: 751–987*, Longman, 1983, p. 4.

7. Wright, C. D., 'Genesis A ad litteram' in Fox, M. and Sharma, M. (eds), *Old English Literature and the Old Testament*, University of Toronto Press, 2012, p. 159.

8. Henry of Huntingdon, *History of the English People 1000–1154*, translated by Greenway, D., Oxford University Press, 2009 (reissued), p. 119.

9. Gillis, M. B., 'Heresy in the Flesh: Gottschalk of Orbais and the Predestination Controversy in the Archdiocese of Reims' in Stone, R. and West, C. (eds), *Hincmar of Reims: Life and Work*, Manchester University Press, 2015, chapter 13.

10. Wood, J., 'Suetonius in the Carolingian Empire' in Power, T. and Gibson, R. K. (eds), *Suetonius the Biographer: Studies in Roman Lives*, Oxford University Press, 2014, pp. 281–3.

11. Newton, S., *The Origins of Beowulf: And the Pre-Viking Kingdom of East Anglia*, Brewer, Cambridge, 1993, pp. 63–4. On remembering genealogies, see Grafton, A., *What Was History? The Art of History in Early Modern Europe*, Cambridge University Press, 2007, p. 112ff. Pupils learning their kings of England are still taught the rhyme 'Willie, Willie, Harry, Ste; Harry, Dick, John, Harry three . . ."

12. As recorded by Bede in his *Ecclesiastical History of the English People*, around 731. Newton, S., *The Origins of Beowulf: And the Pre-Viking Kingdom of East Anglia*, Brewer, Cambridge, 1993, p. 61.

13. Cited in Duby, G., *The Chivalrous Society*, University of California, 1980, p. 154.

14. Karkov, C. E., *The Ruler Portraits of Anglo-Saxon England*, The Boydell Press, 2004, p. 175; Newton, S., *The Origins of Beowulf: And the Pre-Viking Kingdom of East Anglia*, Brewer, Cambridge, 2004, p. 72

15. The Vysehrad Codex, c. 1070–86, Prague Metropolitan Chapter Library.

16. Isaiah, chapter 11, verse 1.

17. Clanchy, M. T., *From Memory to Written Record: England 1066–1307*, Wiley Blackwell, 2013, p. 378 (plate 12); Olivier de Laborderie, *The First Manuals of English History: Two Late Thirteenth Century Genealogical Rolls of the Kings of England in the Royal Collection* (paper from 'Royal Manuscripts' conference at the British Library in 2011, eBLJ, 2014, Article 4, Dec 2016).

18. British Library, Harley MS 7353, f.11.

19. Both examples cited by Bouchard, C. B. in *Those of My Blood: Creating Noble Families in Medieval Francia*, University of Pennsylvania Press, 2001, p. 44.

20. Smith, K. A., *Art, Identity and Devotion in Fourteenth-Century England: Three Women and Their Books of Hours*, British Library and University of Toronto, 2003, p. 175. For a fifteenth-century reference to Christ as a gentleman ('that gentilman Jhesus'), see Berners, J., *The Boke of St Albans* (facsimile of 1486 original), introduction by Blades, W., London, 1901, p. 127.

21. Fox-Davies, A. C., *A Complete Guide to Heraldry*, London, 1909, chapter 31, pp. 479–81.

22. Einhard, *The Life of Charlemagne*, translated by Grant, A. J., 1905, p. 37–8.

23. Baker, D. (ed.), *Portraits and Documents: England in the Early Middle Ages*, Dallas, 1993, p. 112.

24. The woodcut was originally from George the Pious's *Conciones et Scripta*, Wittenberg, 1520. Bodleian Library, University of Oxford, MS Ashm. 34, facing 1r., cited in Woolf, D. R., *Reading History in Early Modern England*, Cambridge University Press, 2000, p. 17.

25. Dürer also made a drawing of what he believed to be Charlemagne's sword, orb, crown and glove, now in the Germanisches Nationalmuseum in Nuremberg. For added realism, he gave details of the exact size of the sword: 'the blade is as long as the piece of string [now lost] that binds this sheet of paper'. See Wood, C. S., *Forgery, Replica, Fiction: Temporalities of German Renaissance Art*, Chicago University Press, 2008, p. 151.

26. 'Oratio de Historia', cited in Grafton, A., *What Was History? The Art of History in Early Modern Europe*, Cambridge University Press, 2007, p. 147.

27. Daston, L., *Classical Probability in the Enlightenment*, Princeton University Press, 1988, p. 320.

28. Grafton, A., *Cardano's Cosmos: The Worlds and Works of a Renaissance Astrologer*, Harvard University Press, 2001, p. 150.

29. Garin, E., *Astrology in the Renaissance: The Zodiac of Life*, Routledge and Kegan Paul, 1976, p. 83ff; Grafton, A., *Cardano's Cosmos: The Worlds and Works of a Renaissance Astrologer*, Harvard University Press, 2001, p. 50ff.

30. Mommsen, T. E., 'Petrarch and the Decoration of the *Sala Virorum Illustrium* in Padua' in *The Art Bulletin*, vol. 34, no. 2, Jun 1952, pp. 95–116. See also France, P. and St Clair, W. (eds), *Mapping Lives: The Uses of Biography*, Oxford University Press, 2004, p. 39.

31. *De Nobilitate* (1440), quoted in Joost-Gaugier, C. L., 'Poggio and Visual Tradition: "Uomini Famosi" in Classical Literary Description' in *Artibus et Historiae*, 6.12, 1985, p. 58.

32. Martin, D. D., *Fifteenth-Century Carthusian Reform: The World of Nicholas Kempf*, Brill, Leiden, 1992, p. 152.

33. Monuments to Piero Farnese (1367) and Niccolò da Tolentino (1456) were also placed in the cathedral.

34. Machiavelli, N., *The Prince*, translated by Marriott, W. K. and Dent, J. M., London, 1958, chapter 14.

35. On loan to the National Gallery, London, from the Longford Collection.

36. For the allegorical potential of Sisyphus, see Simon, E. M., *The Myth of Sisyphus, Renaissance Theories of Human Perfectibility*, Farleigh Dickinson University Press, 2007, pp. 95–109; McMahon, D. M., *Divine Fury: A History of Genius*, Basic Books, New York, 2013, p. 4.

37. Canto 35, verses 25 and 26.

38. Grafton, A., *What Was History? The Art of History in Early Modern Europe*, Cambridge University Press, 2007, pp. 54–5.

39. According to Vico, such bards were called *homeros* after their blindness (Homer was blind), which encouraged them to develop prodigious memories. Vico, G., *The New Science*, Penguin, 2001, p. 382 [section 878].

40. Emerson, R. W., 'History' in *Essays: First Series*, 1841.

41. Vico, G., *The New Science*, Penguin, 2001, pp. 119–20 [section 331].

42. On the innate historicity of the self-sense at this period, see Burke, P., 'Historicising the Self, 1770–1830' in Baggerman, A., Dekker, R. and Mascuch, M., *Controlling Time and Shaping the Self: Developments in Autobiographical Writing Since the Sixteenth Century*, Brill, 2011, pp. 13–32.

43. For the origins of cultural as opposed to political or military history at this time, and of 'the Arts as an Index of Society', see Haskell, F., *History and Its Images: Art and the Interpretation of the Past*, Yale University Press, 1993, p. 201ff. and p. 217ff.

44. Kelly, D., 'The Prehistory of Sociology: Montesquieu, Vico and the Legal Tradition' in *History, Law and the Human Sciences*, London Variorum Reprint, 1984.

45. Turgot, A., *On Universal History*, translated by Meek, R., Cambridge University Press, 1973, p. 90.

46. Ibid., pp. 84, 102.

47. At one end of the spectrum, it resonated with the sceptical philosophy of David Hume, a friend of Turgot, for whom personal identity was but a transient 'bundle' of impressions; at the other end, it corresponded with the 'spontaneous' rococo style in the arts, ever resistant to being subjected to a principle.

48. Daston, L., *Classical Probability in the Enlightenment*, Princeton University Press, 1988, pp. 333–4; Condorcet, N., 'Memoire sur le Calcul des Probabilites' in Bru, B., and Crepel, P. (eds.), *Condorcet: Arithmetique politique, textes rare ou inedites (1767–1789)*, Paris, 1994, pp. 444–448.

49. For the schematic reduction of history to phases, see John Burrow, *A History of Histories: Epics, Chronicles, Romances and Inquiries from Herodotus and Thucydides to the Twentieth Century*, Knopf, New York, 2008, p. 323.

50. de Condorcet, N., *Outlines of an Historical View of the Progress of the Human Mind*, London, 1795, pp. 353–4.

51. Vovelle, M., *The Revolution Against the Church*, Ohio State University, 1991, pp. 102–3.

52. Clay, R., *Signs of Power: Iconoclasm in Paris, 1789–1795*, PhD thesis, University College London, 1999, pp. 209–10.

53. Vovelle, M., *The Revolution Against the Church*, Ohio State University, 1991, p. 98ff.

54. For the development of historical consciousness, see Ziolkowski, T., *Clio the Romantic Muse: Historicising the Faculties in Germany*, Cornell University Press, 2004. According to Ziolkowski (p. 175), the first history of historiography was written in 1812–20 by Ludwig Wachler: *Geschichte der historischen Forschung und Kunst seit der Weiderherstellung der literarischen Cultur in Europa* (*History of the Art of History and its Investigation since the Re-establishment of the Literary Culture in Europe*).

55. Burkhardt, R. W., *The Spirit of System: Lamarck and Evolutionary Biology*, Harvard University Press, 1995, pp. 170–1.

56. Richards, R. J., *Darwin and the Emergence of Evolutionary Theories of Mind and Behavior*, Chicago University Press, 1989, pp. 51, 63, 93.

57. Ibid., p. 52.

58. Ibid., 1989, p. 136.

59. Wallace, A. R., *The Action of Natural Selection on Man*, New Haven, 1871, pp. 15–16. See also Richards, R. J., *Darwin and the Emergence of Evolutionary Theories of Mind and Behavior*, Chicago University Press, 1987, p. 163.

60. Richards, R. J., *Darwin and the Emergence of Evolutionary Theories of Mind and Behavior*, Chicago University Press, 1987, p. 178, 183, 186.

61. 'Mr Darwin's Critics', 1871, quoted in Richards, R. J., *Darwin and the Emergence of Evolutionary Theories of Mind and Behavior*, Chicago University Press, 1987, p. 227.

62. Bell, C., *Essays on the Anatomy of Expression in Painting*, 1806, republished as *Essays on the Anatomy and Philosophy of Expression*, 1824, 1844, discussed by Darwin, C. in *The Expression of the Emotions in Man and Animals*, John Murray, 1872, p. 19.

63. Darwin, C., *The Expression of the Emotions in Man and Animals*, John Murray, 1872.

64. Darwin, C., *The Descent of Man*, John Murray, 1871, vol. 1, p. 67.

65. Chidester, D., 'Darwin's Dogs' in Lloyd, W. and Ratzman, E. (eds), *Secular Faith*, Cascade Books, 2011, pp. 88–93

66. Spencer, H., *Essays on Education and Kindred Subjects*, Dent, London, 1911, p. 154.

67. Ibid., p. 26.

68. Guizot, F., *The History of the Origins of Representative Government in Europe*, translated by Scoble, A. R., introduction and notes by Craiutu, A., Liberty Fund, Indianapolis, 2002.

69. Gossman, L., 'Michelet and Natural History: The Alibi of Nature' in *Proceedings of the American Philosophical Society*, vol. 145, no. 3, 2001, pp. 283–33.

70. Comte, A., *Course de Philosophie Positive*, 1830–42, translated by Martineau, H. as *The Positive Philosophy of Auguste Comte*, 1853.

71. Durkheim, E., *Le Suicide*, Paris, 1897.

72. Taine, H., *History of English Literature*, translated by van Laun, H., Edinburgh, 1872.

73. Taine, H., 'On the Nature of the Work of Art' in *Lectures on Art, Vol. I*, translated by Durand, J., New York, 1875, pp. 33–4.

74. Taine, H., 'On the Production of the Work of Art' in *Lectures on Art, Vol. I*, translated by Durand, J., New York, 1875, p. 104.

75. Spencer, H., *Principles of Psychology*, Longman, Brown, Green and Longmans, London, 1855, pp. 578–9.

76. Smith, C. U. M., 'Herbert Spencer and Henri Bergson' in *Chromatikon VI*, Yearbook of Philosophy in Process, 2010, pp. 191–202.

77. 'Pure duration is the form which the succession of our conscious states assumes when our ego lets itself live, when it refrains from separating its present state from its former states. For this purpose it need not be entirely absorbed in the passing sensation or idea; for then, on the contrary, it would no longer endure. Nor need it forget its former states: it is enough that, in recalling these states, it does not set them alongside its actual state as one point alongside another, but forms both the past and the present states into an organic whole, as happens when we recall the notes of a tune, melting, so to speak, into one another. Might it not be said that, even if these notes succeed one another, yet

we perceive them in one another, and that their totality may be compared to a living being whose parts, although distinct, permeate one another just because they are so closely connected?' 'Time and Free Will' (first published in 1889), in Pearson, K. A. and Mullarkey, J. (eds), *Henri Bergson: Key Writings*, Continuum Books, 2002, p. 100.

78. 'Time and Free Will' (first published in 1889), in Pearson, K. A. and Mullarkey, J. (eds), *Henri Bergson: Key Writings*, Continuum Books, 2002, pp. 76–7.

79. For instance, in one relatively late example, the chairs ranged around the room in Nikolai Ge's *Peter the Great interrogating his son Alexei* (1871, Tretyakov Gallery, Moscow) date from the mid-eighteenth century at the earliest (and are British in style), but the scene itself took place in 1718.

80. Goldstein, J., *The Post-Revolutionary Self: Politics and Psyche in France, 1750–1850*, Harvard University Press, 2005, pp. 162–4. Challenged by Proudhon, P.-J., *What is Property?*, 1840, translated by Kelley, D. R. and Smith, B. G., Cambridge University Press, 2002, pp. 54–5. See also Coleman, C., *The Virtues of Abandon: An Anti-Individualist History of the French Enlightenment*, Stanford University Press, 2014, pp. 287–98.

81. Goldstein, J., *The Post-Revolutionary Self: Politics and Psyche in France, 1750–1850*, Harvard University Press, 2005, p. 158. Cousin's *Premiers essais de philosophie* was published in 1817.

82. Goldstein, J., *The Post-Revolutionary Self: Politics and Psyche in France, 1750–1850*, Harvard University Press, 2005, p. 192.

83. Ibid., pp. 218–22.

84. Ibid., p. 179.

3. THE PUBLICATION OF THE SELF

1. Melton, J. van H., *The Rise of the Public in Enlightenment Europe*, Cambridge University Press, 2001, pp. 240–2.

2. DeJean, J., *Ancients Against Moderns: Cultural Wars and the Making of a Fin de Siècle*, University of Chicago Press, 1997, pp. 57 and 164, note 32.

3. Crow, T., *Painters and Public Life in Eighteenth-Century Paris*, Yale University Press, 1985, pp. 26. A lecture on the relationship between colour and line, given by Philippe de Champaigne in 1671, was one such example.

4. Ibid., pp. 33–4.

5. The exceptional exhibitions took place in 1699, 1704 and 1725. Crow, T., *Painters and Public Life in Eighteenth-Century Paris*, Yale University Press, 1985, pp. 36–9.

6. Cited in Crow, T., *Painters and Public Life in Eighteenth-Century Paris*, Yale University Press, 1985, p. 82.

7. Harrison, C., Wood, P. and Gaiger, J., *Art in Theory, 1648–1815: An Anthology of Changing Ideas*, Wiley-Blackwell, 2001, p. 555.

8. Ibid., pp. 557–8.

9. Crow, T., *Painters and Public Life in Eighteenth-Century Paris*, Yale University Press, 1985, p. 147.

10. The cabinets were designed and made by David Roentgen. Kagan, Y. and Neverov, O., 'An Imperial Affair' in *The Treasures of Catherine the Great*, Hermitage Development Trust, 2000, p. 94.

11. For the slightly earlier but less enduring 'Dusseldorf Gallery', see Gaehtgens, T. G. and Marchesano, L., *Display and Art History: The Dusseldorf Gallery and Its Catalogue*, The Getty Research Institute, 2011.

12. Prohaska, W., *The Kunsthistorisches Museum, Vienna: The Paintings, Volume 2*, Scala, London, 2006, p. 12.

13. McClellan, A., *Inventing the Louvre: Art, Politics and the Origins of the Museum in Eighteenth-Century Paris*, University of California Press, 1994, p. 38ff.

4. THE DISINTEGRATION OF THE SELF

1. Count Delaborde, 1856, quoted in Scharf, A., *Art and Photography*, Penguin Books, 1986, p. 42.

2. Scharf, A., *Art and Photography*, Penguin Books, 1986, p. 152.

3. François Arago, quoted in Scharf, A., *Art and Photography*, Penguin Books, 1986, p. 25.

4. Batchen, G., *Burning with Desire: The Conception of Photography*, Massachusetts Institute of Technology, 1999, p. 27.

5. Driskel, M. P., *Representing Belief*, Penn State University, 1992, pp. 123–31.

6. Scharf, A., *Art and Photography*, Penguin Books, 1986, p. 184.

7. Ibid., p. 182.

8. Ibid., p. 153.

9. Marx, R., *Jules Chéret*, Paris, 1889.

10. 'Definition de neo-traditionnisme' in *Art et critique*, no. 65, 23 Aug 1890, pp. 556–8.

11. Letter to John Dunthorne in *Constable*, Tate Gallery Publications, London, 1993, p. 151.

12. Fourth Lecture at the Royal Institution. Gombrich, E., *Art and Illusion: A Study in the Psychology of Pictorial Representation*, Princeton University Press, 1960, p. 150, cited in Hamblyn, p. 222.

13. Hamblyn, R., *The Invention of Clouds: How an Amateur Meteorologist Forged the Language of the Skies*, Picador, 2001, p. 221.

14. Gilpin, W., 'Essay: On Picturesque Beauty', 1792, translated into French in 1799, in Harrison, C., Wood, P. and Gaiger, J., *Art in Theory, 1648–1815: An Anthology of Changing Ideas*, Wiley-Blackwell, 2000, p. 859.

15. Gage, J., *Colour and Culture*, University of California Press, 1993, p. 209.

16. Ibid., p. 209.

17. Ibid., p. 173. Also Levitt, T., *The Shadow of Enlightenment: Optical and Political Transparency in France*, Oxford University Press, 2009, p. 60.

18. Blanc, C., *Grammaire des arts du dessin*, Paris, 1867, p. 606.

19. Ibid., p. 604.

20. Duret, T., 'Works in Oil and Pastel by the Impressionists in Paris', 1886, cited in Weisberg, G. et al., *Japonisme: Japanese Influence on French Art, 1845–1910*, Cleveland Museum of Art, 1975, p. 118.

21. Edmond de Goncourt, Journal, 9 April 1884.

22. Pissarro criticised Gauguin in Harrison, C., Wood, P. and Gaiger, J., *Art in Theory, 1648–1815: An Anthology of Changing Ideas*, Wiley-Blackwell, 1998, p. 1031.

23. Spira, A., *The Invention of the Self: Personal Identity in the Age of Art*, Bloomsbury Academic, 2020, chapter 14. The debate was revived yet again in the 1970s, when colour photography was first practised as a 'serious' art form, rather than as a 'superficial' medium best suited to advertising and holiday snaps.

24. Chipp, H. B., 'Orphism and Colour Theory' in *Art Bulletin*, vol. 40, 1958, p. 60.

25. Henderson, L. D., 'X-rays and the Quest for Invisible Reality in the Art of Kupka, Duchamp and the Cubists' in *Art Journal*, no. 47, 1988, pp. 328 and 338, note 54.

26. Ibid., p. 328.

27. Vergo, P., *That Divine Order: Music and the Visual Arts from Antiquity to the Eighteenth Century*, Phaidon, 2005, pp. 59–60.

28. Pater, W., 'The School of Giorgione' in *Fortnightly Review*, 22, 1877, p. 528, and *The Renaissance*, 3rd edition, London, 1888, p. 111.

29. Haweis, R. W., *Music and Morals*, London, 1871, p. 32.

30. Ibid., p. 18.

31. Ibid., p. 22.

32. Ibid., p. 33.

33. Giambattista Vico took the same approach to the understanding of history in the eighteenth century. See page 45.

34. Rimington, A., *A New Art Colour Music* (1895), in Colour-Music, Wildside Press, 2004, p. 43.

35. Junod, P., *Counterpoints: Dialogues between Music and the Visual Arts*, Reaktion, 2017, note 80; Vergo, P., *That Divine Order: Music and the Visual Arts from Antiquity to the Eighteenth Century*, Phaidon, 2005, p. 259.

36. Fauchereau, S., *Kupka*, Rizzoli, 1989, p. 19.

37. Frisch, W., *German Modernism: Music and Arts*, University of California Press, 2005, p. 119.

38. Hahl-Koch, J. (ed.), *Arnold Schonberg and Wassily Kandinsky: Letters, Pictures and Documents*, Faber, London, 1984, p. 42.

39. *Reminiscences*, 1913, in Fischer, H. and Rainbird, S. (eds), *Kandinsky: The Path to Abstraction*, Tate, 2006, p. 186.

40. *Reminiscences* quoted in Weiss, P., *Kandinsky and Old Russia*, Yale University Press, 1995, p. 34.

41. Vergo, P., *Kandinsky: Complete Writings on Art*, Da Capo Press, 1994, p. 363.

42. Endell, A., *Vom Sehen: uber Architektur, Formkunst und 'Die Schonheit der grossen Stadt'*, David, H. (ed.), Basel, Birkhauser, 1995, 147, cited in (and translated by) Hand, S., *Embodied Abstraction: Biomorphic Fantasy and Empathy Aesthetics in the Work of Hermann Obrist, August Endell and Their Followers*, PhD dissertation, University of Chicago, 2008, p. 128.

43. Letter to Gabriele Munther, 25 April 1904, quoted in Fischer, H. and Rainbird, S. (eds), *Kandinsky: The Path to Abstraction*, Tate, London, 2006, p. 42.

44. *Reminiscences*, 1913, in Vergo, P., *Kandinsky: Complete Writings on Art*, Da Capo Press, 1994, p. 370.

45. Kandinsky, W., *Concerning the Spiritual in Art*, translated by Sadler, M. T. H., Dover Publications, 1977, p. 9.

46. Besant, A., *The Ancient Wisdom: An Outline of Theosophical Teachings*, London, 1897, partly quoted in Ringbom, S., 'Transcending the Visible: The Generation of the Abstract Pioneers' in Tuchman, M., *The Spiritual in Art: Abstract Painting, 1890–1985*, Abbeville Press, 1993, p. 134.

47. Chladni, E., *Entdeckungen über die Theorie des Klanges* (Discoveries in the Theory of Sound), Leipzig, 1787.

48. Tuchman, M., *The Spiritual in Art: Abstract Painting, 1890–1985*, Abbeville Press, 1993, p. 35.

49. Kandinsky, W., *Concerning the Spiritual in Art*, translated by Sadler, M. T. H., Dover Publications, 1977, pp. 2–3.

50. Besant, A. and Leadbeater, G. W., *Thought Forms*, London, 1905, p. 65.

51. State Pushkin Museum, Moscow. Fischer, H. and Rainbird, S. (eds.), *Kandinsky: The Path to Abstraction*, Tate, London, 2006, p. 115.

52. Milner, J., *Kazimir Malevich and the Art of Geometry*, Yale University Press, 1996, p. 107ff.

53. Malevich, K. S., *Essays, Vol. I*, p. 33, in Bowlt, J., 'The Semaphores of Suprematism: Malevich's Journey into the Non-Objective World' in *ARTnews*, 72, Dec 1973, p. 22; Spira, A., *The Avant-Garde Icon: Russian Avant-Garde Art and the Icon Painting Tradition*, Lund Humphries, 2008, p. 140.

54. Chipp, H. B., *Theories of Modern Art*, London, 1968, p. 342; Spira, A., *The Avant-Garde Icon: Russian Avant-Garde Art and the Icon Painting Tradition*, Lund Humphries, 2008, p. 146.

5. THE DEMOCRATISATION OF THE SELF

1. This tradition can be traced back to the fact that some privileged French manufacturers had been supported as 'state enterprises' since the time of Louis XIV, in contrast to their British equivalents, which were usually private enterprises. Leben, U., *Object Design in the Age of Enlightenment: The History of the Royal Free Drawing School in Paris*, The J. Paul Getty Museum, Los Angeles, 2004, p. 17; Crowston, C., 'From School to Workshop: Pre-Training and Apprenticeship in Old Regime France' in de Munck, B.,

Kaplan, S. L. and Soly, H. (eds), *Learning on the Shop Floor: Historical Perspectives in Apprenticeship*, Berghahn Books, 2007, p. 56ff.

2. Leben, U., *Object Design in the Age of Enlightenment: The History of the Royal Free Drawing School in Paris*, The J. Paul Getty Museum, Los Angeles, 2004, pp. 34 and 77–8.

3. Francoeur, L.-B., *Lineal Drawing and Introduction to Geometry, as Taught in the Lancastrian Schools of France; Translated from the French*, Harvey and Darton, London, 1824, p. 7.

4. Johansson, J.-E., 'F. A. W. Fröbel 1782–1852' in Fleer, M. and van Oers, B. (eds), *International Handbook of Early Childhood Education*, Springer, 2018, p. 1327.

5. The first publication on Pestalozzi's system in English was Synge, J., *The Relations and Descriptions of Forms, According to the Principles of Pestalozzi*, Dublin, 1817.

6. Macdonald, S., *The History and Philosophy of Art Education*, Lutterworth Press, Cambridge, 2004, p. 124.

7. Forty, A., *Objects of Desire: Design and Society Since 1750*, London, 1986, p. 113.

8. Macdonald, S., *The History and Philosophy of Art Education*, Lutterworth Press, Cambridge, 2004, p. 133.

9. Because the 'classical style' has become a 'universal' style, its *regional* origin – mostly with Rome and its Empire (but, ultimately, with Greece) – is often overlooked. Optimistic efforts by its users to *nationalise* the classical style, and therefore to take national credit for it – for instance, by the English architect Inigo Jones (1573–1652), who suggested that Stonehenge was built in a 'proto-classical' style – were relatively rare. Even the Republic of Venice (which did not emerge until the fifth century) could make no claim to it on 'nationalistic' grounds.

10. Redgrave, R., 'Importance of the Study of Botany to the Ornamentalist' in *Journal of Design and Manufactures*, vol. I, March–Aug 1849.

11. *Versuch die Metamorphose der Pflanzen zu erklaren*. Halen, W., *Christopher Dresser*, Phaidon, 1990, p. 12.

12. Dresser, C., *The Art of Decorative Design*, London, 1862, reissued by the American Life Foundation, 1977, p. 40.

13. The Bauhaus manifesto. Naylor, G., *The Bauhaus*, London, 1968, p. 50.

14. For the new fears associated with the individualist art of poetry, see Loewen, D., *The Most Dangerous Art: Poetry, Politic and Autobiography After the Revolution*, Lexington Books, 2010.

15. Kharkhordin, O., *The Collective and the Individual in Russia*, University of California, 1999, p.76ff.

16. From Gastev's 'Our Mission', 1921, cited in Bailes, K. E., 'Alexei Gastev and the Soviet Controversy over Taylorism, 1918–24' in Wood, J. C. and Wood, M. C. (eds), *F. W. Taylor: Critical Evaluations in Business and Management, Vol IV*, Routledge, 2002, p. 311.

17. Milgram, S., 'Anthem in the Context of Related Literary Works' in Mayhew, R. (ed.), *Essays on Ayn Rand's 'Anthem'*, Lexington Books, 2005, p. 139.

18. Fueloep-Miller, R., *The Mind and Face of Bolshevism*, Harper Torchbook, 1965, pp. 208–10.

19. Milgram, S., 'Anthem in the Context of Related Literary Works' in Mayhew, R. (ed.), Essays on Ayn Rand's 'Anthem', Lexington Books, 2005, p. 139.

20. Zamyatin, E., We, translated by Brown, C., Penguin, 1993, p. 124.

21. LEF (Moscow), no. 3 (1923), 54.

6. THE TRANSPERSONALISATION OF THE SELF

1. The engravings from West's painting took five years to emerge, as did the prints from Arthur William Devis's 1807 painting of the same scene.

2. Stravinsky, I., An Autobiography, New York, 1962, pp. 123, cited in Katz, M., Capturing Sound: How Technology has Changed Music, California University Press, 2004, p. 3.

3. Kenkel, K. J., 'The Nationalisation of the Mass Spectator in Early German Film', in Celebrating 1895: The Centenary of Cinema, John Libbey & Co., Sydney, 1998, pp. 155–62.

4. Le Bon, G., La psychologie des foules, 1895, translated into English as The Crowd: A Study of the Popular Mind, Macmillan, New York, 1896.

5. Altman, J. G., '1725: The Politics of Epistolary Art' in Hollier, D. (ed.), A New History of French Literature, Harvard University Press, 1994, p. 417.

6. Camargo, M., 'Where's the Brief? The Ars Dictaminis and Reading/Writing Between the Lines' in Poster, C. and Utz, R. (eds), The Late Medieval Epistle, Northwestern University Press, Illinois, 1996, p. 2.

7. Headrick, D. R., When Information Came of Age: Technologies of Knowledge in the Age of Reason and Revolution, 1700–1850, Oxford University Press, 2000, p. 185.

8. Kronick, D. A., 'The Commerce of Letters: Networks and "Invisible Colleges" in Seventeenth and Eighteenth Century Europe' in The Library Quarterly: Information, Community, Policy, vol. 71, no. 1, Jan 2001, pp. 28–43.

9. Racevskis, R., Time and Ways of Knowing Under Louis XIV, Bucknell University Press, 2010, pp. 91 and 106–7.

10. Letters of 10 June 1671, 31 May 1680, 5 Jan 1689.

11. Boerhaave, H., Dr. Boerhaave's Academical Lectures on the Theory of Physic: Being a Genuine Translation of His Institutes, London, 1744, p. 30.

12. La Mettrie, J. O. de, Man a Machine, translated by Watson, R. A. and Rybalka, M., Hackett Publishing Company, Indianapolis, 1994, p. 31.

13. Cited in Kittler, F., 'The Mechanized Philosopher' in Rickels, L. A., Looking After Nietzsche, State University of New York Press, 1990, p. 195.

14. Brownlee, P. J. (ed.), Samuel F. B. Morse's Gallery of the Louvre and the Art of Invention, Terra Foundation for American Art, 2014.

15. Lepore, J., A is for American: Letters and Other Characters in the Newly United States, Vintage, 2003, p. 157.

16. Pool, I. de S., *Forecasting the Telephone: A Retrospective Technology Assessment of the Telephone*, Ablex Publishing, 1983, pp. 23, 65.

17. CBC Digital Archive, 1975 broadcast.

18. Shea, A., *The Phone Book: The Curious History of the Book That Everyone Uses but No-One Reads*, Perigree Books, 2010, chapter 1.

19. The first automatic exchange centre in the UK was opened in 1912 (at Epsom); the last manual exchange centre in the UK, at Portree on the Isle of Skye, closed in 1976.

20. The key exception was the Scandinavian countries in which private companies were licensed to operate telephone systems, resulting in the highest proportion of telephone users in Europe. For statistics of telephone use in European countries and cities up to 1914, see Wallsten, S., *Ringing in the 20th Century: The Effects of State Monopolies, Private Ownership and Operating Licenses on Telecommunications in Europe, 1892–1914*, Research Policy Working Paper 2690, The World Bank Development Research Group, Oct 2001.

21. Katz, J. (ed.), *Machines that Become Us*, Transaction Publishers, 2006.

22. Waggoner, Z., *My Avatar, My Self: Identity in Video Role-Playing Games*, McFarland & Co., 2009, pp. 13–14.

23. Wurtzel, A. C. and Turner, C., 'Latent Functions of the Telephone: What Missing the Extension Means' in Pool, I/ de S. (ed.), *The Social Impact of the Telephone*, Massachusetts Institute of Technology, 1977, pp. 252–8.

24. Ibid., p. 256.

25. John Henniker Heaton, who was largely responsible for extending the penny post to the whole of the British Empire in 1898 and to the USA in 1908, thereby making long-distance mail possible for all social classes (Read, D., *The Age of Urban Democracy: England 1868–1914*, Routledge, 2014, p. 66, cited in Briggs, A. and Burke, P., *A Social History of the Media*, Polity, Cambridge, 2009, p. 131.

26. Hawthorne, N., *The House of Seven Gables*, Boston, 1851, p. 283. '"Then there is electricity; – the demon, the angel, the mighty physical power, the all-pervading intelligence!" exclaimed Clifford. "Is that a humbug, too?"'

27. Fechner, G., *Nanna, or The Soul-life of Plants*, Leipzig, 1848, and *Zend-Avesta, or the Matters of Heaven and the World Beyond*, 1851.

28. James, W., *A Pluralistic Universe*, Hibbert Lectures at Manchester College on the Present Situation in Philosophy, 1909, Lecture IV. Also cited in Skrbina, D., *Panpsychism in the West*, Massachusetts Institute of Technology, 2007, p. 124. For a critical biography of Fechner, see Heidelberger, M., *Nature from Within: Gustav Theodor Fechner and his Psychophysical World View*, Pittsburg University Press, 2004.

29. Ouspensky, P. D., *Tertium Organum*, 1912, translated from the Russian into English in 1920, Routledge and Kegan Paul, 1981, p. 166.

30. Quoted in James, W., *A Pluralistic Universe*, Hibbert Lectures at Manchester College on the Present Situation in Philosophy, 1909, Lecture IV. The word order is very slightly changed, for the sake of clarity.

31. von Hartmann, E., *Philosophy of the Unconscious*, 1869; Skrbina, D., *Panpsychism in the West*, Massachusetts Institute of Technology, 2007, p. 129.

32. James, W., *A Pluralistic Universe*, Hibbert Lectures at Manchester College on the Present Situation in Philosophy, 1909, Lecture VII.

33. Ibid., Lecture VIII.

34. Ibid.

35. Lowell Lectures, published in 1894.

36. Carpenter, E., *The Art of Creation: Essays on the Self and its Powers*, George Allen, London, 1905, pp. 33–4, cited in Henderson, L. D., 'Vibratory Modernism: Boccioni, Kupka and the Ether of Space' in Clarke, B. and Henderson, L. D. (eds), *From Energy to Information: Representation in Science and Technology, Art and Literature*, Stanford University Press, 2002, p. 149.

37. Page [119]

38. Recent research has attempted to make the link between telephony and telepathy explicit (rather than analogous) by finding (or seeking) evidence to suggest that many people are able to know psychically – before answering a telephone call – who it is that is calling them. Sheldrake, R. and Smart, P., 'Experimental Tests for the Telephone Telepathy' in *Journal of the Society of Psychical Research*, no. 67, 2003, pp. 184–99.

39. See also the Sufi poet Jalaluddin Rumi: 'I died from a mineral and a plant became; I died from a plant, and took a sentient frame; I died from a beast, and donned a human dress; when by my dying did I ever grow less?' cited in Fraser, J. T., *Time: The Familiar Stranger*, University of Massachusetts Press, 1987, p. 221.

40. These questions were raised in the fifteenth century by the scholastic philosopher and theologian William of Vorilong. Dick, S. J., *Plurality of Worlds: The Origins of the Extraterrestrial Life Debate from Democritus to Kant*, Cambridge University Press, 1984, p. 43.

41. James, W., *A Pluralistic Universe*, Hibbert Lectures at Manchester College on the Present Situation in Philosophy, 1909, Lecture IV.

42. Haeckel, E, *The Riddle of the Universe*, Watts, London, 1931, pp. 9–12.

7. THE PSYCHOLOGICAL SELF

1. Wilhelm Wundt (1832–1920) in Germany; Theodule-Armand Ribot (1839–1916) and Pierre Janet (1859–1947) in Paris.

2. Rieber, R. W., *The Bifurcation of the Self: The Theory and History of Dissociation and Its Disorders*, Springer US, 2006, pp. 15–16.

3. Freud, S., *Civilisation and Its Discontents*, Vienna, 1930.

4. Rank, O., *The Double: A Psychoanalytic Study*, translated by Tucker, H., University of North Carolina Press, 1971, p. 4. Freud's comment appears in *The Uncanny* of 1919; Royle, N., *The Uncanny: An Introduction*, Manchester University Press, 2003, pp. 76–7. See also Marcus, L., 'Dreaming and Cinematographic Consciousness' in

Psychoanalysis and History, 3, Jan 2008, pp. 51–68; Gifford, S., 'Freud at the Movies, 1907–1925: From the Piazza Colonna and Hammerstein's Roofgarden to *The Secrets of the Soul*' in Brandell, J. R. (ed.), *Celluloid Couches, Cinematic Clients: Psychoanalysis and Psychotherapy in the Movies*, State University of New York Press, 2004, pp. 147–68.

8. THE LINGUISTIC SELF

1. A remnant of Wilkins's universal language survives in the binomial system of nomenclature for the naming of plants introduced by Carl Linnaeus in the following century. Linnaeus was directly influenced by the English botanist John Ray, who designed the hierarchical names of plants, according to species, for Wilkins's language.

2. Wilkins describes the shortcomings of the Chinese language in his *Essay*, Part IV, pp. 450–2.

3. Locke, *Essay*, chapter III, 1, 5.

4. de Condillac, E. B., *Essay on the Origin of Human Knowledge*, translated and edited by Aarsleff, H., Cambridge Texts in the History of Philosophy, Cambridge University Press, 2001, pp. 164–5.

5. Ibid., pp. 165–6.

6. For the role of onomatopoeia in histories of language from the eighteenth century onwards, see Moore, C., 'An Ideological History of the English Term *Onomatopoeia*' in Adams, M., Brinton, L. J. and Fulk, R. D. (eds), *Studies in the History of the English Language VI*, De Gruyter, 2015, p. 313. Also, in the thought of Giambattista Vico, Danesi, M., *Vico, Metaphor and the Origin of Language*, Indiana University Press, 1993, p. 72.

7. The association with *scindere* was proposed in the sixteenth century but may be incorrect. In English, the word 'scissors' was spelled with an *s* or a *c* (not both) in the thirteenth century. The earliest use of *sc* recorded in the *Oxford English Dictionary* is 1484. It may be older in Old French, from which it derives.

8. Humphrey, N., *A History of the Mind*, Vintage, 1993, p. 100; Lewis, C. S., *Studies in Words*, Cambridge University Press, 1960.

9. James, W., *The Principles of Psychology*, New York, 1890, chapter X, vol. I, p. 304.

10. de Condillac, E. B., *Essay on the Origin of Human Knowledge*, translated and edited by Aarsleff, H., Cambridge Texts in the History of Philosophy, Cambridge University Press, 2001, p. 187.

11. Ibid., p. 190.

12. de Condillac, E. B., *Essay on the Origin of Human Knowledge*, translated and edited by Aarsleff, H., Cambridge Texts in the History of Philosophy, Cambridge University Press, 2001, p. 188.

13. Herder, J. G., *Fragments of Recent German Literature (1767–8)* cited in Forster, M. N., 'Kant's Philosophy of Language?' in *Tijdschrift voor Filosofie*, 74, 2012, p. 502.

14. Zhang, Q., 'About God, Demons and Miracles: The Jesuit Discourse on the Supernatural in Late Ming China' in *Early Science and Medicine*, 4.1., 1999, pp. 1–36; and Zhang,

Q., 'Translation as Cultural Reform: Jesuit Scholastic Psychology in the Transformation of Confucian Discourse on Human Nature' in O'Malley et al. (eds), *The Jesuits: Cultures, Sciences and the Arts, 1540–1773*, University of Toronto Press, 1999, pp. 364–79.

15. The word 'God', *Shang-di*, meaning 'emperor from above', and *Tian-zhu*, meaning 'lord of heaven', were the most common in the sixteenth and seventeenth centuries.

16. While these latter concepts are deeply embedded in European culture, they have of course also been constructed over time. With regard to 'happiness', the root 'hap' originally referred to 'fortune' or 'chance' – something that 'comes to pass', as in 'happen', 'happenstance' and 'haphazard', and (negatively) 'mishap' and 'hapless'; applied to a circumstance rather than a person, the adjective 'happy' can still have this meaning. According to the *Oxford English Dictionary*, its earliest use in this capacity dates to the fourteenth century. The use of 'happiness' as a favoured state of mind does not appear until the sixteenth century.

17. See Rousseau's *Discourse on Inequality*, 1755, translated by Philip, F., Oxford University Press, 2009, Part I, p. 41.

18. Defoe, D., *Mere Nature Delineated or a Body without a Soul*, London, 1726, pp. 38–9.

19. Itard, G., *An Historical Account of the Discovery and Education of a Savage Man*, 1802, quoted in Newton, M., *Savage Girls and Wild Boys*, London, 2002, pp. 115–16.

BIBLIOGRAPHY

Aarslef, H., *From Locke to Saussure: Essays on the Study of Language and Intellectual History*, University of Minnesota, 1982.

Adams, M., Brinton, L. J. and Fulk, R. D. (eds), *Studies in the History of the English Language VI*, De Gruyter, 2015.

Altman, J. G., '1725: The Politics of Epistolary Art' in Hollier, D. (ed.), *A New History of French Literature*, Harvard University Press, 1994.

Ashton, T. S., *The Industrial Revolution*, Oxford University Press, 1997.

Bailes, K. E., 'Alexei Gastev and the Soviet Controversy over Taylorism, 1918–24' in Wood, J. C. and Wood, M. C. (eds), *F. W. Taylor: Critical Evaluations in Business and Management, Vol IV*, Routledge, 2002.

Baker, D. (ed.), *Portraits and Documents: England in the Early Middle Ages*, Dallas, 1993.

Basalla, G., *The Evolution of Technology*, Cambridge University Press, 2002.

Batchen, G., *Burning with Desire: The Conception of Photography*, Massachusetts Institute of Technology, 1999.

Bayer, T. and Verene, D. (eds), *Giambattista Vico: Keys to the New Science*, Cornell University Press, 2009.

Bell, C., *Essays on the Anatomy of Expression in Painting*, 1806, republished as *Essays on the Anatomy and Philosophy of Expression*, 1824, 1844.

Berg, M., *The Age of Manufactures 1700–1820: Industry, Innovation and Work in Britain*, Routledge, 1996.

Berg, M. and Clifford, H. (eds), *Consumers and Luxury: Consumer Culture in Europe 1650–1850*, Manchester University Press, 1999.

Berlin, I., *Three Critics of the Enlightenment: Vico, Hamann, Herder*, Pimlico, 2000.

Berners, J., *The Boke of St Albans* (facsimile of 1486 original), introduction by Blades, W., London, 1901.

Besant, A., *The Ancient Wisdom: An Outline of Theosophical Teachings*, London, 1897.

Besant, A. and Leadbeater, G. W., *Thought Forms*, Londo, 1905.

Blanc, C., *Grammaire des arts du dessin*, Paris, 1867.

Boerhaave, H., *Dr. Boerhaave's Academical Lectures on the Theory of Physic: Being a Genuine Translation of His Institutes*, London, 1744.

Bouchard, C. B., *Those of My Blood: Creating Noble Families in Medieval Francia*, University of Pennsylvania Press, 2001.

Bowler, P., *Evolution: The History of an Idea*, University of California Press, 2003.

Bowlt, J., 'The Semaphores of Suprematism: Malevich's Journey into the Non-Objective World' in *ARTnews*, 72, Dec 1973.

Bricklin, J. (ed.), *Sciousness*, Eirini Press, 2006.

Briggs, A. and Burke, P., *A Social History of the Media*, Polity, Cambridge, 2009.

Brown, M., *Turning Points: Essays in the History of Cultural Expressions*, Stanford University Press, 1997.

Brownlee, P. J. (ed.), *Samuel F. B. Morse's Gallery of the Louvre and the Art of Invention*, Terra Foundation for American Art, 2014.

Burckhardt, J., *The Civilisation of the Renaissance in Italy*, 1860.

Burke, P., *Vico*, Oxford University Press, 1985.

Burke, P., *A Social History of Knowledge: From Gutenberg to Diderot*, Polity, 2004.

Burke, P., 'Historicising the Self, 1770–1830' in Baggerman, A., Dekker, R. and Mascuch, M., *Controlling Time and Shaping the Self: Developments in Autobiographical Writing Since the Sixteenth Century*, Brill, 2011.

Burkhardt, R. W., *The Spirit of System: Lamarck and Evolutionary Biology*, Harvard University Press, 1977.

Burrow, J., *A History of Histories: Epics, Chronicles, Romances and Inquiries from Herodotus and Thucydides to the Twentieth Century*, Knopf, New York, 2008.

Bury, J. B., *The Idea of Progress*, New York, 2008.

Camargo, M., 'Where's the Brief? The *Ars Dictaminis* and Reading/Writing Between the Lines' in Poster, C. and Utz, R. (eds), *The Late Medieval Epistle*, Northwestern University Press, Illinois, 1996.

Campbell, M. B., *Wonder and Science: Imaging Worlds in Early Modern Europe*, Cornell University Press, 2004.

Carneiro, R. L. *The Muse of History and the Science of Culture*, Kluwer Academic, 2000.

Carpenter, E., *The Art of Creation: Essays on the Self and its Powers*, George Allen, London, 1905.

Cassirer, E., *The Individual and the Cosmos in Renaissance Philosophy*, University of Pennsylvania Press, 1972.

Chene, D. D., *Spirits and Clocks: Machine and Organism in Descartes*, Cornell University Press, 2001.

Chidester, D., 'Darwin's Dogs' in Lloyd, W. and Ratzman, E. (eds), *Secular Faith*, Cascade Books, 2011.

Chipp, H. B., 'Orphism and Colour Theory' in *Art Bulletin*, vol. 40, 1958.

Chipp, H. B., *Theories of Modern Art*, London, 1968.

Chladni, E., *Entdeckungen über die Theorie des Klanges* (Discoveries in the Theory of Sound), Leipzig, 1787.

Clanchy, M. T., *From Memory to Written Record: England 1066–1307*, Wiley Blackwell, 2013.

Clarke, B. and Henderson, L. D. (eds), *From Energy to Information: Representation in Science and Technology, Art and Literature*, Stanford University Press, 2002.

Clay, R., *Signs of Power: Iconoclasm in Paris, 1789–1795*, PhD thesis, University College London, 1999.

Cohen, M., *Sensible Words: Linguistic Practice in England, 1640–1785*, John Hopkins University Press, 1977.

Coleman, C., *The Virtues of Abandon: An Anti-Individualist History of the French Enlightenment*, Stanford University Press, 2014.

Comte, A., *Course de Philosophie Positive*, 1830–42, translated by Martineau, H. as *The Positive Philosophy of Auguste Comte*, 1853.

de Condillac, E. B., *Essay on the Origin of Human Knowledge*, translated and edited by Aarsleff, H., Cambridge Texts in the History of Philosophy, Cambridge University Press, 2001.

de Condorcet, N., *Outlines of an Historical View of the Progress of the Human Mind*, London, 1795.

de Condorcet, N., 'Memoire sur le Calcul des Probabilités' in Bru, B. and Crepel, P. (eds), *Condorcet: Arithmétique politique, textes rare ou inédites (1767–1789)*, Paris, 1994.

Coupland, D., *Marshall MacLuhan: You Know Nothing of my Work!*, Atlas & Co., 2010.

Crabbe, M. J. C. (ed.), *From Soul to Self*, Routledge, 1999.

Crary, J., *Techniques of the Observer: On Vision and Modernity in the Nineteenth Century*, Massachusetts Institute of Technology Press, 1992.

Crow, T., *Painters and Public Life in Eighteenth-Century Paris*, Yale University Press, 1985.

Crowston, C., 'From School to Workshop: Pre-Training and Apprenticeship in Old Regime France' in de Munck, B., Kaplan, S. L. and Soly, H. (eds), *Learning on the Shop Floor: Historical Perspectives in Apprenticeship*, Berghahn Books, 2007.

Danesi, M., *Vico, Metaphor and the Origin of Language*, Indiana University Press, 1993.

Darwin, C., *The Descent of Man*, John Murray, 1871.

Darwin, C., *The Expression of the Emotions in Man and Animals*, John Murray, 1872.

Daston, L., *Classical Probability in the Enlightenment*, Princeton University Press, 1988.

Defoe, D., *Mere Nature Delineated or a Body without a Soul*, London, 1726.

DeJean, J., *Ancients Against Moderns: Cultural Wars and the Making of a Fin de Siècle*, University of Chicago Press, 1997.

Desan, S., *Reclaiming the Sacred: Lay Religion and Popular Politics in Revolutionary France*, Cornell University Press, 1990.

Dick, S. J., *Plurality of Worlds: The Origins of the Extraterrestrial Life Debate from Democritus to Kant*, Cambridge University Press, 1984.

Dresser, C., *The Art of Decorative Design*, London, 1862, reissued by the American Life Foundation, 1977.

Driskel, M. P., *Representing Belief*, Penn State University, 1992.

Duby, G., *The Chivalrous Society*, University of California, 1980.

Durkheim, E., *Le Suicide*, Paris, 1897.

Einhard, *The Life of Charlemagne*, translated by Grant, A. J., 1905.

Eliade, M., *The Myth of the Eternal Return: Or, Cosmos and History*, Routledge and Kegan Paul, 1974.

Ellenberger, H. F., *The Discovery of the Unconscious: The History and Evolution of Dynamic Psychiatry*, Fontana Press, 1994.

Elliot, A. (ed.), *Routledge Handbook of Identity Studies*, Routledge, 2014.

Emerson, R. W., 'History' in *Essays: First Series*, 1841.

Emerson, R. K. and McGinn, B. (eds), *The Apocalypse in the Middle Ages*, Cornell University Press, 1992.

Essinger, J., *Jacquard's Web: How a Hand Loom Led to the Birth of the Information Age*, Oxford, 2004.

Fauchereau, S., *Kupka*, Rizzoli, 1989.

Fechner, G., *Nanna, or The Soul-life of Plants*, Leipzig, 1848.

Fechner, G., *Zend-Avesta, or the Matters of Heaven and the World Beyond*, 1851.

Fechner, G., *Religion of a Scientist*, translated by Lowrie, W., Pantheon Books, 1946.

Ffytche, M., *The Foundation of the Unconscious: Schelling, Freud and the Birth of the Modern Psyche*, Cambridge University Press, 2013.

Fischer, H. and Rainbird, S. (eds), *Kandinsky: The Path to Abstraction*, Tate, London, 2006.

Fontana, B., *Benjamin Constant and the Post-Revolutionary Mind*, Yale University Press, 1991.

Forster, M. N., 'Kant's Philosophy of Language?' in *Tijdschrift voor Filosofie*, 74, 2012.

Forty, A., *Objects of Desire: Design and Society Since 1750*, London, 1986.

Fox-Davies, A. C., *A Complete Guide to Heraldry*, London, 1909.

France, P. and St Clair, W. (eds), *Mapping Lives: The Uses of Biography*, Oxford University Press, 2004.

Francoeur, L.-B., *Lineal Drawing and Introduction to Geometry, as Taught in the Lancastrian Schools of France; Translated from the French*, Harvey and Darton, London, 1824.

Franklin, J. H., *Jean Bodin and the Sixteenth Century Revolution in the Methodology of Law and History*, Greenwood Press, 1977.

Fraser, J. T., *Time: The Familiar Stranger*, University of Massachusetts Press, 1987.

Fraser, R., *The Language of Adam: On the Limits and Systems of Discourse*, Columbia University Press, 1977.

Freud, S., *Civilisation and Its Discontents*, Vienna, 1930.

Frisch, W., *German Modernism: Music and Arts*, University of California Press, 2005.

Fueloep-Miller, R., *The Mind and Face of Bolshevism*, Harper Torchbook, 1965.

Gaehtgens, T. G. and Marchesano, L., *Display and Art History: The Dusseldorf Gallery and Its Catalogue*, The Getty Research Institute, 2011.

Gage, J., *Colour and Culture*, University of California Press, 1993.

Gamwell, L. and Solms, M., *From Neurology to Psychoanalysis: Sigmund Freud's Neurological Drawings and Diagrams of the Mind*, State University of New York, 2006.

Garin, E., *Astrology in the Renaissance: The Zodiac of Life*, Routledge and Kegan Paul, 1976.

Gatien-Arnoult, M., *Programme d'un cours de philosophie a l'usage des collèges et des autres établissements d'instruction publique*, Toulouse, 1833.

Gaynesford, M. de, *"I": The Meaning of the First Person Term*, Oxford University Press, 2006.

Gergen, K. J., *The Saturated Self: Dilemmas of Identity in Contemporary Life*, Basic Books, 1991.

Gifford, S., 'Freud at the Movies, 1907–1925: From the Piazza Colonna and Hammerstein's Roofgarden to *The Secrets of the Soul*' in Brandell, J. R. (ed.), *Celluloid Couches, Cinematic Clients: Psychoanalysis and Psychotherapy in the Movies*, State University of New York Press, 2004.

Gillis, M. B., 'Heresy in the Flesh: Gottschalk of Orbais and the Predestination Controversy in the Archdiocese of Reims' in Stone, R. and West, C. (eds), *Hincmar of Reims: Life and Work*, Manchester University Press, 2015.

Goldstein, J., *The Post-Revolutionary Self: Politics and Psyche in France, 1750–1850*, Harvard University Press, 2005.

Gombrich, E., *Art and Illusion: A Study in the Psychology of Pictorial Representation*, Princeton University Press, 1960.

Gossman, L., 'Michelet and Natural History: The Alibi of Nature' in *Proceedings of the American Philosophical Society*, vol. 145, no. 3, 2001.

Grafton, A., *Cardano's Cosmos: The Worlds and Works of a Renaissance Astrologer*, Harvard University Press, 2001.

Grafton, A., *What Was History? The Art of History in Early Modern Europe*, Cambridge University Press, 2007.

Guizot, F., *The History of the Origins of Representative Government in Europe*, translated by Scoble, A. R., introduction and notes by Craiutu, A., Liberty Fund, Indianapolis, 2002.

Habermas, J., *The Structural Transformation of the Public Sphere*, Polity, 2014.

Haeckel, E., *The Wonders of Life*, London, 1905.

Haeckel, E., *The Riddle of the Universe*, Watts, London, 1931.

Hahl-Koch, J. (ed.), *Arnold Schonberg and Wassily Kandinsky: Letters, Pictures and Documents*, Faber, London, 1984.

Halen, W., *Christopher Dresser*, Phaidon, 1990.

Halliwell, M., *Romantic Science and the Experience of the Self*, Ashgate, 1999.

Hamblyn, R., *The Invention of Clouds: How an Amateur Meteorologist Forged the Language of the Skies*, Picador, 2001.

Hand, S., *Embodied Abstraction: Biomorphic Fantasy and Empathy Aesthetics in the Work of Hermann Obrist, August Endell and Their Followers*, PhD dissertation, University of Chicago, 2008.

Harris, R., *Language, Saussure and Wittgenstein: How to Play Games with Words*, Routledge, 1996.

Harrison, C., Wood, P. and Gaiger, J., *Art in Theory, 1648–1815: An Anthology of Changing Ideas*, Wiley-Blackwell, 2001.

von Hartmann, E., *Philosophy of the Unconscious*, 1869.

Haskell, F., *History and Its Images: Art and the Interpretation of the Past*, Yale University Press, 1993.

Haweis, R. W., *Music and Morals*, London, 1871.

Hawthorne, N., *The House of Seven Gables*, Boston, 1851.

Headrick, D. R., *When Information Came of Age: Technologies of Knowledge in the Age of Reason and Revolution, 1700–1850*, Oxford University Press, 2000.

Heehs, P., *Writing the Self: Diaries, Memoirs and the History of the Self*, Bloomsbury, 2013.

Hegel, G. W. F., *Lectures on the Philosophy of World History: Introduction*, translated by Nisbet, H. B., Cambridge University Press, 1984.

Heidelberger, M., *Nature from Within: Gustav Theodor Fechner and his Psychophysical World View*, Pittsburg University Press, 2004.

Hen, Y. and Innes, M., *The Uses of the Past in the Early Middle Ages*, Cambridge University Press, Cambridge University Press.

Henderson, L. D., 'Vibratory Modernism: Boccioni, Kupka and the Ether of Space' in Clarke, B. and Henderson, L. D. (eds), *From Energy to Information: Representation in Science and Technology, Art and Literature*, Stanford University Press, 2002.

Henderson, L. D., 'X-rays and the Quest for Invisible Reality in the Art of Kupka, Duchamp and the Cubists' in *Art Journal*, no. 47, 1988.

Henry of Huntingdon, *History of the English People 1000–1154*, translated by Greenway, D., Oxford University Press, 2009.

Hollier, D. (ed.), *A New History of French Literature*, Harvard University Press, 1994.

Humphrey, N., *A History of the Mind*, Vintage, 1993.

Hunter, R. and Macalpine, I., *Three Hundred Years of Psychiatry 1535–1860*, Oxford University Press, 1964.

Izenberg, G., *Identity: The Necessity of a Modern Idea*, University of Pennsylvania, 2016.

James, W., *The Principles of Psychology*, New York, 1890.

James, W., *A Pluralistic Universe*, Hibbert Lectures at Manchester College on the Present Situation in Philosophy, 1909, Lecture VII.

Johansson, J.-E., 'F. A. W. Fröbel 1782–1852' in Fleer, M. and van Oers, B. (eds), *International Handbook of Early Childhood Education*, Springer, 2018.

Jones, R. F., *Ancients and Moderns: A Study of the Rise of the Scientific Movement in Seventeenth-Century England*, Gloucester, Massachusetts, 1975.

Joost-Gaugier, C. L., 'Poggio and Visual Tradition: "Uomini Famosi" in Classical Literary Description' in *Artibus et Historiae*, 6.12, 1985.

Junod, P., *Counterpoints: Dialogues between Music and the Visual Arts*, Reaktion, 2017.

Kagan, Y. and Neverov, O., 'An Imperial Affair' in *The Treasures of Catherine the Great*, Hermitage Development Trust, 2000.

Kandinsky, W., *Concerning the Spiritual in Art*, translated by Sadler, M. T. H., Dover Publications, 1977.

Karkov, C. E., *The Ruler Portraits of Anglo-Saxon England*, The Boydell Press, 2004.

Katz, J. (ed.), *Machines that Become Us*, Transaction Publishers, 2006.

Katz, M., *Capturing Sound: How Technology has Changed Music*, California University Press, 2004.

Kelly, D., 'The Prehistory of Sociology: Montesquieu, Vico and the Legal Tradition' in *History, Law and the Human Sciences*, London Variorum Reprint, 1984.

Kenkel, K. J., 'The Nationalisation of the Mass Spectator in Early German Film' in *Celebrating 1895: The Centenary of Cinema*, John Libbey & Co., Sydney, 1998.

Kharkhordin, O., *The Collective and the Individual in Russia*, University of California, 1999.

Kittler, F., 'The Mechanized Philosopher' in Rickels, L. A., *Looking After Nietzsche*, State University of New York Press, 1990.

Knowlson, J., *Universal Language Schemes in England and France 1600–1800*, University of Toronto, 1975.

Kronick, D. A., 'The Commerce of Letters: Networks and "Invisible Colleges" in Seventeenth and Eighteenth Century Europe' in *The Library Quarterly: Information, Community, Policy*, vol. 71, no. 1, Jan 2001.

La Mettrie, J. O. de, *Man a Machine*, translated by Watson, R. A. and Rybalka, M., Hackett Publishing Company, Indianapolis, 1994.

Larsen, B. and Flach, S. (eds), *Darwin and Theories of Aesthetics and Cultural History*, Ashgate, 2013.

Leadbeater, C. W., *Man Visible and Invisible*, Theosophical Publishing House, 1942.

Leben, U., *Object Design in the Age of Enlightenment: The History of the Royal Free Drawing School in Paris*, The J. Paul Getty Museum, Los Angeles, 2004.

Le Bon, G., *La psychologie des foules* 1895, translated into English as *The Crowd: A Study of the Popular Mind*, Macmillan, New York, 1896.

Lepore, J., *A is for American: Letters and Other Characters in the Newly United States*, Vintage, 2003.

Levitt, T., *The Shadow of Enlightenment: Optical and Political Transparency in France*, Oxford University Press, 2009.

Lewis, C. S., *Studies in Words*, Cambridge University Press, 1960.

Loewen, D., *The Most Dangerous Art: Poetry, Politic and Autobiography After the Revolution*, Lexington Books, 2010.

Luckhurst, R., *The Invention of Telepathy, 1870–1901*, Oxford University Press, 2002.

Maat, J., *Philosophical Languages in the Seventeenth Century: Dalgarno, Wilkins, Leibniz*, Amsterdam, 1999.

Macdonald, S., *The History and Philosophy of Art Education*, Lutterworth Press, Cambridge, 2004.

Machiavelli, N., *The Prince*, translated by Marriott, W. K. and Dent, J. M., London, 1958.

Makari, G., *Revolution in Mind: The Creation of Psychoanalysis*, Harper, 2008.

Marcus, L., 'Dreaming and Cinematographic Consciousness' in *Psychoanalysis and History*, 3, Jan 2008.

Martin, D. D., *Fifteenth-Century Carthusian Reform: The World of Nicholas Kempff*, Brill, Leiden, 1992.

Martin, R. and Barresi, J., *An Intellectual History of Personal Identity*, Columbia University Press, 2006.

Marx, R., *Jules Chéret*, Paris, 1889.

Mayhew, R. (ed.), *Essays on Ayn Rand's 'Anthem'*, Lexington Books, 2005.

McCall, T. (ed.), *Visual Cultures of Secrecy in Early Modern Europe*, Truman State University Press, 2013.

McClellan, A., *Inventing the Louvre: Art, Politics and the Origins of the Museum in Eighteenth-Century Paris*, University of California Press, 1999.

McCracken, G., *Culture and Consumption*, Indiana University Press, 1990.

McKitterick, R., *The Frankish Kingdoms Under the Carolingians: 751–987*, Longman, 1983.

McKitterick, R., *Carolingian Culture: Emulation and Innovation*, Cambridge University Press, 1994.

McMahon, D. M., *Divine Fury: A History of Genius*, Basic Books, New York, 2013.

Melton, J. van H., *The Rise of the Public in Enlightenment Europe*, Cambridge University Press, 2001.

Meyrowitz, J., *No Sense of Place: The Impact of Electronic Media on Social Behavior*, Oxford University Press, 1986.

Milgram, S., 'Anthem in the Context of Related Literary Works' in Mayhew, R. (ed.), *Essays on Ayn Rand's 'Anthem'*, Lexington Books, 2005.

Moller, A., 'Greek Chronographic Traditions About the First Olympic Games' in Rosen, R. M. (ed.), *Time and Temporality in the Ancient World*, University of Pennsylvania Museum of Archaeology and Anthropology, 2004.

Mommsen, T. E., 'Petrarch and the Decoration of the *Sala Virorum Illustrium* in Padua' in *The Art Bulletin*, vol. 34, no. 2, Jun 1952.

Moore, C., 'An Ideological History of the English Term *Onomatopoeia*' in Adams, M., Brinton L. J. and Fulk, R. D. (eds), *Studies in the History of the English Language VI*, De Gruyter, 2015.

Morris, C., *The Discovery of the Individual, 1050–1200*, University of Toronto, 1972.

Mosshammer, A. A., *The Easter Computus and the Origins of the Christian Era*, Oxford University Press, 2008.

Munck, B. de, Kaplan, S. L. and Soly, H. (eds), *Learning on the Shop Floor: Historical Perspectives in Apprenticeship*, Berghahn Books, 2007.

Mungello, D. E., *Curious Land: Jesuit Accommodation and the Origins of Sinology*, University of Hawaii, 1989.

Naylor, G., *The Bauhaus*, London, 1968.

Newton, M., *Savage Girls and Wild Boys*, London, 2002.

Newton, S., *The Origins of Beowulf: And the Pre-Viking Kingdom of East Anglia*, Brewer, Cambridge, 2004.

Nias, H., *The Artificial Self: The Psychology of Hippolyte Taine*, Legenda, 1999.

Nicholls, A. and Lieblicher, M. (eds), *Thinking the Unconscious: Nineteenth-Century German Thought*, Cambridge University Press, 2010.

Nisbet, R., *History of the Idea of Progress*, Heinemann, 1970.

Norton, R. E., *Herder's Aesthetics and the European Enlightenment*, Cornell University, 1991.

Ogilvie, S. C. and Verman, M. (eds), *European Proto-Industrialisation*, Cambridge University Press, 1996.

Okrent, A., *In the Land of Invented Languages*, Spiegel and Grau, 2009.

Olivier de Laborderie, *The First Manuals of English History: Two Late Thirteenth Century Genealogical Rolls of the Kings of England in the Royal Collection* (paper from 'Royal Manuscripts' conference at the British Library in 2011, eBLJ, 2014, Article 4, Dec 2016).

O'Malley et al. (eds), *The Jesuits: Cultures, Sciences and the Arts, 1540–1773*, University of Toronto Press, 1999.

Ouspensky, P. D., *Tertium Organum*, 1912, translated from the Russian into English in 1920, Routledge and Kegan Paul, 1981.

Passmore, J., *The Perfectibility of Man*, Duckworth, 1972.

Pater, W., 'The School of Giorgione' in *Fortnightly Review*, 22, 1877.

Pater, W., *The Renaissance*, 3rd edition, London, 1888.

Pearson, K. A. and Mullarkey, J. (eds), *Henri Bergson: Key Writings*, Continuum Books, 2002.

Pointer, F. N. L. (ed.), *The History and Philosophy of Knowledge of the Brain and its Functions*, Blackwell, 1958.

Pomper, P., *The Structure of Mind in History: Five Major Figures in Psychohistory*, Columbia University Press, 1985.

Pool, I. de S. (ed.), *The Social Impact of the Telephone*, Massachusetts Institute of Technology, 1977.

Pool, I. de S., *Forecasting the Telephone: A Retrospective Technology Assessment of the Telephone*, Ablex Publishing, 1983.

Poster, C. and Utz, R. (eds), *The Late Medieval Epistle*, Northwestern University Press, Illinois, 1996.

Prohaska, W., *The Kunsthistorisches Museum, Vienna: The Paintings, Volume 2*, Scala, London, 2006.

Proudhon, P.-J., *What is Property?*, 1840, translated by Kelley, D. R. and Smith, B. G., Cambridge University Press, 2002.

Racevskis, R., *Time and Ways of Knowing Under Louis XIV*, Bucknell University Press, 2010.

Rank, O., *The Double: A Psychoanalytic Study*, translated by Tucker, H., University of North Carolina Press, 1971.

Rantanen, T., *The Media and Globalisation*, Sage, 2009.

Read, D., *The Age of Urban Democracy: England 1868–1914*, Routledge, 2014.

Redgrave, R., 'Importance of the Study of Botany to the Ornamentalist' in *Journal of Design and Manufactures*, vol. I, Mar–Aug 1849.

Reed, E. S., *From Soul to Mind: The Emergence of Psychology from Erasmus Darwin to William James*, Yale University Press, 1997.

Reeves, M., *Joachim of Fiore and the Prophetic Future*, London, 1976.

Reeves, M. and Hirsch-Reich, B., *The Figurae of Joachim of Fiore*, Oxford University Press, 1972.

Richards, G., *Mental Machinery: The Origins and Consequences of Psychological Ideas from 1600–1850*, John Hopkins University Press, 1992.

Richards, R. J., *Darwin and the Emergence of Evolutionary Theories of Mind and Behavior*, Chicago University Press, 1989.

Ridley, A., *Nietzsche on Art*, Routledge, 2007.

Rieber, R. W., *The Bifurcation of the Self: The Theory and History of Dissociation and Its Disorders*, Springer US, 2006.

Riegl, A., *Historical Grammar of the Visual Arts*, Zone Books, 2004.

Rimington, A., *A New Art Colour Music*, Wildside Press, 2004.

Ringbom, S., 'Transcending the Visible: The Generation of the Abstract Pioneers' in Tuchman, M., *The Spiritual in Art: Abstract Painting, 1890–1985*, Abbeville Press, 1993.

Roberts, B., *What is Self? A Study of the Spiritual Journey in Terms of Consciousness*, Sentient Publications, 2005.

Robinson, D. N., *An Intellectual History of Psychology*, University of Wisconsin Press, 1981.

Rosenberg, D. and Grafton, A., *Cartographies of Time: A History of the Timeline*, Princeton Architectural Press, 2010.

Rosenfeld, S., *A Revolution in Language: The Problem of Signs in Late Eighteenth-Century France*, Stanford University Press, 2001.

Rousseau, J.-J., *Discourse on Inequality*, 1755, translated by Philip, F., Oxford University Press, 2009.

Royle, N., *The Uncanny: An Introduction*, Manchester University Press, 2003.

Salmon, V., *The Works of Francis Lodwick*, Longman, 1972.

Scharf, A., *Art and Photography*, Penguin Books, 1986.

Seigel, J., *The Idea of the Self: Thought and Experience in Western Experience Since the Seventeenth Century*, Cambridge University Press, 2005.

Sembach, K.-J., *Henry van de Verde*, Thames and Hudson, 1989.

Shea, A., *The Phone Book: The Curious History of the Book That Everyone Uses but No-One Reads*, Perigree Books, 2010.

Sheldrake, R. and Smart, P., 'Experimental Tests for the Telephone Telepathy' in *Journal of the Society of Psychical Research*, no. 67, 2003.

Simon, E. M., *The Myth of Sisyphus, Renaissance Theories of Human Perfectibility*, Farleigh Dickinson University Press, 2007.

Skrbina, D., *Panpsychism in the West*, Massachusetts Institute of Technology, 2007.

Smith, C. U. M., 'Herbert Spencer and Henri Bergson' in *Chromatikon VI*, Yearbook of Philosophy in Process, 2010.

Smith, J. M., *Nobility Reimagined: The Patriotic Nation in Eighteenth-Century France*, Cornell University Press, 2005.

Smith, K. A., *Art, Identity and Devotion in Fourteenth-Century England: Three Women and Their Books of Hours*, British Library and University of Toronto, 2003.

Sobel, D., *Longitude: The True Story of a Lone Genius Who Solved the Greatest Scientific Problem of His Time*, Fourth Estate, 1996.

Solomon, R. C., *Continental Philosophy Since 1750: The Rise and Fall of the Self*, Oxford University Press, 1988.

Sorabji, R., *Self: Ancient and Modern Insights About Individuality, Life and Death*, Oxford University Press, 2006.

Spencer, H., *Principles of Psychology*, Longman, Brown, Green and Longmans, London, 1855.

Spencer, H., *Essays on Education and Kindred Subjects*, Dent, London, 1911.

Spengler, O., *The Decline of the West: Form and Actuality*, London, 1926.

Spira, A., *The Avant-Garde Icon: Russian Avant-Garde Art and the Icon Painting Tradition*, Lund Humphries, 2008.

Spira, A., *The Invention of the Self: Personal Identity in the Age of Art*, Bloomsbury Academic, 2020.

Stack, D., *Queen Victoria's Skull; George Combe and the Mid-Victorian Mind*, Hambledon Continuum, 2008.

Stafford, B. M., *Artful Science: Enlightenment Entertainment and the Eclipse of Visual Education*, Massachusetts Institute of Technology Press, 1994.

Steadman, P., *The Evolution of Designs: Biological Analogy in Architecture and the Applied Arts*, Routledge, 2008.

Steiner, R., *The Evolution of the World and of Humanity*, London, 1923.

Steiner, R., *Oswald Spengler: Prophet of World Chaos*, Anthroposophic Press, 1949.

Steiner, R., *The Christ Impulse and the Development of Ego Consciousness*, Anthroposophic Press, 1976.

Steiner, R., *The Redemption of Thinking*, Anthroposophic Press, 1983.

Stock-Morton, P., *Moral Education for a Secular Society: The Development of 'Morale Laïque' in Nineteenth-Century France*, University of New York Press, 1988.

Stravinsky, I., *An Autobiography*, New York, 1962.

Strawson, G., *Selves*, Oxford University Press, 2009.

Synge, J., *The Relations and Descriptions of Forms, According to the Principles of Pestalozzi*, Dublin, 1817.

Taine, H., *History of English Literature*, translated by van Laun, H., Edinburgh, 1872.

Taine, H., 'On the Nature of the Work of Art' in *Lectures on Art, Vol. I*, translated by Durand, J., New York, 1875.

Taine, H., 'On the Production of the Work of Art' in *Lectures on Art, Vol. I*, translated by Durand, J., New York, 1875.

Taylor, C., *Sources of the Self: The Making of the Modern Identity*, Harvard University Press, 1989.

Teilhard de Chardin, P., *The Phenomenon of Man*, Collins, 1960.

Thiel, U., *The Early Modern Subject: Self-Consciousness and Personal Identity from Descartes to Hume*, Oxford University Press, 2011.

Toynbee, A. J., *Greek Historical Thought*, New American Library, 1953.

Trinder, B., *The Making of the Industrial Landscape*, Phoenix Giant, 1982.

Tuchman, M., *The Spiritual in Art: Abstract Painting, 1890–1985*, Abbeville Press, 1993.

Turgot, A., *On Universal History*, translated by Meek, R., Cambridge University Press, 1973.

Uglow, J., *The Lunar Men: The Friends Who Made the Future*, Faber and Faber, 2002.

Verene, D. P., *The New Art of Autobiography: An Essay on the 'Life of Giambattista Vico Written by Himself'*, Clarendon, 1991.

Vergo, P., *Kandinsky: Complete Writings on Art*, Da Capo Press, 1994.

Vergo, P., *That Divine Order: Music and the Visual Arts from Antiquity to the Eighteenth Century*, Phaidon, 2005.

Vico, G., *The Autobiography of Giambattista Vico*, translated by Fisch, M. H. and Bergin, T. G., Cornell University Press, 1975.

Vico, G., *The New Science*, Penguin, 2001.

Vovelle, M., *The Revolution Against the Church*, Ohio State University, 1991.

Waggoner, Z., *My Avatar, My Self: Identity in Video Role-Playing Games*, McFarland & Co., 2009.

Wallace, A. R., *The Action of Natural Selection on Man*, New Haven, 1871.

Wallsten, S., *Ringing in the 20th Century: The Effects of State Monopolies, Private Ownership and Operating Licenses on Telecommunications in Europe, 1892–1914*, Research Policy Working Paper 2690, The World Bank Development Research Group, Oct 2001.

Weisberg, G. et al., *Japonisme: Japanese Influence on French Art, 1845–1910*, Cleveland Museum of Art, 1975.

Weiss, P., *Kandinsky and Old Russia*, Yale University Press, 1995.

West, D. C. and Zimdars-Swartz, S., *Joachim of Fiore: A Study in Spiritual Perception and History*, Indiana University Press, 1983.

Wolstenholme G. and O'Connor, C. (eds), *Neurological Basis of Behaviour*, London, 1958.

Wood, C. S., *Forgery, Replica, Fiction: Temporalities of German Renaissance Art*, Chicago University Press, 2008.

Wood, J., 'Suetonius in the Carolingian Empire' in Power, T. and Gibson, R. K. (eds), *Suetonius the Biographer: Studies in Roman Lives*, Oxford University Press, 2014.

Wood, J. C. and Wood, M. C. (eds), *F. W. Taylor: Critical Evaluations in Business and Management, Vol IV*, Routledge, 2002.

Wood, P. B., *The Aberdeen Enlightenment: The Arts Curriculum in the Eighteenth Century*, Aberdeen University Press, 1993.

Woolf, D. R., *Reading History in Early Modern England*, Cambridge University Press, 2000.

Wright, A., *Cataloguing the World: Paul Otlet and the Birth of the Information Age*, Oxford University Press, 2014.

Wright, C. D., 'Genesis A ad litteram' in Fox, M. and Sharma, M. (eds), *Old English Literature and the Old Testament*, University of Toronto Press, 2012.

Wurtzel, A. C. and Turner, C., 'Latent Functions of the Telephone: What Missing the Extension Means' in Pool, I. de S. (ed.), *The Social Impact of the Telephone*, Massachusetts Institute of Technology, 1977.

Young, J., *Nietzsche's Philosophy of Art*, Cambridge University Press, 1992.

Zamyatin, E., *We*, translated by Brown, C., Penguin, 1993.

Zhang, Q., 'About God, Demons and Miracles: The Jesuit Discourse on the Supernatural in Late Ming China' in *Early Science and Medicine*, 4.1, 1999.

Zhang, Q., 'Translation as Cultural Reform: Jesuit Scholastic Psychology in the Transformation of Confucian Discourse on Human Nature' in O'Malley et al. (eds), *The Jesuits: Cultures, Sciences and the Arts, 1540–1773*, University of Toronto Press, 1999.

Ziolkowski, T., *Clio the Romantic Muse: Historicising the Faculties in Germany*, Cornell University Press, 2004.

INDEX

The letter *f* following an entry indicates a page that includes a figure.